Jewish Mysticism and Kabbalah

JEWISH STUDIES IN THE 21ST CENTURY
General Editor: Frederick E. Greenspahn

The Hebrew Bible: New Insights and Scholarship
Edited by Frederick E. Greenspahn

Women and Judaism: New Insights and Scholarship
Edited by Frederick E. Greenspahn

Jewish Mysticism and Kabbalah: New Insights and Scholarship
Edited by Frederick E. Greenspahn

Jewish Mysticism and Kabbalah

New Insights and Scholarship

Edited by Frederick E. Greenspahn

NEW YORK UNIVERSITY PRESS
New York and London

NEW YORK UNIVERSITY PRESS
New York and London
www.nyupress.org

Library of Congress Cataloging-in-Publication Data

Jewish mysticism and Kabbalah : new insights and scholarship /
edited by Frederick E. Greenspahn.
p. cm. — (Jewish studies in the 21st century)
Includes bibliographical references and index.
ISBN 978-0-8147-3286-1 (cl : alk. paper) —
ISBN 978-0-8147-3288-5 (e-book : alk. paper) —
ISBN 978-0-8147-3319-6 (e-book : alk. paper)
1. Cabala—History. 2. Mysticism—Judaism—History. 3. Judaism—History.
I. Greenspahn, Frederick E., 1946–
BM526.J49   2011
296.1'6—dc23   2011020470

Contents

Preface

In 1957 Gershom Scholem, a world-renowned expert on Jewish mysticism, came to lecture at the Jewish Theological Seminary of America in New York City. The introduction was delivered by Saul Lieberman, a prominent scholar of Jewish law. Lieberman began with the comment that "mysticism is nonsense, but the history of nonsense is scholarship."[1] Over the past half-century, that remark has become a staple of academic Jewish lore.

It was not always so. In the Middle Ages, Jewish thought was divided into three parallel and, presumably, equal categories—rabbinic, philosophical, and mystical.[2] Nor does Lieberman's point resonate in our own time, when books such as *Kabbalah for Dummies*[3] can be found in mall bookstores, Kabbalah Centres attract celebrities like Madonna, Demi Moore, and Britney Spears, and Chabad Lubavitch is just about everywhere.

Still, Lieberman's attitude did not come out of nowhere. Jewish thinkers have long been suspicious of mystical quests. Two centuries ago, an anonymous work called *Kol Sakal* characterized Kabbalah as a heresy "which is no more believable than the [beliefs of] Christians."[4] And two thousand years before that a Jewish sage warned, "Do not seek what is too wondrous for you nor search for what is hidden from you . . . for you have no business dealing with secrets."[5] The ancient rabbis echoed that sentiment when they speculated about the fact that the Bible begins with the second letter of the Hebrew alphabet: "Why was the world created with the letter *bet*?" they asked; "because just as the letter *bet* (ב) is closed on the sides and open in front, so too you may not inquire what is above or below, what was before and what will be after, but only from the day since the world was created."[6] They cited the case of a child who had wondered about the *ḥashmal*, an obscure term that the prophet Ezekiel mentions as something he saw in the center of a fire (Ezek. 1:4, 27), only to be consumed by a fire that came forth from that very *ḥashmal*.[7] It is hardly surprising, therefore, that they prescribed that "the laws of incest may not be expounded in the presence of three people, the story of creation in the presence of two, nor the chariot in the presence of one, unless he is a sage."[8] Even sages were not necessarily safe, judging from the story of four eminent scholars who had entered a garden (a symbol of esoteric thought) from which only one emerged intact.[9]

Over the past generation, Jewish mysticism has attracted growing academic attention. One reason is that Jewish Studies blossomed on American campuses at about the same time that religious mysticism was attracting heightened attention. Many of those who experienced the spiritual revival of the 1960s are now professors at institutions of higher education, where they have applied academic methods to topics of personal interest. This congruence has yielded both remarkable insights and fierce controversy. In keeping with the purpose of this series, this book strives to make both the fruits of those endeavors and the ensuing debates accessible to audiences beyond the academy.

In the introduction to this volume, after surveying the various expressions of Jewish mysticism, Hartley Lachter describes the contribution of Gershom Scholem, whose importance for the academic study of Jewish mysticism will become clear in the repeated references to his work that fill the following chapters. Scholem's biography also demonstrates the complex interplay between personal motivation and scholarly research. Despite being an arch-rationalist who had little personal sympathy for mystical practice, it was he who, in many ways, brought attention to a phenomenon that had been ignored or dismissed all too often.

The term *mustikos*, which is related to the word *mystery*, comes from a Greek root which means "teach" or "initiate into mysteries." It was originally used for secretive practices in the classical world.[10] Christian tradition borrowed it to refer to the "spiritual" or "hidden meaning."[11]

The classic description of mysticism was provided by William James, who emphasized its concern with achieving "inner union with the divine."[12] Although the ancient Jewish philosopher Philo argued that we cannot know God directly, but only "that He is,"[13] mystical encounters have long been part of Jewish experience. The Bible itself records several direct encounters with God, describing Moses as having spoken with God "mouth to mouth" (Num. 12:8) and having known him "face to face" (Deut. 34:10). He is even said to have seen God from behind (Exod. 24:23) and possibly His feet as well (Exod. 24:10), this after having been told that one may not see God and live (v. 20). Later, Isaiah tells of seeing "the Lord sitting on a throne, high and lifted up, and His train filled the Temple" (6:1), while Ezekiel saw Him amid several creatures (Ezek. 1).

Over the centuries that followed, Jews engaged in a remarkable array of mystical endeavors, as described by Michael Swartz in the following chapter. This was the very period during which rabbinic Judaism produced its most enduring works—the Talmud and the Midrashim. One cannot but wonder whether this environment contributed to the rabbis' concern about what they perceived as dangerous speculation, leading them to issue the warnings mentioned above.

The classical period of Jewish mysticism was, beyond doubt, the Middle Ages, when a book called the *Zohar* was compiled and kabbalistic doctrine given its enduring shape by Isaac Luria. Kabbalistic tradition attributes the *Zohar* to the 2nd-century Palestinian rabbi Shimon bar Yochai. That would certainly support the impression that mysticism was a parallel and possibly competitive stream to the more familiar Jewish tradition as embodied in the Talmud. It was that view which Scholem challenged by demonstrating that the *Zohar* was actually the work of Moshe de Leon, a 13th-century Spanish Kabbalist. As Eitan Fishbane explains in chapter 2, however, more recent scholarship has determined that the *Zohar's* creation was far more complex than previously thought. In so doing, he illustrates how modern scholarship can challenge both religious tradition and its own prior conclusions.

The chapters on Abraham Abulafia and the mystical communities in Safed provide further illumination of this process. In the former, Elliot Wolfson describes recent scholarship's demonstration that alongside the *Zohar's* theosophical (theoretical) Kabbalah there existed another stream, called prophetic by Abraham Abulafia, which is deserving of equal attention. At the same time, Lawrence Fine draws attention to the importance of considering nontheological aspects of the Jewish mystical experience in his discussion of the practice, communal life, and role of women in the 16th-century mystical community at Safed, best known for the teachings of Isaac Luria (the "Ari"), which would become the normative form of kabbalistic theology.

Recent scholarship has itself moved beyond describing the classical forms of Kabbalah in order to explore the breadth of its impact. For example, in the next set of chapters Matt Goldish explains how Kabbalah provided the ideological framework for numerous Jewish messianic movements, and Allison Coudert shows its impact on Christian thinkers and, through them, the development of modern science. Finally, Shaul Magid suggests that the Hasidic movement, which is a modern expression of Jewish mysticism, used the Bible as a way of bringing the Jewish religious tradition, which had focused on the Talmud, into modernity.

We have clearly come a long way from those who thought of mysticism as a primitive form of thought and speculation—as "nonsense," to use Lieberman's term. It is now recognized as an integral part of the Jewish tradition and even a vehicle for Judaism's modernization. Jody Myers reinforces that point in chapter 8 by describing how Kabbalah has drawn on both Jewish and non-Jewish influences in order to flourish in the modern world. Nor has its influence been limited to "exotic" movements, as Hava Tirosh-Samuelson makes clear in her examination of the growing interest in its treatment of divine gender, even if the androgynous elements of its theology are not as deep as some modern thinkers might wish.

The study of Kabbalah thus demonstrates the value of modern scholarship not only for understanding the various forms of Jewish mysticism but also for appreciating the breadth of Judaism as a whole. In so doing, that project has brought several important questions to light:

1. Are the various Jews who have engaged in mystical endeavors connected? In other words, are the groups described in these pages isolated cases of spiritual yearning or outward expressions of an ongoing mystical tradition? Put differently, are these phenomena distinct Jewish mysticisms, or can we speak of a Jewish mystical tradition?

2. How is Jewish mysticism related to so-called normative (rabbinic) Judaism? Are they separate, possibly rival, streams or interconnected parts of a common tradition? Taking that line of reasoning further, can the mystical tradition even be separated from "mainstream" Judaism? After all, Joseph Karo compiled the normative code of Jewish law while living in the 16th-century kabbalistic community at Safed. Analogously, many practices that are mainstays of contemporary Jewish life, such as the Kabbalat Shabbat liturgy which opens Sabbath worship, the Tu Bi-Shevat seder, late-night study on certain holidays, and even the popular phrase *tikkun olam*, originated within the mystical tradition.

3. To what extent is Jewish mysticism related to other traditions? Several chapters of this book allude to the possibility that kabbalistic practices had been borrowed from Christianity or Islam. The reverse may have taken place as well. The messianic claimants Shabbatai Zevi and Jacob Frank, who lived in the 17th and 18th centuries, ended up converting to Islam and Christianity respectively, and one 14th-century scholar claimed that Jesus and his disciples were actually Kabbalists, albeit confused ones.[14] Better documented is Kabbalah's influence on the Christian Renaissance and, through it, on early modern thought.

4. What can these movements teach us about mysticism as a whole? When William James formulated the classical description of mysticism a century ago, he cited evidence from several religious communities, mentioning Hinduism, Buddhism, Mohammedanism, and Christianity by name.[15] Judaism is conspicuously absent from this list. Did James think that Judaism had not produced mystical activity, or was his definition flawed? As we shall see, figures such as the *merkavah* mystics and Abraham Abulafia strove for direct contact with God, a longing that continues in Martin Buber's description of God as the "eternal Thou" (*der ewige du*).[16] Others, however, such as the authors of the *Zohar*, seem to have been more interested in understanding the divine than in experiencing it.

5. Finally, what can these mystical phenomena teach us about Judaism as a whole? Were the Jewish mystics a small handful of heretics, or did they constitute a significant stream of Jewish experience which the rabbis sought to marginalize? Should the latter prove to be true, then we will have to contend with the possibility that our own understanding of Judaism may have been limited by the rabbis' efforts to define what was normative and what was not. If so, then the commitment of modern Jewish Studies to observing and then describing the behavior of actual Jews rather than studying only what their leaders tell them can help us recapture a broader understanding of Jewish life and practice.

These are not simple questions, nor do the results always match our expectations. In the end, that is the value of the scholarly approach—its commitment to starting with evidence rather than beliefs or assumptions and paying attention to what people actually do as well as what their leaders teach. If the conclusions then force us to revise our theories or our categories, that simply demonstrates the self-correcting nature of the scholarly enterprise, where change is ever present and error a sign of vitality rather than a flaw.[17]

To be sure, scholarship's inability to stand still can be confusing. Its ability to let us know more than previous generations knew comes at the expense of proving that these earlier interpretations were inadequate or sometimes incorrect. That, in turn, suggests the possibility that what we know today, including the contents of this book, may be superseded as research continues and our knowledge grows. That may be unsettling—we all crave certainty—but it is also a sign of liveliness, that we continue to learn more as new discoveries emerge out of those that came before. In the epilogue to this book, Pinchas Giller reiterates the value of moving forward with the recognition that it is the achievements of those who came before which enable us to question their conclusions.

There may be those who, like Saul Lieberman more than sixty years ago, dismiss the phenomena described in these pages, questioning whether Chabad is mystical or the Kabbalah Centres Jewish. We should not be put off by the success of such movements, however; that, too, is better recognized as evidence of Judaism's richness and dynamism than its decay. One goal of this book is to share the excitement of understanding where these phenomena fit into the spectrum of Jewish tradition by presenting the current state of our knowledge, even as scholars strive for deeper and broader understanding.

Many individuals have contributed to this project. The seeds of the entire undertaking were sown by Herbert and Elaine Gimelstob, without whose generosity it would have been inconceivable. Alan Berger, Kristen Lindbeck, and Marianne Sanua helped turn that vision into a concrete plan. Their abstract outline was fleshed out with guidance from Arthur Green and Lawrence Fine. As always, Jennifer Hammer participated from beginning to end, ensuring the cohesion and coherence of the resulting product, while Nicole Jacobsen provided visual images that could clarify these ideas and Inbal Mazar ensured that the effort was smoothly and professionally executed. Finally, Barbara Pearl has made my vision her own, contributing her unique warmth and nurturance so that the result could be rewarding, enlightening, and enjoyable. It has been my good fortune to share both the experience and its product with her, along with the entirety of our lives.

NOTES

1. The remark was later published in an appendix to Lieberman's article "How Much Greek in Jewish Palestine?" in *Biblical and Other Studies*, ed. Alexander Altmann (Cambridge, MA: Harvard University Press, 1963), p. 135; see Abe Socher, "The History of Nonsense," *AJS Perspectives* (fall 2006): 32.

2. Profiat Duran, *Ma'aseh Ephod*, ed. Jonathan Friedländer and Jakob Kohn (Vienna: J. Holzworth, 1865), pp. 4–9; cf. Simone Luzzatto's *Discourse on the State of the Jews*, as described by Robert Bonfils, "A Cultural Profile," in *The Jews of Early Modern Venice*, ed. Robert C. Davis and Benjamin Ravid (Baltimore: Johns Hopkins University Press, 2001), pp. 170–71.

3. Arthur Kurzweil, *Kabbalah for Dummies* (Hoboken, NJ: Wiley, 2006); cf. Michael Laitman and Collin Canright, *The Complete Idiot's Guide to Kabbalah* (Indianapolis: Alpha Books, 2007).

4. Talya Fishman, *Shaking the Pillars of Exile, "Voice of a Fool," An Early Modern Jewish Critique of Rabbinic Culture* (Stanford: Stanford University Press, 1997), p. 115.

5. Sirah 3:21–22.

6. *Gen. Rabb.* 1:10

7. B. Ḥag. 13a.

8. *M. Ḥag.* 2:1; cf. the prologue to Origen's commentary to the Song of Songs §1 (ed. R. P. Lawson; Westminster, MD: Newman, 1957, p. 23); and Jerome's letter to Paulinus (letter 53, §8 in *Nicene and Post-Nicene Fathers*, ed. Philip Schaff and Henry Wace, 2d ser. [Edinburgh: T & T Clark, 1893], 6:101).

9. *T. Ḥag.* 2:3–4,; *j. Ḥag.* 2:1, 77b; *b. Ḥag.* 14b; and *Cant. Rabb.* 1:4.

10. E.g., Thucydides, *History of the Peloponnesian War* VI.xxviii.2 (LCL 3:232–33), VI.lx.1 (LCL 3:286–87); Herodotus, *The Persian Wars* VIII.65 (LCL 4:60–61); Strabo, *Geography* XVII.i.29 (LCL 8:82–84).

11. Louis Dupré, "Mysticism," in *Encyclopedia of Religion*, ed. Mircea Eliade (New York: Macmillan, 1987), 10:245–46.

12. William James, *The Varieties of Religious Experience: A Study in Human Nature* [1902] (New York: Random House, 1929), p. 420. The apostle Paul captured that attitude nicely when he wrote, "I live, yet not I but Christ lives in me" (Gal. 2:20).

13. *On Rewards and Punishments* VII.44 (LCL 8:338–39); cf. Maimonides' view that we can only know what God is not (*The Guide of the Perplexed* 1:51, 58, trans. Shlomo Pines [Chicago: University of Chicago Press, 1963]), pp. 112, 134).

14. Profiat Duran, *Kelimat Ha-Goyim*, ed. Adolf Poznanski in *Ha-Ṣofeh* 3, p. 143, as cited by Gershom Scholem, "Zur Geschichte der Anfänge der christlichen Kabbala," in *Essays Presented to Leo Baeck on the Occasion of His Eightieth Birthday* (London: East and West Library, 1954), p. 177, note 2.

15. Ibid., p. 391.

16. Martin Buber, *I and Thou* (New York: Scribner's Sons, 1958), pp. 100–101, cf. p. 112.

17. This is Thomas S. Kuhn's classic point in *The Structure of Scientific Revolutions* (Chicago: University of Chicago Press, 1962).

Introduction: Reading Mysteries

The Origins of Scholarship on Jewish Mysticism

──── HARTLEY LACHTER ────────────────────

Why would someone who does not identify as a Jewish mystic want to study Jewish mystical texts? All modern academics who have chosen to examine texts and ideas from the Jewish mystical tradition have had to address this question in one way or another. As we shall see, a wide range of answers to this question can be inferred from the history of scholarship, but a general feature that academic studies of Jewish mysticism share is the assumption that a detailed examination of Jewish mystical texts and discourse, as it has taken shape in different locations over the course of history, has something important to contribute to our understanding of humanity.

The studies in this volume represent the current state of research in the various subfields of the study of Jewish mysticism. In order to better appreciate their contributions, it is important to understand both the history of Jewish mystical literature and the history of academic scholarship *about* Jewish mystical texts. To that end, we provide a sketch of the history of Jewish mysticism followed by an overview of the main concerns and ideas that gave rise to the academic study of Jewish mysticism as it exists today.

A Brief History of Jewish Mysticism
Biblical Precursors

The Hebrew Bible is a primary source of reflection and inspiration for virtually all branches of Jewish mysticism. Although we must be careful not to conflate the religion of the ancient Israelites with later periods of Jewish history, it remains clear that there are certain elements of continuity. One of the most important ideas of biblical religion that impacted Jewish mysticism is the phenomenon of prophecy and revelatory experience. The texts relating the revelations to Abraham, Isaac, Jacob, Moses, the people of Israel as a whole at Sinai, and the prophetic inspirations and visions of Ezekiel, Daniel, and other prominent personalities in the Bible serve as the foundation for much of the esoteric and mystical traditions of Judaism. The *Zohar*, for example, is organized as a commentary on the Torah, and contains many descriptions of the Divine experience that approximate descriptions of prophetic revelation found throughout the Bible.

1st–7th Centuries: Early Jewish Mysticism and Esotericism

Postbiblical Jewish mysticism and esotericism began in the ancient Near East with a number of important texts that draw upon biblical images, such as Ezekiel's vision of the divine chariot (*merkavah*) and the ascension of Enoch (Gen. 5:21–24). The rabbinic literature of the Talmud and Midrash also contains many images and ideas about the mysteries of the divine realm, the nature of prophecy, the origins of the cosmos, the nature of the human soul, and other matters that went on to have a significant influence on later forms of Jewish mystical discourse.

Rabbinic Literature

A prominent feature of mystical literature is the claim that the knowledge conveyed by the text is "esoteric," meaning secret, restricted, or, in some cases, intellectually incomprehensible. Descriptions of esoteric speculation can be found in a number of places in the Talmud and Midrashim. In one famous example, we read: "forbidden sexual relations may not be expounded before three [or more] people, nor the account of creation [*ma'aseh bereishit*] before two [or more], nor the account of the Chariot [*ma'aseh merkavah*] before one, unless he is a sage who understands through his own knowledge."[1] These categories of forbidden or restricted speculation indicate a tradition, already active in the first few centuries of the Common Era among the rabbinic elite, of secret knowledge regarding God, the creation of the universe, and human sexuality.

The Hekhalot and Merkavah Literature

Another group of Jewish mystical texts from the first centuries of the Common Era discusses the means of traversing the seven courtyards (*hekhalot*) or chambers that surround the divine throne or chariot (*merkavah*). Each stage of the journey involves entering through the gateways between the courtyards, which are guarded by angels. Only those who are fully adept in the proper recitation of the angelic names can enter and exit unharmed. These visions are reported in the names of famous personalities from the rabbinic schools, such as Rabbi Akiva and Rabbi Ishmael. The precise connections between this body of literature and the rabbinic authors are difficult to determine, but most scholars agree that the traditions related in the Hekhalot and Merkavah literature, especially those texts from the *Hekhalot Rabbati* and *Hekhalot Zutarti* collections, date to the rabbinic period.

The *Sefer Yetsirah*

The *Sefer Yetsirah* (Book of Creation), composed sometime between the 2nd and 7th centuries CE, is a short treatise of fewer than two thousand words that discusses the creation of the universe by means of the twenty-two letters of the Hebrew alphabet and the ten "ineffable *sefirot*." It is unclear what the ten *sefirot* exactly are in this context, but they seem to be entities in the divine realm that are incomprehensible to the human mind and yet represent the mysterious nature of God and serve as His tools in the creative process. The focus on the symbolism of the ten *sefirot* and the letters of the Hebrew alphabet in the *Sefer Yetsirah* had a major impact on later Jewish mysticism and Kabbalah.

The *Shi'ur Qomah*

One of the most arcane texts from the ancient period of Jewish mysticism and esotericism is the unusual collection of passages referred to as the *Shi'ur Qomah* (Measure of the Stature). These texts describe the glory of God in the form of a celestial human body of enormous proportions, with names associated with each limb. Anthropomorphic representations of God play an important role in later periods of Jewish mysticism.

7th–11th Centuries: Mysticism in the Geonic Period

Much of what we find from the 7th to the 11th century reflects a strong influence from the rabbinic and Hekhalot/Merkavah sources. Nonetheless, as Gershom Scholem has noted, a number of important ideas that had a significant impact on later Jewish mysticism developed during this period.[2] The first of these, building on ideas that began during the rabbinic period, is the re-conceptualization of the *Shekhinah* (Divine Presence) as more than a name for the presence of God in the world but rather a kind of hypostasis or entity that can interact with God. Furthermore, it was during this period that important notions became widespread: the association between the *Shekhinah* and *Knesset Yisrael* (the community of Israel), the first appearance in Judaism of the idea of reincarnation (*gilgul*), and the application of numerology (*gematria*) to the values of Hebrew letters and words in order to uncover secrets (*sodot*) hidden within biblical texts.

Two important commentaries on the *Sefer Yetsirah* were composed during this period, one by Shabbatai ben Abraham Donnolo (913–ca. 982) and another by Judah ben Barzillai al-Barceloni (late 11th–early 12th century). During the early part of the geonic period, most of the important authors were centered in Babylonia, but later many of these ideas began to spread to the Jewish communities of Europe.

12th–13th Centuries:
Medieval Jewish Mysticism and the Rise of Kabbalah
The Ḥasidei Ashkenaz

A significant development in the promulgation of mystical and esoteric ideas in the Jewish communities of Western Christendom was the emergence of a group in the Rhineland known as the Ḥasidei Ashkenaz (German Pietists). This movement, which was active from roughly 1250 to 1350, had a profound impact on the kabbalistic circles in Spain in the latter part of the 13th century. Its three main figures came from the Kalonymide family, starting with Samuel the Ḥasid (mid-12th century), the son of Rabbi Kalonymus of Speyer, Judah the Ḥasid of Worms (d. 1217), and Eleazar ben Yehuda of Worms, who died between 1223 and 1232. Although little of the literary activity of Samuel the Ḥasid remains, many associate the *Sefer Ḥasidim* (Book of the Pious) with the teachings of Judah the Ḥasid. Eleazar of Worms composed numerous works—some of considerable length—that have survived and serve as the most important evidence of this group's mystical speculations.

The Ḥasidei Ashkenaz placed particular emphasis on ascetic renunciation and ethical discipline. Fasts, abstinence, physical pain and discomfort, and even martyrdom were all regarded as vehicles to enable mystical illumination, especially in the form of visualizing the *Shekhinah*. According to the Ḥasidei Ashkenaz, God's essence is unknowable, and yet He fills all reality and suffuses all being. By practicing ascetic renunciation and contemplating the traditional teachings of the divine mysteries regarding creation, revelation, and the meaning of the Torah, members of this school believed that they could attain the pure love of God in an encounter that was often described in ways that indicate a strong influence from the Hekhalot and Merkavah literature, as well as the *Sefer Yetsirah*. Many scholars believe that the tribulations of the Crusades and the ascetic practices of the surrounding Christian monastic communities had an impact on the particular form of religious and mystical piety of the Ḥasidei Ashkenaz.

Kabbalah in Provence and the *Sefer ha-Bahir*

In the 1180s, a text emerged in the Provence region of southern France that has come to serve as a defining moment in the history of Jewish mysticism and esotericism. This text, known as the *Sefer ha-Bahir* (Book of Brightness), is written in the style of an ancient rabbinic Midrash. The book has a complex origin and contains at least some elements that are believed to reflect ancient Near Eastern Jewish traditions. Determining the exact proportion of the *Bahir* that derives from ancient tradition and specifying the innovation of authors living in 12th-century Europe remains an open question in the scholarly literature. The most significant feature of the *Sefer ha-Bahir* is its focus on the ten *sefirot* as the ten luminous emanations of God that symbolically reveal the realm of inner divine life. The *sefirot* thus become living and dynamic symbols that represent God's unknowable and ineffable secrets. By representing the secret inner life of God as an erotically charged symbolic system of ten gendered divine emanations, the *Bahir* took a decisive step that permanently changed the history of Jewish mysticism.

"Theosophy" is a term employed by scholars to refer to symbolic systems that are understood by their authors to represent concealed aspects of the divine world. Scholars of Jewish mysticism generally use the term "Kabbalah" to refer to those texts, starting with the *Sefer ha-Bahir,* that understand the ten *sefirot* in a theosophic manner, whereas "Jewish mysticism and esotericism" is a broader category which also includes the earlier texts that do not discuss the ten *sefirot* in this way.

In the late 12th century, we also find traditions that associate esoteric speculation with a number of important rabbis in southern France. Abraham ben Isaac of Narbonne (1110–1179), Abraham ben David of Posquières (1125–1198), also know as Rabad, and Jacob Nazir of Lunel (d. late 12th century) are known to have endorsed kabbalistic and mystical teachings, although only a few scattered hints to that effect have been preserved in their own writings. Isaac the Blind (d. ca. 1235), son of Abraham ben David, lived in Narbonne and was the first major rabbi in Europe to specialize in Kabbalah. Most of his teachings were disseminated orally to his students, and only one text, a commentary on the *Sefer Yetsirah,* is regarded as his own composition. This commentary is a notoriously difficult text that discusses the *sefirot* mentioned in the *Sefer Yetsirah* in a theosophical manner. One important contribution found in Isaac the Blind's commentary is the development of the idea that the *sefirot* emanate from an absolutely unknowable aspect of God known as *Ein Sof* ("without end").

Kabbalah in Gerona

In the beginning of the 13th century, Kabbalah spread to Spain when the students of Isaac the Blind moved to Gerona, in the region of Catalonia. Here, for the first time, books were composed on Kabbalah that were designed to bring these ideas to a wider audience. In an intriguing letter sent to his students in Gerona, Isaac the Blind urges them to stop composing books on Kabbalah, for fear that these texts could "fall into the hands of fools or scoffers."[3] Despite Rabbi Isaac's criticism of the literary activities of some of the Gerona Kabbalists, treatises on Kabbalah continued to circulate and soon spread to other communities in Spain. Moreover, the influence of a prominent rabbi such as Nahmanides openly endorsing Kabbalah (he included numerous kabbalistic allusions in his popular commentary on the Torah) was undoubtedly essential for the legitimization of Kabbalah in the Spanish Jewish communities of Catalonia, Aragon, and Castile.

Kabbalah in Castile

In the middle of the 13th century, Kabbalah spread to Jewish communities living in the cities and towns of Castile. Jacob ben Jacob ha-Cohen (mid-13th century) and Isaac ben Jacob ha-Cohen (mid-13th century) became known for their teaching regarding a demonic realm within God from which evil originates. This evil is composed of a set of "*sefirot* of impurity" that parallel the pure *sefirot* of God. Their pupil, Moses of Burgos (ca. 1230/1225–ca. 1300), as well as Todros ben Joseph Abulafia (1220–1298), were significant rabbinic and political leaders of the Castilian Jewish community who wrote important works of Kabbalah. Moses of Burgos was the teacher of Isaac ibn Sahula (b. 1244), author of the famous poetic fable *Meshal ha-Kadmoni* (1281), as well as a kabbalistic commentary on the Song of Songs. Also active in Castile at this time was Isaac ibn Latif (ca. 1210–1280), whose writings strike a delicate balance between kabbalistic symbolism and philosophical speculation.

From the 1270s through the 1290s, a number of important and lengthy kabbalistic books were written by Yosef Gikatilla (1248–1325) and Moshe de Leon (1240–1305). These two figures were among the most prolific of the medieval Kabbalists, and many of their compositions, such as Gikatilla's *Sha'are Orah* (Gates of Light), went on to become seminal works in the history of Kabbalah. This period of remarkable kabbalistic literary productivity took place during the controversy over the study of Aristotelian philosophy, especially as it took shape in the philosophical works of Moses Maimonides, and the pronounced increase in Christian anti-Jewish proselytizing in Western Europe. Both of these events may have been factors in the development of Kabbalah during this decisive moment in its history.

Abraham Abulafia

Abraham Abulafia was born in Spain in 1240 and died some time after 1292. He propounded a kind of Kabbalah that, in addition to many of the typical theosophical motifs, focused on meditative techniques and the recitation of divine names, letter permutation, numerical symbolism of Hebrew letters (*gematria*), and acrostics, designed to bring one to a state of ecstatic union with God and to attain prophetic illumination. The goal of this mystical and prophetic experience was to untie the "knots" binding the soul to the body and the world. According to his own testimony, Abulafia wrote twenty-six books of prophecy based on his mystical experiences. Abulafia traveled widely and may have had messianic pretensions. He attempted to have an audience with Pope Nicholas III in 1280, possibly in order to declare himself the Messiah. In the 1280s, Solomon ben Abraham ibn Adret of Barcelona (ca. 1235–1310) led an attack against him and had Abulafia and his works banned because of his claims that his writings were on a par with those of the biblical prophets. Abulafia was a prolific writer who, in addition to his prophetic works—of which only one, the *Sefer ha-Ot* (Book of the Sign), has survived—wrote many books on topics such as Maimonides' *Guide for the Perplexed*, commentaries on the *Sefer Yetsirah*, and descriptions of meditative techniques.

The *Zohar*

During the late 1200s, a kabbalistic commentary on the Torah that would go on to have a monumental and transformative impact on Judaism and the West began to circulate in Castile. The commentary comprises many texts composed over a period of at least a decade, written in Aramaic in the name of important rabbis from the time of the Mishnah, in the 2nd century CE. The most prominent personality mentioned in this collection of Kabbalistic writings is Rabbi Shimon bar Yochai. By the beginning of the 14th century, this collection of texts came to be known by a number of names, but the one that stood the test of time was the *Sefer ha-Zohar* (Book of Splendor).

A careful reading of the text of the zoharic literature—which, in its printed form, is almost two thousand pages in length—reveals a pronounced influence of Hekhalot and Merkavah imagery, the writings of the Ḥasidei Ashkenaz, the Kabbalists of Provence, Gerona, and Castile, as well as some important medieval Jewish thinkers and philosophers such as Judah Ha-Levi and Moses Maimonides. The text also contains a number of foreign words of Spanish origin. This has led scholars to conclude that most, if not all, of the *Zohar* was composed in Castile toward the end of the 13th century. It is only in the later 1290s and early 1300s that we find citations from the zoharic corpus with any consistency. The earliest citation is in Isaac ibn Sahula's *Meshal ha-Kadmoni* and is taken from a part of the *Zohar* called the *Midrash ha-Ne'elam.*

Gershom Scholem argued that the main body of the *Zohar* was written by Moshe de Leon.[4] This position has been revised by Yehuda Liebes, who argued that the *Zohar* is, in fact, the product of a group of Spanish Kabbalists from the late 13th century, of which Moses de Leon was a prominent member but which also likely included Yosef Gikatilla, Todros Abulafia, Isaac ibn Sahula, Yosef of Hamadan, David ben Yehuda he-Ḥasid, Yosef Shalom Ashkenazi, and Baḥya ben Asher.[5]

The *Zohar* represents in many ways the culmination of a century of tremendous kabbalistic creativity that began in Provence in the late 12th century and ended in Castile in the early 14th century. The long and rambling poetic discourses found in zoharic texts engage with everything from the emergence of the ten *sefirot* from the inner reaches of God and *Ein Sof* to the mysteries of creation, the process of revelation, the mystical meaning of the *mitzvot* (commandments) and meditations on the gendered and highly erotic interactions of the *sefirot* expressed, in particular, as the desire of the *Shekhinah*, the tenth and lowest of the ten *sefirot*, to return to her male counterpart and be reassimilated into God in keeping with trends in Kabbalah from earlier in the 13th century. The *Zohar* argues that it is by means of the actions of Jews in the physical world—especially through the performance of commandments and the study of Torah—that the *sefirot* can be unified and the upper and lower realms perfected. These ideas are delivered in a highly cryptic style that presumes familiarity with many of the main principles of

Kabbalah as well as biblical and rabbinic literature. The *Zohar* encodes its kabbalistic message in a complex set of symbols that are in turn understood to be only the uncovering of mysteries contained within the words and even the letters of the Torah.

14th–16th Centuries:
From the Spanish Expulsion to the Safed Community

By the 14th century, Kabbalah began to spread throughout Western Europe, North Africa, and the Middle East. Treatises such as the anonymous *Ma'arekhet ha-Elohut*, along with the commentary on the Torah by Baḥya ben Asher and the *drashot* (sermons) of Joshua ibn Shu'aib, served to spread Kabbalah to wider audiences. Isaac ben Samuel of Acre's (late 13th–mid 14th century) *Me'irat Einaim* became a seminal exposition of the kabbalistic meaning behind the hints and allusions to secret teachings in the works of Nahmanides.[6] Kabbalah began to spread to Italy in the early 14th century through the works of Menaḥem Recanati, who wrote a popular kabbalistic commentary on the Torah and a book on the mystical meaning of the commandments. Two important works written some time in the second half of the 14th century—the *Sefer ha-Peli'ah*, a commentary on the first section of the Torah, and the *Sefer ha-Kanah*, concerning the kabbalistic meaning of the commandments—argue that both the philosophical and literalist interpretations of Judaism are misguided and that only according to the Kabbalah can Jewish law and tradition be properly understood. A similar sentiment is expressed in 15th century Castile in the writings of Shem Tov ibn Shem Tov, who attacked the philosophical teachings of Maimonides, blaming them for the growing trend of Jewish conversion to Christianity.

Kabbalistic literary activity began to decline in Spain during the 15th century leading up to the expulsion of the Jews in 1492. Although there were important Kabbalists still living in Spain during the mid to late 15th century, many began to migrate even before the expulsion. The exile of the Spanish Jewish community facilitated the spread of Kabbalah to many centers around the Mediterranean.

By the late 1530s, Safed had become the most important center for Kabbalists. Joseph Karo, a Spanish exile who grew up in the vibrant Jewish communities of Adrinopol and Salonika in Greece and became one of the most prominent rabbinic figures of all time, moved to Safed in 1536. There he composed his legal code, the *Shulkhan Arukh*, and served as the head of the Jewish court (*beit din*). Karo was also an accomplished Kabbalist who recorded a series of visions and revelations in a work entitled *Maggid Meisharim* that he claimed to have received from an angelic voice (*maggid*). Solomon ben Moses Alkebetz, the author of the famous Jewish liturgical poem *Lekha Dodi*, sung on Friday nights during the Kabbalat Shabbat service, along with his son-in-law and pupil Moses ben Jacob Cordovero, also moved from Greece to Safed around this time. Cordovero, who studied with Karo, went on to have an enormously productive career as both a teacher and a writer. He composed extensive systematic presentations of kabbalistic ideas, such as his *Pardes Rimmonim* and a multivolume commentary on the Torah entitled *Or Yakar*. He also attracted as his students a number of individuals who would go on to have a tremendous impact on the spread of kabbalistic ideas to the broader Jewish public.

Isaac Luria

Although he spent only a few years in the city of Safed before his death at a young age in 1572, Isaac Luria had an enormous impact on the community of Safed Kabbalists that permanently transformed the history of Jewish mysticism. Luria studied briefly with Cordovero when he arrived in Safed in 1570, but after the latter's death about six months later, Luria quickly became the preeminent Kabbalist of the community. Luria's meteoric rise was not by virtue of his impressive literary production, as his literary output was relatively small. Rather, the force of his impact on the Kabbalists of Safed was through his charismatic personality and the depth and creativity of his ideas, which he taught orally. Not long after Luria's death, hundreds of stories about his spiritual powers, his ability to perform magical wonders, to determine the origin of a person's soul or "soul root," to read a person's fate by the lines on his or her forehead, and other such miraculous tales began to circulate, testifying to the kind of impression Luria made on the imagination of the community. Despite the fact that Luria wrote very little, his teachings spread quickly to the broader Jewish community through the writings of his disciples. Luria's students, especially Hayim Vital, went on to write voluminous compositions based on their master's teachings. These quickly spread Lurianic Kabbalah throughout the Jewish communities of North Africa and Europe.

Luria's kabbalistic teachings were often presented as interpretations of the *Zohar*, although his symbolism of the ten *sefirot* became significantly more complex, with multiple levels and permutations. Luria expanded upon a number of important elements already present in one form or another in zoharic Kabbalah, such as the coming of the Messiah, the process of creation through divine self-contraction (*tzimtzum*), the "shattering of the vessels" (*shevirat ha-kelim*) that took place at a certain stage in the process of creation, the restoration (*tikkun*) of divine light, or "sparks," through Jewish actions and religious practice, and the mystical intention (*kavanah*) necessary for the proper practice of *mitzvot* and prayer. Luria also placed particular emphasis on the notion of *gilgul*, or reincarnation. Like the *Zohar* itself, Luria's Kabbalah contains bold and complex imagery regarding the inner dynamics of the divine realm of the *sefirot* and the potential for Jewish actions to rectify—or destroy—the order of the universe in its relation to God.

Shabbatai Zevi

By the mid-17th century, Kabbalah, especially in the form spread by the disciples of Isaac Luria, was widely disseminated throughout the Jewish world. The strong messianic inclination of Lurianic thinking, coupled with a number of traumatic political events—most notably the Chmielnicki massacres of 1648, which killed thousands and destroyed hundreds of Jewish communities throughout Eastern Europe—contributed to the vast popularity of the messianic movement that developed around the charismatic figure of Shabbatai Zevi. Born in Ismir to a wealthy merchant family in 1626, Zevi distinguished himself early in life as a gifted student. He was also an avid Kabbalist known for his bold tendency to pronounce the divine name aloud. According to historical accounts, Shabbatai Zevi seems to have been afflicted with severe manic depression, and during his manic phases he would engage in bizarre, deliberate violations of the commandments, in one instance marrying himself to a Torah scroll. In the spring of 1665, Shabbatai Zevi arrived in Gaza, where he met Nathan of Gaza, a charismatic Kabbalist and renowned healer of the soul. Both quickly became convinced that Zevi was the Messiah and soon won over many of the local rabbis in Palestine and Jerusalem. Nathan of Gaza, Abraham Miguel Cardozo, and others quickly began to circulate letters and writings, in which they employed kabbalistic symbolism to argue that the Messiah had arrived in the person of Shabbatai Zevi. As the news spread to the Jewish communities of Europe traumatized by disaster and primed for messianic redemption in the form of a grand kabbalistic *tikkun* (restoration), the Sabbatean movement gained many adherents, including a number of highly respected rabbis. In the summer of 1666, Zevi was brought before the Turkish Sultan. The historical accounts of what exactly happened in that meeting are unclear, but the result is certain: Shabbatai Zevi converted to Islam. This devastating disappointment brought the movement to a catastrophic end, with most of Zevi's followers abandoning the hopes they had placed in him. For some, however, the conversion of their Messiah was regarded as a profound kabbalistic mystery that simply needed time to unfold. Those followers of Shabbatai Zevi who continued to believe in his messianic identity generally held their belief secret and are referred to as crypto-Sabbateans. This group developed a complex system of kabbalistic explanation of the life and actions of Shabbatai Zevi. Adherents to the Sabbatean doctrine persisted for several generations, and small numbers still exist today. Another small group of Jews at the time of Zevi's conversion converted to Islam themselves, creating a secret sect known as the Dönme, who outwardly practiced Islam but secretly preserved a form of Sabbatean Kabbalah.

18th-Century Kabbalah

After the Sabbatean debacle in the late 17th century, Kabbalists became more conservative in the way that they discussed and wrote about their mystical ideas, particularly with regard to messianic speculation. Most focused on reconciling the details of Lurianic Kabbalah with the *Zohar* and with the interpretation of works by earlier authorities.

An intriguing school of Kabbalists developed in Jerusalem in the mid-18th century at the Beit El yeshiva under the leadership of the Yemenite Kabbalist Shalom Sha'rabi (1720–1780), who focused on Lurianic Kabbalah, with a particular emphasis on contemplative prayer.[7] Sha'rabi and his school came to be recognized as the main authorities of Kabbalah for Jews living in the Muslim world, and Sha'rabi himself acquired a reputation as a Kabbalist almost on a par with Isaac Luria.

Israel Baal Shem Tov and the Rise of Hasidism

In the mid-18th century, a new social phenomenon in the Jewish world began to take root in Poland-Lithuania, centered around the kabbalistic traditions and the teachings of Israel b. Eliezer Ba'al Shem Tov (the Besht). The Hasidic movement, as it came to be called, emphasized a democratic religious ideal wherein spiritual achievement is attainable through sincerity, piety, and joyful worship. That is not to say that the movement did not have an intellectual component as well—thousands of Hasidic books and treatises were composed in the first few generations, and most of them are infused with kabbalistic motifs and images. As the Hasidic movement gained wide popularity in Eastern Europe throughout the 18th and 19th centuries, many elements of the Kabbalah became widely known to the general Jewish public, and Hasidic masters would often incorporate kabbalistic symbols into their sermons and teachings.

Starting in Podolye, the Besht became famous as a magical healer and wonder-worker—the name "Baal Shem Tov" means "Master of the Good Name" and relates to the kabbalistic notion of the power of divine names. Some Hasidic rabbis became the heads of dynasties that grew over time to include thousands of followers. Some groups still active today, such as Chabad Lubavitch and Breslov, continue to spread their kabbalistically infused teachings to broader Jewish audiences.

Kabbalah in the 20th and 21st Centuries

In addition to the many Hasidic rabbis and disciples of the Beit El yeshiva who remained active into the 20th century, individuals such as Yehuda Ashlag and his disciple and brother-in-law Yehuda Zevi Brandwein continued to develop and spread knowledge about kabbalistic texts and ideas. Ashlag, who was born in Warsaw but moved to Jerusalem in 1920, composed many important texts and commentaries on the works of earlier Kabbalists, including the famous *Maʿalot ha-Sullam* (1945–60) commentary and translation of the *Zohar* in twenty-two volumes, completed by his brother-in-law after Ashlag's death. Brandwein also wrote commentaries on the works of Moses Cordovero and Isaac Luria, as well as a complete library of Lurianic Kabbalah in fourteen volumes. Abraham Isaac Kook, the founding thinker of religious Zionism, was also an avid Kabbalist who sought to apply his mystical teaching in social and political action.

In the late 1960s Philip Berg, born Shraga Feivel Gruberger in Brooklyn, New York, traveled to Jerusalem where he studied with Yehuda Zevi Brandwein. Berg began to open institutes for the study and teaching of Kabbalah, first in Tel Aviv and then throughout the United States and Europe. The branches of Berg's institute came to be known as the Kabbalah Centre,[8] with its main headquarters in Los Angeles, where a number of American celebrities, most notably Madonna, have become associated with the movement. Berg's main goal in developing the Kabbalah Centre is to spread kabbalistic ideas in ways that are comprehensible and practical in daily life. The Kabbalah Centre markets books, classes, online tutorials, "Kabbalah water," and red string bracelets as part of their mission to disseminate kabbalistic teachings as broadly as possible among both Jews and non-Jews. Today the center is co-directed by Berg's sons, Yehuda and Michael Berg.

The History of Scholarship

Jewish scholarship in the Western academic, scientific sense began with a group of researchers in Germany associated with the Wissenschaft des Judentums (Science of Judaism) movement.[9] While their work often displays enormous erudition and wide-ranging knowledge, it is also marked by a number of biases. These scholars wanted to demonstrate through their studies that Jews and Judaism are inherently rational, enlightened, and worthy of inclusion in Western society and culture.[10] As Wolf Landau declared, "Wissenschaft, the clear, pure understanding of religion, is the only justification for our existence as a people."[11] Unsurprisingly, their work tended to emphasize the more rational, philosophical, and scientific aspects of the history of Jewish thought, while downplaying or openly criticizing the nonrational or mystical streams. In 1870 Leopold Zunz asserted that "the cultivation of Wissenschaft alone guards against such aberrations as superstition, excessive literalism and kabbalistic caprice."[12] The work of many Wissenschaft scholars entailed an apologetic presentation of Judaism, designed to argue that Jews deserve full emancipation and inclusion in public life, and that Judaism is not irrational, superstitious, and antiscientific, or a "dead" religious tradition lacking relevance.[13]

Naturally, many Wissenschaft scholars presented Kabbalah and texts like the *Sefer ha-Bahir* and *Sefer ha-Zohar* as embarrassing aberrations. As Heinrich Graetz says in his influential multivolume history of the Jews with regard to the appearance of the *Sefer ha-Bahir*, "This occult science, which made its appearance with a flourish, rests on a deception, at best, on the self-deception of its founders. Its theory is not old, as it pretended, but very modern . . . The Kabbalah is a grotesque distortion of Jewish and philosophical ideas. In order to make it appear ancient and authentic, the compilers had recourse to fraud."[14]

It was within this intellectual context that Gershom Scholem began to build the serious academic discipline of Kabbalah studies.[15] Born in Berlin at the turn of the century to an assimilated and wealthy Jewish family, Scholem chose to "rebel" against his father when, at a young age, he became a Zionist, opposed the German position in World War I, and took a strong interest in Judaism, going so far as to learn Hebrew and seek out instruction from Orthodox Jews.[16] Although Scholem himself chose not to adopt Orthodox religious practice (though he did participate in an Orthodox community for some time during his youth in Berlin), he held deep respect for the dedication to Jewish learning and textual study among the Orthodox Jews, and he felt alienated from his reformist religious upbringing. As Scholem commented in an interview in 1975 on the nature of his own "revolt" against the Jewish world into which he was born, "A person living in a liberal-Jewish, German-assimilationist environment had the feeling that those people were devoting their entire lives to self-delusion."[17] The delusion was, according to Scholem, the possibility of meaningful Jewish integration into German society.[18]

The experiences of his youth informed Scholem's interests as a scholar and his desire to discover the "true" history of Judaism, free from rationalist bias or assimilationist apologetics. In 1923 Scholem immigrated to Palestine, a decision he regarded as essential in enabling him to study Judaism free from his predecessors' apologetic agenda.[19] Counter to the tendencies prominent in the Wissenschaft school, Scholem focused on the historical importance of the "irrational," "mystical," and "symbolic" elements of Judaism—found most prominently in Kabbalah. David Biale has thus dubbed Scholem's approach to the study of Jewish mysticism and its role in Jewish history a "counter-history" that embraced the general outline of the established historical narrative set down by Wissenschaft scholars, but fundamentally revised the role and importance of mystical trends within that narrative.[20] For Scholem, the history of Judaism is driven by the dialectic tensions between conservation and innovation, rationalism and mysticism. Scholem regarded these as *productive* tensions influencing the course of Jewish history.[21] As Biale notes, Scholem held that "Jewish theology, encompassing both rationalism and demonic irrationalism, is anarchistic: it yields no one authoritative formula or dogma. The very vitality of the Jewish tradition lies in this anarchism, since dogma, in Scholem's view, is by definition lifeless."[22] Whereas Scholem's 19th-century predecessors often regarded mysticism and myth "as roadblocks to the forward progress of Jewish history, Scholem sees them as motivating forces."[23]

Scholem's approach to the study of Judaism and his perception that esoteric and kabbalistic discourse plays a decisive and important role in the history of the Jewish people was out of step with Wissenschaft scholarship. Scholem recounts the story of a meeting he had with the then elderly Philip Bloch, a student of Heinrich Graetz, at his residence in Berlin in the early 1920s. Upon seeing Bloch's substantial library of kabbalistic books, Scholem commented: "How wonderful it is, Herr Professor, that you have studied all this!" to which the elderly gentleman replied, "What, am I supposed to *read* this rubbish, too?" About this meeting, Scholem notes in his memoir, "that was a great moment in my life."[24] By this, Daniel Abrams suggests, Scholem meant that "if the most esteemed and elderly scholar in Berlin could speak in such disparaging terms of a body of Jewish literature (in this case Kabbalah), then such overwhelming biases had blinded all serious scholars and prevented them from developing the field. Scholem had found his calling."[25] By choosing to go against the grain of earlier scholarship and study Jewish mystical texts, Scholem substantially redefined the field.[26]

Scholem often characterized the scholarship of his predecessors as a kind of eulogy or death knell, intended to catalogue and thereby put to rest the aspects of Judaism that were out of step with rationalist-enlightenment thinking. Scholem regarded Leopold Zunz and Moritz Steinschneider as prime examples of the "scholars of destruction,"[27] whose work on Judaism resembled the work of "gravediggers and embalmers . . . gathering grasses in the fields of the past, drying them out so that there not remain in them any of the juice of life, and putting them in something which one does not know whether to call a book or a grave. . . Their books, the classical works of the Science of Judaism, are a kind of procession around the dead."[28] Scholem relates the story of a student of Steinschneider, who, "as a young Zionist, was astounded upon seeing his [Steinschneider's] library, and began to lecture his master about the renaissance of the people, its hidden values, and so on. To which the hoary nonagenarian answered, 'Please, sir; we have no other task but to conduct a 'proper funeral' for all that.'"[29] It was Scholem's firm conviction that his predecessors were engaged in a "diligent but lifeless discipline"[30] that sought to "bury" the vital dynamics of classical Judaism in the hopeful expectation of "the liberal messiah"[31] that would bring Jews complete emancipation and render Judaism obsolete. With regard to the tendency of Wissenschaft scholars to obfuscate the mystical elements of Judaism, Scholem declared: "The removal of the pointedly irrational and of demonic enthusiasms from Jewish history, through an exaggerated emphasis upon the theological and the spiritual . . . [t]his is the fundamental, original sin which outweighs all others."[32]

Scholem's scholarship on the messianic movement surrounding the personality of Shabbatai Zevi[33] is a prime example of the kind of role that mystical symbolism and myth can play in Jewish history. Scholem often described Kabbalists as religious anarchists, caught between the two poles of traditional conservation and nihilistic destruction. In Scholem's view, "the Jewish mystic lives and acts in perpetual rebellion against a world with which he strives with all his zeal to be at peace."[34] This tension between the amorphous rapture of mystical encounter and the traditional boundaries of Jewish law and communal life, a tension that Scholem regarded as the secret key to Jewish vitality, took a drastic turn in the minds of the followers of Shabbatai Zevi. The Sabbatean movement saw the secret nihilistic tendencies of Kabbalah come out into the open, expressed as a desire for both liberation from the exile *and* liberation from the restrictions of Jewish law. This desire among the followers of Shabbatai Zevi to assert political and religious autonomy had a lasting impact, according to Scholem, on the history of the Jewish people. In Scholem's view, "the development of Sabbatian nihilism was by no means a purely self-destructive force; on the contrary, beneath the surface of law-lessness, antinomianism, and catastrophic negation, powerful constructive impulses were at work, and these, I maintain, it is the duty of the scholar to uncover."[35] The culmination of "constructive" impulses at work in the Sabbatean movement can be found, according to Scholem, in the development of secular Zionism, and even critical scholarship itself.[36] Scholem's research into the Sabbatean movement became central to his belief that Jewish history is driven more by ideas and events *within* Judaism than it is by those external to it. And, for Scholem, Jewish mysticism is a key aspect of the internal force behind Jewish history and part of the reason why Judaism and *halakha* have been able to survive.[37]

The Task of the Text Scholar

The academic study of Judaism, and Kabbalah in particular, in Scholem's view, requires a careful analysis of the texts with a degree of scientific remove. His painstaking, meticulous attention to the texts and his work uncovering kabbalistic manuscripts, cataloging them, and delineating their history and basic ideas are among his most important contributions.[38] When he began his research program in earnest in the early 1920s, relatively few kabbalistic texts had been printed, and many of those that had been were available in rare and often faulty editions. Most texts remained in manuscript form—a situation that prevails to this day—and Scholem undertook the grueling task of cataloging the manuscripts that had been scattered across Europe and elsewhere. Scholem himself was a famous bibliophile,[39] who amassed a large and important collection of kabbalistic texts that have been preserved in the Scholem Library in Jerusalem.

Scholem's approach to the study of Jewish mystical literature involved a combination of phenomenology, the study of ideas and symbolic structures found in Kabbalistic texts that persist over a long duration,[40] and historical criticism.[41] He describes the task of the scholar of Jewish mysticism in the following manner:

In digging up and evaluating the material, a scholar must make every effort to preserve a critical attitude. For too long before historians became interested in Jewish mysticism, charlatans and cranks were drawn to it. This was of doubtful benefit to the study of Kabbalah. The effort to understand what was here enacted in the heart of Jewry cannot dispense with historical criticism and clear vision. For even symbols grow out of historical experience and are saturated with it. A proper understanding of it requires both a "phenomenological" aptitude for seeing things as a whole and a gift for historical analysis. One complements the other; taken together, they promise valuable findings.[42]

Unlike the "charlatans and cranks," a reference to authors of popular literature on Kabbalah who possessed little or no knowledge of the primary sources of Jewish mysticism and often simply rehashed popular misconceptions (a pursuit for which he had little patience), Scholem dedicated his scholarly career to a meticulous examination of the extant kabbalistic texts in order to illuminate both the broader contours of kabbalistic ideas and the history of the texts from which those ideas emerge.

Scholem's research made major contributions to the understanding of kabbalistic symbolism. He described the kabbalistic conception of the symbol as "an expressible representation of something which lies beyond the sphere of expression and communication, something which comes from a sphere whose face is, as it were, turned inward and away from us. A hidden and inexpressible reality finds its expression in the symbol."[43] Or, as he put the matter elsewhere, "every authentic symbol involves an aspect of mystery. It expresses in brief that which the mouth cannot speak and the ear cannot hear."[44] Symbolic expression in Jewish mysticism thus incorporates an essential element of paradox, in which the ultimate object of the symbol is a divine reality that the Kabbalists themselves maintain is beyond the reach of the human intellect. From the perspective of the Kabbalist, according to Scholem, all reality bears a secret symbolic valence, an aspect of meaning that embodies and conveys a divine mystery incomprehensible to the human intellect.[45] As Scholem remarked, "what makes the *kabbalah* interesting is its power to transmute things into symbols."[46] The Kabbalah reimagines both the physical cosmos as a whole and the particular laws, practices, and sacred texts of Judaism as divine mysteries reflecting the secret realm of God.[47]

One of the definitive characteristics of Kabbalah that distinguishes it from the broader category of Jewish mysticism and esotericism is the symbolic structure of the ten divine luminosities (*sefirot*). Like other symbols, the *sefirot* are not intended to be understood as physical entities or fully comprehensible ideas. Rather, they embody the paradox of all symbols in that the Kabbalists employ them as manifestations and expressions of an infinite and ineffable divine reality. The system of the ten *sefirot* is special within Kabbalah, however, because it constitutes a kind of symbolic language that depicts the dynamic interactions of the inner life of God, a form of myth that scholars often refer to as "theosophy." Scholem took great interest in exploring the kabbalistic theosophy, which he describes as

> a mystical doctrine, or school of thought, which purports to perceive and to describe the mysterious workings of the Divinity, perhaps also believing it possible to become absorbed in its contemplation. Theosophy postulates a kind of divine emanation whereby God, abandoning his self-contained repose, awakens to mysterious life; further, it maintains that the mysteries of creation reflect the pulsation of this divine life.[48]

The system of the ten *sefirot* is thus part of a worldview in which the secret mysteries of both God and the universe can be unlocked. Kabbalah regards itself as the tradition that passes on the knowledge of these divine mysteries. Of particular importance for many Kabbalists is the correlation between theosophic processes and the practices of Judaism. The commandments of Jewish law (*mitzvot*) are understood to reflect the inner life of God.

Theosophies are often associated with what scholars refer to as "theurgy," which connotes the capacity for human actions to influence the divine realm. Kabbalists believe that through the practice of Jewish law one can influence the *sefirot*, drawing them closer to one another, bringing divine blessing or *shefa* (overflow) into the world, and hastening the moment of redemption. As Scholem notes, "the *mitzvoth* are to the Kabbalist symbols in which a deeper and hidden sphere of reality becomes transparent."[49] By infusing symbolic power into the mandates of *halakha*, Kabbalists succeeded, in Scholem's view, in creating a new basis for the practice of Judaism, giving it greater relevance and meaning for many Jews at various points in history.[50] Thus, according to Scholem, "Jewish mysticism in its various forms represents an attempt to interpret the religious values of Judaism as mystical values."[51]

Another important element of Jewish mysticism to which Scholem dedicated significant attention is the centrality of the Hebrew language.[52] As the language of revelation and the ancient tongue of the Israelite ancestors, Hebrew is accorded unique status in Kabbalah. It is regarded as the language of God, a powerful tool of divine creation that both orders and sustains the cosmic order.

Kabbalists who differ in almost everything else are at one in regarding language as something more precious than an inadequate instrument for contact between human beings. To them Hebrew, the holy tongue, is not simply a means of expressing certain thoughts . . . having a purely conventional character, in accordance with the theory of language dominant in the Middle Ages. Language in its purest form, that is, Hebrew, according to the Kabbalists, reflects the fundamental spiritual nature of the world . . . Speech reaches God because it comes from God. All creation—and this is an important principle of most kabbalists—is from the point of view of God, nothing but an expression of his hidden self that begins and ends by giving itself a name, the holy name of God, the perpetual act of creation. All that lives is an expression of God's language—and what is it that Revelation can reveal in the last resort if not the name of God?[53]

The Hebrew language conceals a symbolic dimension, a capacity, as the Kabbalists understand it, to convey "a communication of what is non-communicable."[54] Hebrew is endowed with this unique aspect of transcendent meaning because it is understood to be the very language of God, the tool with which the universe was created and through which all being is sustained. Moreover, Hebrew derives from the name of God (the tetragrammaton), which the Kabbalists regard as "the metaphysical origin of all language."[55] Many Kabbalists embraced the principle that God and His name are identical, as we find, for example, in the *Zohar*, "He and His name are one" (3:291b). The name of God is, paradoxically, a manifestation of the infinite.[56] All of creation and revelation, and the Torah in particular, are understood as elaborations of this divine name, thereby granting every aspect of the cosmic order and the religious life of Judaism a secret, symbolic dimension that at once reflects and impacts the incomprehensible inner life of God.

Another important area of Scholem's studies is the nature and role of mysticism itself in Judaism.[57] Scholarship on religion has traditionally tended to identify mysticism as a religious system that speaks about the experience of union with God (*unio mystica*). There has been a debate about the issue of mystical experience, with some (dubbed "essentialists") arguing for a common "core" experience that all mystics share and others (called "contextualists") maintaining that all mystical experience is conditioned by the historical circumstance of the mystic.[58] Scholem tended toward the contextualist model, arguing that "there is no mysticism as such, there is only the mysticism of a particular religious system . . . That there remains a common characteristic it would be absurd to deny . . . But only in our days has the belief gained ground that there is such a thing as abstract mystical religion."[59]

Scholem imagined three stages in the evolution of religious consciousness.[60] In the first stage, mysticism is unnecessary, since the world is regarded "as being full of gods whom man encounters at every step and whose presence can be experienced without recourse to ecstatic meditation."[61] In the second stage, religion comes to recognize "a vast abyss, conceived as absolute, between God, the infinite and transcendental Being, and Man the finite creature."[62] In the third stage, mysticism develops. According to Scholem's conception, "mysticism does not deny or overlook the abyss; on the contrary, it begins by realizing its existence, but from there it proceeds to a quest for the secret that will close it in, the hidden path that will span it."[63] Mysticism is thus a struggle to overcome, through the discovery of a *secret*, the transcendence of God in order to enter into contact with the divine.

Scholem argued, interestingly, that whereas the Christian and Islamic mystical religions have developed forms of *unio mystica* in which the self of the mystic is understood to be absorbed completely into the infinity of the divine, Jewish mysticism stops short of complete self-annihilation in God. According to Scholem, Jewish mystical experience, often referred to by the term *devekut* (cleaving), "is not union, because union with God is denied man even in that mystical upsurge of the soul, according to kabbalistic theology. But it comes as near to union as a mystical interpretation of Judaism would allow."[64] This led Scholem to advance the position that "Jewish mysticism as such does not exist at all in the sense of direct, unmediated union with the godhead. There is no such thing within the framework of the Jewish tradition, as such a union requires a level of daring which seems impossible within the context of the concepts traditionally accepted by one who calls himself a Jew."[65] More recent scholarship has significantly reconsidered Scholem's construction of mysticism and his assertion that Jewish mysticism lacks the element of *unio mystica*.

In addition to his phenomenological studies, Scholem produced an enormous wealth of valuable research on the history of Jewish mysticism. Although his studies were meticulously detailed and supported by a much more comprehensive evaluation of the texts than many of his predecessors' studies, it is important to note that, before Scholem, earlier scholars had formulated a number of his claims regarding the history of Kabbalah.[66] As David Myers has recently noted, the "narrative of neglect," whereby the scholars of the Wissenschaft des Judentums are depicted as entirely dismissive of Jewish mysticism, is only one facet of 19th century scholarship on Jewish mystical literature. Rather, "it would be much more accurate to place that disregard at one end of a spectrum of 19th century *Wissenschaft* attitudes—at the opposite end of which were various degrees of engagement in the study of Jewish mysticism."[67] Important contributions such as the dating of the *Zohar* to the late 13th century,[68] as well as identifying the important periods in the history of the development of Jewish mysticism, were initiated by some of the very scholars whose work Scholem describes as a "procession around the dead." Moshe Idel has noted that "Scholem's critique of the negative evaluation of Kabbalah in the writings of such representatives of the Wissenschaft des Judentums as Moritz Steinschneider and Heinrich Graetz, although justified, is nevertheless partial. These two giants of Jewish scholarship must be seen not only as critics of Kabbalah but also as two of the founders of its academic study."[69] An interesting note is that although Scholem later rejected Graetz's stance toward the role of mystical trends within Judaism, he also described reading Graetz's *History of the Jews* at the age of thirteen as a powerful experience that introduced him to the world of Jewish history.[70] Scholem's "counter-history," as Biale refers to it, was not a new history but rather a different, and significantly better documented, *interpretation* of an existing historical narrative.

Recent Trends in Scholarship on Jewish Mysticism

More recent scholarship on Kabbalah—though indebted to Scholem—has moved in new directions. Scholarship on Judaism in the late 19th and early 20th centuries was motivated in many cases by theological interests and commitments, in addition to political apologetic concerns.[71] Many of the prominent scholars of Judaism from that period were also ordained rabbis who, in many cases, worked in seminaries.[72] The situation in the academy today, in both the United States[73] and abroad, has changed significantly. New sets of questions are being asked from the perspective of a wider range of academic disciplines. The past thirty or so years have witnessed an expansion of the kinds of interests at stake in the academic study of Jewish mysticism. Contemporary scholarship seeks to enhance our knowledge of humanity, the contours of Western intellectual history, and the phenomenology of religion. To that end, scholars employ new academic tools and methodologies that have been developed within the fields of religious studies, gender studies, philosophy, literary criticism, postmodern hermeneutics, psychoanalysis, anthropology, and sociology, to name a few. Recent studies have also begun to explore contemporary forms of Kabbalah, a subject in which Scholem took surprisingly little interest.[74] These new methodological perspectives are important for a renewed understanding of Jewish mysticism and what it has to contribute to the world of academic knowledge.

In order to understand the significance of the introduction of new methodological perspectives into the study of Jewish mysticism, it is important to consider the purpose of methodological models.[75] They are primarily *tools* designed to help researchers *notice* things in their data that might otherwise escape their consideration. The data under scrutiny are a *discourse*, whether textual, verbal, pictorial, behavioral, or otherwise.[76] Only discursive expressions of one form or another can serve as the subject of critical academic analysis—the inner thoughts and experiences of individuals, without being expressed in some fashion, are inaccessible for the purposes of research. A methodological model or category like "mysticism" is an abstraction, designed to draw attention to features found within the discourses under examination, in order to help researchers perceive the issues at stake. As Jonathan Z. Smith has noted, "scholarly labor is a disciplined exaggeration in the direction of knowledge."[77] What this means is that models such as "mysticism" and "religion" are abstractions or generalizations that, when constructed in complex and multifaceted ways, aid in the study of particular pieces of evidence by drawing attention to elements of the data that might otherwise have gone unnoticed. Mysticism, for example, as an analytical category, might be constructed in different ways by different scholars; all that matters is that each scholar employs the category in ways that serve to produce insightful scholarship.

One could draw a useful comparison between methodological tools as they are employed by academics and maps, which often work best when they do not reflect their territory, be it a city or a body of discourse, in too much detail. Smith cites the fascinating example of the 1979 New York City subway map, which he describes as "one of the least successful experiments in civic map production."[78] The problem with the map was that it was *too* accurate. The subway lines were depicted in their true shape and configuration, with a detailed map of the surface streets of the city superimposed on top. Although the map contained the most complete and accurate information of any subway map before or since, most people found it confusing and unusable. Maps are tools in the service of navigating territory, and that purpose is not necessarily well served simply by reproducing the territory, or data, as accurately as possible. The point of a map is not to help people notice everything but to direct their attention to the features that are essential to the task at hand. As Smith puts it, "maps are structures of transformation, not structures of reproduction. What is at stake is an issue concerning which students of religion have been notably shy, the cognitive power of distortion, or difference, if you prefer the less strident term."[79] A map is not an end in and of itself but rather a means to an end, which is the production of useful research through the imaginative activity of generalization and abstraction. Categories such as "mysticism," "religion," "gender," "power," and "culture" can thus serve as useful tools for the study of human discourse, including the discourses of Jewish mysticism.

Consider, for example, the category of "religion." This term has had a politically fraught history and has been used at times in problematic ways.[80] But when constructed as a nuanced and complex model, it can be a tool for fruitful research. Jonathan Z. Smith has noted that "religion is solely the creation of the scholar's study. It is created for the scholar's analytic purposes by his imaginative acts of comparison and generalization. Religion has no independent existence apart from the academy."[81] Smith offers the following suggestion for how to "imagine" religion and employ it as an abstraction that, through the power of "distortion," helps one notice certain important features of "religious" discourses:

> Religion is the quest, within the bounds of the human, historical condition, for the power to manipulate and negotiate one's "situation" so as to have "space" in which to meaningfully dwell. It is the power to relate one's domain to the plurality of environmental and social spheres in such a way as to guarantee the conviction that one's existence "matters" . . . What we study when we study religion is the variety of attempts to map, construct and inhabit such positions of power through the use of myths, rituals and experiences of transformation.[82]

By operating with such a model of "religion," we can see that all the previously mentioned methodologies can serve as invaluable tools for examining Jewish mystical texts by helping us to understanding how such discourses serve to "construct and inhabit . . . positions of power" and create a "'space' in which to meaningfully dwell" through the development of symbols, theosophies, myths, rituals, and articulations of mystical experiences. As the chapters in this volume amply demonstrate, the academic study of Jewish mysticism has already shed considerable light on these questions. The future directions of the field continue to hold out the promise of teaching us much about Jewish experience, the history of ideas, and the ways that humans have engaged with questions of the human condition.

The historical survey in this chapter has been adapted and reproduced with permission from http://cojs.org/cojswiki/Historical_Periods_of_Jewish_Mysticism. For more comprehensive historical surveys of Kabbalah, to which this one is indebted, see Gershom Scholem, *Kabbalah* (New York: Meridian, 1978), pp. 8–86; idem, *Major Trends in Jewish Mysticism* (New York: Schocken Books, 1954); idem, "The Historical Development of Jewish Mysticism," in *On the Possibility of Jewish Mysticism in Our Time and Other Essays*, ed. Avraham Shapira, trans. Jonathan Chipman (Philadelphia: Jewish Publication Society, 1997), pp. 121–54.

1. *M. Ḥag.* 2:1.

2. Scholem, *Kabbalah*, pp. 31–32.

3. Scholem, *Origins of the Kabbalah*, ed. R. J. Zwi Werblowsky, trans. Allan Arkush (Princeton, NJ: Princeton University Press, 1987), p. 394.

4. See, for example, Scholem, *Major Trends*, p. 159.

5. See Yehuda Liebes, "How the Zohar Was Written," in *Studies in the Zohar*, trans. A. Schwartz, S. Nakache, and P. Peli (Albany: State University of New York Press, 1993), pp. 85–138. Daniel Abrams has recently argued that the history of the texts of zoharic literature is far too complex, both in terms of its redaction and the process of its composition, for this collection to be regarded as a "book" ("The Invention of the 'Zohar' as a Book: On the Assumptions and Expectations of the Kabbalists and Modern Scholars," *Kabbalah* 19 [2009]: 7–142).

6. See Eitan Fishbane, *As Light before Dawn: The Inner World of a Medieval Kabbalist* (Stanford: Stanford University Press, 2009).

7. For a recent study on this subject, see Pinchas Giller, *Shalom Shar'abi and the Kabbalists of Beit El* (Oxford: Oxford University Press, 2008).

8. For a recent study of this movement, see Jody Myers, *Kabbalah and the Spiritual Quest: The Kabbalah Centre in America* (Westport, CT: Praeger, 2007).

9. See Nahum Glatzer, "The Beginnings of Modern Jewish Studies," in *Studies in Nineteenth-Century Jewish Intellectual History*, ed. A. Altmann (Cambridge, MA: Harvard University Press, 1964), pp. 27–45; Ismar Schorsch, *From Text to Context: The Turn to History in Modern Judaism* (Hanover, MA: Brandeis University Press, 1994).

10. See David Biale, *Kabbalah and Counter-History* (Cambridge, MA: Harvard University Press, 1979), pp. 13–25; Michael A. Meyer, "Two Persistent Tensions within the Wissenschaft des Judentums," *Modern Judaism* 24 (2004): 105–19; I. Schorsch, *From Text to Context*, pp. 163–65, 266–93.

11. Cited in Meyer, "Two Persistent Tensions," p. 111.

12. Cited in ibid., p. 112.

13. See Amy Newman, "The Death of Judaism in German Protestant Thought from Luther to Hegel," *Journal of the American Academy of Religion* 61 (1993): 455–84. One interesting exception to the apologetic agenda of Wissenschaft scholarship is Moritz Steinschneider, who was, as Michael Meyer has noted, "totally uninterested in any possible effect of Wissenschaft des Judentums on contemporary Jews and Judaism" ("Two Persistent Tensions," p. 112).

14. Heinrich Graetz, *History of the Jews* (Philadelphia: Jewish Publication Society of America, 1945), 3:556.

15. A sizable body of scholarship has been written on the life and work of Gershom Scholem. See, for example, Biale, *Kabbalah and Counter-History*; Joseph Dan, *Gershom Scholem and the Mystical Dimension of Jewish History* (New York: New York University Press, 1988); Eliezer Schweid, *Judaism and Mysticism according to Gershom Scholem* (Atlanta: Scholars Press, 1985); Paul Mendes-Flohr, ed., *Gershom Scholem: The Man and His Work* (Albany: State University of New York Press, 1994); Steven M. Wasserstrom, *Religion after Religion: Gershom Scholem, Mircea Eliade, and Henry Corbin at Eranos* (Princeton, NJ: Princeton University Press, 1999); Daniel Abrams, "Defining Modern Academic Scholarship: Gershom Scholem and the Establishment of a New(?) Discipline," *Journal of Jewish Thought and Philosophy* 9 (2000): 267–302; idem, "Presenting and Representing Gershom Scholem: A Review Essay," *Modern Judaism* 20 (2000): 226–40; David Myers, "The Scholem-Kurzweil Debate and Modern Jewish Historiography," *Modern Judaism* 6 (1986): 261–86; idem, *Re-Inventing the Jewish Past: European Jewish Intellectuals and the Zionist Return to History* (Oxford: Oxford University Press, 1995), pp. 151–76; Peter Schäfer, "Gershom Scholem und die 'Wissenschaft des Judentums,'" in *Gershom Scholem: Zwischen den Disziplinen*, ed. Peter Schäfer and Gary Smith (Frankfurt: Suhrkamp, 1995), pp. 122–56; Moshe Idel, *Old Worlds, New Mirrors: On Jewish Mysticism and Twentieth-Century Thought* (Philadelphia: University of Pennsylvania Press 2010); Susan Handelman, *Fragments of Redemption: Jewish Thought and Literary Theory in Benjamin, Scholem, and Levinas* (Bloomington: Indiana University Press, 1991).

16. See Gershom Scholem's description of his early political and intellectual interests in his *From Berlin to Jerusalem: Memories of My Youth*, trans. H. Zohn (New York: Schocken Books, 1980); on Scholem's conflict with his father, in particular, see ibid., pp. 84–85.

17. "With Gershom Scholem: An Interview," in *On Jews and Judaism in Crisis* (New York: Schocken Books, 1976), p. 2; see also the discussion in David Myers, "The Scholem-Kurzweil Debate and Modern Jewish Historiography," *Modern Judaism* 6 (1986): 264–66.

18. On this point in Scholem's thought, see Biale, *Kabbalah and Counter-History*, p. 5.

19. See Abrams, "Defining Modern Academic Scholarship," p. 278.

20. See Biale, *Kabbalah and Counter-History*, pp. 11–12, 189–205.

21. See Moshe Idel, "History of Kabbalah and History of the Jews" [in Hebrew], *Theory and Criticism* 6 (1995): 137–48.

22. Biale, *Kabbalah and Counter-History* (2nd ed., 1982), p. 5.

23. Ibid., p. 8.

24. Scholem, *From Berlin to Jerusalem*, pp. 149–50.

25. Daniel Abrams, "Presenting and Representing Gershom Scholem: A Review Essay," *Modern Judaism* 20 (2000): 234.

26. On the question of Scholem as the founder of a "new" field of Kabbalah research, see Abrams, "Defining Modern Academic Scholarship," pp. 267–302.

27. Gershom Scholem, "Reflections on Modern Jewish Studies," in Shapira, *On the Possibility of Jewish Mysticism in Our Time*, p. 59. On the characterization of 19th-century scholarship as an "academic mortician" of Judaism, see Biale, *Kabbalah and Counter-History*, p. 8; Abrams, "Defining Modern Academic Scholarship," p. 270 n. 3; Idel, *Old Worlds, New Mirrors*, 103–105.

28. Scholem, "Reflections on Modern Jewish Studies," p. 59.

29. Ibid., p. 60.

30. Ibid., p. 64.

31. Ibid., p. 62.

32. Ibid., p. 63.

33. Scholem composed a sizable monograph on this subject, *Sabbatai Sevi: The Mystical Messiah* (Princeton, NJ: Princeton University Press, 1973).

34. Scholem, *Major Trends*, p. 34.

35. Scholem, "Redemption through Sin," in idem, *The Messianic Idea in Judaism* (New York: Schocken Books, 1971), p. 84.

36. Ibid.

37. See Myers, *Re-Inventing the Jewish Past*, pp. 162, 171–72.

38. On Scholem's philological methodology and its independence from his broader political and religious aims, see Abrams, "Defining Modern Academic Scholarship."

39. See Malachi Beit-Arie, "Gershom Scholem as Bibliophile," in idem, *Gershom Scholem: The Man and His Work*, pp. 120–27.

40. On the phenomenology of Jewish mysticism, see Elliot Wolfson, "Structure, Innovation, and Diremptive Temporality: The Use of Models to Study Continuity and Discontinuity in Kabbalistic Tradition," *Journal for the Study of Religions and Ideologies* 6, no. 18 (winter 2007): 143–67, esp. the comments on p. 156.

41. See Wasserstrom, *Religion after Religion*, 26–28.

42. Gershom Scholem, *On the Kabbalah and Its Symbolism* (New York: Schocken Books, 1965), p. 3; see also Moshe Idel's comments, *Kabbalah: New Perspectives* (New Haven, CT: Yale University Press, 1988), p. 11.

43. Scholem, *Major Trends*, p. 27.

44. Scholem, "The Historical Development of Jewish Mysticism," p. 140.

45. On Scholem's emphasis on the role of symbolism in Kabbalah and its connection to Reuchlin, see Idel, *Old Worlds, New Mirrors*, pp. 85–88; on the relationship between Scholem's approach to kabbalistic symbolism and Franz Molitor, and the connection this has to a "Christian emphasis on the centrality of mystery," see ibid, pp, 110–13.

46. "With Gershom Scholem: An Interview," p. 48.

47. See Scholem, *Major Trends*, pp. 27–28.

48. Ibid., p. 206.

49. Ibid., p. 28.

50. On Scholem's turn to myth in Jewish history, see Wasserstrom, *Religion after Religion*, pp. 123–24.

51. Scholem, *Major Trends*, p. 10.

52. Scholem addressed this issue in many places in his work; an important articulation of his views on this subject is in "The Name of God and the Linguistic Theory of the Kabbalah," *Diogenes* 79 (1972): 59–80; 80 (1972): 164–94. See also Biale, *Kabbalah and Counter-History*, pp. 89–92; Elliot Wolfson, *Language, Eros, Being: Kabbalistic Hermeneutics and Poetic Imagination* (New York: Fordham University Press, 2004), pp. 25–26; Idel, *Old Worlds, New Mirrors*, pp. 23–24, 168–75; Handelman, *Fragments of Redemption*, pp. 76–78, 82–92.

53. Scholem, *Major Trends*, p. 17.

54. Scholem, "The Name of God," p. 61.

55. Ibid., p. 63.

56. See Wolfson, *Language, Eros, Being*, p. 123.

57. On Scholem's tendency toward a "mystocentric" interpretation of Judaism, see Wasserstrom, *Religion after Religion,* esp. pp. 36, 53, 239–41.

58. On this issue, see Stephen Katz, ed., *Mysticism and Philosophical Analysis* (New York: Oxford University Press, 1978).

59. Scholem, *Major Trends*, p. 6.

60. For a discussion of the "Hegelian" character of Scholem's conception of the place of mysticism in the history of religion, see Moshe Idel, "'Unio Mystica' as a Criterion: Some Observations on 'Hegelian' Phenomenologies of Mysticism," *Journal for the Study of Religious Ideologies* 1 (2002): 21–23. See also idem, *Old Worlds, New Mirrors*, 125–28.

61. Scholem, *Major Trends*, p. 7.

62. Ibid.

63. Ibid.

64. Scholem, *The Messianic Idea in Judaism*, pp. 203–204.

65. Scholem, *On the Possibility of Jewish Mysticism*, p. 7.

66. Important in this respect are the works of Adolph Frank and Solomon Munk; see Idel, *Kabbalah: New Perspectives*, pp. 8–9. On the important contributions of Scholem's predecessors, see Biale, *Kabbalah and Counter-History*, pp. 25–32.

67. David N. Myers, "Philosophy and Kabbalah in Wissenschaft des Judentums: Rethinking the Narrative of Neglect," *Studia Judaica* 16 (2008): 57.

68. As David Myers points out ("Philosophy and Kabbalah in Wissenschaft des Judentums," p. 69), David Joël advanced the argument that the *Zohar* must have been written in the 13th century in his *Die Religionsphilosophie des Sohar und ihr Verhältnis zur allgemeinen jüdischen Theologie* (Leipzig: O. L. Fritzsche, 1849). On the relationship of Scholem's scholarship on the *Zohar* to his predecessors, see Abrams, "Defining Modern Academic Scholarship," pp. 291–99.

69. Idel, *Kabbalah: New Perspectives*, p. 10. Moshe Idel has also pointed out the important and underappreciated work of Scholem's predecessor, Moses Gaster (1856–1939), in a recent study, "Moses Gaster on Jewish Mysticism and the Book of the Zohar" [in Hebrew], in *New Developments in Zohar Studies*, ed. Ronit Meroz, *Te'uda* 21/22 (2007): 111–27.

70. See Scholem's description of his first encounter with this book in his *From Berlin to Jerusalem*, p. 37. It is worth noting that mysticism, though negatively valenced, plays an important role in Graetz's reconstruction of the history of both Judaism and Christianity; see Jonathan Elukin, "A New Essenism: Heinrich Graetz and Mysticism," *Journal of the History of Ideas* 59 (1998): 135–48.

71. See Meyer, "Two Persistent Tensions," pp. 105–11; Moshe Idel, "'That Wondrous, Occult Power': Some Reflections on Modern Perceptions of Jewish History," *Studia Judaica* 7 (1998): 57–70.

72. See David Myers, *Resisting History: Historicism and Its Discontents in German-Jewish Thought* (Princeton, NJ: Princeton University Press, 2003), p. 28.

73. On the history of the academic study of Judaism in America, see Frederick E. Greenspahn, "The Beginnings of Judaic Studies in American Universities," *Modern Judaism* 20 (2000): 209–25.

74. See Boaz Huss, "Ask No Questions: Gershom Scholem and the Study of Contemporary Jewish Mysticism," *Modern Judaism* 25 (2005): 141–58.

75. For a discussion of the use of models in contemporary scholarship on Jewish mysticism, see Wolfson, "Structure, Innovation, and Diremptive Temporality," pp. 143–67.

76. See Kocku von Stuckrad, "Discursive Study of Religion: From States of the Mind to Communication and Action," *Method and Theory in the Study of Religion* 15, no. 3 (2003): 255–71.

77. Jonathan Z. Smith, *Relating Religion: Essays in the Study of Religion*, (Chicago: University of Chicago Press, 2004), p. 175.

78. Ibid., pp. 58–60 n. 115.

79. Ibid. p. 59.

80. See J. Z. Smith's discussion of the term "religion," in "Religion, Religions, Religious," in *Critical Terms for Religious Studies*, ed. Mark C. Taylor (Chicago: University of Chicago Press, 1989), pp. 269–84.

81. Jonathan Z. Smith, *Imagining Religion: From Babylon to Jonestown* (Chicago: University of Chicago Press, 1982), p. xi. See the discussion by Elliot Wolfson in his "Structure, Innovation, and Diremptive Temporality," pp. 148–49.

82. Jonathan Z. Smith, *Map is Not Territory: Studies in the History of Religions* (Chicago: University of Chicago Press, 1993), p. 291.

Jewish Mysticism Takes Shape

Ancient Jewish Mysticism

——— MICHAEL D. SWARTZ ———

A number of years ago I asked students in an introductory class on Jewish mysticism to define mysticism in their own words. One student ventured a particularly memorable definition. Mysticism, he suggested, was "stuff too weird to believe." This statement was impressive not because it is a good definition of mysticism; rather, it exposes an underlying criterion that has often been used, consciously or unconsciously, to designate a given phenomenon as mystical. Modern, sophisticated scholars are sometimes prone to argue that a given literature should be characterized as mystical based precisely on this student's criteria.[1]

At the same time, the very strangeness of a phenomenon we call mystical can be valuable in helping us understand it. This student's explanation of mysticism has a certain validity in that it reminds us that when we study a religion—especially an ancient one—we enter a different world. Entering that world changes our own familiar notions of what religion is supposed to be about. Indeed, this is one of the attractions of studying the literature of ancient Jewish mysticism.

The study of ancient Jewish mysticism, like most modern studies of Jewish mysticism, begins with Gershom Scholem's masterpiece *Major Trends in Jewish Mysticism*.[2] Although scholars had noticed this phenomenon since the 19th century, it was Scholem who brought it out of obscurity and argued that it was an essential part of Jewish history. According to Scholem, the first stage in the long, controversial history of Jewish mysticism was found in a type of visionary literature written at the time of the formation of classical rabbinic Judaism, when the foundation of what we now know as Judaism was being forged in the Mishnah and the Talmud. This is a fascinating possibility, because it means that Judaism during this period was far more diverse than we once thought.

Classical rabbinic Judaism developed in the wake of the trauma of the destruction of the Temple in Jerusalem in 70 CE. Its center of gravity is Torah, seen as an active process of reading, study, and debate. Torah is the mediating principle between God and Israel, between creation and revelation.

But in the past century scholars have discovered texts, not only from scrolls buried in the desert but also from the libraries of Europe and the Middle East, that tell the story of a different, though related, form of Jewish culture. This story is one of myth and magic, elements we do not often associate with the civilization of the rabbis. We call these texts the Hekhalot literature, after the heavenly "palaces" (*hekhalot*), that they describe, and we call the phenomenon *merkavah* mysticism, for the name of the divine throne that this literature seeks to describe. These texts tell stories of ancient rabbis who traveled through the seven layers of heaven, saw God on His glorious chariot-throne, and conjured angels that gave them great powers of wisdom and memory.[3]

Although Jewish mysticism is often equated with Kabbalah, Merkavah mysticism developed centuries before the Kabbalah and has little in common with it. Whereas the Kabbalah began in the 12th and 13th centuries in Provence and Spain, Merkavah mysticism developed in Palestine and Babylonia between the 3rd and 7th centuries. Whereas the Kabbalah is interested in the inner dynamics of the divine personality and the abstract and symbolic contemplation of the nature of God, Merkavah mysticism developed before the philosophical and spiritual concepts that shaped Kabbalah entered the mainstream of Jewish intellectual life. Hekhalot literature, in contrast, concerns the concrete vision of God and His retinue and the rituals for bringing angels down to earth.

Visions of God

The authors of the Hebrew Bible believed that it was possible to see God directly in anthropomorphic form.[4] At Mt. Sinai, according to the Bible, Moses, Aaron, Aaron's sons, and the seventy elders of Israel ascended the mountain and "saw the God of Israel; under His feet was a pavement of sapphire" (Exod. 24:9–11). In the book of Isaiah, the prophet sees God "seated on a high and lofty throne" (Isa. 6:1) in the Temple. On seeing God's face, Isaiah fears for his life, perhaps acquainted with the tradition in Exodus 33:20 in which God tells Moses, "no one may see Me and live." He is then purified by an attending angel. In chapters 1–3 of the book of Ezekiel, the prophet, who is on the banks of the river Chebar, sees God on a traveling throne borne by fiery beings.

These texts were the most foundational sources for the early Jewish visionary tradition that flourished in the rabbinic period. In postbiblical Jewish tradition, the heavenly throne came to be known as the *merkavah*.

Descriptions of the *merkavah* and the angelic liturgy surrounding it inspired several texts in the Dead Sea Scrolls, including a liturgical cycle known as the Songs for the Sabbath Sacrifice.[5] The ancient rabbis had little doubt that the ancient Israelites had seen God in this way. According to one Midrash, "A maidservant saw at the Red Sea what Isaiah and Ezekiel did not see."[6] The Babylonian Talmud tells a story in which Rabbi Ishmael sees God sitting on His throne in the Temple.[7]

But these visions of God are initiated by God Himself, not by anyone who wanted to see God directly. In the apocalyptic literature of the Second Temple period, angels sometimes take biblical heroes such as Enoch on guided "tours of heaven," showing them where they keep the snow and hail, where they keep the souls of the righteous, and other cosmic secrets.[8] But rabbinic literature of the next several centuries shows little recognition of those traditions. At what point, then, did Jews think it was possible to ascend to heaven at will and see the heavenly hosts and the divine throne? This question is significant for the history of Jewish mysticism, for one essential element of Jewish mysticism is considered to be the human attempt to approach the sphere of the divine.[9]

Evidence for this idea from rabbinic literature itself is difficult to identify. The evidence most cited for this idea is a cryptic story in the Tosefta, a collection of traditions that supplemented the Mishnah. The second chapter of Mishnah *Ḥagigah* identifies bodies of religious knowledge that may be imparted only in very exclusive circles of disciples, including Ezekiel's vision of God. The Tosefta adds several details to these regulations. In the case of Ezekiel, the Tosefta tells a mysterious story about four famous rabbis of the second century CE:

Four entered the *pardes*: Ben Azzai, Ben Zoma, *Aḥer*, and Rabbi Akiba. One glimpsed and died, one glimpsed and went mad,[10] one glimpsed and cut the shoots. And one went up safely and went down safely.

Ben Azzai glimpsed and died; about him scripture says: "Precious in the eyes of the Lord is the death of His faithful ones" (Ps. 116:15). Ben Zoma glimpsed and went mad; about him scripture says: "If you find honey, eat only what you need, [lest you be sated with it and vomit it]" (Prov. 25:16). Elisha glimpsed and cut the shoots; about him scripture says: "Do not let your mouth cause your body to sin" (Eccles. 5:5). Rabbi Akiba went up safely and went down safely; about him scripture says: "Draw me after you, let us run; [the king has brought me to his chambers]" (Song 1:4).[11]

From the early centuries of the rabbinic period to the present day, this enigmatic story has served as a kind of tabula rasa for our understanding of mystical and visionary dimensions of rabbinic civilization. One of the suppositions of these studies has been that if we can decipher this story we can determine if the early rabbis, the intellectuals responsible for Jewish law as we know it, were also mystics who cultivated visions of the divine throne and pursued ecstatic journeys through the heavens.[12] But the story provides precious few details.

We know a few facts about the story. The term *pardes*, an early loanword from Persian, means "orchard." Each of the figures in the story is familiar from other rabbinic texts. Rabbi Akiba was one of the founders of the mishnaic tradition and a rabbinic hero, known by tradition as a "Scholar, Saint, and Martyr."[13] His colleagues, Ben Azzai and Ben Zoma, are the source of numerous teachings and stories. *Aḥer*, as the passage subsequently makes clear, is a term meaning "the other one" for Elisha ben Abuya, who was notorious in rabbinic literature for having been a prominent rabbi who became a heretic.[14] But what is this *pardes*—a physical place, a metaphor of some sort, or a term for a spiritual state or supernatural location? What exactly did three of the four rabbis "glimpse"? Why did those three meet with tragic fates—assuming that "cutting the shoots" means some form of transgression?

Later rabbinic traditions are of little help in understanding the original meaning of this story. The Tosefta and the Palestinian Talmud follow the story with further stories that suggest only that the *pardes*, whether a real place or a metaphor for a kind of activity, is fraught with danger. At the same time, the story does not discourage the reader entirely from entering it. The story implies that if one is somehow like Rabbi Akiba, entry to the *pardes* is possible. But the variety of interpretations they offer suggest that the meaning of the passage was lost, even to the editors of the Tosefta.

A brief passage in the Babylonian Talmud (*b. Ḥag.* 14b) leads in a somewhat different direction. After quoting the *pardes* story, the Talmud relates:

> Rabbi Akiba said to them, "When you arrive at the pure marble stones, do not say, 'water, water,' as it is said, 'He who speaks untruth shall not stand before my eyes'" (Ps. 101:7).

It was Gershom Scholem who brought the *pardes* story to prominence by suggesting that it constituted valid historical evidence for early Jewish visionary practice.[15] Scholem related Rabbi Akiba's warning about the marble plates in the Babylonian Talmud to a similar passage found in Hekhalot literature. These remarkable texts describe journeys undertaken by early rabbis, such as Rabbi Akiba and especially his contemporary Rabbi Ishmael, through seven layers of heaven, known as *hekhalot* ("palaces" or "temples"), to the throne-room of God. The rabbis travel from palace to palace, warding off hostile angelic guardians at each of the gates, and finally reach the divine throne-room, where they see God Himself seated on his chariot-throne, the *merkavah*.

Earlier generations of scholars had argued that this literature was written in the early Middle Ages, well after the ancient rabbis, by marginal groups influenced by Islamic throne mysticism.[16] Scholem showed, however, that the Hekhalot texts belonged to late antiquity. He further argued that this literature represents a window into the inner spiritual life of the central shapers of Rabbinic Judaism. A text called *Hekhalot Zutarti* describes a crucial moment when the traveler is invited to enter the sixth palace, whereupon it seems to him as if millions of waves of water are raining down on him. But those waves are an illusion, and it is only the marble plates with which the walls of the palace were covered.[17] Scholem argued that this passage preserved the original meaning of Rabbi Akiba's warning in the Babylonian Talmud's version of the story and that the term *pardes* stands for Paradise or the inner chambers of heaven. So Scholem thought that these texts were records of visions cultivated by mystical circles within the rabbinic elite and attributed to the ancient rabbis.

But since Scholem advanced this argument for the existence of an esoteric mystical tradition within the heart of early Rabbinic Judaism, there has been a great deal of debate. Most prominently David J. Halperin argued that Talmudic literature does not prove that visionary mysticism was practiced by the early rabbis.[18] So for clear evidence that ancient Jews believed that human beings can travel at will to heaven, we must look at the Hekhalot literature itself.

Hekhalot Literature

The Hekhalot texts appear in medieval manuscripts. Although these texts are attributed to rabbis who lived in the 2nd century CE, they were almost certainly not written by those rabbis.

The major Hekhalot texts have been published by Peter Schäfer.[19] He discovered that this literature did not begin as separate, "original" texts written by a single author but together make up a complex network of smaller texts that are organized in different ways into larger units. This means that a Hekhalot text is not the product of a single author, recording his experiences and simply attributing them to famous rabbis. Rather, they were composed from a wide variety of literary forms, instructions for ritual practices, myths, and interpretations.

Keeping this in mind, we can identify a few main streams of Hekhalot texts. The two main types are (1) ascent texts that describe how a rabbi traveled to the divine throne-room, and (2) adjuration texts that provide instructions for conjuring an angel known as the Prince of the Torah (*Sar ha-Torah*), who will grant the practitioner wisdom and skill in learning Torah. There is also a text called the *Shi'ur Qomah*, which describes in graphic detail the measurements of God's body.

Ascent

The paradigmatic ascent text is the *Hekhalot Rabbati* (Greater [Book of the] Palaces). The *Hekhalot Rabbati* lays out the scheme of the divine palaces:

> [The] God of Israel dwells in seven *hekhalot*, a chamber inside a chamber, and at the gate of each *hekhal* there are eight guards of the doorway at the right side of the lintel.[20]

At each gate there are ferocious angels who guard that *hekhal* against intruders. The premise of the text is that any qualified human being can ascend through those heavens to the *merkavah*. The human traveler who wishes to go to the divine throne-room must appease those angels and present the proper credentials. These credentials take the form of elaborate names of God. These names come largely from the Jewish magical tradition. We must remember that angels are essentially bureaucrats. The way to impress a bureaucrat is to show him a document with the signature of the authority. That is what these magical names are.

At a crucial point in the journey, the traveler encounters a particularly frightening angel, as in this passage from the *Hekhalot Rabbati*:

> When a man wishes to descend to the *merkavah*, the angel 'Anafiel opens the gates to the seventh *hekhal*; and the Holy Creatures lift their 512 eyes against him—their eyes are like bolts of lightning—darting out from the eyes of the Cherubim of the Mighty One and the Ofanim of the Divine Presence—they are like torches of light and burning embers.

That man trembles and shakes, is awestruck and terrified, and is faint and falls. But 'Anafiel and the sixty-three guards of the seventh *hekhal* support him, and all of them assist him and say: "Do not fear, beloved human being! Enter and see the King in His beauty, and you will not be burned."[21]

An essential element, the overriding emotion in this passage, is the profound fear the traveler feels. The passage also demonstrates a curious paradox: Despite the dangers, God wishes for the approach of the adept: "Do not fear, beloved human." This paradox reminds us of the *pardes* narrative; the story warns of the danger but still holds out the possibility that under the right circumstances the rewards of the journey can be acquired.

Not all Hekhalot texts are organized around the journey through seven *hekhalot*. One of the most unusual texts in this literature is the *Shi'ur Qomah* (The Measurement of the Body), which relates the size of God's body in graphic fashion. Each part of the divine body is given a specific measurement in *parsangs* (Persian miles), as well as an esoteric name:

The left ankle of the Creator is named 'TRQM, may He be blessed. It is 190,000,000 *parsangs* tall, which equals 43,250 *sheqalim*. From His ankles to the knee of the Creator, may He be blessed, is called GMGY, may He be blessed, and has a height of 600,000,080 *parsangs*.[22]

It is explained that one of the divine *parsangs* equals 1,640,000,025,000 terrestrial *parsangs*. The text seems to have been written for the purpose of liturgical recitation and also contains several hymns. The *Shi'ur Qomah* represents an extreme example of anthropomorphic tendencies prevalent in Hekhalot literature, as well as its tendency to ascribe gargantuan dimensions to heaven and its inhabitants.[23] In all these texts, God is localized—that is, He dwells in a specific place in heaven—and invisible.

Hymnology

One of the most important components of Hekhalot literature is the unusual hymns praising God and describing the celestial beings. One of the main reasons the traveler ascends is to participate in the heavenly liturgy, based on the *qedushah*, the sanctification sung by the angels in Isaiah 6 and Ezekiel 3.

Another major text, *Ma'aseh Merkavah*, consists mostly of esoteric prayers framed by a narrative of the vision of the heavens and the cultivation of the angel of the Torah. The hymns in this text draw from the earliest stage of post-biblical Hebrew liturgical poetry, called *piyyut*.[24] This style uses parallelism, the main characteristic of biblical poetry, as well as a steady rhythm, usually of four feet, to convey the praise of God and the participation of both angels and humans in this praise. One hymn in *Ma'aseh Merkavah* expresses it in this way:

> Be blessed, God, great, mighty, and strong,
> King, exalted in beauty, magnificent in glory.
> In glory You spoke and the world came into being;
> With the breath of Your lips You established the firmament,
> and Your great name is pure and exalted
> over all those above and all those below.
> Angels stand in heaven,
> and the righteous are sure in their remembrance of You,
> and Your name hovers over them all.[25]

This hymn begins with the theme of God's creation of heaven and earth. The parallelism counterpoises God's creation of heaven with the creation of earth and His sovereignty over "all those above and all those below." The hymn thus emphasizes that God, especially His divine name, which plays an important role in the text, transcends both the angelic community in heaven and the human worshipers (the "righteous"). This reinforces the idea that underlies the text: that humans have the right to praise God in correspondence with the angelic liturgy.

In fact, evidence has emerged that the poets of the early synagogue were aware of Hekhalot literature. A recently published *piyyut* from about the 6th century includes details that could only have come from the *Hekhalot Rabbati* in some form; it mentions not only "seven palaces" but also angelic "guards" to which one must "show a seal." This text not only shows that the poets knew Hekhalot literature, but helps place the narrative in the *Hekhalot Rabbati* in Amoraic Palestine.[26]

The *Sar-Torah*

The final major type of text in this literature consists of rituals and incantations for more conventionally practical purposes, especially the cultivation of great powers of memory and skill in learning Torah by means of the conjuration of an angel, the Prince of the Torah (*Sar-Torah*), an important element in a society in which the study of texts is central. These draw heavily on the Jewish magical tradition; but unlike magical texts from late antiquity and the early Middle Ages, they take the form of stories in which Rabbi Ishmael and his colleagues learn and perform *Sar-Torah* rituals and encounter the angels of wisdom and Torah.

These instructions usually involve extensive preparatory rituals. The practitioner is instructed, sometimes by an angel, to purge himself of all traces of impurity by elaborate rituals of seclusion, fasting, bathing, and avoidance of infinitesimal traces of menstrual impurity (*niddah*):

> Whoever wants [the secret of the *Sar-Torah*] to be revealed to him must sit fasting for forty days, perform twenty-four immersions every day, and not eat anything defiling. He must not look at a woman and must sit in a totally dark house.[27]

These rituals go well beyond those prescribed in rabbinic law for ritual purity. The object of these rituals of purification is to prepare the individual for the encounter with the angel, who will tolerate no contamination in his presence. The same concept underlies the sacrificial system in the ancient Temple. In order to approach the potent presence of God, the priests and the people had to be ritually pure. But in this case the purity is transferred from the realm of the public ritual to the private sphere.

The Book of Formation

One additional text is usually included in descriptions of ancient Jewish mysticism, although whether it is directly related to Hekhalot literature is not clear. This legendary text is called the *Sefer Yetsirah* (Book of Formation).

In the Talmud it is said that two rabbis, Rav Hanina and Rav Oshaya, occupied themselves with the *Sefer Yetsirah*,[28] or "laws of formation" (*hilkhot yetsirah*),[29] on the eve of the Sabbath and by means of it made a three-year-old calf and then ate it. This brief tale contains no further details, however, about what this book or set of laws might be. In the 10th century, a brief and mysterious text known as the *Sefer Yetsirah* began to appear. During the early Middle Ages, this text had become the subject of several commentaries and studies by Jewish scientists, philosophers, and mystics.[30] Eventually the *Sefer Yetsirah* provided key inspiration and terminology for the kabbalistic tradition, which adopted the text's term *sefirot* as well as many of its main concepts.[31]

The subject of *Sefer Yetsirah* is the process by which God formed the universe out of ten mathematical entities, known as *sefirot belima*. The term uses a new word, *sefirah*—meaning "number," from the root *spr*, "to count"—which was to become an essential term in Kabbalah. The term *belima* comes from Job 26:7 and could mean "closed" (that is, "ineffable"), "unpronounceable," or "basis." The text goes on to speak of three (or four) primordial elements, "twenty-two elemental letters," and "thirty-two paths of wisdom" as components of creation. The text is then taken up with metaphysical, mathematical, and linguistic permutations of these components.

The question of the origin and history of the *Sefer Yetsirah* has confounded scholars from the Middle Ages to modern times. Although tradition ascribes the book to the patriarch Abraham, relatively few specifically Jewish references are found in the text. Aside from a few terms for God and scattered biblical allusions, the text seems to resemble certain esoteric forms of spirituality that flourished in the Hellenistic world. But it does not resemble Hebrew texts of the rabbinic period.[32] Scholars have also noticed similarities to texts written in Arabic in the 8th and 9th centuries during a revival of Greek esoteric cosmological ideas.[33] As a result, they have suggested widely divergent dates for the text, ranging from the 1st century[34] to the 2nd or 3rd centuries[35] to the early Muslim era.[36]

Does the *Sefer Yetsirah* belong in the category of early Jewish mystical texts? The text bears little resemblance to the Hekhalot literature; it does not concern a journey to the divine throne or the conjuration of angels, nor does it speculate on the topography of the heavens. Unlike the Hekhalot texts, however, *Sefer Yetsirah* does offer an explicit indication of how it is to serve as a source of meditation:

> Understand with wisdom and be wise with understanding. Test them and investigate them, and get the matter clearly worked out and restore the Creator to his place.[37]

The meditation described here seems to be the intellectual contemplation of the relationships between the letters and numbers spelled out in the texts, which will lead to a proper understanding of creation or even the restoration of God's rulership.[38] If the dating of the *Sefer Yetsirah* is ever determined with greater certainty, we may be able to place it into the early history of Jewish mysticism. Nonetheless, it undoubtedly influenced medieval Jewish mystical and philosophical thought deeply. Rationalistic philosophers such as Saadia Gaon and Moses Maimonides wrote commentaries on the book; and the Kabbalah took the text as foundational, adopting the term *sefirah* and changing its meaning to refer to the attributes of God.

Ancient Jewish Mysticism?

Should we call this diverse, bizarre literature mysticism? If we apply my student's criterion, this is clearly "Stuff too weird to believe." But what does it mean to historians of religion?

This literature lacks several elements usually associated with mysticism. One of these is a sense of the interior self approaching the divine. There is no reason to suppose that the authors did not actually believe that Rabbis Ishmael and Akiba went up to heaven, encountered angels, and saw the *merkavah*. In fact, some of the purity rituals assume that what happens to the physical body affects what happens to the person in heaven. Although the heroes of these texts approach the presence of God, they do not achieve the kind of unification or attachment with God that we find in other mystical traditions. God is still remote and impersonal.

The sole claim to mysticism in this literature is based on the idea, advanced especially by Scholem, that its authors experienced visions of the *merkavah* and transcribed them as the Hekhalot literature. It may be that one of the premises behind this argument is that the details in this literature are so bizarre that they must have been the product of an inner, irrational, or subconscious process of contemplation. But in recent years this theory has come under a great deal of criticism. David J. Halperin argues that the purpose of the ascent texts was not to engender a mystical trance but to provide a mythic justification for the *Sar-Torah* practices, which he considers to be the "center" of Hekhalot literature.[39] Peter Schäfer emphasizes the liturgical function of the ascent.[40] Most striking, Martha Himmelfarb argues that "the Hekhalot literature should be understood not as rites to be enacted but as stories to be repeated."[41]

Most likely, the states of mind that produced this literature are irrecoverable. More to the point, this literature is not the product of individual authors. It is most probable that the *Sar-Torah* texts were meant to be used. But the ascent texts give us precious little information about how they would be used to achieve a vision of the *merkavah*. So it is best to see them as excellent sources of rituals, sacred stories, and theologies that we would not have known otherwise. This approach may not enable us to reconstruct the individual experiences of the ancient authors, but it does yield insights into the culture of Judaism in the age of the Talmud.

One of the most important of the influences on this literature is the Temple, its priesthood, and its sacrificial system, which had long been destroyed when the Hekhalot literature developed. The word *hekhal* can mean both palace and Temple, and it is likely that the *hekhalot* were considered to be the heavenly equivalent of the Temple or, more accurately, its celestial prototype. In biblical times the Temple was considered to be God's place of residence on earth, where His Glory (*kavod*), the Presence of God, could appear when the priests invoked Him. Ancient Jews believed that when they held sacrifices that presence came down to the sanctuary to bless Israel. Ritual purity played an essential role in this system. The elaborate process of expiation at the altar was designed to purify the Temple and assure the proper environment for that Presence.[42] The elaborate washings, the sprinkling of blood, the spreading of incense—all these activities allowed the priests to approach God. Not only was impurity dangerous to the human being, but if God encountered the demonic forces of chaos, He had no choice but to react. Making a mistake in performing the ritual had serious consequences. This is the basis of the story of Nadav and Abihu, the sons of Aaron who, in Leviticus 10:1–3, offered "strange fire" to the Lord. The Temple, therefore, was a dangerous place, but the ancient Jews believed that it was the only place where humanity could approach God physically.

Conclusion

But what happened to the Presence of God when the Temple was destroyed? A Midrash tells us: The Divine Presence, known to the rabbis as the *Shekhinah*, departed outward from the Holy of Holies and then upward to heaven.[43] Other sources tell of a Temple in heaven where the angels are still holding sacrifices and reciting a heavenly liturgy.[44] If we remember that in early Jewish mysticism God was located somewhere in heaven and that the word *hekhal* can mean both "palace" and "temple," we can see why these magicians and mystics thought it was necessary to go through such extraordinary purifications. We can also see why they thought that the journey to the divine throne would be so dangerous. The angels personify the impersonal wrath of the Potent Presence in reaction to the invasion of its pure realm. If one came too close, one could go mad or die, just like three of the rabbis who entered the *pardes*. But if the practitioner succeeded, he could meet angels who would turn an ordinary person into a great scholar or be part of the divine service in heaven and "see the King in His beauty." Despite these affinities with the theology of the ancient priesthood, it is unlikely that priests actually wrote this literature.[45] It does mean, however, that the authors of these texts held the priesthood in high regard, unlike many of the rabbis of the time.[46] Some of them were most likely members of a secondary elite, who drew upon both rabbinic values and popular religious traditions.[47]

The authors of the Hekhalot literature apparently believed that travel to the divine throne and direct apprehension of God were possible in their lifetimes. They may have intended their elaborate stories, hymns, and rituals to be used as inspirations for mystical visions or simply as stories of their heroes. But they certainly meant to say that it was possible to bridge the distance between the divine and human worlds.

NOTES

1. Cf. Northrop Frye, *Fearful Symmetry: A Study of William Blake* (Boston: Beacon, 1965), pp. 3–9, on the tendency of earlier scholars to attribute the complexities of Blake's imagery to his "mystical" frame of mind.

2. Gershom Scholem, *Major Trends in Jewish Mysticism*, 2nd ed. (New York: Schocken Books, 1954), pp. 40–79; see also idem., *Jewish Gnosticism, Merkavah Mysticism, and Talmudic Tradition*, 2nd ed. (New York: Jewish Theological Seminary of America, 1965).

3. For a more detailed overviews of *hekhalot* literature, see Peter Schäfer, *The Hidden and Manifest God: Some Major Themes in Early Jewish Mysticism* (Albany: State University of New York Press, 1992); David J. Halperin, *Faces of the Chariot: Early Jewish Responses to Ezekiel's Vision* (Tübingen: Mohr, 1988); and Michael D. Swartz, "Mystical Texts," in *The Literature of the Sages, Second Part: Midrash, Aggada, Targum, Berakhot, Varia*, ed. Shmuel Safrai, Joshua Schwartz, and Peter Tomson (Assen: Royal Van Gorcum, 2006), pp. 391–418.

4. For a useful survey of biblical and rabbinic attitudes to visions of God, see Elliot Wolfson, *Through a Speculum That Shines: Vision and Imagination in Medieval Jewish Mysticism* (Princeton, NJ: Princeton University Press, 1994), pp. 13–51.

5. On the *merkavah* in the Dead Sea Scrolls, see Lawrence H. Schiffman, *Reclaiming the Dead Sea Scrolls: The History of Judaism, the Background of Christianity, and the Lost Library of Qumran* (Philadelphia: Jewish Publication Society, 1994), pp. 351–66; and Michael D. Swartz, "The Dead Sea Scrolls and Later Jewish Magic and Mysticism," *DSD* 8 (2001): 1–12. On the Songs of the Sabbath Sacrifice, see Esther Eshel et al., *Discoveries in the Judaean Desert XI: Qumran Cave 4 VI: Poetical and Liturgical Texts, Part I* (Oxford: Clarendon, 1998).

6. *Mekhilta de-Rabbi Ishmael, Shirata* 3 (ed. Horowitz-Rabin, p. 126).

7. *B. Ber.* 7a.

8. On these texts, see Martha Himmelfarb, *Ascent to Heaven in Jewish and Christian Apocalypses* (New York: Oxford University Press, 1993).

9. See Scholem, *Major Trends*, pp. 7–8.

10. Literally, "was afflicted."

11. *T. Ḥag.* 2:3 (ed. Lieberman).

12. The best analysis of this story is David J. Halperin, *The Merkabah in Rabbinic Literature* (New Haven, CT: American Oriental Society, 1980). On the concepts of mysticism and mystical experience and how they have been applied with regard to Rabbinic Judaism and its milieu, see Michael D. Swartz, *Scholastic Magic: Ritual and Revelation in Early Jewish Mysticism* (Princeton, NJ: Princeton University Press, 1996), pp. 15–18.

13. This was the subtitle of Louis Finkelstein's 1936 biography of Akiba (New York: Atheneum, 1970).

14. On legends of Elisha ben Abuya, see Alon Goshen-Gottstein, *The Sinner and the Amnesiac: The Rabbinic Invention of Elisha ben Abuya and Eleazar ben Arach* (Stanford: Stanford University Press, 2000); Jeffrey L. Rubenstein, *Talmudic Stories: Narrative Art, Composition, and Culture* (Baltimore: Johns Hopkins University Press, 1999), 64–104; Jeffrey L. Rubenstein and Yehuda Liebes, *Hatato shel Elisha: Arba'ah she-Nikhnesu la-Pardes ve-Tiv'ah shel ha-Mistiqah ha-Talmudit* (Jerusalem: Akademon, 1990).

15. Scholem, *Major Trends*, pp. 52–53; idem, *Jewish Gnosticism*, pp. 14–19.

16. See Heinrich Graetz, "Die mystische Literatur in der gaonäischen Epoche," *Monatsschrift für Geschichte und Wissenschaft des Judenthums* 8 (1859): 67–78, 103–18, 140–53.

17. The text from *Hekhalot Zutarti* appears in Peter Schäfer, *Synopse zur Hekhalot-Literatur* (Tübingen: Mohr, 1981), §408. The passage was cited in connection with the *pardes* story by the 10th-century rabbinic authority Hai ben Sherira Gaon (B. Lewin, ed., *Otzar ha-Geonim*, pt. 2 [*Hagigah*], 4:14); and by the 11th-century Talmudic commentator Hananel ben Hushiel's commentary to *b. Hagigah* 14b.

18. Halperin, *The Merkabah in Rabbinic Literature*. Halperin's conclusion has been challenged, particularly by C. R. A. Morray-Jones (*Transparent Illusion: The Dangerous Vision of Water in Hekhalot Mysticism* [Leiden: E. J. Brill, 2002]), but his research has called into serious question the thesis that the rabbis practiced ecstatic visions of the *merkavah*.

19. Peter Schäfer, *Synopse zur Hekhalot-Literatur* (Tübingen: Mohr, 1981); idem, *Genizah-Fragmente zur Hekhalot-Literatur* (Tübingen: Mohr, 1984). All passages from Hekhalot literature in this chapter are cited from these editions, with the exception of the *Shi'ur Qomah*, which is quoted from Martin Samuel Cohen, *The Shi'ur Qomah: Texts and Recensions* (Tübingen: Mohr, 1985).

20. Schäfer, *Synopse*, §206.

21. Ibid., §248.

22. Cohen, *Shi'ur Qomah: Texts and Recensions*, pp. 30–31; on the text, see Martin Samuel Cohen, *The Shi'ur Qomah: Liturgy and Theurgy in Pre-Kabbalistic Jewish Mysticism* (Lanham, MD: University Press of America, 1983).

23. On anthropomorphism and the gargantuan proportions of the deity in the *Shi'ur Qomah*, see Howard M. Jackson, "The Origins and Development of *Shi'ur Qomah* Revelation in Jewish Mysticism," *Journal for the Study of Judaism* 31 (2005): 373–415.

24. For introductions to *piyyut*, see J. Yahalom, *"Piyyut* as Poetry," in *The Synagogue in Late Antiquity*, ed. Lee I. Levine (New York: Jewish Theological Seminary of America, 1987), pp. 111–26; and Michael D. Swartz and Joseph Yahalom, *Avodah: Ancient Poems for Yom Kippur* (University Park: Pennsylvania State University Press, 2005), pp. 1–15.

25. Schäfer, *Synopse* §587. On this passage see Swartz, *Mystical Prayer*, pp. 145–47, 171–84.

26. Michael Rand, "More on the Seder Beriyot," *Jewish Studies Quarterly* 16 (2009).

27. Schäfer, *Synopse*, §314.

28. *B. Sanh.* 65b.

29. *B. Sanh.* 67b.

30. For a survey of the history of the *Sefer Yetsirah* and its reception, as well as a selection of the vast bibliography on the subject, see Joseph Dan, "Three Phases of the History of the Sefer Yezira," *Frankfurter Judaistische Beiträge* 21 (1994): 7–29.

31. The text exists in three main rescensions, one of which was redacted by Saadiah Gaon; the so-called shorter rescension is usually thought to reflect the earlier form of the text. For a comprehensive edition and the best account of the redactional state of the text, see Peter Hayman, *Sefer Yeṣirah: Edition, Translation, and Text-Critical Commentary* (Tübingen: Mohr-Siebeck, 2004).

32. On the influence of neo-Pythagorean and Hermetic spirituality, see Shlomo Pines, "Points of Similarity between the Exposition of the Doctrine of the Sefirot in the Sefer Yezira and a Text of the Pseudo-Clementine Homilies," *Proceedings of the Israeli Academy of Sciences and Humanities* 7 (1989): 63–14.

33. See, esp., Steven Wasserstrom, "*Sefer Yeṣirah* and Early Islam: A Reappraisal," *Journal of Jewish Theology and Philosophy* 3 (1993): 1–30.

34. Yehuda Liebes, *Torat ha-Yeṣirah shel Sefer Yeṣirah* (Jerusalem: Schocken Books, 2000).

35. Peter Hayman, "The Temple at the Center of the Universe," *Journal of Jewish Studies* 37 (1986): 176–82.

36. For a summary of the arguments for this dating as well as further evidence, see Wasserstrom, "*Sefer Yeṣira* and Early Islam."

37. *Sefer Yetsirah,* §4 (Hayman, *Sefer Yeṣirah*, pp. 60–61; Hayman's translation is adapted here).

38. Cf. Hayman, "Temple." On the idea in rabbinic literature that human thought can affect the nature of God's sovereignty, see Moshe Idel, *Kabbalah: New Perspectives* (New Haven: Yale University Press, 1988), pp. 156–66.

39. See Halperin, *Faces of the Chariot*, pp. 376–83.

40. Schäfer, *Hidden and Manifest God.*

41. Himmelfarb, *Ascent to Heaven*, 109. This argument is spelled out in Martha Himmelfarb, "Heavenly Ascent and the Relationship of the Apocalypses to Hekhalot Literature," *HUCA* 59 (1988): 73–100.

42. On this concept, see Baruch A. Levine, *In the Presence of the Lord* (Leiden: Brill, 1974); and idem, *The JPS Torah Commentary: Leviticus* (Philadelphia: Jewish Publication Society, 1989).

43. *Avot de-Rabbi Natan* (ed. Schechter), version A, chap. 34.

44. On these sources, see Victor Aptowitzer, "The Celestial Temple as Viewed in the Aggadah" in *Binah 2: Studies in Jewish Thought*, ed. Joseph Dan (New York: Praeger, 1989), pp. 1–29.

45. Cf. Rachel Elior, *The Three Temples: On the Emergence of Jewish Mysticism* (Portland, OR: Littman Library of Jewish Civilization, 2005).

46. On the status of the priesthood in Hekhalot literature and its relationship to narrative in *Hekhalot*, see Ra'anan Boustan, *From Martyr to Mystic: The Story of the Ten Martyrs, Hekhalot Rabbati, and the Making of Merkavah Mysticism* (Tübingen: Möhr-Siebeck, 2005), pp. 99–147.

47. For this argument applied to the authors of the Sar-Torah literature, see M. D. Swartz, *Scholastic Magic, Ritual, and Revelation in Early Jewish Mysticism* (Princeton, NJ: Princeton University Press, 1996). Recently, James R. Davila has argued that the Hekhalot tradition is the product of a class of shamanistic practitioners (*Descenders to the Chariot: The People behind the Hekhalot Literature* [Leiden: Brill, 2001]).

2

The *Zohar*

Masterpiece of Jewish Mysticism

EITAN P. FISHBANE

Certain works of the human imagination reorient the culture of reading, rising as classics in the terrain of letters and interpretation. Reaching across the ages, the classic reverberates with an enduring beauty; its artistry makes a claim on each new generation, and it awakens fresh engagement with the mystery and authority of the past. Crafted in late-13th-century Spain, the *Zohar* is one of a handful of texts in the history of Judaism that achieved such an essential impact. The unquestioned masterpiece of Jewish mysticism, the *Zohar* is nothing less than one of the most significant compositions produced by the Jews in more than two thousand years of creativity. From the time of its mysterious emergence in Castile, the *Zohar* was regarded as a sacred text, a work whose place in the canon was only superseded by Scripture; it was perceived to hold a status comparable to the talmudic-midrashic corpora of late antiquity.[1] What is more, the *Zohar* was believed by its medieval receivers to be a part of that classical Jewish literature, the recovered mystical voice of the ancient tannaitic sages, a book authored by the revered master Rabbi Shimon bar Yochai. It was not until modern academic scholarship on the Kabbalah that this belief was successfully challenged—first in the 19th century by the German scholars Adolph Jellinek and Heinrich Graetz and then in detail by Gershom Scholem, the pioneer of the field as it exists today.[2]

Shortly upon its initial circulation by the 13-century-kabbalist Rabbi Moshe de Leon—distributed first as selected pamphlets and passages from a supposedly larger work—the community of pious readers accepted the prominent authorship of bar Yochai, and the text was absorbed into the canon of paradigmatic and sacred works of the rabbinic tradition. The immense significance of this moment in the reception history of the *Zohar* cannot be underestimated, insofar as the acceptance of tannaitic authorship had the automatic effect of constructing the cultural memory of the generations that would follow. Once we see the clear grounds for medieval author-ship of the *Zohar* (and I will discuss that in due course), we realize the degree to which projecting authorship into the past had the radical result of trans-forming perceptions of the historically real. Generations of traditional read-ers encountered the sages and landscape represented in the text and believed that they were sitting before a record of the rabbis of the 2nd-century Land of Israel, a historically true account of the tannaitic world.³ Of course, scholars of talmudic-midrashic literature may well say that the same principle holds with regard to that corpus, although I would suggest that the *Zohar* reflects a more complete process of invention than the reconstructed vignettes of rab-binic literature.⁴

The *Zohar* is marked by two dominant genres, each of which serves, in part, to situate the text in the literary world of rabbinic antiquity. The first of these, and by far the weightier in terms of sheer volume, is the mystical-midrashic genre. Modeled on the homiletical and exegetical forms of clas-sical Midrash, this is an entirely new mode of kabbalistic discourse, blend-ing metaphysical rumination on the inner workings of divine reality with an interpretive technique rooted in older midrashic creativity. What emerges from this fusion is an altogether different and brilliant construction of dis-course, a lyrical and playful theological imagination that works homiletically out of a bold engagement with Scripture. In contrast to the many other kab-balistic works that were produced in 13th-century Spain, the *Zohar* articu-lates the theological system of the *sefirot* through the voice of midrashic exegesis, a method that not only successfully represents the text as a work of antiquity but also fashions a hitherto unknown type of discourse: a midrashi-cally driven exploration of mystical symbols and inner-divine dynamics. For although the midrashic method was a well-established model in Jewish let-ters, the aim of homiletical creativity in the *Zohar* was to uncover a symbolic subtext about the intradivine realm, believed to be latent in the Torah. A cen-tral component of this new rhetoric is also the mythology of *sefirot*, a man-ner of reflecting on the divine dimensions that is markedly different from the rhetoric adopted in other kabbalistic texts of this period. In the *Zohar*, the realm of the *sefirot* assumes a powerful new dynamism—a supernal world in which the androgynous nature of Divinity is represented as a mythic drama of inner divine sexual yearning and union in which the cosmic battle of good and evil is subsumed within the divine self and wherein the perennial ema-nation of divine life from the depths of infinity is articulated with a radiant poetic charge. In the *Zohar*, the symbolic language of Kabbalah is opened to full flower. The symbols and myths of earlier Kabbalah are expressed with an unprecedented dynamism and imaginative force; the inner life of God is narrated and envisioned with a fresh and bold mythological voice.

The second major genre of the *Zohar* is the fictional narrative, the epic tale of Rabbi Shimon bar Yochai and his disciples wandering the roads of ancient Galilee in search of mystical wisdom. Presented in a highly fragmented structure, the narrated moments most often lead into and out of extended discourses of the mystical Midrash. More often than not, the fictional scene provides an opening into—or a closure for—the kabbalistic homily of one of the companions. But these units of narration are far more than mere excuses for the exegetical discourses; they constitute an art form unto themselves, a new aesthetic of language reaching toward birth. In the narratives of the *Zohar* we observe the quest for new kabbalistic insight; the construction of Rabbi Shimon as a saintly master of otherworldly power, the attempt to utilize fresh tools of rhetoric and representation. Searching for Torah on the road, the companions frequently encounter mysterious strangers who turn out to be exalted mystical masters in disguise; the narrative scenes often dramatize the power and ambivalence involved in the disclosure of secrets. The authors of the *Zohar* resurrect the world of 2nd-century Galilee within the poetic eye of a medieval imagination presented through the veil of pseudepigraphy.

Kabbalistic Theology and Mythology

The *Zohar* constitutes the culmination of more than a century of kabbalistic thinking and creativity in medieval Europe and perhaps much longer, if we are to believe at least some of the Kabbalists' own claims about the oral reception of their esoteric tradition. Having developed in the writings of the earliest kabbalistic authors in southern France and then among the circle of mystics that lived in the Catalonian town of Gerona, the theological system of the *sefirot* came to maturation in the *Zohar* and the related works of late-13th-century Castile. In this medieval kabbalistic thinking we observe a remarkably different theological conception than was established in previous Jewish thought, closest perhaps in approach to the 3rd-century Neoplatonism of Plotinus and its medieval reverberations many centuries later. In the *Zohar* and its antecedents, God is represented as a dynamic flow of cosmic energy—composed of ten identifiable dimensions or stages of emanation (the *sefirot*)—always in flux from a primordial source of Infinity, unfolding in progressively greater manifestation through these ten *sefirot* until birth is given to the lower world. *Ein Sof* (lit., "without end"; the Infinite One) is the source of all, and it is the lifeblood of all reality, circulating through Divinity and the totality of the cosmos. From the mystery of that Infinity, the *Zohar* teaches, a spark flashed in the darkness—the colors of all that would be exploded in a wondrous array. From the most infinitesimal point of concentration, the containment of all future Being in complete potentiality, the rivers of divine life were opened—the concealed spring of the universe overflowed with an energy too immense to contemplate. *Keter* (Crown), *Ḥokhmah* (Wisdom), *Binah* (Understanding), *Ḥesed* (Love), *Gevurah* (Severity), *Tiferet* (Beauty), *Netzaḥ* (Eternity), *Hod* (Splendor), *Yesod* (Foundation), *Malkhut* (Kingship)—these are the ten dimensions of Divinity (the *sefirot*) that flow forth in a stream of emanation from *Ein Sof*, the well of Infinity. They are the ten rivers of cosmic light, the ten chambers of the inner divine self (Figure 2.1).

The Kabbalists never tire of emphasizing that these ten are one; they are not to be understood as separate entities, despite the considerable length to which the mystics go to explicate their individual features. It is all one. Indeed, this refrain of oneness is repeated numerous times on virtually every page of the *Zohar*; the ten rungs of divine life are contained in the mystery of oneness. But it is important to underscore that the standard Hebrew terminology I have just employed above—a vocabulary that is used extensively in the Hebrew kabbalistic literature of 13th-century Spain—is clearly avoided in the pages of the *Zohar*. This avoidance, including the absence of the term *sefirot* itself, is certainly part of the *Zohar*'s attempt to disguise its medieval origins, to separate itself from the distinctive markers of 13th-century conventions and forms. Nevertheless, the clusters of images and symbols associated with these *sefirot* are used with great liberty in the *Zohar*, and the constellation of symbolic discourse is readily apparent to the experienced reader of medieval Kabbalah.[5] For despite the fact that the *Zohar* uses the word *dargin* (rungs) instead of *sefirot* (along with other Aramaic variations) and employs interchangeable images in place of the most recognizable sefirotic names, the subject of the text is clear, and the *Zohar* presents the drama of an inner divine mythology with a dynamism and life that was not attained in earlier kabbalistic creativity. In the rhythmic Aramaic voice of the *Zohar*, divinity is represented as brimming with interior struggle and yearning. Male lover (*Tif'eret*) and female beloved (*Shekhinah/Malkhut*) pine for each other with poetic romance, and the actions of Jews in the lower world are thought to stimulate union or separation of those divine forces above. The life of God is represented as a dance of sexual intimacy, a drama of eros between gendered and personified dimensions of the divine realm that is most easily com-

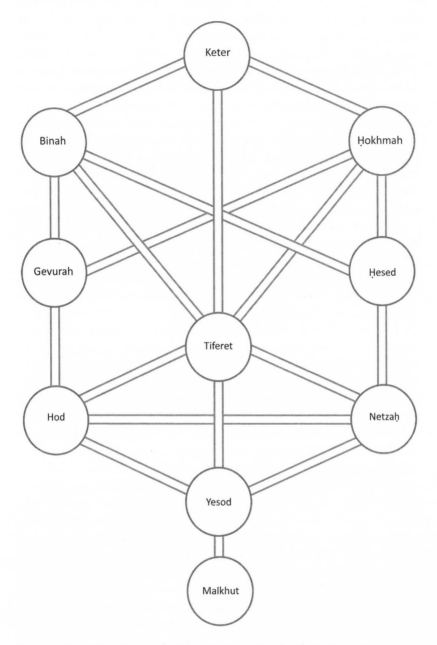

Figure 2.1. The Sefirot. Designed by Nicole Jacobsen, Florida Atlantic University.

pared to the mythological narratives of ancient Greece. And yet the *Zohar* constantly disavows these distinctions, claiming that the different, sexually charged *sefirot* are nothing but faces of the one, indivisible, divine organism.

The other prominent dimension of zoharic mythology is the perennial cosmic struggle between good and evil, metaphysical forces that are rooted in particular components of the tenfold divine structure.[6] The divine self, like the world of human experience, is depicted as dominated by a tense polarity between the Right Side (*Ḥesed*—Love/Compassion) and the Left Side (*Gevurah/Din*—Severity/Judgment); the ideal is the restoration of a proper harmony between these two forces of the cosmos, a harmony that is ultimately a dominance of the Right Side (*Ḥesed*) over the Left Side, even a subsumption and reintegration of the Left into the Right.[7] In this sense, it is *Ḥesed* that dominates when all is restored and perfect in the cosmos. The ideal and redeemed state of God and world is one of love and compassion. This is all the more powerful given that the Left Side is believed to give birth to the demonic, havoc-wreaking forces of the cosmos; the reintegration of the Left Side of God into the Right Side is the ultimate victory over the demonic forces and an obliteration of the severe face of evil.

The notion that evil derives from, and is even located within, the deity is a startling conception in the history of Jewish thought. This was one of the signature ideas of Castilian Kabbalah in general and of the *Zohar* in particular. Moreover, this divide between left and right is gendered in zoharic Kabbalah (as it is for Kabbalah more broadly). The ideal absorption of the forces of severity and evil into the forces of compassion and grace is articulated as an absorption of the female dimension of God back into the masculine. In this way, the Attribute of Judgment (*middat ha-din*) is constructed as female and subordinate to the masculine Attribute of Grace/Compassion (*middat ha-Ḥesed*). The perfected state of divinity is an androgynous masculine, the ultimate maleness of God thus understood to relocate femininity back into the masculine,[8] a return to the primordial paradigm reflected in the way biblical Eve is drawn from the original body of Adam. For just as the first man was believed to reflect the upper divine image and paradigm, so, too, is the secret of divine gender indicated in the masculinity of primal man from whose body emerges the female. This theory of gender symbolism functions in some tension with the mythic drama of inner-divine courtship, marriage, and sex that the *Zohar* narrates. *Tif'eret* and *Shekhinah* are depicted as lovers in quest of each other. Ultimately, however, the moment of sexual union enables the restoration of the original singular maleness of the deity. The female is understood to constitute a subcomponent of the unified male God.[9]

The Question of Authorship

The historical provenance of the *Zohar* is one of the most palpable wedge issues that exist between modern academic scholars and the community of traditional readers and believers. For the faithful, it is nothing short of blasphemous to dispute the antiquity of the *Zohar*; Rabbi Shimon bar Yochai's authorship of the text and its position in the classical culture of Rabbinic Judaism is sacrosanct and integral to the traditional perception of Jewish history and textuality. To explode this belief is to unmoor religious memory and collective understandings of the paradigmatic and sacred past. And yet it is just such an explosion that lies at the heart of 20th- (and 21st-) century scholarship on this monumental text. Responding to the hypotheses and reflections of his predecessors (particularly the embittered judgments asserted by Heinrich Graetz), Gershom Scholem laid the foundation for all subsequent research into the problem of zoharic origins and authorship, in much the same way that he did for virtually every other major area of inquiry in the study of Jewish mysticism. Starting with his earliest Hebrew and German articles in the 1920s and culminating in his magisterial *Major Trends in Jewish Mysticism* in 1941, Scholem set out to demonstrate why the *Zohar* was a medieval and not a 2nd-century work, and why, in his view, authorship of the text is solely attributable to the late 13th-century Castilian Kabbalist Rabbi Moshe de Leon. In making this bold claim, Scholem marshaled convincing evidence based on linguistic and thematic criteria. He showed, for example, that the author of the *Zohar* did not have direct knowledge of the geography of the Land of Israel, a startling fact given the traditional claim that the text was authored by a sage living and wandering in that land! Scholem points out that the characters walk absurd distances in short periods of time, that the author did not have a proper understanding of direction and proximity in the holy land. He observes that the author of the *Zohar* confuses the mountains of Kurdistan with the mountains of Palestine, that the representations of natural phenomena in the zoharic adventures are far more consonant with the plant life of Spain than they are with that of the Middle East.

Among the linguistic criteria observed by Scholem is another phenomenon that reveals the confused historical knowledge of the zoharic author, one that supports the thesis that the *Zohar* was not written by a 2nd-century mystic. In a clear attempt to relocate the text in antiquity and to remove it from the literary conventions and forms of medieval Judaism, the author fashions an Aramaic that is unlike any other usage in rabbinic literature. Whereas the Kabbalists of medieval Europe wrote in a distinctive Hebrew, the *Zohar* was composed in an Aramaic that attempts to replicate the language of the Babylonian Talmud and the Targumim, while simultaneously creating a completely idiosyncratic and invented mode of rhetoric, one with hitherto unseen words, phrases, and syntactical constructions. But the author of the *Zohar* clearly was not aware that the tannaitic mystics (most famously represented in the Merkavah/Hekhalot corpora) would not (and did not) write esoteric texts in Aramaic. In that era, Aramaic was the language of the populace, the spoken vernacular of the unlettered. It was Hebrew which was the literary language of the times, and it was Hebrew that was employed by the authors of the mystical-esoteric texts from this period. A text like the *Zohar*, which aims to construct a veil of concealment over its own discourse, a secrecy that covers the wisdom to be revealed, would certainly not have been composed in the language of ordinary people. To the contrary, it would seem that the author(s) thought of the *Zohar*'s Aramaic as a way to maintain the secrecy and the aura of mystery around the text; precisely because the texts of 13th-century Spain were primarily composed in Hebrew, the strange Aramaic form underscored the esotericism and *otherness* of the text and its subject.[10] Indeed, even apart from the matter of chronological dissimulation, the Aramaic of the *Zohar* functions to instill an atmosphere of mystery. The rhythms and tones of the text cast a secretive mist over the encounters and teachings represented, and I suggest that the author(s) sought to stimulate just such a sense of mystery in the readers of the work.[11]

In making his assessment, Scholem noted still other features that point to a medieval dating of the text. Scholem observed the use of numerous philosophical concepts and turns of phrase that did not enter into Jewish usage until the Middle Ages, syntactical and idiomatic constructions that are thinly veiled Aramaic translations of distinctive medieval Hebrew forms and expressions; traces of Arabic and Muslim influence (which would have been anachronistic in the 2nd century), as well as a few instances of zoharic expression that betray a knowledge of Spanish (Castilian). Perhaps the most convincing piece of philological evidence emphasized by Scholem is the stunning similarity between the *Zohar* and the Hebrew writings of Rabbi Moshe de Leon. For despite the fact that the *Zohar* achieves a lyricism and dynamism not reached in de Leon's Hebrew works, the similarities in phrasing, syntax, and theme are indeed overwhelming. For a variety of reasons spelled out by Scholem, it is clear that de Leon's works were not simply influenced by an existing zoharic text; the signature manners of the *Zohar* are organic to de Leon's stylistic method in his Hebrew books. Moreover, there is no Kabbalist whose writings more closely resemble the *Zohar* in thought and compositional approach.

Many of Scholem's foundational insights still hold true and have guided the development of research for subsequent generations of scholars. And yet much has changed as well. Yehuda Liebes suggested a bold new approach in his 1982 article, "How the Zohar Was Written," an essay that dramatically shifted scholarly assumptions about and approaches to the question of authorship.[12] Liebes put forth the groundbreaking argument that the *Zohar* was quite probably composed by a group of Kabbalists, of which Moshe de Leon was a central part. Liebes himself acknowledged the extraordinary connection between de Leon and the *Zohar*, and affirmed that de Leon should still be viewed as the author of the great majority of the zoharic composition.[13] But Liebes articulated convincing arguments for the hypothesis that several other Castilian Kabbalists also had a hand in this authorship—including such prominent figures as Yosef Gikatilla, Bahya ben Asher, Yosef of Hamadan, and David ben Yehuda he-Ḥasid.[14] Most significant, Liebes proposed and effected the shift in scholarly emphasis from asking "Who wrote the *Zohar*?" to "How was the *Zohar* written?" Liebes suggested that a real-life circle of mystics stands behind the *Zohar*'s fictionalized group of wanderers; he even went so far as to hypothesize that Rabbi Todros Abulafia of Toledo may have been the real-world model for the figure of Rabbi Shimon bar Yochai in the text.[15] In shifting our attention to the "how" of zoharic composition, Liebes underscored the idea that the text was likely written as the collaboration of a mystical fraternity, the product of fellowship and shared spiritual purpose.

In more recent developments, Ronit Meroz has taken the conclusions of Liebes in exciting new directions. Meroz argues that the *Zohar* reflects many more compositional layers than was previously assumed; she has inaugurated a new kind of literary archeology, which utilizes the diversity of manuscript evidence to claim that different strata of the *Zohar* were written over the course of many years—indeed, over the span of numerous generations.[16] In the research of Meroz, the supposed unity of the zoharic literature (leaving aside the major distinctions already observed by Scholem) has been challenged, thereby raising new questions as to how the *Zohar* came to achieve its ultimate form. Indeed, as Daniel Abrams has argued, the very nature of the manuscript evidence points to the provocative notion that the *Zohar* did not achieve the status of a "closed book," a canonized text with the shape and borders encountered by modern readers, until it was first printed in the 16th century.[17] At that pivotal moment, the printers of the Mantua and Cremona editions of the *Zohar* collated a diverse set of manuscripts to fashion the book we now refer to as the *Sefer ha-Zohar*. Prior to that time, Abrams argues, the work existed as a loose constellation of manuscript fragments and passages, not necessarily reflecting some underlying base text that was composed by the Castilian Kabbalists of the late 13th century. A disparate array of strata and sources (most of which, to be sure, were authored by those Castilian Kabbalists) existed as a non-unified literary landscape; the Mantua and Cremona editors gave new order and shape to that literature, thereby forming a new entity known as the *Sefer ha-Zohar*.

At this juncture I highlight the most recent major contribution of Elliot Wolfson to the question of authorship and composition. In a fascinating new article that offers a critical edition of a hitherto neglected source, Wolfson reveals striking affinities between the *Zohar* and a text known as *Sha'arei ha-Zaqen* (The Gates of the Elder).[18] Like the narrative about Shimon bar Yochai and his wandering disciples, a story in which the drama of the text revolves around the master who reveals the secrets, the *Sha'arei ha-Zaqen* centers upon such a revered figure, one that suggests the existence of a real-world circle of Kabbalists who may have been one of the primary envisioned models for the authors of the *Zohar*. Furthermore, in addition to the figure of Shimon bar Yochai, the *Zohar* dramatizes the persona of another elderly master of secrets, the much discussed old man of its commentary on *parashat Mishpatim* (the *Sabba de-Mishpatim*).

A Literary Approach to the Zohar

As I have outlined above, zoharic scholarship to this point has focused on the historical question of authorship; the conceptual universe of zoharic theology, mythology, and symbolism; the exegetical dimensions of the text; the nature of mystical experience; and the representation of gender and sexuality with the human and the divine realms. Relative to this prodigious research, we are still in the early stages of our appreciation of the *Zohar* as a work of the literary imagination, as a product of poetic and narrative artistry.[19] This is, after all, one of the central threads of zoharic textuality; the rhythm of the work is set by the alternation between the mystical Midrash and the fictional representation of Shimon bar Yochai and his band of Galilean disciples. It is to this *desideratum* of scholarship that my own work is directed; I seek to develop a poetics of zoharic narration, an understanding of the narrative tapestry and the techniques whereby the authors take us into the imagined world of mystery and mystical disclosure.

As intimated earlier, the fiction of the *Zohar* portrays a quest for wisdom, the sojourn of a group of mystics through the ancient Galilee in search of a deeper understanding of divine truth in the cosmos. This point is essential,

I believe, to an appreciation of the dynamic interplay between the *Zohar's* narrative and exegetical modes. The narrated anecdotes and tales most often depict a moment of mystical discovery, an insight that is presented to the companions through an encounter of one sort or another. Frequently this takes place through an interpersonal encounter with a stranger along the road. The companions meet a figure who does not appear to be a kabbalistic sage but turns out to be the bearer of some extraordinary level of mystical knowledge and teaching. In one instance, a donkey driver reveals himself to be a great sage; in another a small child delivers a profound homily and rebukes the rabbis for their shortcomings in piety; and in yet another scene the companions are guided to safety in the desert by a man who subsequently delivers a stunning kabbalistic discourse. In all these cases, the moment of teaching is represented as a great surprise, a wondrous and unexpected discovery, a revelation that is greeted with intense emotional and rhetorical drama on the part of the companions. In still other instances, a few examined here, kabbalistic meaning is extracted from an experience in the natural world. The companions encounter a particular phenomenon of nature, and this moment of engagement serves as a stimulus for new associations in theological and cosmic meaning. In these instances, we observe the interdependent relationship between the exegetical and narrative modes, as well as the way in which the lines of discourse are drawn and bridged by a removed narrator and editor.

With this is mind, I turn to a paradigmatic textual case. Framed as a homily on the opening chapter of Exodus, this pericope begins by citing the language of that biblical text: "A new king arose over Egypt who did not know Joseph." We may note, first of all, that, like a great many exegetical moments in classical midrashic literature, the citation of the verse is presented in the removed voice of an editor; the interpretive voice of the specific sage whose reference is only cited as such *after* the anonymously uttered biblical verse. And in keeping with earlier midrashic models, the zoharic text immediately shifts to a particular rabbinic voice, in this case, that of Rabbi Yosi, who offers a kabbalistic reading of the biblical words. Rabbi Yosi links the verse in Exodus with a seemingly unrelated formulation in Psalm 104—"He makes His angels spirits"; such a method of correlation between distant biblical verses was also a typical technique of the older homiletical Midrashim. It is the use of the present tense (*oseh*, "makes") that attracts the preacher's attention, and he asserts that God is constantly creating angelic messengers to be in charge of different elements of the universe. And this, Rabbi Yosi argues, is how we should understand the statement in Exodus 1:8. Because all phenomena and happenings of the earthly realm are the mirrored reflections of the heavenly domain, the rise of a new king in Egypt reflects the moment in which a celestial purveyor was appointed over the demonic, impure elements of the cosmos, a cluster of negative forces represented by the symbolic word "Egypt." For just as there is an Egypt below, so, too, is there an Egypt above. Rabbi Yosi then parses the second half of the verse, "who did not know Joseph" (*asher lo yada et yosef*): because the purveyor of cosmic impurity comes from "the place of Separation" (*atar de-peiruda*) or the evil Other Side of the cosmic structure, he is characterized as one who does not know Joseph, the symbolic representation of divine perfection, righteousness, holiness, and sexual purity, the frequent term of choice to refer to the *sefirah Yesod*, the locus of male sexuality within the divine self. As is the way of the *Zohar*, the straightforward meaning (*peshat*) of the biblical text, and indeed of the whole earthly world, is read as a doorway into a deeper understanding of the divine mysteries and the workings of the cosmos. In this case, the polarity between earthly Joseph and the subsequent Pharaoh of earthly Egypt reflects a heavenly polarity between the ultimate forces of Good and Evil, of purity and impurity, in the universe.

But it is to the relationship between this interpretation and the narrative that follows that I want to call our attention. Immediately upon the conclusion of Rabbi Yosi's kabbalistic interpretation of the biblical verse, the voice of the text shifts from quoted speech to a removed narration of the journeying companions. Having just been the speaker of exegesis, Rabbi Yosi now becomes the subject of a fictional scene that carries the purpose of anchoring the foregoing hermeneutical assertions in the living context of the road, in an encounter with the vibrant phenomena of the natural world, the moment of discovery wherein cosmic meaning is extrapolated from the physical-sensory experience of the companions:

> Rabbi Elazar and Rabbi Yosi were traveling on the road, and they arose with the light to continue walking. They saw a star running from one side and another star from the other side. Rabbi Elazar said, "The time has now arrived for the stars of morning to praise their Master. They are running out of fear and awe for their Master, to praise and to sing to Him." As it is written: "When the morning stars sang together, and all the divine beings shouted for joy" (Job 38:7). Because they are all in one unity, they praise Him.[20]

At this point, we are still hard-pressed to discern a link between the exegesis regarding the figure of Joseph and the narrated encounter with the sunrise and morning stars. Here the lyrical voice of the *Zohar* comes to the fore;

we are drawn into the pastoral imagination of the text, into an evocation of natural rhythms of the world as a seemingly pure celebration of physical wonderment. The stars are personified only to the extent that they are the hyper-literal realization of Job's use of imagery; we have yet to see these natural phenomena as portals to *meta*physical understanding. But that transition takes place almost immediately as the interpreter (presumably still in the voice of Rabbi Elazar) offers a correlated metaphysical reading of Psalm 22:6. Here we also see the association to the Joseph exegesis:

> "For the leader; on the doe of the dawn. A Psalm of David" (Ps. 22:6)—
> "Doe of the dawn": For when the face of the East shines and the darkness of night withdraws, there is one purveyor for the east side, and he draws forth a single thread of light from the south side until the sun comes and emerges and breaks through the windows of heaven and illumines the world. And that thread of light causes the darkness of night to withdraw.

In these lines we still see the *Zohar* in lyrical thrall to the mysterious rhythms of nature; the majestic experience of sunrise is represented as the sublime craft of heavenly officers, the unfolding threads of light a meditation on the slow and wondrous passage from the depths of night to the rise of morning. In the instrumental role of the appointed purveyor (*memanne*), we observe the rhetorical link between the foregoing exegesis regarding the "new king who did not know Joseph" and the lyrical representation of sunrise prompted by the moment in the narrative in which the stars are beheld. This association is significant in that it begins to crystallize the manner in which the *Zohar* moves from one thought to another, from the hermeneutical to the narrative-lyrical and back again. Through the powerful hand of the purveyor, the speaker evokes the drama of that radiant breaking through, the passage of increasing illumination through the "windows" of the firmament, the shining of the "face" of the East.

Utilizing such metaphoric depiction endows the sunrise in the East with a quality of personified life, a living face that is aglow with awakened energy. Thus far, the *Zohar* speaks within the ordinary bounds of nature; there may be heavenly officers in charge of the mundane cycle, but we have yet to pass into the realm of theosophical knowledge, of the extrapolation of inner divine mysteries from the happenings and structures of the world. But this is indeed the next step in the zoharic speaker's exegetical process; the poetic evocation of the natural realm, first fueled by the narrated encounter of the companions with the wonder of an emergent daylight, leads the *Zohar* on an inexorable stream of association to the dynamics of the divine *sefirot*. With this we return to the opening focus of the reflection—the "doe of the dawn" (*ayelet ha-shaḥar*) and her symbolically potent emergence in the predawn light that divides the night from the day:[21]

> Then the doe of the dawn [*ayelet ha-shaḥar*] comes out, and a black light emerges in the darkness to join with the day, and the day is illuminated. And the light of day subsumes and draws that doe [*ayelet*] into itself.

With this depiction of the doe that comes out at the earliest moment of dawn, Rabbi Elazar has begun the interpretive move so characteristic of zoharic exegesis. The sun is a well-known symbol for the masculine *sefirah Tiferet* in kabbalistic hermeneutics, and the darkness of night (further symbolized elsewhere by the moon) and the *ayelet* are standard symbols for the *Shekhinah*, the feminine dimension of Divinity, the partner of *Tiferet*. The breaking through of dawn's light is the first gesture of love and eros between *Tiferet* and *Shekhinah*; this moment culminates in the union of male and female, here characterized as the drawing in of the female, the reabsorption and enclosure of the feminine within the masculine that is such a dominant gender paradigm in kabbalistic symbolism, despite the fact that it clearly runs counter to the workings of earthly heterosexuality.

And so the natural phenomenon of sunrise is understood to reflect a supernal dynamic within the divine self, the process of the two inner-divine lovers uniting as one light. But as the lovers separate, following the climactic moment of union, they immediately yearn for each other; they lament the sorrow of their parting. It is in this way that the *Zohar* magnificently reflects on the meaning of Psalm 22 and the enigmatic juxtaposition of the *ayelet ha-shaḥar* in verse 1 with the passionate call of the psalmist in verses 2 and 3, the exclamation of yearning for a God who has seemingly abandoned the individual to his crying and his anguish. The *Zohar* makes this exegesis of the Psalm explicit in the lines that follow:

> And it was about this doe, [about the moment] when she withdraws from the daylight that subsumed her, that David sang his song. As it is written: For the leader; on the "doe of dawn." And what did he say? "My God, my God, why have you abandoned me?" For the doe of dawn (*ayelet ha-shaḥar*) has withdrawn from the light of day.

The cry over divine absence in Psalm 22:2–3 is understood to be a direct response to the symbolic meaning of verse 1. The doe that emerged at dawn's light, that was enveloped and subsumed in the radiance of the rising sun, has returned to her hiding place. In the symbolism of the *Zohar*, the *Shekhinah* who had been united in love with *Tiferet* has now withdrawn from the fully risen sun, and her lover, *Tiferet,* cries out in anguished yearning, "My God, my God, why have You abandoned me?"

Though somewhat marginal to my specific literary concerns here, it certainly behooves us to recall the centrality of this Psalm to Christian thinking about the Passion of Christ. In Matthew 27, Jesus utters a blended Hebrew and Aramaic version of these words on the cross at the height of his suffering, and Christian exegetes have long understood Psalm 22 to be a prefiguration of the crucifixion. Seen through the lens of later Christian theology, the language of Psalm 22 and Matthew 27 reflects an *inner* divine cry—a calling out of yearning from the divine Son to the divine Father. It is in this respect that there exists a striking parallel between the zoharic exegesis and the Christian model. In the passage from the *Zohar* it is also an *inner* divine cry that takes place—one sefirotic dimension of Divinity cries out in anguish over the absence of his lover; it is *Tiferet* who utters an exclamatory lament for the withdrawn *Shekhinah*. A veiled correlation, to be sure, though one wonders whether this exegesis may reflect some measure of response to Christian thinking, especially in light of our growing appreciation for the likelihood that the Christian majority culture in medieval Spain may have influenced the zoharic literature.

At this point, the voice of the text shifts again from Rabbi Elazar's homiletical monologue back to a voice that seemingly stands outside the text or, at the very least, outside the interior of narrative action. This third-person voice serves to enclose the exegesis of Rabbi Elazar, and indeed returns us to the original context within which the teaching about the *ayelet ha-shaḥar* was articulated:

> As they were walking, the day became light, and the time for [morning] prayer arrived. Rabbi Elazar said, "Let us pray and then walk on." They sat and prayed. Afterward, they stood up and [continued] walking.

As we find rather frequently in the *Zohar*, the narrated action here is conveyed in a simple staccato rhythm; unlike the many instances in which the authors apply their considerable poetic artistry (as we have just observed in the *Zohar*'s depiction of the sunrise and its correlated metaphysical drama), the narrator here seems merely interested in sealing up one piece of discourse and opening another. The intentional act of sitting to pray functions here as a gesture of pause and focus in the narrative rhythm, and it evokes its own intrigue. One would assume that the companions would have needed to stand for parts of the morning service (as is stipulated by rabbinic law) before rising again to continue walking.

But the moment of prayer and the act of sitting[22] are most notable for our purposes insofar as they function to complete the pericope; after the companions stand and continue walking, Rabbi Elazar launches into an unrelated metaphysical discourse. The interrelated acts of sitting and praying mark the rise of the sun to full daylight; it is clearly the recognition of that light that prompts Rabbi Elazar's suggestion that they pray before walking further. In this way the act of morning prayer seals and brings to dramatic conclusion the discourse that it follows. For having first beheld the rushing stars of dawn within the context of the fictional tale, Rabbi Elazar's kabbalistic teaching was a theological-metaphysical reflection on the gradual emergence of daylight, a mystical rumination stimulated by an experience in the natural world. Returning to the third-person voice (for we recall that the encounter with the morning stars was first narrated in the third-person), the completion of sunrise is acknowledged and responded to with ritual gesture and speech.

In conclusion, I have set out here to examine the contours and borders of zoharic discourse through consideration of one paradigmatic pericope. I have sought to show the manner in which the *Zohar* is crafted as a tapestry of exegesis, narrative, and lyricism—how the narrative dramatizes the energy and process of mystical discovery. The fictional dimension of the *Zohar* is by no means incidental to the creative power of the text; instead, it is within the shapes and wonders of worldly exploration that the divine mysteries are revealed—the narrative of journey and the lyrical representation of the natural realm serve to lead the kabbalistic exegete into the discovery of metaphysical associations. Through this lens of analysis, which has been remarkably underdeveloped in zoharic scholarship, we see the workings of an organic and protean literary aesthetic, a textual weave that still awaits appreciation as one of the pivotal masterworks in the broad history of religious literature.

1. On this question, see the analyses in Boaz Huss, *Like the Radiance of the Sky: Chapters in the Reception History of the Zohar and the Construction of Its Symbolic Value* (Jerusalem: Ben-Zvi Institute and Bialik Institute, 2008).

2. Scholem's findings were summarized in his *Major Trends in Jewish Mysticism* (New York: Schocken Books, 1954), pp. 156–204 and notes. Also see the highly important discussion in Isaiah Tishby, *The Wisdom of the Zohar*, trans. David Goldstein (Oxford: Oxford University Press, 1989), 1:13–23. For a recent and extremely detailed history of scholarship on the zoharic authorship, see Daniel Abrams, "The Invention of the *Zohar* as a Book: On the Assumptions and Expectations of the Kabbalists and Modern Scholars," *Kabbalah: Journal for the Study of Jewish Mystical Texts* 19 (2009): 7–142.

3. On the relationship between historical objectivity and received cultural memory in medieval Judaism, see Yosef H. Yerushalmi, *Zakhor: Jewish History and Jewish Memory* (Seattle: University of Washington Press, 1982), pp. 31–52.

4. On this question in rabbinic literature, see Richard Kalmin, "Saints or Sinners, Scholars or Ignoramuses? Stories about the Rabbis as Evidence for the Composite Nature of the Babylonian Talmud," *AJS Review* 15 (1990): 179–205.

5. On this notion of symbolic clusters and the construction of a new religious language through sefirotic terminology, see the remarks of Arthur Green, *A Guide to the Zohar* (Stanford: Stanford University Press, 2004), p. 56.

6. The two most prominent discussions of this issue in kabbalistic mythology are Gershom Scholem, *On the Mystical Shape of the Godhead: Basic Concepts in the Kabbalah* (New York: Schocken Books, 1991), pp. 56–87; and Tishby, *The Wisdom of the Zohar*, 1:447–74, 509–12.

7. This topic has been examined at great length in the writings of Elliot Wolfson; see, for example, "Left Contained in the Right: A Study in Zoharic Hermeneutics," *AJS Review* 11 (1986): 27–52; *Through a Speculum That Shines: Vision and Imagination in Medieval Jewish Mysticism* (Princeton, NJ: Princeton University Press, 1994), pp. 326–92; *Language, Eros, Being: Kabbalistic Hermeneutics and Poetic Imagination* (New York: Fordham University Press, 2005), pp. 142–89 and notes.

8. This insight has been powerfully argued by Elliot Wolfson; see the above-mentioned works, as well as the more detailed consideration of Wolfson's work in Hava Tirosh-Samuelson's chapter in this volume.

9. The broader subject of mythological creativity and the place of myth in the mystical imagination have also been explored in stimulating ways in recent scholarship. These developments have, among other things, ventured to show the ways in which kabbalistic mythology functions within an organic tradition from rabbinic antiquity, despite the fact that the specifics of theological doctrine are dramatically different. See, for example, Yehuda Liebes, *Studies in Jewish Myth and Jewish Messianism* (Albany: State University of New York Press, 1993), pp. 1–64; Elliot R. Wolfson, "Coronation of the Sabbath Bride: Kabbalistic Myth and the Ritual of Androgynisation," *Journal of Jewish Thought and Philosophy* 6 (1997): 301–44; Michael Fishbane, *Biblical Myth and Rabbinic Mythmaking* (Oxford: Oxford University Press, 2003), pp. 275–92.

10. On the Aramaic of the *Zohar*, see Ada Rapoport-Albert, "Late Aramaic: The Literary and Linguistic Context of the Zohar," *Aramaic Studies* 4 (2006): 5–19; Yehuda Liebes, "Hebrew and Aramaic as Languages of the Zohar," ibid., pp. 35–52; Charles Mopsik, "Late Judeo-Aramaic: The Language of Theosophic Kabbalah," ibid., pp. 21–33 (first published in French in 1999).

11. See Melila Hellner-Eshed, *A River Flows from Eden: The Language of Mystical Experience in the Zohar*, trans. Nathan Wolski (Stanford: Stanford University Press, 2009), pp. 157–88.

12. Yehuda Liebes, *Studies in the Zohar*, trans. Stephanie Nakache (Albany: State University of New York Press, 1993), pp. 85–138.

13. On the shift in Liebes's opinion about this matter, see Abrams, "The Invention of the *Zohar* as a Book," p. 71.

14. Also see Moshe Idel, "Kabbalistic Material from the School of R. David ben Yehuda he-Ḥasid" [in Hebrew], *Jerusalem Studies in Jewish Thought* 2 (1983): 169–207.

15. Liebes, *Studies in the Zohar*, pp. 135–38.

16. See Ronit Meroz, "Der Aufbau des Buches Sohar," *PaRDeS: Zeitschrift der Vereinigung für jüdischen Studien* 11 (2005): 16–36.

17. Abrams, "The Invention of the *Zohar* as a Book," p. 107.

18. Elliot Wolfson, "The Anonymous Chapters of the Elderly Master of Secrets: New Evidence for the Early Activity of the Zoharic Circle," *Kabbalah: Journal for the Study of Jewish Mystical Texts* 19 (2009): 143–278, esp. pp. 172–83.

19. That said, however, quite a number of important advances have been made. Among an array of other works, Yehuda Liebes's groundbreaking study, "The Messiah of the *Zohar*" (in *Studies in the Zohar*, pp. 1–84 and notes) powerfully demonstrated that the representation of Shimon bar Yochai as the "great one" of his, and indeed all, generations was critical to the life of the text and to the depth of its reception among generations of devoted readers. Other elements of the literary approach are present in Liebes, "Zohar and Eros" [in Hebrew], *Alpayyim* 9 (1994): 67–119. This last essay explores the playfulness of the narrative strata, including the use of humor in zoharic creativity. Other important contributions to the literary approach, or to the study of the narrative content, include Mati Megged, *The Darkened Light: Aesthetic Values in the Zohar* [in Hebrew] (Tel Aviv: Sifriyat Poalim, 1980); Mordechai Pachter, "Between Night and Morning: A Literary Analysis of a Zoharic Text" [in Hebrew], in *The Age of the Zohar*, ed. Yosef Dan (Jerusalem: Hebrew University Press, 1989), pp. 311–46; Naomi Tene, "Constructions of the Story in the Zohar" [in Hebrew] (Ph.D. dissertation, Bar Ilan University, 1993); Michal Oron, "Set Me as a Seal upon Your Heart: The Poetics of the Zohar in *Sabba de-Mishpatim*" [in Hebrew], in *Masu'ot: Studies in the Literature of Kabbalah and Jewish Thought Dedicated to the Memory of Prof. Efrayim Gottlieb*, ed. Michal Oron and Amos Goldreich (Jerusalem: Mossad Bialik, 1994), pp. 1–24; Eliane Amado Lévy-Valensi, *La Poétique du Zohar* (Paris: Éditions de l'Éclat, 1996); Pinchas Giller, "Love and Upheaval in the Zohar's *Sabba de-Mishpatim*," *Journal of Jewish Thought and Philosophy* 7 (1997): 31–60; Aryeh Wineman, *Mystic Tales from the Zohar* (Philadelphia: Jewish Publication Society, 1997); Boaz Huss, "A Sage Is Preferable to a Prophet: R. Shimon bar Yochai and Moses in the Zohar" [in Hebrew], *Kabbalah: Journal for the Study of Jewish Mystical Texts* 4 (1999): 103–39; Ronit Meroz, "Zoharic Narratives and Their Adaptations," *Hispania Judaica Bulletin* 3 (2000): 3–63; Gil Anidjar, *"Our Place in al-Andalus, Kabbalah, Philosophy, Literature in Arab Jewish*

Letters (Stanford: Stanford University Press, 2002), pp. 166–218; Eitan P. Fishbane, "Tears of Disclosure: The Role of Weeping in Zoharic Narrative," *Journal of Jewish Thought and Philosophy* 11 (2002): 25–47; David Greenstein, "Aimless Pilgrimage: The Quotidian Utopia of the *Zohar*" (Ph.D. dissertation, New York University, 2003), esp. pp. 105–44; Hellner-Eshed, *A River Flows from Eden*; Wolfson, *Language, Eros, Being,* esp. pp. 1–45, 190–260, and notes (Wolfson's work in this monograph opens up the dynamic forces of poetic imagery and contemplative imagination in the Kabbalah; his quest to "craft a poetics of Kabbalah" and its relation to one of Scholem's many programmatic remarks, is articulated on pp. xi–xiv); Oded Yisraeli, *The Interpretation of Secrets and the Secret of Interpretation: Midrashic and Hermeneutic Strategies in Sabba de-Mishpatim of the Zohar* [in Hebrew] (Los Angeles: Cherub, 2005), pp. 51–112; Ronit Meroz, "The Weaving of a Myth: An Analysis of Two Stories in the *Zohar*" [in Hebrew], in *Study and Knowledge in Jewish Thought,* ed. Howard Kreisel (Be'er-Sheva: Ben Gurion University of the Negev Press, 2006), 2:167–205; Michal Oron, "The Motif of the *Yanuqa* and Its Meaning in the Zohar" [in Hebrew], in *Ḥiddushei Zohar,* ed. Ronit Meroz (Tel Aviv: Tel Aviv University Press, 2007), pp. 129–64; Joel Hecker, "Kissing Kabbalists: Hierarchy, Reciprocity, and Equality," in *Love—Virtual and Real—in the Jewish Tradition,* ed. Leonard J. Greenspoon, Ronald A. Simkins, and Jean A. Cahan (Omaha, Nebr.: Creighton University Press, 2008), pp. 171–208; Nathan Wolski, "Mystical Poetics: Narrative, Time, and Exegesis in the Zohar," *Prooftexts* 28 (2008): 101–28; idem, "Don Quixote and Sancho Panza Were Walking on the Way: El Caballero Andante and the Book of Radiance (*Sefer HaZohar*)," *Shofar* 27 (2009): 24–47; and Eitan P. Fishbane, "The Scent of the Rose: Drama, Fiction, and Narrative Form in the Zohar," *Prooftexts* 29 (2009) 324–61.

20. *Zohar* 2:10a–10b.

21. Compare this text to the parallel analyzed in Mordechai Pachter, "Between Night and Morning," pp. 311–46.

22. See the parallel to the *Sha'arei ha-Zaqen* (as mentioned by Moshe Cordovero) cited in Wolfson, "The Anonymous Chapters of the Elderly Master of Secrets," p. 147 n. 23.

3

Abraham ben Samuel Abulafia
and the Prophetic Kabbalah

ELLIOT R. WOLFSON

Abraham Abulafia, the self-proclaimed prophet with messianic pretenses, was born in Saragossa, Spain, probably in late 1239 or early 1240 and died sometime after 1291, the last year for which we have any evidence of his life.[1] The time that Abulafia was active is the precise moment in Jewish history that witnessed an impressive proliferation of mystical speculation and practice in several geographical settings both within the Land of Israel and in the Diaspora, especially on the European continent. In contrast to most other masters of esoteric lore from this period, about whom we know more of their literary productions than their biographies, we have a relative wealth of information about Abulafia's personal life, largely owing to the meticulous fashion by which he documented his life experiences. Given Abulafia's fecund imagination, however, it is probably wise to exercise a measure of doubt regarding the factual veracity of some of his claims. Alternatively expressed, Abulafia's construction of history—both individual and collective—is such that fantasy is not easily disentangled from facticity.

Here I will note only some of the highlights of his intellectual and spiritual odyssey. In 1260 he departed from the Iberian Peninsula and set out to Palestine, hoping to cross the Sambatyon River in an effort to locate the ten lost tribes of ancient Israel. Raging battles in the region forced Abulafia to leave Acre and journey to Greece and Italy. The time spent in those countries constituted a period of extensive and concentrated study of philosophical works, especially Maimonides' *Guide of the Perplexed*, under the tutelage of Hillel of Verona. This treatise became a cornerstone of his own thinking, as attested to by the fact that he eventually composed no fewer than three commentaries on it, *Sitrei Torah*, *Ḥayyei ha-Nefesh*, and *Sefer ha-Ge'ullah*. Sometime in the 1260s Abulafia returned to Catalonia, settling in Barcelona, where he continued his study of Jewish philosophy, including Baḥya Ibn Paquda's *Book of the Duties of the Heart*, a treatise that incorporated aspects of Sufi pietism,[2] elements of which have been detected in his own meditational practice.[3]

In the 1270s, Abulafia began to immerse himself (probably through the guidance of Baruch Togarmi) in Jewish mystical and magical treatises, including, for instance, the *Sefer Yetsirah*, together with several kabbalistic commentaries, the *Pirqei Hekhalot de-Rabbi Ishmael*, *Shimmush Torah* and *Shimmush Tehillim*, *Sefer ha-Bahir*, *Sefer Raziel*, and *Sefer ha-Razim*.[4] Sometime in the late 1270s Abulafia left Spain and traveled back to Italy and Sicily, where he spent the rest of his life teaching students and writing numerous treatises expounding his unique brand of mysticism, which he eventually called "prophetic Kabbalah" (*qabbalah nevu'it*).

Typological Classification and Modern Scholarship

It has become routine in modern scholarship to distinguish sharply between two kinds of Kabbalah—the theosophic and the ecstatic. The former is focused on visual contemplation of the ten hypostatic powers of the Godhead and the latter on the cultivation of meditative practices that lead to prophetic-unitive states. Whereas Gershom Scholem limited these types to the second half of 13th-century Spain, Moshe Idel has expanded the historical categories, arguing that they are the two phenomenological trends in Jewish mysticism more generally. What has not been sufficiently noted by these and other scholars is that Abulafia himself is the Kabbalist most responsible for this typological classification. As I have noted elsewhere, this distinction is particularly prominent in a passage that occurs in the *Iggeret ve-Zo't li-Yehudah*, an epistle that Abulafia wrote to Judah Salomon in the late 1280s.[5] It was published by Adolph Jellinek in 1853[6] and has served as an important source for subsequent historians who have attempted to depict the development of medieval Jewish mysticism in terms of these typological classifications. In it Abulafia distinguished between two types of Kabbalah, the tradition of divine names (*qabbalat ha-shemot*) and the tradition of the emanations (*qabbalat ha-sefirot*).

It is important to emphasize that the tone of this letter is entirely polemical and self-justificatory; that is, the purpose of the document is to legitimate the author's own enterprise in the eyes of his readers. It is in the context of this letter that Abulafia responds in a rather acerbic manner to the criticism directed at him by Solomon ben Abraham ibn Adret. The strategy Abulafia adopted to promote his own intellectual agenda was to demarcate his orientation over and against the views of others, including the Talmudists, philosophers, and Kabbalists primarily interested in expounding the doctrine of the *sefirot*. The distinction between the two types of Kabbalah has to be seen as part of this larger project.

Appreciating the highly polemical nature of this context provides a key for understanding the rhyme and reason of Abulafia's adoption of a typological approach. The sharp angle of Abulafia's presentation is determined by the immediate concern to validate his own position; hence he distinguishes his own Kabbalah from that of the opposing party. In an effort to legitimate his own teaching and thereby defend himself against the attacks of Ibn Adret, who is to be counted among those who focus exclusively on *qabbalat ha-sefirot*, Abulafia may have exaggerated the difference between his own brand of Kabbalah and those of the other Kabbalists. This is not to suggest that he advocated or even remotely intimated that the two kinds of Kabbalah could be reduced to a single religious phenomenon.[7] The scholarly tendency to bifurcate these two types of Kabbalah is due to the extreme contrast found in Abulafia's own epistle;[8] as I have argued, however, this formulation was shaped by his immediate concern to justify himself in light of the criticism of a leading rabbinic authority who belonged to the other camp. Indeed, even in this document there is evidence that Abulafia embraced a more comprehensive understanding of Kabbalah that comprised both *qabbalat ha-shemot* and *qabbalat ha-sefirot*. Thus, for example, in one passage he asserts that there are four bases of knowledge—sense experience (*murgash*), reason (demonstrable truth; *muskal*), conventional opinion (*mefursam*), and received tradition (*mequbbal*). The last item consists of a source of knowledge that is not only unique to the Jewish people, but, as Abulafia is quick to point out, hidden from most of the rabbis involved in the study of Talmud. That tradition (*qabbalah*) is divided into two parts: (1) "knowledge of God by way of the ten *sefirot*, which are called the shoots, and the one who separates them, the one who cuts the shoots, and they reveal the secret of unity"; and (2) "knowledge of God by way of the twenty-two letters, from them and their vowels and accents the names and the seal are compounded."[9] Both these components constitute the nature of Kabbalah and are included in the *Sefer Yetsirah*.

There is no doubt regarding Abulafia's acceptance of the essential place occupied by *torat ha-sefirot* in the taxonomy of the kabbalistic tradition. The consummate master of esoteric knowledge must know the "mysteries of the names and the seal together with the *sefirot*."[10] Although Abulafia recognizes both components as part of Kabbalah, he clearly gives priority to the former over the latter. Thus, he observes that the "first part [*sefirot*] is prior in time with respect to the study of the tradition, but the second [*otiyyot*] is prior to the first in terms of level, for it is the goal of the existence of select human beings. The one who reaches it is the one whose intellect is actualized, and he is the one to whom the Lord of everything revealed Himself and disclosed to him His secret."[11]

In another passage in the same work, Abulafia describes the two types of Kabbalah in an even somewhat more conciliatory manner: "My intention in this epistle that has been sent as a gift in honor of the distinguished sage and faithful colleague R. Judah Salomon is to notify him and all who see it that I have already received the first part [that consists of] knowledge of the *sefirot* that have been mentioned before I received the second part, for the second is not found until the first is found even though there is a great connection between the two like the connection of the animal soul and the rational."[12] In the continuation of this passage, Abulafia compares philosophy and the two types of Kabbalah to the three souls—vegetative, animal, and rational—as well as to the three divisions of Jews—the Israelites, Levites, and priests. Both metaphors express the hierarchical view adopted by Abulafia that placed prophetic Kabbalah as the goal of human endeavor and the apex of spiritual achievement. But just as the three kinds of soul and the three divisions of Jews form organic wholes, so, too, are the three kinds of knowledge one entity in which every part is essential to the organism. The ultimate purpose of the human being is to acquire knowledge of the divine, and each one of these three elements—philosophy, the Kabbalah of the *sefirot*, and the Kabbalah of the *shemot*—contributes to the process, although clearly the most perfect expression of that knowledge is attained only by virtue of the last of these paths.

Abulafia's Messianic Pretensions and His Relation to Christianity

Late in the year 1270, Abulafia had a vision that initiated intense mystical and messianic activity for the following two decades, epitomized by what I consider to be his imaginary attempt to meet Pope Nicholas III around the time of Rosh Hashanah in 1280, which is recounted in the beginning of his *Sefer ha-Edut* and alluded to poetically in the first stanzas of *Sefer ha-Ot*.[13] Evidence suggests that he considered 1291 as the year when his messianic mission would be fully realized, especially around March (corresponding to the Hebrew month of Nisan, 5051), but apparently nothing actually materialized, and we do not hear about him after that time. Abulafia's messianic speculation is multifaceted, but in this brief account I will focus on the negative and positive christological overtones of his views on redemption.

The relationship to Christianity that one may elicit from Abulafia's works is as complex as that of other Spanish Kabbalists of his time,[14] especially the Castilian Kabbalists who participated in what scholars are now calling the zoharic circle.[15] Not only did Abulafia recognize the part that Christianity played in salvation history, typified, for instance, in the association of Jesus with the sixth day, as opposed to the Jewish Messiah, who is the Sabbath,[16] but certain passages point to Abulafia's fascination with and appropriation of Christian doctrines, especially trinitarian imagery, even if we concede that these passages are themselves part of his polemical strategy.[17] There is also the possibility that some of the techniques he incorporated into his contemplative regimen reflect hesychastic exercises that he may have learned in his sojourn in Greece.[18] Beyond these tactics, however, Abulafia occasionally characterized Christianity with stock derogatory images, referring, for instance, to Jesus as the "bastard son of a menstruant."[19] The Christian savior is identified as Satan, which, for Abulafia (following Maimonides), is the allegorical representation of the material body or the imagination.[20] By contrast, the Jewish Messiah represents the intellect, which is the source of truth. Moreover, in *Or ha-Sekhel*, Abulafia employs a widely circulated medieval tale of three rings in order to undermine the credibility of Christianity and Islam as adequate expressions of the truth and to indicate that even Judaism in its present state did not possess the truth (symbolically represented by a pearl) in its entirety; however, in the messianic era, religious faith will be cleansed of its illusions and Judaism will manifest itself as the superior expression of monotheism.[21] In Abulafia's scheme, all three Abrahamic faiths instruct about the theological truth—he states explicitly that Jesus and Muhammad both harbored the intention to unify the Name[22]—but only Judaism is the "universal religion" through which the "divine overflow moving the universal speech" is established in the world.[23] Just as all created entities derive from God and yet are distinct, so, too, do the nations share a common nature but each is diverse. Abulafia argues, accordingly, that every ethnic group must remain faithful to its own religious customs and cultural-linguistic vocation, but in the future, in the days of the "final redeemer"—an expression we can presume refers to Abulafia himself[24]—all three liturgical communities will know the name of God.[25] In line with other medieval Jewish thinkers, Abulafia viewed Christianity as presenting the greater assault on the belief in God's oneness, and thus his critiques of this faith are far more strident that his comments about Islam;[26] indeed, at times he even refers to Christians as idolaters, a view that was shared by others in the Middle Ages, including Maimonides.[27]

In one extraordinary passage, Abulafia writes that the "Greek Christians" call the Messiah "anti-Christ," for he "stands opposite [Jesus] to indicate to everyone that his saying to the Christians that he is God and the son of God is a complete lie, for he did not receive the power from the unique name, but rather all his power hangs on the image of the Teli, the serpentine constellation, which is hanging on the tree of knowledge of good and evil."[28] The true Messiah, by contrast, is suspended from the tree of life. As several scholars have argued, it would seem that the intent of this text is that Abulafia is the Jewish messianic figure who rises to expose the deceit of the Christian savior; the former corresponds to the Tree of Life, the intellect or form, and the latter to the Tree of Knowledge, the imagination or matter, also represented by the astrological image of the Teli.[29]

In the same context, Abulafia satirically renders the eucharistic images of the bread and wine, the body and blood of Christ (related typologically to the dreams of Pharaoh's baker and cupbearer, which were interpreted by Joseph). The bread is identified as the *corpus daemones*, which he glosses as the "bodies of demons, the opposite of *dominus*, whose matter is spiritual and divine."[30] Rather than being the body of God (*corpus domini*), Jesus is the body of the demon, the force of Satan, which, for Abulafia, connotes the imaginative faculty that has the capacity to deceive.[31] Christians are denigrated as "fools" for thinking that the powers they venerate are divine; the bread, which is a matter of carnal desire, is offered as a *sacrificio*, but it is, in fact, *sheqer officio*, that is, "false worship" (*avodat sheqer*). By deifying Jesus, therefore, Christians are guilty of bearing false witness, as their *sacramentum* is veritably an "erroneous lie (*sheqer mendo*)." The *secreto* (*śqryto*) can be transposed into the name *christo* (*qrśto*), which Abulafia decodes as a hybrid of the Hebrew *sheqer* and the Latin *tu*, that is, "you are a lie." On the basis of this word play, the fallacy of the Trinity is laid bare: "Thus they say to him 'you are a lie' [*sheqer attah*], for [the word] *sheloshah* [three] is numerically equal to *sheqer we-khazav* ['lie and deception'].[32] Whoever thinks that God is divisible into two, three, or more persons is an idolater and a heretic."[33] Abulafia similarly undermines the eucharistic symbol of the wine by transposing (through the principle of numerical equivalence) the word *ha-sarigim* ("vines") into *sarei moah*. ("princes of the brain") or *sarei yovel* ("princes of the jubilee"), which is also *sar magiyah* ("prince of magic"), echoing another long-standing polemical association of Jesus (or Christians more generally) with the power of magic.[34]

Alongside such strident attacks, there is ample evidence that Abulafia was also intrigued by Christianity and recognized its spiritual power in the terrestrial realm. This is substantiated by his aforementioned attempt to gain an audience with Pope Nicholas III. Abulafia's report that the meeting never took place because of the Pope's death is confirmed by Vatican sources that place the demise of the Pope on August 22, 1280, and in a manner that is consistent with Abulafia's account. This verification, however, does not necessarily substantiate the historical veracity of his entire claim.[35] At best, what we may glean from the corroboration is that Abulafia's imaginary tale was, in part, woven from historical data. Far more crucial than affirming the factual veracity of Abulafia's narrative is the need to grasp the function such a meeting occupied in the landscape of his imagination. Let us also recall that a decade before the date of the alleged encounter Abulafia already had a revelation in which he was commanded by God to go to the Pope in order to convert him to Judaism. We can plausibly reconstruct Abulafia's thought process: if the head of the Church could be convinced of the viability of his messianic teaching, then the redemption (in the distinctive way that he was interpreting it) would be realized and the transition from the mundane to the sacred could take place.

But what did Abulafia really mean when he spoke of the Messiah? Did he envision substantial modifications in the natural order or in the social conditions of the Jewish people vis-à-vis the other nations? To assess this issue properly, one must be mindful of the esoteric character of Abulafia's thought, a point that can be viewed from at least two perspectives. First, one cannot refute that he was committed to exposing many secrets related to the dissemination of the knowledge of the Name, which included meditational instruction, but it also cannot be denied that he insisted that some secrets cannot be fully disclosed in writing.[36] The second and, in my judgment, more important matter is that he embraced the notion that a secret cannot be disclosed as secret unless something of the secret is withheld.[37] Applying this insight to the messianic secret, I would argue that despite the fact that Abulafia availed himself of the standard rhetorical expressions concerning a personal redeemer, the salvation of which he spoke is an altered state of consciousness, achieved principally through the practice of letter-combination (ḥokhmatha-ṣeruf). On this score, the Messiah is not a literal historical figure, the proverbial one who is coming in the future, but instead a metaphorical denotation of the intellect or, to be more exact, the process of conjunction that unites the human and divine. Anyone who attains the state of unification can be considered to have achieved the status of the anointed one, and it is in this sense that Abulafia identifies himself as the Messiah—that is, he is the one to reveal the knowledge of the Name that facilitates the ecstatic experience which renders every individual messianic. Redemption, therefore, is primarily of a spiritual-individualistic as opposed to a geopolitical and communal nature.[38] To be sure, there is some modification in the historical arena, but salvation is not primarily about effecting a change in the temporal conditions of the people of Israel; on the contrary, to be saved means to have a conversion of spirit, a transformation of the heart, that divests one's soul of its corporeal imprisonment and attachment to the physical realm of space and time.

Abulafia's spiritualized and individualized messianism was informed by the philosophical notion of conjunction, which he likely derived primarily from his reading of Maimonides, though one should not rule out the possibility of Christian influence.[39] This possibility is supported by the aforementioned fact that Abulafia utilized Christian motifs and symbols, such as the doctrine of the trinity, in his own writings. Moreover, at the very end of *Iggeret ve-Zo't li-Yehudah*, Abulafia even speaks of the "Kabbalah of the other nations."[40] The content of that Kabbalah is not entirely clear, but of interest is that Abulafia utilizes this terminology, and I assume he is referring to Christian nations, although I cannot be absolutely certain. However we are to interpret this reference, what is clear is that the phenomenon of a Kabbalah promulgated by non-Jews stands in marked contrast to Abulafia's repeated insistence that the transmission of the knowledge of the Name, which is at the center of his prophetic Kabbalah, is limited to the Jews or, to be even more precise, to male Jews who bear the sign of the covenant on their flesh. It seems reasonable to conclude that the Kabbalah of the other nations cannot encompass the critical gnosis and the ensuing possibility of prophetic attainment, for if one were to suggest otherwise, then there would be no way to make sense of a position that Abulafia repeats on many occasions in his writings.

Transmission of the Name and the Angelic Status of the Jews

Based on the correlation of the covenant of the tongue and the covenant of the male organ, a correlation first enunciated in the *Sefer Yetsirah* and reiterated in kabbalistic sources from the Middle Ages to the present, Abulafia asserts that the divine name (*YHWH*) can only be transmitted to one who is circumcised. Abulafia delineates the hierarchy of human attainment in his work *Imrei Shefer*. The context wherein this comment appears is his affirmation of an archaic root of Jewish esotericism concerning the link between the secret of circumcision and knowledge of the four-letter divine name:

"The explicit name is the soul of Israel, and Israel the soul of the seventy nations . . . the nations are the soul of every irrational living being, and the living being a soul for the vegetative, and the vegetative a soul for every inanimate being, and the inanimate being has no soul."[41] Predictably, the issue is cast in another passage from the same work in decidedly linguistic terms: "Know that if all the languages are conventional, the holy language is natural . . . for it is not possible that there not be a natural language whence all the languages derive, and it is like the matter for all of them, nor is it possible that there not be a natural script whence all scripts emerge in the image of the primal Adam from whom all human beings were created."[42] Just as Hebrew is the "natural language," that is, the language of creation and thus the basis for all other languages,[43] which, by contrast, are deemed to be "conventional," so the Jewish people represent the ethnicity that embodies the human ideal most fully. This standing is connected more specifically to their possession of the divine name, which is expressed somatically as the inscription of the sign/letter of the covenant on the male organ[44] and psychically as the envisioning of the Name in the imagined form of the divine *anthropos*.[45] This possession, which Abulafia and other Kabbalists considered unique to the Jewish people, facilitates the actualization of their angelic potentiality.[46]

It is incumbent upon me to note that even in passages where Abulafia ostensibly embraces the philosophical anthropology of Maimonides, careful scrutiny reveals that he reinterprets the latter in a manner that shows greater affinity with the particularism of the esoteric tradition than with the universalism of medieval rationalism. Thus, to cite one of numerous possible examples, in the context of describing the unique status of the human being (*adam*) vis-à-vis other species, Abulafia duly notes that the distinguishing mark of *Homo sapiens* is linked to the fact that a person can think and speak.[47] In the continuation of this discussion, he states (echoing the language of the *Sefer Yetsirah*) that "there is no speech in man apart from the twenty-two holy letters and apart from the five movements that move them in the five places of the mouth."[48] Abulafia does affirm that all the languages are contained in the Hebrew letters, and hence one can speak of the manifold forms of speech ensuing therefrom,[49] an idea expressed poignantly in the numerological equivalence of the expressions *ṣeruf ha-otiyyot* ("permutation of the letters") and *shiv'im leshonot* ("seventy languages").[50] This does not, however, alter the fact that he privileged Hebrew over all the languages such that speech in its most perfect form—whether mental, oral, or graphic—is a unique cultural possession of the Jews among all the nations of the world. Having rendered the philosophical position in ethnocentric terms, it comes as no surprise that he concludes, "There is no intellect in man without speech, and there is no understanding of speech without knowledge of the secrets."[51] In other words, without knowledge of the Hebrew letters, which comprise the essence of Torah, there is no knowledge of the secrets, and without knowledge of the secrets there is no conjunction with the Active Intellect, no receiving of the intellectual overflow of the holy spirit. One cannot attain the level of prophecy unless one has received the tradition concerning the knowledge of the Name, but only the one who is circumcised in the flesh can receive it.[52]

The special status of circumcision and esoteric knowledge of the Name is a motif affirmed in a number of passages in Abulafia's corpus, as we find, for example, in the following text from *Otsar Eden Ganuz*: "Thus it was appropriate to make the covenant of circumcision with us . . . the physical covenant, and to cleave to the spiritual from it, which is knowledge of the Name."[53] Similarly, in *Imrei Shefer*, Abulafia reiterates the point: "Thus Abraham our patriarch, the beginning for every master of the covenant, was circumcised in the commandments of God, and since there is in the secret of the covenant of circumcision a first principle concerning the knowledge of the instruction about the explicit Name, it is written, 'the secret of the Lord is for those who fear Him, and to them He makes His covenant known' (Ps. 55:14), and this secret is revealed from the words *eser sefirot belimah* [ten ineffable enumerations]."[54] The burden of circumcision as the cultural marker of identity as well as the contextualization of the covenant of the one (*berit yaḥid*), or the covenant of unity (*berit yiḥud*), according to a passage in the *Sefer Yetsirah* in the covenant of the tongue (*milat lashon*) and in the covenant of the foreskin (*milat maʿor*), forged the thematic bond between esotericism and phallo-eroticism. It is precisely because Abulafia categorically did not reject the literal circumcision of the flesh that one cannot sever the connection between *berit lashon* and *berit maʿor* in his thought, even though he affirms the superiority of the former over the latter. As he puts it in *Mafteaḥ ha-Raʿayon*:

> The intention of creation was not complete until after the giving of Torah, and similarly the [human] creature is not complete until he circumcised himself and removed the foreskin from himself. And [in this act] two covenants are comprised, the covenant of circumcision to perfect the formation of the attributes of the body and the covenant of the tongue to perfect the formation of the attributes of the soul. The covenant of circumcision in perfection came to us by means of Abraham our patriarch, and the covenant of the tongue [came to us] in perfection by means of Moses our master.[55]

The rite of circumcision, which perfects the human creature (and obviously in this context the reference can only be to the Jewish male), comprises the two covenants mentioned in the *Sefer Yetsirah*, the covenant of the foreskin, which is associated with Abraham, and the covenant of the tongue, which is associated with Moses.[56] The phallo-centric dimension is underscored in the continuation of the passage when Abulafia remarks that those "who are included in the ones circumcised in the commandments of Torah"—and surely only one who bears the covenantal mark on the phallus could be included in this category—have the "eyes of the heart" capable of apprehending the divine light.

The anti-Christian slant of Abulafia's position is demonstrated in his interpretation of the verse "And you shall circumcise the foreskin of your hearts" (Deut. 10:16), "for it mediates between the covenants. The head is created from fire in which is the covenant of the tongue, and the stomach is created from water, which is the covenant of circumcision, and the body is created from spirit in which is the covenant, Torah, the life and sustenance in the faculty of the heart."[57] Circumcision of the heart does not replace circumcision of the flesh but rather serves as the mediation between the covenant of the foreskin and the covenant of the tongue. One who is not corporeally branded by the former cannot attain the spiritual perfection of the latter, and hence the light of God is not perceptible except to the eyes of the heart of one who is circumcised.

Many more texts could be adduced to prove the point, but what I have cited is sufficient. In the last analysis, Abulafia is not completely coherent, for he also embraces the Maimonidean approach, and thus he identifies the divine image with which Adam was created as the faculty of reason that is naturally shared by all humans. On this basis, he resisted positing an ontological distinction between souls of the gentiles and souls of the Jews; the former, like the latter, are intellects capable of attaining the disembodied state of conjunction. And yet, as we have seen, other passages indicate that he did not consistently affirm this perspective. We must conclude, therefore, even though his vision may be considered universal, promoting a more expansive and utopian idea of Judaism that is not restricted by culturally specific ritual practice and theological belief, it would be incorrect to ignore his own ethnocentrism, which is rooted in the Jewish mystical tradition that he transmitted and elaborated.

Mystical Path of Prophetic Kabbalah

Somewhat improbably, Abulafia was able to combine the basic tenets of Maimonidean religious philosophy with esoteric doctrines and mystical practices (mediated chiefly through the works of the Rhineland Jewish

Pietists but also through select treatises of Catalonian and Castilian Kabbalists that either preceded or were contemporary with him) to produce his distinctive understanding of Kabbalah as a path, a way to attain knowledge of the Name. In a manner closer to Judah Halevi than to Maimonides, he maintained that the knowledge of this Name, which is the essence of the tradition, is not grasped by speculation shared universally by all nations, but by a prophetic vision unique to the people of Israel.[58] Moreover, insofar as this Name is equated with the Torah,[59] and the Torah is composed of the twenty-two letters of the Hebrew alphabet, we may surmise that this identification implies the belief that the vital life force of all existence consists of the "holy tongue," the "mother of all languages"[60] that Abulafia considered "natural" in contrast to all the other seventy languages that are derived from Hebrew and are assigned the status of "conventional."[61] On this point, Abulafia is simply inconsistent: all languages are comprised within Hebrew, and hence secrets pertaining to the Name can be found in every language,[62] but Hebrew is still privileged as the one language that is essential and not contingent.

Abulafia taught that by means of the practice connected to receiving the Name, the discipline of letter combination, one can be conjoined to the outpouring of intellectual light,[63] a unifying experience that, both conceptually and experientially, relates to the contemplative ideal of *devekut* (conjunction), whose epistemological and ontological contours he configured on the basis of philosophical assumptions elicited from Jewish and Muslim sources wherein the Aristotelian and Neoplatonic currents are intertwined, for example, Avicenna, Averroës, Abraham Ibn Ezra, and, above all others, Maimonides.[64] In the peak experience, the practitioner is transformed into the angelic guide, the Active Intellect, personified in the figure of Metatron, the creator-angel about whom there is intentional confusion regarding its relationship to the glory, the angel of the Lord (*mal'akh yhwh*), that is, the "angel whose name is YHWH," the intermediary between human and divine that assumes corporal shape in the imagination at the moment of prophetic vision.[65] Referring to this process in *Ḥayyei ha-Olam ha-Ba*, Abulafia writes: "It is known that we, the community of Israel, the congregation of the Lord, know in truth that God, blessed be He and blessed be His name, is not a body or a faculty in a body, and He never materializes. But His overflow creates a corporeal intermediary, and it is an angel in the moment of the prophecy of the prophet."[66] The ambiguity that one may discern in Abulafia's demarcation of the object of the unitive experience as either God or the Active Intellect may be explained by the fact that he viewed the latter as the visible vehicle by which the invisibility of the former is manifest in space and time. In the moment of divine appearance, the line separating the two is blurred. As Abulafia himself put it in *Sefer ha-Ḥesheq*:

> All these matters emanate from the Active Intellect, which informs the person about the truth of the substance of his essence by means of the permutation of the letters and the mentioning of the names without doubt, until the person is restored to the level of intellect so that he may be conjoined to him in the life of this world in accord with his capacity and in the life of the world-to-come in accord with his comprehension.[67]

Following Maimonides, Abulafia portrays the imagination in negative, indeed at times explicitly satanic, terms, but, like his philosophical guide, he also accepts that this faculty plays a crucial role in the mechanics of prophecy (with the exception of Moses) as the angelic intermediary[68] that bridges spirit and matter, intellect and body.[69] Thus, in one passage wherein the prophetic vision is discussed in terms of a mirror or a body of water, through word play Abulafia links together imagination (*dmywn*), demon (*dymwn*), and medium (*mdwyn*).[70] According to another passage, Abulafia notes that the expressions *demut* ("image"), *shem dimyon* ("name of the imagination"), and *shefa* ("overflow") all equal 450,[71] a numerical equivalence that drives home the point that the imaginal form envisioned by the prophet-mystic is the concretization—indeed, "incarnation" would not be an inappropriate term as long as we understand the latter in terms of an imaginal rather than a material body, that is, a theophanic apparition that is configured as real in the specter of the imagination[72]—of the divine effluence. Also relevant here is the grouping of the terms *mal'akh*, *adam*, and *saṭan*.[73] The justification to juxtapose these three is that the human is situated between the two, since he has the capacity to be one or the other, an elaboration of a basic postulate of rabbinic anthropology concerning the good and evil inclinations lodged within each person's heart. For Abulafia, the two inclinations, *yeṣer ha-tov* and *yeṣer ha-ra,* also identified as the good angel (*mal'akh ṭov*) and the bad angel (*mal'akh ra'*) or as the scale of merit (*kaf zekhut*) and the scale of debt (*kaf ṭovah*),[74] correspond to matter and form, the imagination and intellect, both of which are sealed within the divine name *YHWH*.[75] Just as the Active Intellect displays the warp and woof of this twofold comportment,[76] so each human being psychically possesses a dual potential to act in accordance with either the angel from the right or the angel from the left.[77] The goal is to actualize the angelic potential over and against the satanic, to subjugate the imaginative faculty to reason,[78] thereby facilitating the ocular apprehension of the letters *yhwh*.[79]

Note that the prophetic (ecstatic) vision is predicated on a harnessing of the intellect and imagination, not the eradication of the latter by the former. The harnessing is possible because at root opposites are identical in their difference, a basic sensibility that Abulafia shared with other Kabbalists of his time. The point is epitomized in his observation that one who visualizes Metatron in the "countenance of the living man" comes to know that "death is life, and that life, too, is death, and that if the living die, the dead shall live."[80] According to Abulafia's esoteric teaching, the roots of which can be discerned in Togarmi's *Maftehot ha-Qabbalah*,[81] from the perspective of ordinary consciousness, the two impulses ought to be treated as being in conflict, and hence it is appropriate to speak of one as truth and the other as deceit; from the perspective of enlightened mindfulness, however, the two impulses are manifestations of one light, and hence the contrast between truth and deceit collapses.

In *Otsar Eden Ganuz*, Abulafia links this insight to the depiction of the *sefirot* in the *Sefer Yetsirah* (1:7): "their end is fixed in their beginning, and their beginning in their end, like the flame bound to the coal"; "the secret of the 'coal' (*gahelet*) is 'truth' (*emet*), and the secret of the bond (*qesher*) is deceit (*sheqer*), as in the matter of our existence, that is, in deceit there is truth."[82] Abulafia discerns the secret of the paradoxical identification of opposites in the self-consuming description of the *sefirot*,[83] an idea that he substantiates by noting the numerical equivalence of *gahelet* ($3 + 8 + 30 + 400 = 441$) and *emet* ($1 + 40 + 400 = 441$), on the one hand, and, on the other, by the transposition of *qesher* into *sheqer* (they are composed of the same consonants and thus numerically equivalent, since both equal 600). The unity of the *sefirot* bespeaks the metaphysical truism that is reflected empirically in the fact that in every falsehood there is truthfulness.

For the sage, truth and deception are not binary opposites, as he knows that truth is the mediation between what is true and what is false (the three matrix letters—that is, the letters that serve as the material substratum for all the other letters—*alef*, *mem*, and *shin* are decoded as the acrostic *emet makhri'a sheqer*, meaning "truth determines falsehood"), and hence he has the capacity to ascertain the deceptive truth (*ha-emet shiqri*) that is the truthful deception (*ha-sheqer ha-amitti*).[84]

The pietistic ideal that emerges from this gnosis is one of transformation as opposed to obliteration, the intellect guiding rather than annihilating the imagination. As Abulafia puts it in the concluding sentence in his advisory note in the introduction to the third part of *Sitrei Torah*, "On account of this it is necessary for every person to have a revealed and a concealed matter."[85] From the vantage point of the soul that is not yet enlightened, the revealed and concealed must be kept apart, and thus the model of redemption entails liberating the intellect from the imagination—this is the figurative understanding of the exodus from Egypt[86]—but from the vantage point of the soul that is enlightened, the revealed and concealed are to be united, and thus the model of redemption entails transmuting good into evil.

In *Ḥayyei ha-Olam ha-Ba*, Abulafia relates the unity of opposites to the scriptural instruction to craft the two cherubs from one piece of gold (Exod. 25:18–19): "The matter of the two cherubs alludes to the Presence (*ha-shekhinah*), they are cause and effect, male and female, and therefore they were hammered in one body with two forms, and they saw one another, and God was between them."[87] The soul transformed into this angel realizes the integration of opposites in its own being and thereby imitates the divine. Abulafia refers to this awareness as the "secret of inversion" or the "inversion of attributes,"[88] predicated on the realization that opposites are one, that the attribute of the right is the attribute of the left and the attribute of the left is the attribute of the right, since above we cannot properly speak of an autonomous left that is not comprised within the right.[89]

The esoteric wisdom consists of apprehending that there is one essence that is composed of two facets. The time of this realization, we read in several of his treatises, is the split second, the indivisible point, an eternity more fleeting than the blink of the eye. In *Sefer ha-Malmad*, Abulafia provides more insight into the nature of this time by echoing the talmudic association of the blink of the eye and twilight: "We have also received that twilight indicates that it is without time, for the meaning of twilight is that its moment is like a blink of the eye."[90] It is precisely in and from that site, whence one gains access to the secret of the world-to-come, that one may discern the line that divides and thereby conjoins light and dark, day and night,[91] the angelic and satanic capacities of the human being. In the time of twilight, a time that is without time, the interim between life and death, opposites are identified in the difference of their identity to the extent that they are differentiated in the identity of their difference.

In a passage from *Otsar Eden Ganuz*, Abulafia addresses this point in slightly different language: "Every enlightened person knows that the human being possesses these three types of existence, as we have remarked. Hence, at times he is a human and his actions confirm that they are human actions, and at times he is Satan for his actions are satanic actions that are injurious to himself and to others, and at times he is an angel, for his actions are angelic actions that are beneficial to himself and to others, and this is well understood."[92] In other contexts, Abulafia identifies the satanic and angelic as two faces of Metatron, sometimes portrayed as the attributes of mercy and judgment, and thus we may assume that, in grouping together human, angel, and Satan, what he intends is that an individual can emulate either dimension of Metatron. This symbolism may relate as well to Abulafia's portrayal of Christianity as demonic, which he associates (as I noted above) with its idolatrous nature, that is, the worship of the image (the term Abulafia often uses is *demut*) of the divine body, a characterization that is based, in turn, on the assumption that the tenets of this Abrahamic faith originate in the imagination rather than reason.[93] In an ironic twist, the religion that dogmatically professes the incarnation of God in human form is placed on the level of Satan as opposed to Adam, whereas the religion upon whom the prophetic tradition has been bestowed expresses its adamic nature by actualizing the capacity to conjure the angelic body, the anthropomorphic configuration of the incorporeal, in the imagination.[94] It is feasible, then, to surmise that the three terms, *adam*, *mal'akh*, and *satan*, signify the struggle on the psychological plane between the evil and good inclinations, which corresponds to the battle on the theological plane between Christianity and Judaism, Jesus of Nazareth and the Messiah of Israel, the seals of the sixth and seventh days of the week, the material tree of knowledge and the spiritual tree of life.[95] The threefold distinction can also be cast in temporal terms that were commonplace in the cosmological order that Abulafia derived from Maimonides: the satanic corresponds to corruptible matter and is thus subject to time, the angelic corresponds to the incorruptible intellect and is thus not subject to time, and the human being is a composite of matter and intellect that is thus both subject to and not subject to time;[96] or, to put it in different terminology, the human being has the capacity to eternalize the temporal by temporalizing the eternal.

Mystical gnosis of the Name, which is achieved as a result of the technique of letter-combination, entails a state of intellectual conjunction that Abulafia also designates by the rabbinic notion of eschatological fulfillment in the "life of the world-to-come."[97] Although the latter retains something of its original connotation in Abulafia's scheme, he was far more interested in utilizing the phrase to denote an interior state of spiritual transformation occasioned by the triumph of intellect over imagination, spirit over body, an orientation that is attested to as well in other medieval Jewish philosophical exegetes, poets, and Kabbalists.[98] Abulafia does not go so far as to negate entirely the nationalistic aspects of the messianic ideal, but it is clear from his writings that his messianism is primarily mental in nature. Physically, the mystic experiences the illumination as being anointed with oil, and thus the one who is illumined is not only capable of being redeemed prior to the historical advent of the Messiah, but such an individual pneumatically attains the rank of the messianic figure.[99] The anointment also denotes the mystic's priestly status;[100] indeed, in the unitive state, the ecstatic assumes the role of high priest,[101] the position accorded Metatron in the celestial Temple, the angelic vice-regent summoned by Abulafia as the object of conjunction.[102]

We may conclude, therefore, that the phenomenon of anointment comprises three distinct, though inseparable, aspects of the pneumatic metamorphosis—messianic, priestly, and angelic. For Abulafia, moreover, how this takes place is critical to his understanding of the prophetic-messianic experience, as the enlightened mind, the soul unfettered from the chains of corporeality, receives the surfeit of the holy spirit, which is identified in Abulafia's system as the Active Intellect, the angelic Metatron, and the wheel of letters that is the Torah scroll in its idealized form.[103] The experience of mystical union may be viewed in four ways: to cleave to the Name, to be conjoined with the intellect, to be transformed into the creator-angel, and to be incorporated within the textual embodiment of the word of God.[104]

NOTES

1. The specifics of Abulafia's biography have been usefully reviewed in Harvey J. Hames, *Like Angels on Jacob's Ladder: Abraham Abulafia, the Franciscans, and Joachimism* (Albany: State University of New York Press, 2007), pp. 29–53. For discussion of the main tenets of Abulafian Kabbalah, see Gershom Scholem, *Major Trends in Jewish Mysticism* (New York: Schocken Books, 1954), pp. 119–55; Moshe Idel, *The Mystical Experience in Abraham Abulafia* (Albany: State University of New York Press, 1988); idem, *Language, Torah, and Hermeneutics in Abraham Abulafia* (Albany: State University of New York Press, 1989); Elliot R. Wolfson, *Abraham Abulafia: Kabbalist and Prophet—Hermeneutics, Theosophy, Theurgy* (Los Angeles: Cherub, 2000).

2. See, most recently, Diana Lobel, *A Sufi-Jewish Dialogue: Philosophy and Mysticism in Baḥya Ibn Paqūda's Duties of the Heart* (Philadelphia: University of Pennsylvania Press, 2007).

3. Scholem, *Major Trends*, pp. 147, 384 n. 105; Idel, *Mystical Experience*, pp. 14, 24, 46 n. 59, 104; idem, *Studies in Ecstatic Kabbalah* (Albany: State University of New York Press, 1988), pp. 43 n. 30, 74–76, 79, 91–101, 105–107, 126, 144 n. 22; Harvey J. Hames, "A Seal within a Seal: The Imprint of Sufism in Abraham Abulafia's Teachings," *Medieval Encounters* 11 (2006): 153–72; Elliot R. Wolfson, "Kenotic Overflow and Temporal Transcendence: Angelic Embodiment and the Alterity of Time in Abraham Abulafia," *Kabbalah: Journal for the Study of Jewish Mystical Texts* 18 (2008): 167–68.

4. Abraham Abulafia, *Sheva Netivot ha-Torah*, in Adolph Jellinek, *Philosophie und Kabbala*, part 1 (Leipzig: Heinrich Hunger, 1854), p. 21; idem, *Oṣar Eden Ganuz* (Jerusalem, 2000), p. 98; idem, *Or ha-Sekhel* (Jerusalem, 2001), pp. 95–96.

5. Wolfson, *Abraham Abulafia*, pp. 99–102.

6. Adolph Jellinek, *Auswahl kabbalistischer Mystik*, part 1 (Leipzig: A. M. Colditz, 1853).

7. Contrary to the erroneous presentation of my view, I have never suggested adopting a homogeneous approach that eradicates all difference. My point is rather that the dominant perspective that polarizes the so-called theosophic and ecstatic Kabbalists fails to take seriously the many shared doctrines that may be traced to a common wellspring of esoteric tradition with much older roots.

8. Moshe Idel already noted that the typological approach exemplified in *Ve-Zo't li-Yehudah* is based on Abulafia's religious struggle with Solomon ben Abraham ibn Aderet (the Rashba) and his consequent desire to demonstrate the superiority of his own Kabbalah ("Defining Kabbalah: The Kabbalah of the Divine Names," in *Mystics of the Book: Themes, Topics and Typologies*, ed. Robert A. Herrera [New York: Peter Lang, 1993], pp. 109–10). See also Gershom Scholem, *The Kabbalah of Sefer ha-Temunah and Abraham Abulafia* [in Hebrew], ed. Joseph Ben-Shlomo (Jerusalem: Akadamon, 1965), p. 99. In spite of this recognition on the part of both Scholem and Idel, both accept and uncritically apply Abulafia's distinction more generally.

9. Jellinek, *Auswahl kabbalistischer Mystik*, p. 15 (Hebrew section).

10. Ibid., p. 14.

11. Ibid., p. 16.

12. Ibid., p. 17.

13. Both texts have been printed in Abraham Abulafia, *Maṣref ha-Sekhel ve-Sefer ha-Ot* (Jerusalem, 2001); see idem, *Sefer ha-Edut*, pp. 57–58 and *Sefer ha-Ot*, p. 2. For an analysis of these texts and the historical event it purports to chronicle, see Moshe Idel, "Abraham Abulafia and the Pope," *AJS Review* 7–8 (1982–83): 1–17 (Hebrew section); and idem, *Studies in Ecstatic Kabbalah*, pp. 45–47.

14. Scholem, *Major Trends*, p. 129; Idel, *Studies in Ecstatic Kabbalah*, pp. 33–44; Wolfson, *Abraham Abulafia*, pp. 131–33 n. 101; Hames, *Like Angels*; Robert Sagerman, "Ambivalence toward Christianity in the Kabbalah of Abraham Abulafia" (Ph.D. dissertation, New York University, 2008).

15. From many homilies included in the zoharic literature we discern themes that suggest an affinity to christological symbols and concepts, for example, the threefold unity of the divine and the iconic depiction of the invisible as the mystery of faith in which the pious practitioner physically and spiritually participates. The very same texts, however, are replete with the demonization of Christianity as the locus of an inherent impurity, often illustrated by the image of menstruation, the earthly embodiment of Satan or Samael, the archangel of Edom or Esau, as well as the theological denigration of Christian piety by identifying it with idolatry. See Yehuda Liebes, *Studies in the Zohar*, trans. Arnold Schwartz, Stephanie Nakache, and Penina Peli (Albany: State University of New York Press, 1993), pp. 139–61; Elliot R. Wolfson, *Language, Eros, Being: Kabbalistic Hermeneutics and Poetic Imagination* (New York: Fordham University Press, 2005), pp. 255–60; idem, *Venturing Beyond*, pp. 135–54.

16. Abraham Abulafia, *Mafteaḥ ha-Ḥokhmot* (Jerusalem, 2001), p. 64; and see Idel, *Studies in Ecstatic Kabbalah*, p. 51, where the text is cited in the name of *Mafteaḥ ha-Shemot* extant from MS New York, JTSA 843, fol. 80a.

17. Scholem, *Major Trends*, p. 129; Wolfson, *Abraham Abulafia*, pp. 131–33 n. 101. See also the text I adduce in ibid., p. 189, and my comments in note 26 there.

18. Idel, *Mystical Experience*, pp. 14, 24, 40 (in that context, a crucial difference is drawn between the contemplative practice of Abulafia, on the one hand, and that of Yoga, Sūfism, and Hesychasm, on the other), 80, 176–77 n. 338. Gershom Scholem suggested that the gazing at the navel as a means to concentrate attested to in Abulafia (*Ḥayyei ha-Olam ha-Ba*, 2nd ed. [Jerusalem, 1999], p. 164) may reflect a similar technique in Christian Hesychasm, which he characterizes as "the wisdom of permutation in Christian garb and with Christian content," referring to Gregory Palamas (1296–1359) as the "Christian Abulafia" (*The Kabbalah of Sefer ha-Temunah and Abraham Abulafia*, pp. 169–70). Idel rejects the surmise of Scholem regarding this practice, even though he does acknowledge the likelihood of the influence of Hesychasm on Abulafia (*Mystical Experience*, p. 35).

19. Abraham Abulafia, *Sefer ha-Ḥayyim*, in *Maṣref ha-Sekhel*, p. 83; idem, *Mafteaḥ ha-Shemot* (Jerusalem, 2001), p. 130; Idel, *Studies in Ecstatic Kabbalah*, pp. 52–53; Wolfson, *Venturing Beyond*, p. 137 n. 27; Sagerman, "Ambivalence," pp. 61–62.

20. Idel, *Studies in Ecstatic Kabbalah*, pp. 45–61.

21. Ibid., pp. 48–50.

22. Abulafia, *Oṣar Eden Ganuz*, p. 192.

23. Abulafia, *Or ha-Sekhel*, p. 34.

24. See Abraham Berger, "The Messianic Self-Consciousness of Abraham Abulafia: A Tentative Evaluation," in *Essential Papers on Messianic Movements and Personalities in Jewish History*, ed. Marc Saperstein (New York: New York University Press, 1992), p. 251.

25. Abulafia, *Mafteaḥ ha-Shemot*, p. 81. Regarding this passage, see Berger, "The Messianic Self-Consciousness," p. 252; and Idel, *Studies in Ecstatic Kabbalah*, p. 50.

26. But see Abulafia, *Sefer ha-Ḥayyim*, p. 83: "Raziel the son of Sham'uel discerns the blessing and the curse, he discerns the bastard son of a menstruant, he discerns Jesus and Muḥammad."

27. Abraham Abulafia, *Sitrei Torah* (Jerusalem, 2002), pp. 59–60, and compare the analysis of this text in Sagerman, "Ambivalence," pp. 266–68. See also Moshe Idel, *Messianic Mystics* (New Haven: Yale University Press, 1998), pp. 62, 97–99; Wolfson, *Venturing Beyond*, pp. 61-62; and idem, "Kenotic Overflow," pp. 162–63.

28. Abulafia, *Mafteaḥ ha-Shemot*, p. 130.

29. Idel, *Studies in Ecstatic Kabbalah*, p. 52; Hames, *Like Angels*, pp. 80–81; Sagerman, "Ambivalence," p. 107. See Abulafia, *Sitrei Torah*, p. 144, and idem, *Mafteaḥ ha-Sefirot* (Jerusalem, 2001), p. 85, where the Teli is connected to the "copper serpent" (Num. 21:9), whose power is magic; idem, *Mafteaḥ ha-Tokhaḥot* (Jerusalem, 2001), p. 8. On the astrological symbol of the Teli in Abulafia, see Idel, *Studies in Ecstatic Kabbalah*, pp. 77–78; and Wolfson, *Abraham Abulafia*, p. 145 n. 135. The connection of this image and Jesus has been explored most extensively by Sagerman, "Ambivalence," pp. 183, 259–68, 276–79, 281, 285–87, 294–96, 299, 302, 305, 307–13, 316, 318, 323, 327–31, 335–37, 340, 348–70, 421–22, and 461–64.

30. Abulafia, *Mafteaḥ ha-Shemot*, p. 131. I mention this text briefly in *Venturing Beyond*, p. 63 n. 195.

31. On the identification of the imagination (*dimyon*) as the *daemon* in Abulafia, see his *Oṣar Eden Ganuz*, p. 121; and Idel, *Language*, pp. 21, 56–57. See also idem, *Studies in Ecstatic Kabbalah*, pp. 34, 38; and Wolfson "Kenotic Overflow," p. 147.

32. That is, the numerical value of both expressions is 635.

33. Abulafia, *Mafteaḥ ha-Shemot*, pp. 132–33. The passage is partially translated and discussed in Hames, *Like Angels*, p. 82.

34. Abulafia, *Mafteaḥ ha-Shemot*, p. 134. On the association of Jesus and/or Christianity and magic, see the sources cited in Wolfson, *Venturing Beyond*, pp. 44 n. 112, 140–41, and further reference to Abulafia cited on p. 141 n. 47.

35. Idel offers this argument (*Messianic Mystics*, p. 98).

36. Wolfson, *Abraham Abulafia*, pp. 54–57, 72–73.

37. Ibid., pp. 81–93.

38. Berger, "The Messianic Self-Consciousness," p. 253; Idel, *Studies in Ecstatic Kabbalah*, pp. 52–53; idem, *Messianic Mystics*, pp. 58–100, 295–307; idem, "'The Time of the End': Apocalypticism and Its Spiritualization in Abraham Abulafia's Eschatology," in *Apocalyptic Time*, ed. Albert I. Baumgarten (Leiden: Brill, 2000), pp. 155–85. See also Moshe Idel, *Hasidism: Between Ecstasy and Magic* (Albany: State University of New York Press, 1995), pp. 209–10.

39. Berger, "The Messianic Self-Consciousness," p. 254.

40. Jellinek, *Auswahl kabbalistischer Mystik*, p. 28.

41. Abraham Abulafia, *Imrei Shefer* (Jerusalem, 1999), pp. 48–49. Compare the formulation in idem, *Oṣar Eden Ganuz*, pp. 72–73.

42. Abulafia, *Imrei Shefer*, pp. 67–68.

43. Compare Abulafia in *Ḥayyei ha-Nefesh* (Jerusalem, 2001), p. 67; idem, *Mafteaḥ ha-Ra'yon* (Jerusalem, 2002), pp. 24, 42–43.

44. On the nexus between circumcision and intellectual conjunction, which is expressed mystically as cleaving to the Name, see Wolfson, *Abraham Abulafia*, pp. 87–90, 194–95, 216–20.

45. See the Abulafian text translated and analyzed in Scholem, *Major Trends*, pp. 136–38; Idel, *Mystical Experience*, pp. 95–100, 103–104; and Wolfson, *Abraham Abulafia*, pp. 167 n. 197, 208.

46. Wolfson, *Abraham Abulafia*, pp. 65–68. In *Ḥayyei ha-Olam ha-Ba* (Jerusalem, 1999), p. 53, Abulafia depicts the ontic difference between Jew and non-Jew in terms of the rabbinic legend that the Sinaitic theophany resulted in the removal of the filth with which the primordial serpent inseminated Eve from the Jews in contrast to the other nations (*b. Yevamot* 103b). Abulafia discusses this older legend under the rubric "the secret of illicit sexual relations" (*sitrei arayot*), one of the three subjects considered esoteric by some in the rabbinic academy. For an extensive analysis of *sitrei arayot* in Abulafia's writings, see Moshe Idel, "The Kabbalistic Interpretation of the Secret of 'Arayot in Early Kabbalah" [in Hebrew], *Kabbalah: Journal for the Study of Jewish Mystical Texts* 12 (2004): 155–85.

47. Abulafia, *Mafteaḥ ha-Ra'yon*, p. 17.

48. Ibid., p. 18.

49. Ibid., p. 38.

50. Abulafia, *Or ha-Sekhel*, p. 85; idem, *Imrei Shefer*, p. 185; idem, *Oṣar Eden Ganuz*, pp. 77, 313, 381; idem, *Sheva Netivot ha-Torah*, p. 4; Idel, *Language*, p. 142 n. 47.

51. Abulafia, *Mafteaḥ ha-Ra'yon*, p. 21.

52. Abulafia, *Imrei Shefer*, p. 29.

53. Abulafia, *Oṣar Eden Ganuz*, p. 286.

54. Abulafia, *Imrei Shefer*, p. 48.

55. Abulafia, *Mafteah ha-Ra'yon*, p. 14.

56. On the two covenants and their respective correlation with Abraham and Moses, see Abulafia, *Osar Eden Ganuz*, pp. 285–86, partially translated and analyzed in Wolfson, *Language, Eros, Being*, pp. 139–40.

57. Abulafia, *Mafteah ha-Ra'yon*, p. 15. See also idem, *Hayyei Olam ha-Ba*, pp. 107–109. In the continuation of the passage, circumcision of the heart is connected to the comprehension of the "secret of the rotation of the letters and their reversal" (*sod gilgul ha-otiyyot we-hippukham*), which is depicted further as the exclusive worship of God.

58. Judah HaLevi, *Sefer ha-Kuzari*, translated, annotated, and introduced by Yehuda Even Shmuel (Tel-Aviv: Dvir, 1972), IV.15, p. 172, and see the brief but incisive characterization in Harry A. Wolfson, *Studies in the History of Philosophy and Religion*, ed. Isadore Twersky and George H. Williams (Cambridge, MA: Harvard University Press, 1977), 2:141.

59. It should be noted that the equation of Torah and the tetragrammaton affirmed by Abulafia and his disciples is accepted as well by Kabbalists that have been placed into the school of theosophic Kabbalah according to the reigning typological classification adopted by contemporary scholars of Jewish mysticism. This is one of several main principles shared by the different trends of medieval Kabbalah, a sharing that at least problematizes to some degree the sharp distinctions made between so-called theosophic and ecstatic Kabbalists.

60. Abulafia, *Mafteah ha-Hokhmot*, p. 60.

61. Idel, *Language*, pp. 12–14, 16–27, 143–45 n. 55, 146 n. 71; Wolfson, *Abraham Abulafia*, pp. 58–59, 62–64.

62. Abulafia, *Hayyei ha-Nefesh*, p. 10.

63. For a discussion of the phenomenon of receiving God's name according to the prophetic Kabbalah, set against the background of the philosophical notion of the continuous chain of being, see Moshe Idel, *Enchanted Chains: Techniques and Rituals in Jewish Mysticism* (Los Angeles: Cherub, 2005), pp. 76–109.

64. Idel, *Mystical Experience*, pp. 124–34; idem, *Studies in Ecstatic Kabbalah*, pp. 1–31.

65. For a discussion of this aspect of Abulafia's understanding of prophecy, see Idel, *Mystical Experience*, pp. 89–90, 100–104. With respect to the matter of the angelic body beheld in the prophetic vision, there is an interesting affinity between Abulafia's Kabbalah and Islamic mysticism, especially Shi'ite esotericism as presented by Henry Corbin. See Wolfson, *Language, Eros, Being*, p. 239.

66. Abulafia, *Hayyei ha-Olam ha-Ba*, p. 49.

67. Abraham Abulafia, *Sefer ha-Hesheq* (Jerusalem, 2002), p. 8.

68. See, especially, the words of Moses Maimonides, *The Guide of the Perplexed*, translated with an introduction and notes by Shlomo Pines, with an introductory essay by Leo Strauss (Chicago: University of Chicago Press, 1963), II.6, pp. 264–65: "Thereby we have stated plainly to him who understands and cognizes intellectually that the imaginative faculty is likewise called an *angel* and that the intellect is called a *cherub*. . . . We have already spoken of the fact that every form in which an *angel* is seen, exists *in the vision of prophecy*" (emphasis in original). On Maimonides' identification of the angelic form seen and/or heard in prophecy as either the Active Intellect or the imaginative faculty, an imprecision that doubtlessly influenced Abulafia, see Howard Kriesel, *Prophecy: The History of an Idea in Medieval Jewish Philosophy* (Dordrecht: Kluwer, 2001), pp. 236–37.

69. The positive valorization of imagination can be seen, for instance, in Abulafia's explanation of the "image" and "likeness" with which Adam was created according to the biblical account (Gen. 1:26): "Thus it has been explained that the matter of the image (*selem*) is the form of intellect (*surat sekhel*), and the matter of the likeness (*demut*) is the image of knowledge (*dimyon da'at*), for it is known that intellect and imagination are the image and likeness" (in *Sitrei Torah*, p. 21). To grasp the import of the last sentence, one must bear in mind that the expressions *ha-sekhel we-ha-dimyon yedu'im* and *selem u-demut* both numerically equal 616.

70. Abulafia, *Osar Eden Ganuz*, p. 121, cited in Idel, *Language*, pp. 21, 56–57; and see idem, *Studies in Ecstatic Kabbalah*, pp. 35–39.

71. Abulafia, *Osar Eden Ganuz*, p. 83.

72. This point is missed by the criticism of my use of the term "incarnation" to characterize kabbalistic thinking on the part of Moshe Idel, *Ben: Sonship and Jewish Mysticism* (London: Continuum, 2007), pp. 59–61. For a more detailed discussion of the angelic incarnation in Abulafia, see Wolfson, "Kenotic Overflow," pp. 147 and 159–60.

73. On this threefold classification in Abulafia, see the passages from *Mafteah ha-Shemot* and *Sefer ha-Melis*, cited and analyzed in Idel, *Studies in Ecstatic Kabbalah*, pp. 38–39. See also *Sefer ha-Malmad* (Jerusalem, 2002), p. 18, where Abulafia speaks of the "matter of prophecy" in the threefold manner of the "creation of the human body," the "creation of Satan," and the "creation of the angel."

74. Abulafia, *Imrei Shefer*, p. 26; compare his *Sheva Netivot ha-Torah*, p. 9: "The judge sits on two thrones of judgment and he judges by two attributes . . . and they are called the attribute of judgment and the attribute of mercy . . . the scale of merit and the scale of debt."

75. Idel, *Mystical Experience*, pp. 96–97; idem, "Kabbalistic Interpretation," p. 161 n. 507.

76. Abulafia repeatedly uses the image of the warp and woof (*sheti wa-erev*) to characterize form and matter. For instance, see *Or ha-Sekhel*, p. 94. In a number of contexts, the expression *sheti wa-erev* is transposed into *berit esaw*, that is, the "covenant of Esau." See *Perush Sefer Yesirah Almoni mi-Yesodo shel Rabbi Avraham Abula'fiyah*, ed. Israel Weinstock (Jerusalem: Mosad ha-Rav Kook, 1984), p. 29; Abulafia, *Osar Eden Ganuz*, pp. 9, 286.

77. *Perush Sefer Yesirah*, p. 29.

78. On the collaboration between intellect and imagination, the angel and Satan, see the text from *Osar Eden Ganuz* cited in Idel, *Language*, p. 19.

79. Wolfson, *Abraham Abulafia*, pp. 167–68 n. 197.

80. Abraham Abulafia, *Ish Adam*, in *Masref ha-Sekhel*, p. 44; and see Wolfson, *Abraham Abulafia*, p. 220 n. 125.

81. See the important passage from Togarmi's *Maftehot ha-Qabbalah* transcribed in Scholem, *Kabbalah of Sefer ha-Temunah*, p. 234, and the reverberation of his chain of associations in Abulafia, *Osar Eden Ganuz*, p. 110.

82. Abulafia, *Osar Eden Ganuz*, p. 20.

83. See Itamar Gruenwald, "Some Critical Notes on the First Part of *Sēfer Yesirā*," *Revue des Études juives* 132 (1973): 492; Wolfson, *Abraham Abulafia*, pp. 143–44.

84. Abulafia, *Osar Eden Ganuz*, p. 111.

85. Abulafia, *Sitrei Torah*, p. 151.

86. Idel, *Language*, p. 69.

87. Abulafia, *Ḥayyei ha-Olam ha-Ba*, p. 152.

88. Wolfson, *Abraham Abulafia*, p. 59 n. 167.

89. Abulafia, *Sitrei Torah*, p. 132. For the full citation, see the reference to my work in the previous note.

90. Abulafia, *Sefer ha-Malmad*, p. 21; cf. *b. Berakhot* 2b and *b. Shabbat* 34b.

91. See Abulafia, *Perush Sefer Yeṣirah*, p. 24, cited in Idel, *Language*, p. 41. On the representation of the time cycle in terms of diurnal and nocturnal rotation, see the extended discussion in Abulafia, *Sefer ha-Ḥesheq*, pp. 7–8.

92. Abulafia, *Oṣar Eden Ganuz*, p. 90. See ibid., p. 56, and compare *Perush Sefer Yeṣirah*, p. 32: "And when you attach the serpent to Adam and Eve, you find that man is a satan just as satan is a man [*ha-adam saṭan eḥad ka'asher ha-saṭan adam eḥad*]." The passage is cited in Idel, *Studies in Ecstatic Kabbalah*, p. 37, from MS Paris, Bibliothèque Nationale héb. 768, fol. 11a. See also *Ḥayyei ha-Olam ha-Ba*, p. 141: "Every man is satan, every satan a man [*kol adam saṭan kol saṭan adam*]."

93. Wolfson, *Venturing Beyond*, pp. 62–63; Idel, *Studies in Ecstatic Kabbalah*, pp. 45–61; idem, *Messianic Mystics*, pp. 62, 97–99.

94. On the vision of the human form and prophecy in Abulafian Kabbalah, see Idel, *Mystical Experience*, pp. 95–100.

95. Idel, *Studies in Ecstatic Kabbalah*, pp. 51–52. On the correlation of the tree of knowledge and the tree of life with Cain and Abel, see Abulafia, *Imrei Shefer*, p. 65.

96. *Ner Elohim* (Jerusalem, 2002), pp. 85–86.

97. Scholem, *Major Trends*, pp. 131–35; Wolfson, *Abraham Abulafia*, pp. 54–55.

98. See Dov Schwartz, "The Neutralization of the Messianic Idea in Medieval Jewish Rationalism" [in Hebrew], *Hebrew Union College Annual* 64 (1993): 37–58; Wolfson, *Abraham Abulafia*, p. 39 n. 95, with specific reference to Abraham Ibn Ezra's understanding of the secret (*sod*) of conjunction (*devequt*), and p. 91, where I argue that the more spiritualized interpretation of the traditional eschatological term "world-to-come" is an approach shared by Abulafia and other masters of esoteric lore of his time who are classified by modern scholars (following the typological scheme proffered by Scholem and Idel) as "theosophic Kabbalists."

99. Gershom Scholem rightly points out that the "state of ecstasy as described by Abulafia . . . carries with it something like an anticipatory redemption." (*Major Trends*, p. 142).

100. On the priestly status of the Messiah in Abulafia's writings, see Idel, *Messianic Mystics*, pp. 94–97.

101. Abulafia, *Ḥayyei ha-Olam ha-Ba*, p. 67.

102. Idel, *Mystical Experience*, pp. 116–19; idem, *Messianic Mystics*, pp. 65–77, and see, especially, the passages from Isaac of Acre cited and analyzed in Idel, *Messianic Mystics*, pp. 303–306; and Wolfson, *Language, Eros, Being*, p. 241.

103. Idel, *Language*, pp. 34–41, 79–80, 163 n. 33; idem, *Absorbing Perfections: Kabbalah and Interpretation* (New Haven: Yale University Press, 2002), pp. 348–50.

104. On Abulafia's use of the expression "word of God" to designate the Active Intellect, see Idel, *Language*, p. 33. See also Wolfson, *Abraham Abulafia*, p. 141. On the identification of the visionary and the Torah in the supreme state of ecstasy, see Scholem, *Major Trends*, p. 141.

4

New Approaches to the Study of Kabbalistic Life in 16th-Century Safed

LAWRENCE FINE

The Historical Setting

In the 15th century Jews began to migrate to Turkey and the lands of the Ottoman Empire in significant numbers from various parts of Europe. What accounts for this migration? Listen to the words of a certain Isaac Zarfati of Edirne in a letter he wrote in 1454 urging his fellow Jews in Ashkenaz to settle in the empire. His impassioned plea graphically portrays the dismal realities of Jewish life in Europe during this period and reflects the Ottomans' generally benevolent attitude toward Jews.

> I have heard of the afflictions, more bitter than death, that have befallen our brethren in Germany—of the tyrannical laws, the compulsory baptisms, and the banishments which are of daily occurrence. I am told that when they flee from one place a yet harder fate befalls them in another. . . . Brothers and teachers, friends and acquaintances! I, Isaac Zarfati, though I sprang from a French stock, yet I was born in Germany and sat there at the feet of my esteemed teachers. I proclaim to you that Turkey is a land wherein nothing is lacking and where, if you will, all shall yet be well with you. The way to the Holy Land lies open to you through Turkey. Is it not better for you to live under Muslims than under Christians? Here every man may dwell at peace under his own vine and fig tree. Here you are allowed to wear the most precious garments. In Christendom, on the contrary, you dare not even venture to clothe your children in red or blue, according to our taste, without exposing them to the insult of being beaten black and blue, or kicked green and red, and therefore, are you condemned to go about meanly clad in sad, colored raiment. . . . and now, seeing all these things, O Israel, why do you sleep? Arise! And leave this accursed land forever![1]

The reign of Sultan Bayezid II, between 1481 and 1512, coincided with the most significant Jewish migration in the late medieval, early modern period. Massive migrations were set off with the expulsion of the Jews from Spain in 1492 and the subsequent mass conversion of Portugal's Jewish community in 1497. Although many sought refuge in Italy and North Africa, the vast majority made their way to the Ottoman Empire. Of these weary and desperate exiles, Bayezid is alleged to have made the following oft-quoted remark: "You call Ferdinand [of Spain] a wise king; him, who by expelling the Jews has impoverished his country and enriched mine!"[2] When the Ottomans conquered most of the Near East, including the Land of Israel, in 1516–17, Ottoman Jews were able to settle there under the relative security and protection of the Ottoman authorities. One might expect that the greatest beneficiary of these developments would be the Jewish community in Jerusalem. But that was not the case. Instead, Safed, a small city in the northern part of the country, became the primary center of new settlement and communal life beginning in the early decades of the 16th century. By mid-century, Safed swelled in population with thousands of Jews who had come from all over Europe and the Ottoman Empire.[3]

The Geographical Setting

The village of Safed lies nestled high in the eastern mountains of the Upper Galilee, twenty-five miles northwest of Tiberias, thirty miles east of the Mediterranean Sea. It commands the high ground just west of the great African-Syrian rift, which, in Israel, stretches from the Hula Valley in the north to the Sea of Galilee, down to the Dead Sea. The old Jewish quarter of the city, with its labyrinth of narrow, winding streets and reconstructed 16th-century synagogues, sits upon the eastern slope of a mountain. In the valley below lies an ancient cemetery where, even today, Jews make pilgrimage to the graves of Safed's leading Kabbalists.

An anonymous Italian Jew provides us with an especially detailed and colorful description of Safed, which he visited in the year 1495. It has wonderful value as a rich picture of the town and its environs. Of particular interest is what he has to say about the graves of various important sages that dotted the landscape:

> Safed is built on the slopes of a mountain and is a great city. The houses are small and modest, and when the rain falls it is impossible to walk about town on account of the dirt, and also because it is on the hillside. It is also

difficult to go out in the markets and the streets even during the summer, for you must always be climbing up or down. However, the land is good and health giving and the waters are quite good. And this is the absolute truth: I saw men in Safed who are far older than sixty or seventy years. . . . The holy congregation numbers about three hundred householders, and most of the Jews have shops of spices, cheese, oil, and sundry pulses and fruits. . . . Around Safed there are many caves in which great and pious men have been buried. . . . About six miles from Safed is a certain village called Meron, where very great and pious saints whose names I shall mention are buried. . . . we entered a certain cave in which twenty-two scholars lie, and they said that these were the disciples of Rabbi Shimon bar Yochai of saintly and blessed memory; and near the spot on the hillside there is an extremely fine monument, which can be seen as far as Safed.[4]

This report provides evidence of one of the most prominent factors that accounted for the appeal of Safed to Jewish émigrés, namely, traditions concerning the presence of the burial sites of numerous biblical and rabbinic figures. Of these, the most important from a kabbalistic point of view was the aforementioned burial site of Rabbi Shimon bar Yochai, the main figure and teacher of the *Zohar*. Without question, the tradition that Shimon bar Yochai had lived, taught, and was buried not far from Safed contributed significantly to its importance for Kabbalists.

An altogether different factor that contributed to the flourishing of the Safed community in the 16th century was economic. Safed became a leading center of textile manufacturing for the empire and beyond. Conditions in Safed for the development of the textile industry were exceptional, including the existence of streams and springs that could provide water power and clear running water for the processing of woolen cloth. The textile industry dominated the commercial life of Safed and made for a flourishing economy insofar as it employed large numbers of people.[5]

Finally, because of its strategic importance to the Ottomans, the authorities sought to keep Safed well protected. In 1549, during the reign of Suleiman the Magnificent, a wall was constructed, and Turkish soldiers guarded against the perpetual threat of marauders from neighboring villages. It appears to have provided insufficient protection, however, as evidenced by the request of the Jewish community to build a fortified section for Jewish homes that could be locked at nightfall. Sometime in the middle of the century, the Ottoman district ruler erected such a fortress, or *khan*, near the Jewish quarter, within which some of Safed's Jews presumably lived. Thus, relatively secure conditions existed until the last quarter of the century when the disciplined control of the authorities in Istanbul began to fail. In the meantime, however, the Jewish community in Safed enjoyed a significant degree of prosperity and peace.

New Directions in Scholarship

Many of the chapters in this book raise specific scholarly issues that have been contested in the past or are currently the subject of debate. In this chapter I take a slightly different approach by focusing on some of the relatively new ways that scholarship has conceptualized Safed Kabbalah and approached its study. These new directions are inextricably bound up with a focus on aspects of the Safed experience to which much of the earlier scholarship paid relatively little attention and which it implicitly tended to regard as having peripheral importance. Among the points I seek to make is that, far from being peripheral, these aspects were absolutely central to Safed Kabbalah as well as to our understanding of it. The lens through which the Safed experience is now viewed has grown wider as scholarship over the last number of years has broadened its vision and scope. I thus want to identify and discuss several of these features, including the following: social community, autobiography and biography, ethics, ritual innovation, and questions of women and gender. Although these features are by no means altogether unique to Safed, they manifested themselves in particularly vivid and consequential ways in the life of this mystical community.

Social Community and the Social Body

I use the expression "mystical community" deliberately because in Safed we encounter not simply individual pietists, practitioners, and religious thinkers but a true *community* of Kabbalists in possession of a distinctive and self-conscious collective identity. This phenomenon is reflected in the fact that many of Safed's Kabbalists—perhaps most—belonged to some intimate intentional fellowships, or *ḥavurot*, that developed there. In reflecting upon the nature of social companionship as portrayed in the narrative portions of 13th-century zoharic literature, Arthur Green remarks that Rabbi Shimon bar Yochai's fellowship "is one of a series of such circles of Jewish mystics, stretching back in time to Qumran, Jerusalem, Provence, and Gerona, and forward in history to Safed, Padua, Miedzybozh, Bratslav, and again to Jerusalem."[6]

This is, to be sure, an alternative and relatively new way of conceptualizing the history of Jewish mystical tradition, namely, in terms of the circles and communities of individuals who came together under the inspiration of Kabbalah. As has frequently been pointed out by now, the pioneering scholars of Kabbalah in the 20th century, including Gershom Scholem, Alexander Altmann, and George Vajda, exhibited a strong tendency to study Kabbalah significantly (although not exclusively) in terms of its mythic, theological, and metaphysical *ideas*.[7] This tendency ought to be understood within the context of a broader early- and mid-20th-century approach to the study of religion that was preoccupied with religious ideas at the expense of actual religious communities and their practices. The latter were more likely to have been left to cultural anthropologists and their study of "primitive" communities. Happily, in recent years scholarship has begun to expand its interest beyond the body of ideas in Kabbalah to many new objects of inquiry, including what I call the *social* body.

Let me elaborate upon this phenomenon as it expressed itself in Safed. Although Kabbalah permeated the air of Safed in the 16th century in general, and few could have been left untouched by the powerful currents surrounding them, many chose to associate themselves with one of the several intentional fellowships that emerged there. We presume that such individuals sought to devote themselves to a more disciplined and rigorous style of spiritual life than did others. Most of the individuals whose names appear with any frequency in the kabbalistic literature are likely to have been associated with one or another of the groups we know about. From a sociological point of view, these fellowships served to institutionalize kabbalistic life to a certain degree, helping to define the direction that piety ought to take and to channel religious energy in a disciplined way. From a psychological point of view, they must have served as both a means of support and a source of peer pressure to live the proper life. As one scholar, Zvi Werblowsky, long ago observed, "The social habits and values of the Safed kabbalists helped to integrate the individual mystic in an ideal, normative community which gave him spiritual security and support, and which provided him with a fund of energy and discipline on which he could constantly draw."[8] There is reason to believe that the rules and rites that these groups practiced inspired members of the wider community in Safed and even beyond to engage in similar pietistic practices.

Some of these circles were under the spiritual guidance of particular personalities, such as Moses Cordovero (1522–1570) and Eleazar Azikri (1533–1600).[9] The latter, a disciple of Cordovero's in kabbalistic studies, organized two different fellowships in Safed, one under the name *Ḥaverim Maqshivim* (The Hearkening Companions), the other *Sukkat Shalom* (The Tent of Peace). Others appear to have been more loosely structured around some specialized goal. Thus, the "Fellowship of Penitents" that Abraham Berukhim (ca. 1515–ca. 1593) informs us about sought to achieve atonement through certain especially severe ascetic practices.[10] This particular group exemplifies one of the central features that characterized the Kabbalists of 16th-century Safed, that is, their deep and pervasive sense of sinfulness. Unusual and dramatic penitential practices evolved in Safed for the purpose of enabling individuals to purify their souls and atone for their sins.[11] Berukhim also tells us about a group whose dedicated purpose seems to have been to rejoice at the conclusion of every Sabbath. An anonymous authority indicated: "There is a group that goes out on the night of the festival of *Simḥat Torah* for the purpose of singing and dancing in the presence of the Torah scroll in every synagogue."[12]

In his instructions to his circle of disciples, Moses Cordovero enjoined the following: "Let a person commune with one of our companions every day for the purpose of conversing about devotional concerns."[13] Likewise, "a person ought to discuss with this same companion, every Sabbath eve, what he did each day of that past week. From there he should go forth to welcome the Sabbath Queen."[14] Attesting to the special relationship that these companions were supposed to cultivate with one another, Cordovero also taught that "a person ought to converse in Hebrew with the fellow companions at all times."[15] An anonymous teacher encourages individuals to "commune each and every day with a friend while in a state of reverence for God."[16]

By far the most significant fellowship from a historical point of view was the circle of approximately forty individuals who gathered around Isaac Luria (1534–1570).[17] Luria was the most influential Kabbalist of the 16th century and one of the several most important in the entire history of Kabbalah. Born in Jerusalem, Luria emigrated to Egypt with his mother following the death of his father. In Egypt, Luria became a rabbi, studying under the most prominent Egyptian rabbinic authority of the day, David ibn Zimra (ca. 1480–1573). Luria was active in a circle of rabbis and scholars around ibn Zimra, collaborated in the writing of various works of Jewish law, and eventually began to pursue an interest in Kabbalah. He spent his last years in Egypt largely in contemplative seclusion on a small island in the Nile. It is during this time that he appears to have begun to develop his distinctive mystical ideas and practices. He left Egypt for Safed in late 1569 or early 1570 and studied with Moses Cordovero until the latter's death about six months after Luria's arrival. Following Cordovero's death, Luria almost immediately became the most significant kabbalistic teacher in Safed, filling the void left by his own teacher's passing. Luria's circle had an elaborate social structure. According to Luria's chief disciple, Hayyim Vital (1543–1620), this brotherhood was divided into four, hierarchically ordered groups. The first, and most important, was composed of eleven men, whose names Vital provides. It was to these individuals that Luria imparted his most esoteric kabbalistic teachings and concerning whom he had the highest expectations for spiritual attainment.

From the evidence we have, it is clear that Luria was exceedingly concerned that his disciples treat one another with the utmost consideration and love. He appears to have regarded strife among them as a critical impediment to accomplishing not only the goal of individual self-perfection but as, importantly, the goal of cosmic redemption to which his teachings were directed. Toward this end, he enjoined his disciples to seek to treat one another with love. Listen to the words of Hayyim Vital:

> My teacher, may his memory be for a blessing, cautioned me and all the brethren [*haverim*] who were with him in this fellowship that before praying the morning service, we should take upon ourselves the positive commandment "... and you shall love your neighbor as yourself" [Lev. 19:18]. He should concentrate upon loving every member of the House of Israel as he loves himself, for on account of this, his prayer will ascend, bound up with all the prayers of Israel. By this means his soul will be able to rise above and effect [cosmic] healing [*tikkun*]. And especially when it comes to the love of our brethren, each and every one of us must bind himself to the others as if he were one limb within the body of this fellowship. My teacher, of blessed memory, went out of his way to caution me concerning this matter. And if any fellow, God forbid, was in distress, or if there was any illness in his house or among his children, all should share in his trouble and pray on his behalf; similarly, in all matters, each of the fellows should be mindful of his fellows.[18]

According to these views, Luria's companions constituted an *organism*, a single body whose "limbs" depended on one another to function properly. The integrity of the fellowship was thus compromised by the absence of love among its members. Luria and his disciples regarded themselves as having an intimate link to the (fictional) fellowship of disciples (*hevraya*) described in the literature of the *Zohar*, composed several centuries earlier in 13th-century Spain.[19] In fact, we know that Luria taught his disciples that theirs were the reincarnated souls of the disciples of Rabbi Shimon bar Yochai, the central teacher at the heart of the zoharic community. Luria's disciples believed that they were engaged in completing the task of cosmic redemption (*tikkun*) which Shimon bar Yochai and his disciples had sought to accomplish. Here, then, we have a striking example of a mystical "social body" and its self-understanding. The *collective* efforts of these individuals were directed at cultivating the intentions, behaviors, and practices that would not only purify their own souls but would also bring about their vision of cosmic restitution and redemption. While Luria's fellowship was the most significant example of intentional brotherhoods in 16th-century Safed—indeed, in the whole of late medieval, early modern Judaism—it may nevertheless be regarded as representative of the important role that mystical community occupied more generally during this period.

Autobiography and Biography

At the risk of appearing to contradict what I have just said about the importance of studying kabbalistic social communities, I wish to draw attention to the significance of the *individual* in the 16th century. This is best illustrated by way of the autobiographical and biographical literature produced by Safed's Kabbalists. Although we have only fragmentary and limited autobiographical traditions from among earlier Kabbalists, in Safed we have no fewer than three substantial autobiographical diaries, from Joseph Karo, Hayyim Vital, and Eleazar Azikri. In addition, we have highly significant, if loosely organized, biographical evidence in connection with several figures, most prominently Isaac Luria. The existence of this literature calls upon us to appreciate the importance of scholarly focus on the individual lives and personalities of Jewish mystical figures. In the case of Safed, we are fortunate to have a great deal of information not only about these diary writers but also about a number of other colorful personalities. These materials constitute evidence about the emerging sense of individual identity that is characteristic of the late Middle Ages and the early modern period. But such evidence also richly illuminates the local kabbalistic culture of Safed in especially interesting and valuable ways. It is worth noting that in recent years we have witnessed a strong interest in the autobiographical genre in Jewish Studies and religious studies more generally.[20]

Hayyim Vital is best known as Isaac Luria's chief disciple. Vital is responsible for having preserved and composed several different versions of his master's teachings. These are among the most important evidence for Lurianic

Kabbalah as well as for biographical traditions about Luria himself, as we shall see below. But Vital also wrote a number of books of his own, including one that has come down to us as the *Sefer ha-Hezyonot* (Book of Visions). It amply displays Vital's rather considerable regard for himself—while at the same time revealing his substantial self doubts. The former is apparent in the very first diary entry:

> The following are the events that befell me from the day of my birth, on the first day of the month Heshvan in the year 5303 from the creation [1542]. While my father, of blessed memory, was still in the Diaspora, before he came to the Land of Israel, he had as his guest a great sage by the name of Hayyim Ashkenazi, who said to him: "Know that you are destined to reside in the Land of Israel. There a son will be born to you. Call him Hayyim after my name. He will be a great sage, without peer in his generation."[21]

Or consider the following entry:

> The year 5350 [1590]. A man by the name of Rabbi Shealtiel Alsheikh came from Persia. He is a man who sees visions even while he is awake, a man of discernment; a sage and saint who spends all his days in fasting. He told me that his visions always show him that the redemption of Israel depends on me, as does the return of Israel in repentance. They tell him of the high state of my soul. Even until now, in the year 5370 [1610], he writes letters to me regarding his visions in the matter of my soul and the matter of redemption.[22]

I offer one brief example of the biographical impulse in Safed in connection with Isaac Luria. Luria's students regarded him as a saintly individual who possessed extraordinary occult skills and charismatic abilities.[23] These are described in anecdotal fashion but are nevertheless quite detailed and elaborate. Here, for example, is a report about Luria by Hayyim Vital:

> Concerning his attainments, it is impossible for one to relate them even in general terms, much less in detail. However, these are the wondrous and true things that I witnessed with my own eyes: He knew how to make a future soul appear before him, as well as the soul of a living or deceased person, from among the early as well as later sages. He could inquire of them whatever he wished concerning knowledge of the future and secret mysteries of the Torah. The prophet Elijah, may he be a blessing, would

also appear to him and teach him. He could also recognize the letters on the forehead and was adept at the science of physiognomy, as well as at recognizing the lights that are upon the skin and body of an individual. He was also skilled at recognizing the lights in the hair, the chirping of birds, and the language of trees and plants. He understood the speech even of inanimate things, as Scripture says: "For the stone shall cry out of the wall [and the beam out of the timber shall answer it]" [Hab. 2:11]. [He knew] the language of the burning candle and the flaming coal. He was able to see the angels who announce all the proclamations from on high, as is well known, and to converse with them. His knowledge was expert concerning all the plants and the genuine remedies [they provide]. There are many other such things that cannot even be related. Those who hear of them will not believe them when told. I have recorded that which my eyes have seen in all truth.[24]

In another version, Vital adds that Luria "knows all the deeds that people have performed or will perform in the future, [for] he can discern the thoughts of individuals even before they are carried out." In addition, he was able to determine the transmigrations (*gilgulim*) through which the souls of individuals had passed, the sins that had been committed in the past, and the current state of their souls. As Hayyim Vital's dream diary makes clear, Luria was also considered to have expertise in dream interpretation. He applied himself to a careful and extensive study of plant life, teaching in some detail about the particular characteristics of plants and the beneficial effect each one had upon a person's physical health. In sum, Luria is described in these accounts as having been skilled at inducing various types of direct revelatory experiences, as having engaged in different types of divinatory activities, that is, in discerning the meaning of signs from the natural world, and as having had an intimate familiarity with the natural world.

These types of traditions about Luria preserved by his disciples have often been characterized as "legendary," even in the scholarly literature, because of the array of occult and supernatural skills attributed to him.[25] Such a view— which lumps together these kinds of anecdotal traditions with truly legendary works composed in the 17th century—misses the mark. In my view, such an approach fails to appreciate the significant differences between the earliest biographical traditions about Luria by his actual disciples and the subsequent hagiographies, works of exaggerated praise that bear little or no relationship to what we actually know about the man. The latter were produced decades removed from Luria's life by individuals who had never even seen him. By contrast, Vital's account of Luria exemplifies traditions by disciples who studied with Luria and represent ways in which they actually perceived and experienced him. They are thus biographical in the sense that his disciples are describing what they experienced as well as their understanding of those experiences. By contrast, the authors of two well-known hagiographical collections of stories about Luria, *Shivhei ha-Ari* and *Toldot ha-Ari*, were more or less *inventing* portraits of Luria that were rooted in folk traditions that evolved after his death.[26]

The autobiographical diaries authored by Joseph Karo, Eleazar Azikri, and Hayyim Vital, along with the biographical traditions such as we have in Isaac Luria's case, collectively attest to the powerful sense of the individual in this culture and the power that certain individuals could have in relationship to the community (or communities) of Kabbalists. In the course of the 17th and 18th centuries, the role of such personalities would become even more vivid. In the 17th century, for example, the messianic pretensions and charismatic behavior of the Turkish Jew Shabbatai Zevi (1626–1676) would incite widespread turmoil in the Jewish world. And in the 18th century in Eastern Europe, the individual personalities and charismatic qualities of the Hasidic masters (*rebbe* or *tsaddik*) would become absolutely central to the explosive success of that movement.

Ethics and the Ethical Body

One of the most prominent features of Safed Kabbalah was the profound concern for ethical behavior and the proper cultivation of personal spiritual traits. Earlier Kabbalists—including those whose teachings comprise the literature of the *Zohar* in the 13th century—had certainly taken an interest in ethics. But not until the 16th century do we find a more self-conscious and systematic effort to bring together kabbalistic metaphysical principles and ethical values and practice. This is dramatically affirmed by the development and profusion of a new genre of literature in Safed, which has come to be called in Hebrew *musar ha-Kabbalit*, or ethical Kabbalah. Moses Cordovero, Elijah de Vidas, Eleazar Azikri, and Hayyim Vital produced highly influential and popular books intended to demonstrate the way in which kabbalistic theology informs and transforms traditional Jewish ethical practice.

I illustrate this genre by referring to the first such book composed in Safed, authored by Cordovero and titled *Tomer Devorah* (The Palm Tree of Deborah).[27] This relatively short treatise consists of ten chapters, each one dedicated to exploring the spiritual significance and ethical application of one of the ten *sefirot*. It exerted enormous influence upon the subsequent development of this genre of kabbalistic literature. The very opening of the book lays bare the metaphysical and anthropological principles that serve as the basis for Cordovero's approach:

> Imitate your Creator. Then you will enter the mystery of the supernal form, the divine image in which you were created. If you resemble the divine in body but not in action, you distort the form. People will say of you: "A lovely form whose deeds are ugly." For the essence of the divine image is action. What good is it if your anatomy corresponds to the supernal form, while your actions do not resemble God's? So imitate the acts of *Keter* (the first *sefirah*, "Crown"), the thirteen qualities of compassion alluded to by the prophet Micah: "Who is a God like you, delighting in love? You will again have compassion upon us. You will hurl all our sins into the depths of the sea."[28]

We discover here a distinctively kabbalistic understanding of the biblical and rabbinic notions that human beings are created in God's image. From the kabbalistic perspective, every individual's body and entire persona is a microcosm of the divine "body" and persona, that is, the structure of the ten *sefirot*. As such, the human body resembles and parallels—in an earthly form—the divine "anatomy." Cordovero begins by challenging individuals to fulfill the potential with which every person is endowed by acting in ways that resemble God's actions, namely, in moral ways. Insofar as every human "limb" is patterned after its corresponding divine "limb," each interpersonal gesture is capable of being divine in nature. For example, every feature of the human face, corresponding to the divine face, should "behave" in such a way as to promote ethical interpersonal relations:

> Your forehead should not be tense at all, but rather always resemble the forehead of the [Divine] Will, so that you soothe everyone. Even if you come across angry people, soothe and calm them with your goodwill. For the forehead of the [Divine] Will constantly accepts and soothes the harsh powers, reintegrating them. So should you soothe those overwhelmed by anger. . . . Derive the power to be genial with others. If your character is somewhat harsh, people will not be soothed . . .
> Your ears should always be tuned to hear the good, while rumors and gossip should never be let in, according to the secret of sublime [that is, Divine] listening. There, no harsh shouting enters, no tongue of evil leaves a blemish. So listen only to positive, useful things [and] not to things that provoke anger.

. . . Your face should always be shining. Welcome each person with a friendly countenance. For with regard to *Keter Elyon*, the supernal Crown, it is said: "In the light of the king's face is life." No redness or harsh judgment gains entrance there. So, too, the light of your face should never change; whoever looks at you will find only joy and a friendly expression. Nothing should disturb you.[29]

We know about the importance of ethical life in Safed, however, not only from the formal literary works of ethical Kabbalah but also from anecdotal evidence concerning some of the fellowships to which we referred earlier. Once again I illustrate this dimension of 16th-century Kabbalah by referring to the brotherhood of Isaac Luria. In addition to being reputed to have had the charismatic skills that I described earlier, Luria also gained a reputation for possessing an exemplary moral character and is described as having exceedingly strong ethical concerns. We have already seen his concern that his disciples treat one another with love and compassion. Safed literature is replete with anecdotal material describing his ethical teachings as well as his personal ethical habits. For example, Hayyim Vital relates the following in Luria's name:

The most important of all worthy traits consists in an individual behaving with humility, modesty, and with the fear of sin to the greatest possible degree. He should also, to the utmost degree, keep his distance from pride, anger, foolishness, and evil gossip; and even should he have a significant reason for behaving harshly, he ought to refrain from acting in this way. He should also abstain from idle conversation, even though it is not as important as the previous admonition. And he should not lose his temper, even with the members of his own household.[30]

Spiritual perfection thus entailed cultivating one's emotional life in particular ways. Luria appears to have been especially concerned with the importance of avoiding anger. Again, Hayyim Vital:

The quality of anger, aside from serving as an obstacle to mystical inspiration altogether, [has other injurious consequences]. My teacher, of blessed memory, used to be more exacting when it came to anger than with all other transgressions, even in a situation where a person loses his temper for the sake of some religious obligation. This is because all other transgressions injure only a single limb of the body, whereas the quality of anger injures the soul in its entirety, altering its character completely. This is the issue: when an individual loses his temper, his holy soul deserts him altogether; in its place a spirit of an evil nature enters. And this is the esoteric meaning behind the verse: "Thou that tearest thyself in thine anger" [Job 18:4]. For such a person actually tears the soul, rendering it unfit at the moment of his wrath and anger.[31]

Other evidence suggests that cultivation of the proper emotional life was crucial to Luria's conception of spiritual practice. With respect to sadness, he taught as follows: "Melancholia is, by itself, an exceedingly unpleasant quality of personality, particularly in the case of an individual whose intention is to acquire esoteric knowledge and experience the Holy Spirit. There is nothing that impedes mystical inspiration—even for someone who is otherwise worthy of it—as much as the quality of sadness."[32]

On the contrary, joy in the fulfillment of the commandments ought to exceed the happiness one might experience through material wealth: "When an individual carries out any precept, be it the study of Torah or prayer, he ought to be joyful and spirited, more than if he had acquired money, or found thousands of gold pieces."[33]

In my view, the attribution to Isaac Luria of these particular qualities (and his concern that his disciples cultivate them) reflects the particular preoccupations of Luria and his fellowship. Similarly, the interpersonal themes in Cordovero's *Palm Tree of Deborah* attest to actual concerns of the kabbalistic community in Safed more generally. These are not simply a litany of generic moral conventions; they capture a discrete cultural milieu, a particular cluster of social concerns and tensions. Thus, for example, the emphasis on avoiding melancholy and serving God in joy may be seen as a way of counteracting the strong tendency toward guilt and self-reproach that we know characterized the Safed community. The special concern for modesty and humility repeatedly mentioned in our sources takes on heightened significance in the context of a culture where more than a few egos loomed large. The internecine rivalry in evidence among certain members of Luria's brotherhood helps put into focus Luria's warning about loving one another. As such, this collection of traditions about Luria's own behavior, and his exhortations to cultivate a certain type of spiritual life, must be read as more than a set of stereotypical pietisms. They serve as one measure of some of the psychological and social conflicts that beset this community.

Ethical values, as well as emotional behaviors, are, to some degree, social constructions, that is, they represent expectations for behavior that are learned within the context of a particular cultural setting. Emotions are performed, as it were, in the sense that they are a function of the ways in which people are taught and are expected to behave in relationship to others. As such, they are a matter of public discourse, always evolving and being acted out in dynamic, interactional ways. The values and attitudes embodied in the traditions described here thus go to the heart of some of the most significant spiritual issues with which Luria and his circle of disciples were concerned. The exploration of such social and psychological features helps to bring this community to life for us by drawing our attention to the lived experience of these individuals.

Ritual Innovation

We justifiably think of contemporary Judaism in America as characterized by extraordinary ritual innovation and experimentation. But 16th-century Safed was also one of those particularly dynamic historical moments in which religious creativity and originality flourished. Many of the ritual, devotional, and liturgical practices that were innovated in the 16th century exerted immense influence upon subsequent Jewish life—not only among Kabbalists and Hasidim but also in Jewish communities more generally. The most familiar example of this is Kabbalat Shabbat (Welcoming the Sabbath), the liturgy that serves as a prelude to the Friday evening service. But there are many others, including rites at the table for the three festive Sabbath meals, the midnight vigil known as *Tiqqun Hatsot*, nighttime study vigils for the festivals of Shavuot (*Tiqqun Leil Shavu'ot*) and Hoshanah Rabbah, the "minor day of Atonement" (*Yom Kippur Qatan*), special rites at grave sites, penitential rituals, and numerous meditative and liturgical practices of different types. These were all in the realm of superogatory traditions, that is, they went beyond standard Jewish practice, although over time many of these assumed normative status by the communities that embraced them. Of considerable note is that the contemporary Jewish interest in ritual creativity has been nourished in significant part by a similar revival of interest in the mystical tradition. The result has been the rediscovery and rejuvenation of such ritual practices as the midnight study vigil for the festival of Shavuot and the custom of *Ushpizin*, welcoming divine, sefirotic "guests" into one's Sukkah on the festival of Sukkot.

Women and Questions of Gender

Studies of Jewish culture are increasingly and appropriately being informed (to varying degrees) by questions of women, gender, and sexuality. A virtual revolution is beginning to take place in the conceptualization of that culture now that heightened attention is being paid to these topics, including the role of women. Scholarship in the field of Jewish mysticism has also begun to contribute in significant ways to this endeavor. As the chapter in this book by Hava Tirosh-Samuelson demonstrates, a remarkable stream of diverse and original scholarly writing has emerged in the past decade or so that explores notions of the divine feminine in kabbalistic literature. But what about the place of actual women in the history of Kabbalah and Hasidism? Here there are considerable challenges, primarily owing to the paucity of our sources. Gershom Scholem, the preeminent scholar of Jewish mystical tradition in the 20th century, famously asserted that there were no female Jewish mystics because no females had written mystical treatises.[34] In my own work, I have sought to frame the question differently. If we do not limit ourselves to the question of authorship but ask instead about how women living in a kabbalistic culture were affected by their environment, as well as how they may have influenced their environment, we are confronted by a series of new possibilities. Consider, for example, the case of the Lurianic community, several aspects of which we have already described.

As with so much of Judaism, Lurianic Kabbalah was conceived of by men and virtually exclusively for men. Luria had no female disciples. Nevertheless, women were clearly implicated in a variety of ways in Safed ritual in general and Lurianic ritual in particular. After all, Luria's male disciples had mothers, wives, daughters, sisters, and aunts. And living with and among male Kabbalists, these women must be presumed to have adopted both kabbalistic views of the world and kabbalistic practices to some degree, just as women in non-kabbalistic rabbinic communities shared in their Weltanschauungen and ritual lives. Moreover, insofar as Jewish women have always had a certain degree of agency and spheres of influence—especially within the home—there is good reason to assume that women exerted influence upon those with whom they lived. In my view, we must therefore expand our notion of what it meant to be a Kabbalist to include women who participated in the kabbalistic community in one way or another.[35]

In the case of Lurianic Kabbalah, for example, there is clear evidence that women were implicated in a wide range of rituals that had kabbalistic significance and meaning, from lighting candles on the Sabbath and other rites at the Sabbath table, to matters of sexual practice. Nevertheless, we do not have the evidence to inform us concerning what these practices might have meant to the women themselves. Thus, we would like to know how very particular notions of sexuality and sexual relations—including anxieties about sex— may have had an impact on women's lives. Was Isaac Luria's wife curious about why sexual relations were essentially limited to Friday nights, whereas non-kabbalistic wives could have sexual relations with their husbands on other nights of the week? Did she wonder why their bed was positioned in a partic-ular way—that is, with one's head toward the east, one's feet to the west, one's right hand southward, and one's left hand southward, corresponding to vari-ous *sefirot*—during marital relations? What did she make of the fact that her husband required twelve loaves of challah to be placed on the Sabbath table? Did Luria's mother understand the meaning of his kissing her hands after he returned from welcoming the Sabbath Bride on Sabbath eve? Did the wives of Luria's disciples regard themselves as representing and embodying the female divine presence, the *Shekhinah* or, in Lurianic parlance, *Nuqba de-Ze'ir*? Could this have elevated their status in the eyes of their husbands or in their own eyes? These and many more questions can be asked of Lurianic culture. We do not have clear answers—or even, in most cases, any answers at all. But it is nevertheless imperative to pay close attention to the (regrettably sparse) sources that provide evidence suggesting the women's involvement and to explore as far as possible the intriguing and important questions prompted by such evidence. What we can say with absolute certainty, however, is that women performed acts and engaged in activities that were imbued with pro-found kabbalistic meaning, at least as far as kabbalistic men were concerned.

We do have limited, but nevertheless rich, evidence of several women in Safed and its environs having had visionary experiences and having engaged in occult activities.[36] This evidence is found in Hayyim Vital's dream diary to which we have referred earlier. In a diary entry from the year 1570, he informs us, for example, that a wise woman in Safed named Soniadora could foretell the future, interpret dreams, and was expert in the art of divining from drops of oil on water. Vital consulted her concerning his own future spiritual attainments by asking her to "cast a spell over the oil as was cus-tomary." Vital also described the visionary experiences of a woman named Rachel, the sister of Judah Mishan, one of Luria's disciples:

On Sabbath morning, I was preaching to the congregation in Jerusalem. Rachel, the sister of Rabbi Judah Mishan, was present. She said that dur-ing the whole of my discourse, there was a pillar of fire above my head;

Elijah was at my right hand to support me. When I had finished they both departed . . . This woman was known to see visions, spirits, and angels, and she was accurate in most of her reports, from the time that she was a young girl until now that she has grown into womanhood.[37]

Several other women in Safed and Damascus are said to have experienced visionary dreams, typically having to do with confirming Vital's greatness. In addition, we have several reports by Vital about women who experienced auditory revelations. One woman in Damascus, the daughter of a certain Raphael Anav, is said to have had visions while awake, through the medium of souls and angels, as well as an auditory experience of the prophet Elijah at the moment of a Sabbath eve celebration. Still another woman, Franseza Sarah, "a saintly woman (*'ishah ḥasidah*), used to have visions while awake, and would hear a voice speak to her. And most of her words were true."

Taken together, these and other stories about women are remarkable insofar as they suggest a picture quite different from what we might have expected. At least some women evidently gained reputations for having visionary dreams, visions of light, auditory revelations of angels, departed souls, and the prophet Elijah, and were expert at certain types of divination. Almost always identified by name, and as the daughter, sister, or wife of a particular individual, these women were clearly part of the community rather than lone, marginal individuals behaving in deviant ways. Aside from their intrinsic interest, most striking about these reports is that they provide evidence that some 16th-century women engaged in religious practices beyond the boundaries of home and family.

Embodied Experience

The categories of concern I have identified here in connection with Safed reflect a few of the significant developments in the study of religion as a whole over the recent past. New approaches to the study of Jewish religious culture in general, and Jewish mysticism in particular, represent growing interest among students of religion in the nature of social community, religious personalities, ethical discourse, religious rituals of all types, and gender and sexuality, among other matters. What these diverse phenomena have in common is that they go beyond older conceptions of religion that reach back into 19th-century Europe. These conceptions reflected a historically Christian perspective, in which theology and faith were of paramount importance. By contrast these areas of inquiry, and the new methodological approaches they engender, reflect an interest in understanding religion not primarily as a set of beliefs but as lived experience.[38] Put differently, these categories of concern lead us in the direction of appreciating religious life as *embodied* experience, that is, as ways in which individuals not only think about reality but also how they experience it physically, interpersonally, emotionally, and expressively.

NOTES

1. The complete text of this letter is in F. Kobler, ed., *A Treasury of Jewish Letters: Letters from the Famous and the Humble* (New York: Farrar, Straus & Young, 1952), 1:283–85.

2. This famous report is attributed to Bayazid's courtiers by Eliyahu Capsali, *Seder Eliyahu Zuta*, ed. A. Shmuelevitz (Jerusalem, 1975), 1:240. Immanuel Aboab ascribes it to Bayazid himself in his *Nomologia, o Discursos legales compuestos* (Amsterdam, 1629), p. 195.

3. For a fuller discussion of these historical events, see Lawrence Fine, *Physician of the Soul, Healer of the Cosmos—Isaac Luria and His Kabbalistic Fellowship* (Stanford: Stanford University Press, 2003), pp. 19–24.

4. Abraham Yaari, *Iggrot Erets Yisrael* (Ramat Gan: Masada, 1971), pp. 144–60. I have drawn on the English translation found in K. Wilhelm, ed., *Roads to Zion* (New York: Schocken Books, 1948), pp. 15–27.

5. The definitive study of Safed's textile industry is Shmuel Avitsur, "Contributions to the History of the Woolen Textile Industry in Salonika" [in Hebrew], *Sefunot* 12 (1971–78): 147–68. For more on this topic, see Fine, *Physician of the Soul,* pp. 47–49.

6. Arthur Green, *A Guide to the Zohar* (Stanford: Stanford University Press, 2005), p. 72. Concerning this phenomenon, see also Rachel Elior, *Jewish Mysticism: The Infinite Expression of Freedom* (Oxford: Littman Library of Jewish Civilization, 2007), pp. 51–54.

7. Concerning this question, see Fine, *Physician of the Soul,* pp. 7–15.

8. R. J. Z. Werblowsky, *Joseph Karo: Lawyer and Mystic* (Oxford: Oxford University Press, 1962), p. 62.

9. With respect to Cordovero's circle, see Lawrence Fine, *Safed Spirituality* (Mahwah, NJ: Paulist Press, 1984), pp. 30–38. Azikri's mystical life is studied in Mordecai Pachter, *Millei de-Shemaya le-Rabi Eleazar Azikri* (Tel Aviv: Miflaim Univeristaim, 1991); and Moshe Idel, *Studies in Ecstatic Kabbalah* (Albany: State University of New York Press, 1988), pp. 132–34.

10. Fine, *Safed Spirituality,* pp. 47–53.

11. Concerning this subject, see Fine, *Physician of the Soul,* esp. chap. 5; idem, "Penitential Practices in a Kabbalistic Mode," in *Seeking the Favor of God,* ed. Mark J. Boda, Daniel K. Falk, and Rodney A. Werline (Atlanta, GA: Society of Biblical Literature, 2008), 3:127–48.

12. Fine, *Safed Spirituality,* p. 59.

13. Ibid., p. 36

14. Ibid.

15. Ibid., p. 38.

16. Ibid., p. 58.

17. The Lurianic fellowship is studied in detail in Fine, *Physician of the Soul*. On Lurianic Kabbalah, see the valuable study by Shaul Magid, *From Metaphysics to Midrash: Myth, History, and the Interpretation of Scripture in Lurianic Kabbala* (Bloomington: Indiana University Press, 2008). The scholarship of Gershom Scholem on Isaac Luria has recently been edited by Daniel Abrams as *Lurianic Kabbalah: Collected Studies by Gershom Scholem* (Los Angeles: Cherub, 2008).

18. Fine, *Physician of the Soul*, pp. 91–92.

19. Concerning the *Zohar*'s fellowship, see Melila Hellner, *A River Flows from Eden: The Language of Mystical Experience in the Zohar* (Stanford: Stanford University Press, 2009). For a discussion of the relationship between the companions of the *Zohar* and the Lurianic fellowship, see Fine, *Physician of the Soul*, chap. 9.

20. For recent studies of Jewish autobiography, see *Hebrew Ethical Wills*, expanded and with a new introduction by Lawrence Fine (Philadelphia: Jewish Publication Society, 2006), pp. 8–12; Natalie Zemon Davis, *Women on the Margins: Three Seventeenth-Century Lives* (Cambridge, MA: Harvard University Press, 1995); Mark Cohen, ed., *The Autobiography of a Seventeenth-Century Venetian Rabbi: Leon Modena's Life of Judah* (Princeton, NJ: Princeton University Press, 1988); Mark Moseley, *Being for Myself Alone: Origins of Jewish Autobiography* (Stanford: Stanford University Press, 2006); and Michael Stanislawski, *Autobiographical Jews: Essays in Jewish Self-Fashioning* (Seattle: University of Washington Press, 2004).

21. Louis Jacobs, *The Schocken Book of Jewish Mystical Testimonies* (New York: Schocken Books, 1997), p. 153.

22. Ibid., p. 156.

23. Concerning Luria's charismatic and saintly reputation, see Fine, *Physician of the Soul*, esp. chap. 5; Jonathan Garb, "The Cult of the Saint in Lurianic Kabbalah," *Jewish Quarterly Review* 98 (2008): 203–29.

24. Hayyim Vital, *Sha'ar Ruah. ha-Qodesh*, translated in Fine, *Physician of the Soul*, pp. 93–94.

25. See Fine, *Physician of the Soul*, p. 383 n. 21.

26. Concerning these two hagiographical works, see Fine, *Physician of the Soul*, pp. 2, 84–86, 383 nn. 18–21.

27. For a complete English translation of this work, see Louis Jacobs, *The Palm Tree of Deborah* (London: Valentine, Mitchell, 1960). For a recent discussion of Cordovero's book, see Elliot R. Wolfson, *Venturing Beyond: Law and Morality in Kabbalistic Mysticism* (Oxford: Oxford University Press, 2006), pp. 196–98, 312–13; this book also contains an important discussion of kabbalistic ethics.

28. This translation is slightly adapted from Daniel Matt, *The Essential Kabbalah* (San Francisco: Harper San Francisco, 1995), p. 83.

29. Ibid., pp. 84–85.

30. Hayyim Vital, *Sha'ar ha-Mitsvot*, translated in Fine, *Physician of the Soul*, p. 90.

31. Vital, *Sha'ar Ruah ha-Qodesh*, translated in Fine, *Physician of the Soul*, p. 90.

32. Ibid., p. 91.

33. Ibid. 34. Gershom Scholem, *Major Trends in Jewish Mysticism* (New York: Schocken Books, 1954), pp. 37–38.

34. Gershom Scholem, *Major Trends in Jewish Mysticism* (New York: Schocken Books, 1954) pp. 37–38

35. For important examples of studies that explore the world of actual women in Jewish mystical tradition or that bear upon the question of women's lives, see Fine, *Physician of the Soul*; Talya Fishman, "A Kabbalistic Perspective on Gender-Specific Commandments: On the Interplay of Symbols and Society," *Association for Jewish Studies Review* 7 (1992) 199–245; Sharon Koren, "Mystical Rationales for the Laws of Niddah," in *Women and Water: Menstruation in Jewish Life and Law*, ed. Rahel S. Wasserfall (Hanover, NH: Brandeis University Press, 1999), pp. 101–21; Ruth Lamdan, *A Separate People: Jewish Women in Palestine, Syria, and Egypt in the Sixteenth Century* (Leiden: Brill, 2000); Chava Weissler, *Voices of the Matriarchs: Listening to the Prayers of Early Modern Jewish Women* (Boston: Beacon, 1988); Malkah Shapiro, *The Rebbe's Daughter: Memoir of a Hasidic Childhood*, translated and with an introduction by Nehemia Polen (Philadelphia: Jewish Publication Society, 2002); Nathaniel Deutsch, *The Maiden of Ludmir: A Jewish Holy Woman and Her World* (Berkeley: University of California Press, 2003); J. H. Chajes, *Between Worlds: Dybbuks, Exorcists, and Early Modern Judaism* (Philadelphia: University of Pennsylvania Press, 2003); and Morris M. Faierstein, "*Maggidim*, Spirits, and Women in Rabbi Hayyim Vital's *Book of Visions*," in *Spirit Possession in Judaism: Cases and Contexts from the Middle Ages to the Present*, ed. Matt Goldish (Detroit: Wayne State University Press, 2003).

36. On this subject, see Fine, *Physician of the Soul*, pp. 120–22.

37. Translated in ibid., p. 120.

38. As a stellar representative of this trend in Jewish scholarship, see Maria Diemling and Giuseppe Veltri, eds., *The Jewish Body: Corporeality, Society, and Identity in the Renaissance and Early Modern Period* (Leiden: Brill, 2009). An earlier, important groundbreaking work on this subject is Howard Eilberg-Schwartz, ed., *People of the Body: Jews and Judaism from an Embodied Perspective* (Albany: State University of New York Press, 1992).

Becoming Modern

Mystical Messianism

From the Renaissance to the Enlightenment

———— MATT GOLDISH ————

Almost all significant Jewish messianic movements from Abraham Abulafia until recent times deeply involved mysticism or Kabbalah. As a result, messianic movements and thought have become part of the story of Jewish mysticism since the 13th century.

The destruction of the Second Temple in 70 CE and the loss of Jewish sovereignty in Judea caused the messianic idea to gradually lose its military and political immediacy. The Messiah became an increasingly spiritual and miraculous figure. The emergence of Kabbalah in the 13th century offered an ideological framework in which to place messianic hopes along with powerful symbols and terms about the Messiah. In this way, messianism and mysticism became inextricably bound together for centuries.

Although "Renaissance" and "Enlightenment" are not necessarily meaningful terms for Jewish history, they are a convenient way to describe the period between the fall of Constantinople to the Ottomans in 1453 and the rise of the Hasidim in the 1740s. Although messianic movements are sometimes defined by the existence of an actual Messiah figure in the midst of a large group of believers, there are also periods of messianic agitation, prediction, and expectation that lack an actual Messiah figure.

Jewish Messianism Until the 15th Century

The idea of the Jewish Messiah originated in the Hebrew Bible. The term *mashiah* is used there to describe those anointed with oil to take the offices of king, priest, or prophet. Over time, the idea became most associated with kingship. During periods of exile or subjugation the Israelites would pray for God to send a powerful messianic king to redeem them. This idea became more complex in the writings of the later biblical prophets. For example, it incorporated the return of all Jews, including the ten northern Israelite tribes who were "lost" in the Babylonian exile. Later authors embellished the scenario with tales of the "sabbatical river" (the Sambatyon), which flowed violently with enormous stones all week. On the Sabbath, however, the river remained quiet as the Ten Tribes waited for God to give them the signal to cross and fight the apocalyptic wars in preparation for the Messiah.[1]

After the Babylonian exile of the 6th century BCE, there was no true Israelite king. In the 2nd century BCE the Hasmoneans (the "Maccabees") took on a messianic role as both high priests and pseudo-kings. A variety of messianic expectations and pretenders flourished as the Jewish Commonwealth lost much of its independence to Rome. This process occurred during the two centuries that preceded the destruction of the Second Temple by the Romans in 70 CE. Most of these scenarios imagined a repetition of the Hasmonean success in expelling meddling foreign powers through military strength. A new breed began to appear, however, whose conjectured messianic scenario involved events more spiritual than military. These included some of the authors of the Dead Sea Scrolls, individuals like John the Baptist who withdrew from corrupt city life, and, most fatefully, Jesus of Nazareth, who taught that the revolution in the human condition would come through meekness and humility rather than power and force.[2]

Although our information about Jewish messianic movements between Bar Kokhba (d. 135 CE) and the Crusades is somewhat spotty, we know that both the militant and the spiritualist strains continued. A number of important local movements, based mainly on the military messianic model, occurred in the Middle East during this period. These included a group of messiahs in Persia during the 8th century. Isaac Abu Issa, Yudghan (Yehuda), and Mushka led a political uprising whose ultimate goal appears to have been the recapture of Jerusalem. Sari'a (Serenus), a Syrian who advocated radical revisions of Jewish law and life, was another 8th-century militant messiah. In the 12th century, David al-Ro'i (Alroy), a Kurdish Jew, gained fame and widespread support for his messianic mission by performing feats of magic. In a famous epistle directed to the Yemenite Jewish community, Maimonides discussed the characteristics of messianic figures who appeared in France (though there is some debate about the location), Spain, and Yemen in the 11th and 12th centuries. The missions of these messiahs are military at some times and spiritual at others.[3]

A major development in Jewish messianism occurred in the 13th century with the appearance of the ecstatic Kabbalist Abraham Abulafia in Spain, Italy, and other areas. Abulafia created a new paradigm and a powerful example of prophetic messianism which, though much berated in his own time, influenced Jewish messianic thought and activity straight through the Hasidic movement.[4] The other 13th-century development with pivotal implications for the future was the appearance of the *Zohar*, the fundamental work of Spanish Kabbalah. It presents an extensive and highly mystical conception of the Messiah, which, together with the figure of Abulafia, decisively shifted the focus of Jewish messianism away from the military and concrete and toward the spiritual and mystical.[5]

This spiritual and mystical sense of the Messiah, presented in the unique terminology, symbolism, and ideas of Kabbalah, was characteristic of almost all Jewish messianic movements from Abulafia's time until the 20th century. The Kabbalah gave extra impetus to messianic impulses in the late Middle Ages by presenting a spiritualized, mystical redemption scenario. The world of the spirit rather than that of the body is where God will act in the end of days. In this vision, the Jews, increasingly unempowered in the physical world, are the masters of the future, for they have learned the workings of the divine realm through the Kabbalah.

Jewish Messianism under the Impact of Ottoman Islam and Iberian Christianity

When the city of Constantinople, the capital of Eastern Christendom, fell to the Muslim Ottomans in 1453, Christians around the world were shocked. The gospel, which was meant to spread throughout the world, was now losing ground to the Muslims on an enormous scale. The Christians' dismay increased as more and more cities fell to the Ottomans, who became deeply entrenched in Europe itself. What could it mean when Islam, with its own conversionist philosophy of *jihad*, overthrew centers of Christian life? Clearly God was sending a message—perhaps even a messianic or apocalyptic message about the coming age. The amazement was naturally reflected on the Muslim side as euphoria and triumphalism, sometimes expressed as *mahdism*, a belief somewhat akin to Christian Millenarianism and messianism.[6]

These monumental shifts were not lost on the Jews. For example, there are records of significant messianic activity in Sicily around 1455–56. Although there are few details—the reliable records are largely from dull archival sources—we do know that a considerable group of Jews boarded ships from Sicily to the Land of Israel at that time out of messianic motives. Other indications of the impact caused by the fall of Constantinople appear in letters from the early 16th century, reflecting the importance of the Ottoman conquests in Jewish messianic thought. (Muslim or Ottoman forces are commonly spoken of in the aggregate as "The Turk"):

You must know, and have surely heard—for it was predicted to you before-hand—how the Turk has captured the city of Rhodes in Romany, and all the atrocities he committed there. He now fights in Hungary . . . We have also heard how he sent messengers to Sicily with a message of peace; but if they would not accept it he would come upon them in war . . . Here [in Jerusalem] this has become known, and the rumor has spread among the gentiles. Letters arrived for the ambassador of the King of Naples from the King of Poland [reporting that] the Sambatyon River is now constantly calm, that four of the [Lost Ten] Tribes have now passed over it, and five more are preparing to cross it.[7]

Other letters from the same group similarly report that the Sambatyon River stopped flowing on Rosh Hashanah in 1453. They also tell how the Jew-ish king in "India" (a generic term for unknown parts of the world) was beat-ing the Christian king, Prester John, and capturing his lands as part of the messianic process.[8] Though these reports are imaginary, they clearly reflect the significance of the Ottoman conquests of 1453 and after in fostering a Jewish messianic atmosphere. They are also kabbalistic, since some of the authors are known Kabbalists and the letters themselves are replete with kab-balistic references.[9]

These letters and other documents reflect a messianic atmosphere in Italy and the Land of Israel, but much of the same expectation existed in Spain in the second half of the 16th century. Inquisitorial documents speak of Jewish converts to Catholicism (*conversos*) sharing such expectations in the 1460s. Around that time, the Spanish Jews are reported to have received letters from Constantinople that the Messiah had been born there. They maintained that when the Messiah arrived in Spain there would be enormous bloodshed, and the Spaniards would be punished for their cruelty to the Jews and *conversos*. A Turkish antichrist would also soon arise who would destroy the Christians and their churches but favor the Jews. Whether these beliefs had a mystical basis is unclear, but they definitely show the ongoing sense that Islam and the Ottomans had a key role in the Jewish messianic imagination of the time. This positive valuation of the Ottomans was compounded by the fact that Jews who suffered persecution in Spain could find refuge and live as Jews in Turkish lands.[10]

A more clearly mystical Jewish messianic agitation appeared among a group of Spanish Kabbalists known to scholars as the Circle of the Respond-ing Angel (*Ḥug Mal'akh ha-Meshiv*, or the *Sefer ha-Meshiv* Circle). The mem-bers of this group were deeply involved in magic and prophecy, particularly activities involving dream questions and the commanding of angels or other heavenly beings. They were intensely anti-Christian and anti-philosophical, but, as recent scholarship has shown, they were also deeply affected by Christian theology. According to legend, a figure associated with this group, Rabbi Joseph della Reina, attempted to use practical Kabbalah (the magical manipulation of divine names and talismans) to bring the Messiah. Though recent research has undermined the origin of this story, the tale was very popular and suggests a strong sense of the relationship that people perceived between Kabbalah and the Messiah.[11]

The expulsion of the Jews from Spain in 1492 and their subsequent forced conversion in Portugal in 1497 created a major crisis in the Jewish world, giving further impetus to messianic expectations. One of the great leaders of Spanish Jewry in that generation, Don Isaac Abarbanel, wrote three separate treatises about the Messiah shortly after he left Spain and went to live in Italy. Abarbanel expresses himself as an acute messianist but not as a Kabbalist—that is, his message is not couched in the terms, symbols, and ideas of the Kabbalah.[12] His calculations of the Messiah's arrival include 1453 as an important moment in the process and a possible end date of 1503, 1547, or 1559. Although one recent scholar has warned against overinterpreting the significance and impact of Abarbanel's messianism, it is clearly connected with the Spanish expulsion as well as other important historical events, and it influenced other Jews.[13]

Although Abarbanel was not really a Kabbalist, several major Kabbalists from the generation of the expulsion also promoted a messianic program, sometimes by calculating expected dates when the Messiah would arrive. Foremost among these was Rabbi Abraham ben Eliezer ha-Levi, who traveled in North Africa and the Land of Israel and wrote extensively of the expected messianic arrival in the 1520s. A recent find in the Cairo Geniza revealed work by another figure, probably from ha-Levi's circle, writing about the same time, who had acute messianic expectations. These mystics wove together an esoteric Bible interpretation of Kabbalah with a keen awareness of current events to convey a sharp sense that the signs of redemption were everywhere.[14]

Another important messianic movement after the expulsion involved a group of Spanish *conversos* and *conversas* around 1499 or 1500. They believed that God would send the Messiah to redeem them as well as the Jews. Again, a strong mystical and prophetic streak typifies this group, who lived in the dangerous frontier between Catholicism and Jewish beliefs. Most of the leading figures were women, especially Ines of Herrera and María Gomez. These women experienced mystical visions of the coming messianic age and urged their fellow *conversos* to return to Jewish practice so that they might be saved when the day of redemption arrived. They were part of a larger *converso* messianic stream that lasted at least into the 17th century.[15]

The first major messianic figure to appear after the expulsion was Asher Laemmlein Reutlingen, an Ashkenazi Jew living in northern Italy. His movement peaked from 1500 to 1502 but, apparently, it had nothing to do with the fate of Spanish Jewry, as Laemmlein detested Sephardim. His Kabbalah featured magical elements from the Italian tradition. Nowhere does he mention the expulsion from Spain, nor does he use the Spanish work *Zohar*. The influence of his movement was widespread at the time. In a famous passage written in the late 16th century, the Prague scholar David Gans recalls that his grandfather destroyed his special *matzah* oven during the Laemmlein episode because he expected to be in the Holy Land by the following Passover.[16]

We have already seen some of the messianic excitement that showed up in the Jewish world in the 1520s in the letters mentioning Constantinople, the writings of Rabbi Abraham ben Eliezer ha-Levi, and the Geniza fragments. This excitement probably had to do with a number of factors, some within the Jewish community and some from outside. Recent research has pointed out that Christian messianism, or Millenarianism, and Muslim *mahdism* were also peaking in this era. Some Jews took the split in the Catholic Church led by Martin Luther to signal an impending apocalypse. Many Christians and Muslims, as well as Jews, saw the monumental clash between the Hapsburg emperor Charles V and the Ottoman sultan Suleiman the Magnificent to be a step in the messianic process. For many Christians, Charles played a messianic role, and many Muslims saw Suleiman as a *mahdi*.[17] What is certain is that the next major stage of Jewish messianism involved a great deal of interaction with non-Jewish leaders.

David Reubeni and Solomon Molkho

In the spring of 1525 a man appeared in Rome claiming to be David of the (Lost) Tribe of Reuben, brother of King Joseph of that tribe. He said he had come to Europe to acquire canons—and perhaps Jewish soldiers—for an assault on the Ottoman forces in Jerusalem. The implications of this constellation of claims are numerous. Nobody has ever figured out precisely who David Reubeni was, where he was from, or what was really behind his "mission." He was clearly aware, however, that any scheme against the Ottomans, and especially one with messianic implications such as the capture of Jerusalem, would get a favorable hearing in Christian Europe. The highly practical nature of his request, reflecting a factual grasp concerning the distribution of large firearms, gave his claims a ring of truth. The messianic connotations of his lineage as well as his alleged assignment created an aura of sanctity as well as pragmatism around Reubeni. His decision to come to Rome indicates an audacious certainty that the Pope would entertain his tale. What is perhaps most amazing about the whole episode is that Pope Clement VII did indeed take him seriously and sent him along with a letter of introduction to King João III of Portugal!

The arrival in Portugal of a guest of state who was an openly practicing Jew, decades after all Jews were supposed to have converted or left the country, caused an enormous tumult among the Portuguese *conversos*. They were certain that Reubeni was the harbinger of the Messiah, if not the Messiah himself. Many of them began to behave recklessly, allowing their Christian neighbors to see them performing Jewish rites and even crossing the Portuguese-Spanish border to reclaim property as the new era seemed to dawn. Reubeni played his role to the hilt. He went so far as to throw a Spanish priest out the window when the priest challenged Reubeni's purpose. It is not surprising that the Portuguese king, though he could not ignore an introduction from the Pope, took a dim view of these occurrences. He kept Reubeni cooling his heels for many months and ultimately dismissed him—that is, expelled him—without granting him anything.

Was Reubeni a mystic? Although there is only poor testimony that he might have had a hand in Kabbalah, he certainly conducted himself in the manner of a mystic. He fasted a great deal, prayed for long stretches, carried out secret symbolic ceremonies at important religious sites such as the Temple Mount and the Gates of Rome, and hinted at complex secret meanings to his activities.[18]

Among the *conversos* whose soul was set afire by the strange figure of Reubeni was a young secretary of the king named Diogo Pires. He went home at night and dreamed that God had destined him for a role in the unfolding messianic drama playing out before him in Portugal. When he came to Reubeni for instructions on how to proceed, the latter warned him not to do anything further that would anger the king and endanger David's mission. Pires, being a true mystical personality, interpreted this to mean that he must make himself a Jew and join the proceedings in that manner. Pires went home and circumcised himself. He awoke, euphoric, in a pool of blood. When he recovered from the operation, he took on a Jewish name—Solomon Molkho—and found secret passage out of the country. He went to the

Ottoman Empire and studied intensively for several years at the talmudic academies of Salonica and Constantinople.

Molkho must have been a very unusual person, with a brilliant mind and highly charismatic personality. As a *converso* born in Portugal around 1500, his previous knowledge of Judaism could not have been substantial. Within only a few years of beginning his studies, however, Molkho's knowledge of Torah, Talmud, and Kabbalah was so extensive and his oration so magnetic that people came from all over to learn from him. Several of his sermons and writings, which reflect the depth and grandeur of his ideas, have been preserved. Much of his thought deals allegorically with the *converso* condition and the redemption that will come to *conversos* and Jews with the messianic advent. Molkho's classical Christian education left its mark on his thought, along with his deep Jewish learning.

Now, as a baptized Iberian Christian who had openly reverted to Judaism, the last thing Molkho should want to do is return to Christian lands. If you have followed the pattern of Molkho's messianic personality, however, it will surprise you not at all that this is precisely what he did. He made his way to Ancona, Venice, and Rome, preaching and declaring the imminence of redemption. Rome, of course, was the lion's den for a heretical Catholic, but naturally, in addition to showing up in the city, Molkho sought out the Pope himself. If Reubeni's ability to achieve an audience with the Pope and gain his support seems almost miraculous, Molkho's success in becoming a favorite guest of the Pope is almost beyond comprehension.

Molkho so impressed Pope Clement with his personality, wisdom, and messianic mysticism that the Pope protected him from the Inquisition for an extended period. Eventually the Pope could no longer protect him, and Molkho was dragged out to be burned at the stake. As the smoke cleared later that day, a guest in the Pope's chambers was shocked to observe none other than Molkho himself, alive and well, walking around. The Pope—the spiritual leader of the entire Catholic Church—had saved a heretic by sending a ringer, now quite dead, to perish in his place!

In 1530 Reubeni and Molkho met up once again. It must have been an odd occasion. Reubeni had failed miserably on his mission and could hardly hold on to his dignity among the formerly enthusiastic Italian Jews. Molkho, once the self-conceived protégé of the Reubenite, was now a famous and respected figure. The details of precisely what transpired between the two messianists will probably never be known, but they did decide to carry out a joint expedition to visit the Holy Roman Emperor Charles V—probably the most powerful man on earth at that time. Charles was holding the imperial diet at Regensburg, and Reubeni and Molkho made their way to that place. The principal Jewish community representative at the diet, Josel of Rosheim, officially dissociated himself from the two voyagers and fled out of fear for the possible consequences of their visit. Though the emperor did receive them, they did not succeed in convincing Charles to convert to Judaism and support their campaign. Instead, the emperor had Molkho shipped off to Mantua, where he was really burned at the stake, and Reubeni sent to Spain, where he apparently died years later in an inquisitorial prison.[19] Thus ended one of the strangest, most public, and most mystical episodes in the history of Jewish messianism.

Safed and Italy

Among the scholars at the Salonica and Constantinople academies when Molkho arrived there were several important Kabbalists. One of the foremost among them was Rabbi Joseph Taitatzak, who had apparently been involved with the Responding Angel circle back in Spain. While any messianic proclivities are shrouded in his thought, he did bring the technique of exploiting heavenly mentors (*maggidim*) to his new home. One of those in the academy who would experience possession by a *maggid* throughout much of his life was the renowned legalist Rabbi Joseph Karo, author of the standard law code *Shulḥan Arukh*. Karo was deeply impressed by Solomon Molkho and his martyrdom, as well as by the mystical and magical ideas wielded by Molkho, Taitatzak, and other Iberian Kabbalists. Although earlier scholars have not described Karo as having any significant messianic doctrine, one recent author has made an extensive case for Karo's deep-seated messianism. There are certainly messianic traces in the writings of Karo's close associate, Rabbi Solomon Alkabetz, author of the classic Sabbath hymn *Lekhah Dodi*, and in the decision of Karo, Alkabetz, and others from their group to make *aliyah* to the Land of Israel in the 1530s.[20]

When the Karo group arrived in Palestine, a significant number of mystics had already assembled in Jerusalem. The presence of a rapacious Ottoman governor there, however, made living conditions superior in Safed in the north of the country, which is where Karo's company settled. Safed was also next to Meron, traditionally understood as the burial place of the 2nd-century Rabbi Shimon bar Yochai, purported author of the *Zohar*. A considerable group of Kabbalists as well as other Torah scholars gathered around the great Karo over the following decades, creating one of the most powerful spiritual enclaves in history.[21]

This amazing gathering of minds took on potent new dimensions with the arrival of Rabbi Isaac Luria Ashkenazi (called the AR"I) in Safed in 1569. Though he was a young man about thirty-six years of age at the time of his arrival and he died about two and a half years later, Luria's impact on both the Safed community and the entire Jewish world was immense. Luria was a brilliant Talmudist as well as an outstanding Kabbalist, but his greatest gifts were in the realms of imagination and charisma. Within a very short time of his arrival, some of the greatest mystics of Safed had placed themselves at his feet as students—most notably, the exceptional Rabbi Hayyim Vital Calabrese. The Kabbalah Luria taught was composed of powerful images about God, creation, the human soul, and redemption. Much of Luria's astounding originality centered on the construction of a highly detailed and mystically intricate myth around the seeds of ideas that were known from the Talmud or earlier Kabbalah.[22]

Gershom Scholem, the father of academic Kabbalah studies, taught that Luria was deeply messianic but in a manner that was sublimated within a theology of expulsion and redemption. The origins of this theology, according to Scholem, are to be found in the trauma of the Spanish expulsion, whose shock waves still influenced the Jewish world almost a century later. Though some have argued against Scholem, other contemporaries definitely felt that Luria himself was destined to be the Messiah.[23] Interestingly, it appears that Luria thought his student, Vital, would be the Messiah. These messianic tensions can be traced in the hagiographic work *In Praise of the AR"I* and in Vital's autobiography.[24] It is difficult to know how widespread such beliefs were, but Luria's astonishing learning and charisma made the idea seem plausible.

There is a tradition that the AR"I himself predicted the coming of the Messiah in 1575, a date that others had lighted upon as well. One of these was the famed Italian Kabbalist Mordecai Dato, who calculated that the numerical equivalent of the last two sentences of the prophetic Book of Daniel came to 5335, the Hebrew year corresponding to 1575. Dato adds other reasons for his prediction of 1575, and almost all his voluminous writings are suffused with the acute expectation of the messianic advent in that year. He was supported by the anonymous kabbalistic work *'Avodat ha-Kodesh* as well as calculations by others.[25] Although Dato was not especially influential, he was well known in his time, and his voice joined the chorus surrounding the AR"I and other messianic circles to create a dense atmosphere of mystical expectation in the early 1570s. It was all left unfulfilled.

Interlude: Some Scholarly Debates

During the ninety years between the 1575 expectation and the outbreak of the Sabbatean movement in 1665, few messianic pretenders appeared in the Jewish world. The messianic anticipation of the Luria era continued to smolder throughout the lifetime of Luria's protégé Vital, who died in 1620. Some minor figures turned up here and there, and a new wave of expectations began to build in the 1640s. This lull, however, seems like an appropriate moment to mention some historiographical debates about Jewish messianism in this period.

In a famous article titled "Messianic Postures of Ashkenazim and Sephardim," the chancellor of the Jewish Theological Seminary, Gerson Cohen, differentiated between the traditions of Ashkenazi Jews (those living in Germany, Northern France, and sometimes Northern Italy and Poland) and the traditions of Sephardi Jews (those of Spain, and, for his purposes, areas of the Middle East) with regard to messianic activity during the Middle Ages.[26] He says that during that period not only did the Ashkenazim not spawn messianic pretenders but their literature on messianism was "quiescent." Insofar as it appeared at all, it was prophetic and speculative in nature. The Sephardim and Middle Eastern Jews, on the other hand, experienced a multitude of public messianic calculations and active movements featuring messianic pretenders during the same period. While Cohen's argument purports to refer only to the Middle Ages, he does mention that the movements we have just discussed—Reubeni, Molkho, the Safed Kabbalists—as well as Shabbatai Zevi in the 17th century, were all focused in the Sephardic world.

Against Cohen's thesis, Elisheva Carlebach of Columbia University has pointed out that the phenomena counted by Cohen as being of a messianic nature are unduly limited. For example, collective migrations to the Holy Land have usually had messianic causes, even when the sources do not mention them. In the Middle Ages there were at least two such migrations from Ashkenazi lands, one from Germany in 1210–11 and another from Northern Italy in the early 14th century. The corpus of writings from which Cohen draws information about Jewish messianism is also quite narrow. In particular, Christian sources often tell us about movements that go unmentioned or barely reported in the Jewish sources. One reason for this is that Christians antagonized Jews by pointing out the failed messiahs whom the Jews chose over Jesus. Ashkenazi authors, not wishing to supply their enemies with ammunition, tended to be much more reticent in their recollection of such movements. At least one event in Ashkenaz is recounted through Sephardic sources. Even the categories "Ashkenaz" and "Sepharad" are too facile and must not be so simply divided. For example, Northern Italy, where the Ashkenazi Asher Laemmlein appeared, was home to Ashkenazim, Sephardim, and native Italiani Jews. Many other messianic movements and agitations that do not fall into Cohen's categories occurred in Italy in earlier centuries.[27]

Gershom Scholem also had a grand theory about Jewish messianism after the expulsion from Spain which has been quite controversial. He suggested that the shock of the Spanish expulsion caused a wave of messianic response, which included the writings of Abarbanel and ha-Levi, as well as the movements of Reubeni and Molkho. He also said that it was this ordeal that fused Kabbalah and messianism together for centuries to come.

Scholem points out that, before the period of the expulsion, "the mystical meditations of the Kabbalists on theogony [the origins of God] and cosmogony [the origins of the cosmos] . . . produced a non-Messianic and individualistic mode of redemption or salvation."[28] In other words, before the expulsion, Kabbalah was focused on the individual mystic's experience, not on the national or universal redemption ushered in by the Messiah. The Kabbalists may have thought that their work on the cosmic repair of the spiritual universe would bring redemption to the world, but not in an apocalyptic messianic fashion. But "after the Exodus from Spain," Scholem explains, "Kabbalism underwent a complete transformation. A catastrophe of this dimension, which uprooted one of the main branches of the Jewish people, could hardly take place without affecting every sphere of Jewish life and feeling."[29] Scholem points out various ways that Kabbalah was changed by the expulsion, among which was the Kabbalists' idea of redemption and messianism:

> After the catastrophe of the Spanish Expulsion . . . it also became possible to consider the return to the starting-point of creation [for which the Kabbalists strive] as the means of precipitating the final world-catastrophe, which would come to pass when that return had been achieved by many individuals united in a desire for "the End" of the world. A great emotional upheaval having taken place, the individual mystic's absorption could have been transformed, by a kind of mystical dialectics, into the religious aspiration of the whole community.[30]

In other words, the expulsion from Spain, according to Scholem, caused the Kabbalists to look outside themselves and their personal mystical experience, and see their work as something that could effect an apocalyptic shift in history. Their spiritual power could induce a catastrophe that would precipitate the messianic advent. In this way, the expulsion caused the Kabbalah to become fused with messianism.

When the Messiah failed to manifest himself in the generation following the expulsion, in Scholem's view, the impulse to search out the redemptive process went underground, as it were. It resurfaced half a century later in the form of Luria's Kabbalah, with its emphasis on the themes of exile and redemption. "The concrete effects and consequences of the catastrophe of 1492 were by no means confined to the Jews then living. As a matter of fact, the historic process set in place by the expulsion from Spain required several generations—almost an entire century—to work itself out completely."[31]

The themes of exile and redemption, and the myths in which they are embedded, reappear and provide the symbolic underpinning of the Sabbatean movement, which appeared in 1665–66. According to Scholem, Sabbateanism took Jewish messianic impulses to their ultimate consummation, rupturing the fabric of Jewish legal and communal boundaries and catapulting the Jewish world into the antinomian frontiers of modernity.[32]

Though many scholars have criticized pieces of the argument, Moshe Idel has been the main critic of this great theoretical framework. He points out that the first great messianic movement after the expulsion was led by an Ashkenazi Jew, Asher Laemmlein, who was based in Italy and despised Sephardim, so this could hardly be a response to the expulsion. Moreover, Ha-Levi, Reubeni, and Molkho were all active more than thirty years after the expulsion, so this, too, does not appear to reflect a direct response. The idea that Luria—who was an Ashkenazi Jew—was responding to the Spanish expulsion more than three-quarters of a century after the event is extremely unlikely. Idel points out that Scholem's own interpretation of Luria's central myth as a tale of divine exile is speculative and not necessarily correct. In addition, Idel brings evidence that few people were familiar with the details of Lurianic Kabbalah at the time Shabbatai Zevi appeared, nor was Shabbatai himself a Lurianic Kabbalist. The details of both Scholem's theory and Idel's critique enter a complex world of kabbalistic interpretation which we will leave aside, but both have been highly influential in the study of Jewish history and thought.[33]

Scholem's work has raised other historiographical questions about messianism. One is whether crisis is indeed the regular trigger for messianic movements. Scholars have pointed out, for example, that the Crusades appear to have brought on only minor messianic episodes, whereas the enormous Sabbatean movement came at a relatively calm time for many Jewish communities. Another question has to do with the insularity of Jewish messianism. Scholem's picture suggests that there is an internal logic and impetus to the series of messianic agitations from 1492 until 1666, and that outside forces—with the exception of cataclysms such as the Spanish expulsion—had little or no effect on those events. Others, such as David Ruderman, have shown that Jews, Christians, and Muslims were constantly looking across at one another and at the great world events for signs and portents concerning their own messianic scenarios.[34] These debates, of course, have implications that go far beyond Jewish history and thought or the messianic context.[35]

Finally, Idel has pointed out repeatedly that Scholem is interested almost exclusively in apocalyptic messianism—that is, the kind of messianic thought or movement that involves a disruption of the entire world order, physical and spiritual. Idel thinks that much messianism, especially mystical messianism, does not involve rupture or revolution. This argument speaks to the very definition of messianism in any culture.

The Sabbatean Outbreak

Several messianically charged events occurred during the 1640s and 1650s that shook the Jewish world. Some rabbis had predicted the messianic advent in 1648, but instead, a disaster occurred in the Jewish world that year. The Ukrainian uprising of Bogdan Chmielnicki swept across Poland, and many thousands of Jews were murdered by the rampaging Cossacks. Tens, if not hundreds, of thousands of Polish Jews were left dead, destitute, or displaced, their lives ruined. Meanwhile, in Western Europe, messianic and Millenarian agitation continued among both Christians and Jews. Much of this anticipation of the messianic advent was happening in England, the Low Countries, and Germany. One of the most significant developments was the appearance of a book by the Amsterdam rabbi Manasseh ben Israel, reporting that some of the Lost Tribes had been discovered in South America. Manasseh speculated about the significance of this finding, coupled with other news of the Lost Tribes from diverse parts of the world. One thing was certain for Manasseh: this was a portent of the coming redemption. His book caused a wave of excitement among Christian Millenarians, who were certain of the same thing, though their scenario involved a Second Coming whereas his involved a first appearance of the Messiah.[36]

Far away from this Jewish-Christian commotion, in the Turkish port city of Izmir, the stirrings of what would soon become the largest Jewish messianic movement since Christianity were afoot. In 1648, a young yeshiva student named Shabbatai Zevi had told a small group of his friends that he believed he was the Messiah. A few listened, but nothing further came of this brief incident for another seventeen years. Shabbatai, meanwhile, started showing symptoms of a bipolar personality that landed him in trouble. Between 1651 and 1654, for reasons unknown but probably connected to the strange things he did in his euphoric states, he was expelled from Izmir. He made his way to Salonica, the great center of Jewish life in the Ottoman Empire, where his ordinarily dignified character and scholarship in Talmud and Kabbalah won him friends. His ecstasies again brought trouble upon him, however, and he was expelled from Salonica for performing some extremely odd ceremonies in public—an early example of the "strange deeds" that would become a hallmark of his persona. The scandals in Izmir and Salonica were repeated in Constantinople in 1658, where Shabbatai remained for about eight months before being expelled. He declared at that time that God had vouchsafed to him a new Torah for the messianic era, an extremely dangerous proposition in the eyes of Jewish communal leaders.

Shabbatai briefly returned to Izmir in 1662, then wandered more in the Ottoman Jewish communities. He stayed for a time in Egypt, where he was apparently in a relatively stable state of mind. He was befriended by the head of the community, Raphael Joseph Chelebi, who was impressed with him. Shabbatai proceeded to Jerusalem, where he lived for about a year before the community dispatched him back to Egypt, in 1664, to raise money. There he married Sarah, a Polish refugee of dubious reputation who had been telling everyone that she was destined to marry the Messiah. Around this time there was excitement at the Chelebi's court about a prophet and spiritual healer named Nathan Ashkenazi, who had appeared in the city of Gaza. Nathan, all of twenty-two years of age at the time, was already renowned in the Land of Israel and in Egypt for his brilliant mastery of Kabbalah, his ability to help those whose spirits were troubled, and his prophetic powers. Shabbatai rushed to see him, certain that Nathan would help him overcome the demons that haunted his heart. Instead, Nathan told Shabbatai that he was indeed the Messiah.

The two spent several weeks together discussing this situation; apparently Shabbatai needed to be convinced to manifest himself in this role. In the spring of 1665, at the Shavuot holiday, Nathan experienced a prophetic possession by a heavenly messenger and announced publicly that Shabbatai Zevi was the Messiah. The combination of the dramatic prophecy and the high esteem in which Nathan and Shabbatai were held gave the first impetus to the movement. The rabbis present that Shavuot night took this event seriously and reported it to others. Because these rabbis were highly respected in their circles, the news spread rapidly: the Messiah had appeared in the Land of Israel. Nathan experienced other prophecies, and soon he wrote a letter to Raphael Chelebi in Egypt describing Shabbatai's messianic design in detail. Nathan's letter was replete with references to both the classical zoharic Kabbalah and the Kabbalah of Rabbi Isaac Luria.

While Nathan stayed in Gaza and wrote, Shabbatai and several of the rabbis who had been present on Shavuot night went on the road to Safed, Aleppo, and Izmir. Everywhere they went, waves of excitement broke out and gripped the communities. In many places Jews of all descriptions fell into prophetic ecstasies and convulsions, testifying about Shabbatai's exalted calling. These fits were highly dramatic and sometimes incorporated physical or mental feats that seemed impossible in the course of nature. Letters were dispatched around the Jewish world about Shabbatai and the miraculous prophecies surrounding the Messiah's revelation. Reports of the reappearance of the Ten Lost Tribes were often appended to these letters.

Shabbatai, for his part, made his way from Izmir to Constantinople (Istanbul), the capital of the Ottoman Empire, where the Jews expected him to appropriate the reins of government from the sultan and commence their redemption. This, of course, would include retribution on the Jews' enemies, regathering the Lost Tribes, and rebuilding the Temple in Jerusalem. Shabbatai's arrival in Constantinople was anticipated by the Turkish authorities, and he was brought in as a prisoner in February 1666. The Great Vizier, Ahmed Koprülü, sentenced Shabbatai to prison for rebellion and causing agitation in the Jewish community. When his cell in Constantinople turned into a pilgrimage center for throngs of expectant Jews from all over, he was moved to a prison in Gallipoli. This, however, did little to alleviate the situation. The Jews had Messiah fever, and it was a small matter to pay off the guards and turn the Gallipoli fortress into a reception center for Shabbatai's admirers. Believers around the Jewish world waited with baited breath for Shabbatai to manifest himself and usher in the messianic era. The voices of opposition to Shabbatai found themselves fighting a losing battle.

Eventually, Nehemiah Kohen, a competing messianic pretender from Poland, blew the whistle on Shabbatai, who was hauled up before the vizier's court once again. The commotion, disturbance to trade, and purported threat to the sultan's authority had reached the ears of the sultan, who took a personal interest in the matter. When Shabbatai was threatened with execution for his sedition, an apostate Jew in the royal service told him that he might save himself by converting to Islam. This is what he did. The sultan excused Shabbatai and gave him a government stipend.[37]

Sabbateanism after Shabbatai's Apostasy

Responses to the apostasy took two main directions. The vast majority of Jews, once they had become convinced that the news was true, dejectedly returned to their former lives, ridiculed by their Christian and Muslim neighbors for their credulity. Communal leaders declared Sabbatean theology to be heretical and hazardous to Torah values. A surprising number of Jews, however, continued to believe that Shabbatai had converted as a sort of kabbalistic mission into the realms of evil, and he would soon return from this temporary state to rule the world as the Jewish redeemer. Support for this position was provided in complex works of kabbalistic Sabbatean theology by Nathan of Gaza and Abraham Miguel Cardozo, the two main theologians of the movement. The "believers" found each other and joined in groups despite the official Jewish community's condemnation of Shabbatai and everything connected with him. While the rabbis in one town were issuing excommunications and bans against the Sabbateans, the rabbi of a nearby town might himself be an unapologetic believer.[38]

As the years passed, the believers were forced into more secrecy. Certain towns, including Adrianople (Edirne), Salonica, Kastoria, Livorno, and Modena, became centers of underground Sabbateanism. Often the focus of Sabbatean faith was the home of a Sabbatean leader or theologian, such as Nathan or Cardoso. In Modena it was the study hall of Rabbi Abraham Rovigo, where a series of faithful visionaries, dreamers, and prophets poured out their revelations. These were duly recorded and passed along to a network of believers that extended from Poland to Greece and sometimes beyond. Cells of Sabbatean believers were active in the Netherlands, England, Morocco, Yemen, Libya, and elsewhere, sometimes well into the 18th century. The movement would flare up anew when Nathan, Cardozo, or a Sabbatean adventurer like Nehemiah Hiyya Hayon (1655–ca. 1730) would appear in a community. Around 1700 there was even a mass movement of Sabbateans and their adherents to the Land of Israel in anticipation of Shabbatai's reappearance.[39]

As the believers increasingly took on the disposition of a clandestine sect, they became known for certain qualities. One of these was secrecy and duplicity. Nathan assured the believers that the situation warranted lying and keeping the faith underground in the face of persecution. Shabbatai himself created a hybrid secret identity as a Muslim who still believed in some sense in his own messianic identity rooted in Judaism.[40] Another quality of the group was ritualized antinomianism, that is, the deliberate transgression of

Jewish law in a ceremonial manner, intended not for enjoyment, but to show faith in Shabbatai's new Torah of the messianic age. These practices were inspired largely by Shabbatai's own "strange actions." Some Sabbatean groups were even accused of holding orgies and transgressing other moral laws of Judaism—a charge which may not be fully without basis. Several important rabbis lashed out against the widespread study of Kabbalah, which they held partly responsible for the Sabbatean debacle. Some recent scholars, however, have noted that Sabbateanism actually served to *spread* the study of Kabbalah, which had been much more limited before 1665.[41]

Nathan died in 1673, still trying to explain why the Messiah had failed to manifest himself on any of the dates that Nathan had predicted. Shabbatai died in 1676, never having entirely reconciled his Jewish, Muslim, and messianic personas. One might think that this would put an end to the movement but, once again, the kabbalistic theology of the faith kept it alive. In the world of mysticism death is nothing more than a surface appearance, and thousands continued to believe that Shabbatai's apparent physical departure was a mere chimera designed to fool those of weak faith into abandoning him.

The kabbalistic writings of Nathan, Cardozo, and other Sabbatean thinkers were so sophisticated and profound that they continued to be read, even by rabbis who had no interest in Sabbateanism.[42] This trend was aided by the fact that the Sabbateans often couched their messianic faith in kabbalistically coded terms that outsiders would not recognize. It thus became difficult to convince people—even rabbinic scholars—that a Sabbatean tract really was heretical and sectarian. The most famous example of this is the commentary on Jewish festivals called *Ḥemdat Yamim*, a Sabbatean-influenced work that is still used widely today. The most notable example of a non-Sabbatean reader of Sabbatean theology is Rabbi Moses Hayim Luzzatto (1707–1747), one of the most influential Jewish authors of the 18th century. Luzzatto was a controversial figure, and other forms of messianism were brewing in his own circle—but he was apparently not a Sabbatean believer.[43]

In addition to the Sabbateans who stayed within the Jewish community, two other groups appeared that ultimately led believers out of Judaism altogether. Although these movements take us beyond the period under consideration here, they belong to the aftermath of Sabbateanism and thus may not be ignored altogether.

The first of these was the Dönme, a group of followers, mainly in Adrianople and Salonica, who chose to follow Shabbatai into Islam. The Dönme created their own hybrid Sabbatean-Muslim identity which has lasted until today, though the Dönme communities are no longer truly coherent. These groups sought out leaders from among Shabbatai's closest followers and relatives, particularly his brother-in-law, Jacob Philosoph (known as Querido), whom many believed to be a reincarnation of Shabbatai. Ultimately the Dönme split into three groups, all of which practiced Islam in public and performed secret Sabbatean rituals until the early 20th century.[44]

The second of the Sabbatean groups that ultimately left Judaism, at least in part, was the Frankists, followers of the Polish-born, Turkish-trained leader Jacob Frank (1726–1791). Frank began as an undistinguished frontier guide and wagon driver in the regions of southern Poland that bordered the Ottoman Empire. He probably encountered Sabbateans in his youth, and as a young man he traveled to Salonica where he met the Dönme leaders. Possessed of boundless self-confidence, bravado, physical strength, and charisma, Frank returned to Poland and gathered many believers, especially those of less distinction and education. He was in direct competition with other figures (especially from the Eibeschütz family) who were attempting to impose their own leadership on this group. Frank referred to himself as "The Third," implying a succession in which Shabbatai was the first and Jacob Querido the second. Frank gloried in the persona of a *prostak*, an ignoramus who is nevertheless more clever and quick-witted than those of fine education. His writings suggest, in fact, that he knew quite a bit of the Jewish tradition. Frank's group eventually split in half, as some converted to Catholicism (again, like the Dönme, maintaining their Sabbatean faith) and the rest remained Frankist Jews. Frankism survived into the early 19th century under the leadership of Frank's daughter, Eva, but was thereafter formally disbanded.[45]

Conclusion

Jewish messianism was associated with Kabbalah from the high Middle Ages through the beginnings of modernity. A number of major movements formed around messianic pretenders during this period, each with its unique kabbalistic or mystical proclivities. This period also saw a number of moments of messianic excitement when no Messiah figure was forthcoming. These cycles of messianic enthusiasm parallel similar waves in the Christian and Muslim worlds, sometimes in tandem and sometimes in disparate peaks and valleys. Messianism played an important role in both the spiritual life of Jews and in their daily existence. They constantly hoped and prayed for redemption from their painful lot in life, expecting the Messiah to appear any day. When the Messiah did appear, as happened on so many occasions, he often departed leaving his people more spiritually bereft than before. The revolutionary condition of messianic times opened the door for radical shifts in Jewish thought and behavior which often threatened the established leadership. The most extreme case of radical behavior occurred in the Sabbatean movement, and the great scholar of that movement, Gershom Scholem, saw in it the rupture that led to Jewish modernity. Although tracing the Jewish Enlightenment (*Haskalah*) back to the Sabbatean movement has proved very controversial, the messianic impact on the Hasidic movement is now widely accepted by scholars.[46]

NOTES

1. See Harris Lenowitz, *The Jewish Messiahs, From the Galilee to Crown Heights* (Oxford: Oxford University Press, 1998), pp. 9–14; Raphael Patai, *The Messiah Texts* (New York: Avon, 1979); William Horbury, *Jewish Messianism and the Cult of Christ* (London: SCM Press, 1998), chap. 1; Sigmund Mowinckel, *He That Cometh: The Messiah Concept in the Old Testament and Later Judaism* (New York: Abingdon, 1954), pt. 1.

2. See Lenowitz, *Jewish Messiahs*, chap. 2; Horbury, *Jewish Messianism*, chaps. 2–4; Mowinckel, *He That Cometh*, pt. 2; Marc Saperstein, ed., *Essential Papers on Messianic Movements and Personalities in Jewish History* (New York: New York University Press, 1992), sec. 2.

3. See Lenowitz, *Jewish Messiahs*, chap. 3–4; Saperstein, *Essential Papers*, secs. 3–5.

4. See chapter 3 in this volume; Moshe Idel, *Messianic Mystics* (New Haven: Yale University Press, 1998), chaps. 2–3; Elliot Wolfson, *Abraham Abulafia: Kabbalist and Prophet* (Los Angeles: Cherub, 2000); and Gershom Scholem, *Major Trends in Jewish Mysticism* (New York: Schocken Books, 1941), Fourth Lecture.

5. Scholem, *Major Trends*, Fifth and Sixth Lectures; Yehuda Liebes, *Studies in the Zohar* (New York: State University of New York Press, 1993), chap. 1.

6. See, e.g., Nancy Bisaha, *Creating East and West: Renaissance Humanists and the Ottoman Turks* (Philadelphia: University of Pennsylvania Press, 2004), chap. 4; Cornell Fleischer, "Shadows of Shadows: Prophecy in Politics in 1530s Istanbul," *International Journal of Political Economy* 13, no. 1–2 (2007): 51–62; idem, "The Lawgiver as Messiah: The Making of the Imperial Image in the Reign of Süleymân," in *Soliman le magnifique et son temps/Süleymân the Magnificent and His Time*, ed. G. Veinstein (Paris: École du Louvre et École des Hautes Études en Schiences Sociales, 1990), pp. 157–77.

7. Aaron Z. Aescoly, *Jewish Messianic Movements: Sources and Documents on Messianism in Jewish History from the Bar Kokhba Revolt until Recent Times* [in Hebrew], 2nd ed. (Jerusalem: Bialik Institute, 1987), p. 339.

8. Aescoly, *Messianic Movements*, pp. 317, 341–43.

9. Material for this paragraph is drawn from ibid., pp. 305–56.

10. Aescoly, *Messianic Movements*, pp. 318–19.

11. Ibid., pp. 126–32; Aescoly, "Inquiries into the Doctrine of *Sefer ha-Meshiv*" [in Hebrew], *Sefunot* 2, no. 17 (1983): 185–266.

12. See Idel, *Messianic Mystics*, pp. 138–39.

13. On Abarbanel, see Abba Hillel Silver, *A History of Messianic Speculation in Israel,* 2nd ed. (Gloucester, MA: Peter Smith, 1978), pp. 116–30, esp. p. 125; Benzion Netanyahu, *Don Isaac Abravanel: Statesman and Philosopher,* 3rd ed. (Philadelphia: Jewish Publication Society, 1953), pt. 2, chap. 4; Eric Lawee, "The Messianism of Isaac Abarbanel, 'Father of the [Jewish] Messianic Movements of the Sixteenth and Seventeenth Centuries,'" in *Millenarianism and Messianism in Early Modern European Culture,* Vol. 1, *Jewish Messianism in the Early Modern World,* ed. M. Goldish and R. H. Popkin (Dordrecht: Kluwer, 2001), pp. 1–39.

14. See Scholem, *Major Trends,* beginning of Seventh Lecture; Silver, *History of Messianic Speculation,* pp. 110–16, 130–33; Ira Robinson, "Two Letters of Abraham ben Eliezer ha-Levi," in *Studies in Medieval Jewish History and Literature,* ed. I. Twersky (Cambridge, MA: Harvard University Press, 1984), 2:403–22; Isaiah Tishby, *Messianism in the Time of the Expulsion from Spain and Portugal* [in Hebrew] (Jerusalem: Shazar Center, 1985); Saperstein, *Essential Papers,* chap. 11 (translates part of Tishby's Hebrew work); Idel, *Messianic Mystics,* pp. 132–44. Idel states that neither Abarbanel nor the author of Tishby's genizah pages was a Kabbalist. This does not mean, however, that they were not mystics of any type, nor do all scholars agree with Idel.

15. See Haim Beinart, *Chapters in Judeo-Spanish History* (Jerusalem: Magnes, 1998), pp. 500–765; Renée Levine Melammed, *Heretics or Daughters of Israel? The Crypto-Jewish Women of Castile* (Oxford: Oxford University Press, 1999) chap. 3; Lenowitz, *Jewish Messiahs,* pp. 97–99, 101–102; Matt Goldish, "Patterns in Converso Messianism," in idem, *Jewish Messianism in the Early Modern World,* pp. 41–63.

16. See Idel, *Messianic Mystics,* pp. 140–42; Lenowitz, *Jewish Messiahs,* pp. 99–101; Ephraim Kupfer, "The Visions of Rabbi Asher ben Me'ir Known as Laemmlein Reulingen" [in Hebrew], *Koveṣ al Yad* (n.s.) 8 (1976): 385–423.

17. See note 7 above, and David Ruderman, "Hope Against Hope: Jewish and Christian Messianic Expectations in the Late Middle Ages," in *Exile and Diaspora: Studies in the History of the Jewish People Presented to Haim Beinart,* ed. A. Mirsky, A. Grossman, and Y. Kaplan (Jerusalem: Ben-Zvi Institute, 1991), pp. 185–202; reprinted in D. Ruderman, ed., *Essential Papers on Jewish Culture in Renaissance and Baroque Italy* (New York: New York University Press, 1992), pp. 299–323; Moshe Idel, "Introduction," in Aescoly, *Messianic Movements,* pp. 13–14; Hayim Hillel Ben-Sasson, "The Reformation in Contemporary Jewish Eyes," *Proceedings of the Israel Academy of Sciences and Humanities* 4 (1971): 239–326; Geoffrey Parker, "The Place of Tudor England in the Messianic Vision of Philip II of Spain," *Transactions of the Royal Historical Society* (6th series) 12 (2002): 167–221.

18. On this point see the testimonies of eyewitnesses, especially Giambattista Ramussio, in Aescoly, *Messianic Movements,* p. 405.

19. On Reubeni and Molkho, see *The Story of David Reubeni* [in Hebrew], ed. A. Z. Aescoly, 2nd ed., with introductions by Moshe Idel and Elias Lipiner (Jerusalem: Bialik Institute, 1993); Aescoly, *Messianic Movements,* 357–434; Lenowitz, *Jewish Messiahs,* chap. 5; Idel, *Messianic Mystics,* pp. 144–52; Rivka Schatz-Uffenheimer, *The Messianic Idea from the Expulsion from Spain* [in Hebrew] (Jerusalem: Magnes, 2005), chap. 2.

20. See R. J. Z. Werblowsky, *Joseph Karo: Lawyer and Mystic,* rev. ed. (Philadelphia: Jewish Publication Society of America, 1977); Mor Altshuler, "'Revealing the Secret of His Wives': R. Joseph Karo's Concept of Reincarnation and Mystical Conception," *Frankfurter Judaistische Beiträge* 31 (2004): 91–104; idem, "Prophecy and Maggidism in the Life and Writings of R. Joseph Karo," *Frankfurter Judaistische Beiträge* 33 (2006): 81–110.

21. See Werblowsky, *Joseph Karo*, chap. 4; Solomon Schechter, "Safed in the Sixteenth Century: A City of Legists and Mystics," in idem, *Studies In Judaism,* 2nd series (Philadelphia: Jewish Publication Society, 1908), pp. 202–306; Meir Benayahu, *Yosef Behiri* [in Hebrew] (Jerusalem: Yad ha-Rav Nissim, 1991).

22. See Scholem, *Major Trends,* Seventh Lecture; Lenowitz, *Jewish Messiahs,* chap. 6; Idel, *Messianic Mystics,* pp. 162–82; Lawrence Fine, *Physician of the Soul, Healer of the Cosmos: Isaac Luria and His Kabbalistic Fellowship* (Stanford: Stanford University Press, 2003); and idem, *Jerusalem Studies in Jewish Thought* [in Hebrew] 10 (1992), which is dedicated to Lurianic Kabbalah.

23. See the sources in the previous note.

24. See M. Benayahu, ed., *Sefer Toledot ha-Ar"i* [in Hebrew] (Jerusalem: Ben-Zvi Institute and the Hebrew University, 1967); A. Klein and J. Machlowitz Klein, eds., *Tales in Praise of the Ar"i* (Philadelphia: Jewish Publication Society, 1970); M. Faierstein, ed. and trans., *Jewish Mystical Autobiographies* (New York: Paulist Press, 1999), pp. 3–263 (Book of Visions of Rabbi Hayim Vital); Harris H. Lenowitz, "A Spirit Possession Tale as an Account of the Equivocal Insertion of Rabbi Hayyim Vital into the Role of Messiah," in *Spirit Possession in Judaism: Cases and Contexts from the Middle Ages to the Present,* ed. M. Goldish (Detroit: Wayne State University Press, 2003), pp. 197–212.

25. See Yoram Jacobson, *Along the Paths of Exile and Redemption: The Doctrine of Redemption of Rabbi Mordecai Dato* [in Hebrew] (Jerusalem: Bialik Institute, 1996); Silver, *History of Messianic Speculation,* pp. 135–38; David Tamar, "Expectations for the Year of Redemption in 335 [1575] in Italy" [in Hebrew], in idem, *Studies in the History of the Jewish People in Eretz Israel and in Italy* (Jerusalem: Rubin Mass, 1986); Idel, *Messianic Mystics,* p. 169.

26. Gerson Cohen, "Messianic Postures of Ashkenazim and Sephardim," *Leo Baeck Memorial Lecture* (New York: Leo Baeck Institute, 1967); reprinted in idem, *Studies in the Variety of Rabbinic Cultures* (Philadelphia: Jewish Publication Society, 1991), pp. 271–98, and in Saperstein, *Essential Papers,* pp. 202–33.

27. Elisheva Carlebach, "Between History and Hope: Jewish Messianism in Ashkenaz and Sepharad," *Annual Lecture of the Victor J. Selmanowitz Chair of Jewish History* (New York: Touro College, 1998).

28. Scholem, *Major Trends,* p. 245

29. Ibid, p. 244.

30. Ibid, pp. 245–46.

31. Ibid, p. 246.

32. Ibid., pp. 244–51; Scholem, "Redemption Through Sin," in idem, *The Messianic Idea in Judaism* (New York: Schocken Books, 1971), pp. 71–141 and passim.

33. Moshe Idel, "Religion, Thought, and Attitudes: The Impact of the Expulsion on the Jews," in *Spain and the Jews,* ed. E. Kedourie (London: Thames and Hudson, 1992), pp. 123–39; idem, "Introduction," in Aescoly, *Messianic Movements*; idem, "'One from a Town, Two from a Clan': The Diffusion of Lurianic Kabbala and Sabbateanism—A Re-examination," *Jewish History* 7, no. 2 (1993): 79–104; idem, *Messianic Mystics,* chaps. 4–6.

34. Ruderman, "Hope Against Hope."

35. Idel, *Messianic Mystics*, chap. 1; Ruderman, "Hope Against Hope"; Lenowitz, *Jewish Messiahs*, pp. 5–9; Matt Goldish, *The Sabbatean Prophets* (Cambridge, MA: Harvard University Press, 2004), prologue and chapters 1–2.

36. David S. Katz, *Philosemitism and the Readmission of the Jews to England, 1603–1655* (Oxford: Clarendon, 1982); Lucien Wolf, *Menasseh Ben-Israel's Mission to Oliver Cromwell* (London: Macmillan, 1901); Goldish, *Sabbatean Prophets*, chap. 1; Jacob Barnai, *Sabbateanism—Social Perspectives* [in Hebrew] (Jerusalem: Shazar Center, 2000), chap. 1.

37. All this is laid out in astonishing detail in Gershom Scholem, *Sabbatai Sevi: The Mystical Messiah* (Princeton, NJ: Princeton University Press, 1973), chaps. 1–6. See also David Halperin, *Sabbatai Zevi: Testimonies to a Fallen Messiah* (Oxford: Littman Library, 2007); Idel, *Messianic Mystics*, chap. 6; Barnay, *Sabbateanism, Social Perspectives* (Jerusalem: Zalman Shazar Center for the History of Israel, 2000); Goldish, *Sabbatean Prophets*; and, on Shabbatai's conversion to Islam, Marc David Baer, *Honored by the Glory of Islam: Conversion and Conquest in Ottoman Europe* (Oxford: Oxford University Press, 2008), chap. 6.

38. See Scholem, *Sabbatai Sevi*, chaps. 7–8; David J. Halperin, ed. and trans., *Abraham Miguel Cardozo: Selected Writings* (New York: Paulist Press, 2001); Chaim Wirszubski, *Between the Lines: Kabbalah, Christian Kabbalah, and Sabbatianism* [in Hebrew] (Jerusalem: Magnes, 1990), sec. 3; Isaiah Tishby, *Studies in Kabbalah and Its Branches*, vol. 2 (Jerusalem: Magnes, 1993), sec. 3; Yehuda Liebes, *On Sabbateanism and Its Kabbalah: Collected Essays* [in Hebrew] (Jerusalem: Bialik Institute, 1995).

39. See Scholem, *Sabbatai Sevi*, chaps. 7–8; idem, *Studies and Texts concerning the History of Sabbetianism and Its Metamorphoses* [in Hebrew] (Jerusalem: Bialik Institute, 1982); idem, *Researches in Sabbateanism* [in Hebrew], ed. Y. Liebes (Tel-Aviv: Am Oved, 1991), chaps. 3–7; *Sefunot* 3–4 (1961), and all the work of Meir Benayahu in *Sefunot* 14 (1971–77); *The Sabbatian Movement and Its Aftermath: Messianism, Sabbatianism and Frankism*, vols. 1–2 (Hebrew and English; = *Jerusalem Studies in Jewish Thought* vols., 16–17 (Jerusalem: Hebrew University, 2001); *Kabbalah* 8 (2003); Bezalel Naor, *Post-Sabbatian Sabbatianism* (Spring Valley, NY: Orot, 1999).

40. Liebes, *On Sabbateanism*; idem, *Studies in Jewish Myth*, chaps. 2–5; Avraham Elqayam, "'Bury My Faith,' A Letter from Shabbatai Zevi in Exile" [in Hebrew] *Pe'amim* 55 (1993): 4–37.

41. See Idel, "'One from a Town'"; Zeev Gries, *The Book in the Jewish World, 1700–1900* (Oxford: Littman Library, 2007), chaps. 4–6 and passim.

42. See Isaiah Tishby, *Messianic Mysticism: Moses Hayim Luzzatto and the Padua School*, trans. M. Hoffman (Oxford: Littman Library, 2008) chaps. 4–5. Maoz Kahana spoke on this topic at the Fifteenth World Congress of Jewish Studies (Jerusalem, August 2009), and I believe he is preparing to publish his work.

43. Isaiah Tishby, *Paths of Faith and Heresy* (Hebrew; Jerusalem: Magnes, 1982); idem, *Messianic Mysticism*; Liebes, *On Sabbateanism*, chaps. 5–8; Elisheva Carlebach, *The Pursuit of Heresy: Rabbi Moses Hagiz and the Sabbatian Controversies* (New York: Columbia University Press, 1990).

44. Scholem, *Messianic Idea*; Marc David Baer, *The Dönme: Jewish Converts, Muslim Revolutionaries, and Secular Turks* (Stanford: Stanford University Press, 2010); *Kabbalah* 8 (2003).

45. Scholem, *The Messianic Idea*; H. Levine, ed. and trans., *The Kronika—On Jacob Frank and the Frankist Movement* (Jerusalem: Israel Academy of Sciences and Humanities, 1984); *Kabbalah* 9 (2003); Lenowitz, *Jewish Messiahs*, chap. 8. H. Lenowitz has also published a series of articles on Frankism and uploaded a complete translation of the "Sayings of the Lord," the most important Frankist document, on the Internet at http://www.languages. utah.edu/kabbalah/protected/dicta_frank_lenowitz.pdf.

46. See Scholem, *Major Trends*, Ninth Lecture; Idel, *Messianic Mystics*, chap. 7; Mor Altshuler, *The Messianic Secret of Hasidism* (Leiden: Brill, 2006); Liebes, On Sabbateanism, chaps. 11–12.

6

Hasidism

Mystical and Nonmystical Approaches
to Interpreting Scripture

SHAUL MAGID

The history and literature of Hasidism are two of the most extensively researched areas of Jewish mysticism. Historians, sociologists, anthropologists, psychologists of religion, ethnographers, and theologians have
examined Hasidism as a Marxist critique of rabbinic culture; a rereading of
classical Kabbalah; a form of Jewish revivalism; a conservative response to,
and extension and normalization of, Sabbateanism; a mystical psychology;
and a source for modern existential philosophy.[1]

From the beginning, scholarship on Hasidism has been divided into two
basic camps. Gershom Scholem examined Hasidism as a branch of Jewish
mysticism even as Martin Buber, one of the most prominent earlier examin-
ers of Hasidism in the first decades of the 20th century, tried to downplay
the mystical elements in Hasidism by suggesting that it is better described
as a form of religious existentialism. Scholem's chapter on Hasidism in his
seminal *Major Trends in Jewish Mysticism* ("The Latest Phase") is indicative
of his general approach. Calling Hasidism a "mystical psychology," Scholem
claimed that although it is based on the Jewish mystical tradition it did not
add anything new to the history of Kabbalah. Other scholars have weighed
in, all claiming in one way or another (mostly contra Buber) that Hasidism
does constitute a form of Jewish mysticism although its relationship to classical Kabbalah is a more vexing problem.[2]

In a recent work that offers a schematic view of the mystical origins of
Hasidism as well as Hasidism as a field of research, Rachel Elior illustrates
the complex relationship between Hasidism and the mystical traditions
upon which it is based. She writes, "These mystical innovators set out to
contribute something new to the mystical outlook and its implications on
earth. The novelty of the Ba'al Shem Tov's approach was that it replaced the
dualistic mystical perception of good and evil, exile and redemption, with

a new holistic perception based on three essential theological elements: the entirety of the divine presence everywhere; the accessibility of the hidden divine realm to every member of the community; and the essential equality of all modes of divine worship."[3] Although such declarative statements may not fully encapsulate a tradition that is quite variegated and multivalent, her point is well taken and largely correct; that is, Hasidism is surely a link in the chain of the Jewish mystical tradition but one that in some ways undermines or revises the basic metaphysical framework of previous Kabbalah.

The other camp was initiated largely by Ben Zion Dinur and Simon Dubnow. These scholars, among many others that followed, examined Hasidism as a social phenomenon and maintained that the only way to understand it as a movement was to view it in its historical, social, and socioeconomic context, using external Polish, Russian, Ukrainian, and Galician sources to verify the claims that the Hasidim made about themselves. In a recent essay reviewing what can be called the new phase of the controversy, Yohanan Petrovsky-Shtern called these two camps *Ḥasidei dekokhvaya* (star-struck Hasidism) and *Ḥasidei deʾarʿa* (earth-bound Hasidism).[4]

Both groups function within the discipline of history. The first group is devoted to the internal sources of Hasidism, largely viewing them diachronically as carriers of an age-old tradition of Jewish mysticism. *Ḥasidei dekokhvaya* scholars are interested in terms such as *devekut* and concepts such as the *tzaddik* and how Hasidim adapted or revised classical kabbalistic metaphysics. Though interested in the historical and cultural context in which these changes emerged, they are generally less skeptical of internal sources. The *Ḥasidei deʾarʿa* scholars take a synchronic view and are less interested in the "ideas" as abstract entities, maintaining that all ideas must be viewed as emerging from particular social and cultural contexts.

Though sympathetic to both, I find myself generally inclined toward the *Ḥasidei dekokhvaya* approach, largely as a consequence of my interests and training. While it is certainly true that Hasidism is deeply influenced and connected to the Jewish mystical tradition (even the *Ḥasidei deʾarʿa* scholars acknowledge that) and can be examined in that light, Hasidism is also a modern example of a new traditional way of reading the Bible that has received little attention. For example, while Zev Gries has offered important insights into the structure of Hasidic publishing, specifically its choice of organizing Hasidic homilies according to the weekly Torah portion, scholars have paid less attention to the way Hasidism contributes to and perhaps even spearheads a traditionalist revival of the Hebrew Bible. In this sense Hasidism may be viewed as a response (whether conscious or not is hard to determine) not only to religious modernity in general but also to the critique of Scripture that serves as one of modern religion's ideational foundations.

Below I will argue that Ya'akov Yosef Katz of Polnoy (d. 1792), one of the most influential masters of the first generation of Hasidim, had a particular understanding of Hasidism's relation to Scripture that in subsequent generations became the unspoken frame of much of Hasidic literature. His approach stands in direct opposition, both structurally and substantively, to Moses Mendelssohn's Bible project and to later biblical criticism.[5] The extent to which he was aware of either of these is unknown to me. Yet, in another sense, both the progressive modern reformers and the Hasidic masters—separated by both ideology and geography—are engaged in a similar project of reinserting the Bible into the center of Jewish intellectual life.[6] It is also significant to note here that Ya'akov Yosef, one of the most celebrated disciples of the Ba'al Shem Tov, was not a noted Kabbalist before "converting" to Hasidism as was, for example, his contemporary Dov Baer (the Maggid) of Mezritch. He was a noted pietist and ascetic, as well as a respected halakhic jurist, and was intimately familiar with the corpus of kabbalistic writing, but he was not known to be mystically inclined.

Whereas most early modern and modern meta-halakhic literature is based on, or interprets, Scripture, the centrality of Scripture that dominated the medieval and early modern world of biblical exegesis (Saadia Gaon, Rashi, Rashbam, Ibn Ezra, Nahmanides, Gersonides, Bahya ibn Asher, Seforno, and others) gave way to the dominance of Talmud, responsa literature, Kabbalah, pietism, and Musar for many learned Jews living deep inside the Jewish textual tradition. In most traditional Jewish institutes of higher learning in the modern period, at least until the second half of the 20th century, the Hebrew Bible, or *Humash*, was not studied systematically. It was assumed that one knew (often by memory) his Scripture (until recently these institutes of higher learning were exclusively for boys) and that one had looked through the classical medieval commentators (largely on one's own), but a careful analysis of Bible was not the concern of traditional Jewish education until very recently.[7] Enlightenment works such as Moses Mendelssohn's German translation of the Hebrew Bible and its accompanying commentary (*Biur*) and the rise of biblical criticism (beginning, perhaps, with Spinoza and then extending through modernity among Protestants and later Catholics and Jews) brought the Bible back into focus for progressive Jews in the modern period (including, of course, Zionists), and we can safely say that the Hebrew Bible plays a prominent role in the construction of these modern Judaisms.[8] Of course, these movements are shunned by Hasidic leaders and their communities as heretical.[9] And yet Hasidism is engaged in its own Bible revolution, framing its unique perspective through creative and often daring readings of the scriptural narrative. I use Ya'akov Yosef of Polnoy not only because he is one of the most celebrated of the early Hasidic masters but also because I believe he inaugurates a particular revolution in reading the Hebrew Bible that has become standardized in subsequent Hasidic literature.

Ya'akov Yosef Katz of Polnoy's Toldot Ya'akov Yosef and the Return to Scripture

Ya'akov Yosef Katz of Polnoy is considered one of the most important disciples of the Ba'al Shem Tov, or Besht, and a major architect of early Hasidism. A well-known and respected rabbinic scholar, jurist (*av beit din*), and ascetic pietist, he "converted" to Hasidism after an encounter with the Besht.[10] His commentary on the Book of Exodus (*Ben Porat Yosef;* 1781) contains one of the earliest versions of the famous letter of the Besht that arguably served as the touchstone of the Hasidic movement. Unlike his contemporary, the younger Dov Baer (the Maggid) of Mezritch, Ya'akov Yosef did not attract a large circle of followers, and it was Dov Baer and not Ya'akov Yosef who was chosen as the Besht's successor. Yet Ya'akov Yosef is widely known as the most important ideological architect of early Hasidism through his widely read Torah commentary *Toldot Ya'akov Yosef* (1780).[11] His Hasidic commentaries are uncharacteristically replete with complex and sometimes lengthy digressions on Talmudic passages (*sugyot*) both halakhic and aggadic, medieval talmudic commentaries, Kabbalah, and the entire body of medieval and early modern pietistic literature.[12] It is also a book with a very definite agenda, responding to traditional critics of the nascent Hasidic movement by defending Hasidism as the necessary corrective to the wayward state of Jewish spiritual life.[13]

Ya'akov Yosef was particularly fond of two works of Torah homilies that are consistently cited throughout his work: the 16th-century pietist and mystic Moshe Alsheikh's *Sefer Alsheikh* and the Torah commentaries of Ephraim of Lunshitz, who lived and preached in Poland in the late 16th century.[14] He also often refers to the Torah commentary of Isaac Abarbanel, a 15th-century leader of Iberian Jewry. In fact, it appears that Ya'akov Yosef modeled his commentary on Abarbanel, who characteristically begins his exegesis in the medieval scholastic mode by posing a series of questions which he proceeds to answer in his homily (more on this below).

Although Ya'akov Yosef cites kabbalistic works such as the *Zohar* and Lurianic Kabbalah quite frequently, one would be hard-pressed to call his work kabbalistic or mystical in any conventional sense. Mystical literature, though cited frequently, is often not central but is usually engaged as part of the larger body of classical Jewish literature.[15] For example, a comment by the medieval Tosafists (a group of 12th-century French sages who glossed the Babylonian Talmud) can just as easily warrant his sustained attention as a mystical or esoteric idea from the *Zohar*. Whereas his contemporary, Dov Baer, was a much more mystical and charismatic personality, whose works are replete with mystical and ecstatic observations, Ya'akov Yosef is more grounded and his work more focused on what he considered the two essential challenges of Hasidim: first, to gain legitimacy from the rabbinic elite— of which he was a part before his conversion to Hasidism—without which Ya'akov Yosef thought Hasidism had no chance of success. This may, in part, be behind his long and learned digressions on rabbinic sources. Though he likely wrote that way before converting to Hasidism, maintaining that style in light of his ostensible commitment to the masses after becoming a disciple of the Besht seems curious. It also may inform the way he tries to situate Hasidism in the trajectory of the classical pietism of Alsheikh and Lunshitz, both of whom were well respected and widely read in his period. Second, he believed that a firm commitment to the unlearned masses was an essential core of his master's innovative project and one to which he was ideologically committed. One way he addresses this is to develop a form of tzaddikism (worship of the righteous one, or *tzaddik*) that views Jewish society as comprising two distinct groups: the elite and the masses, both of whom need each other. The former he calls "men of form" (*anshei ṣura*) and the latter "men of matter" (*anshei ḥomer*).[16] The Aristotelian form/matter dichotomy, which he likely gleaned from Maimonides and other medieval sources, is deployed to both describe and construct his historical and geographical context. He lived in a world where the rabbinic elite dominated the intellectual discourse and the masses were largely ignored. On the one hand, he had to convince the elite that reaching out to the masses was not simply an act of kindness but an essential part of their own identity, a central tenet of their vocation, and crucial for the welfare of Israel.[17] And he wanted to curb the growing hatred among the masses (including the wealthy) for the learned rabbis.[18]

The most serious challenge to Hasidism in its early period was its rejection by the rabbinic elite, perhaps most forcefully illustrated in the Gaon of Vilna's 1777 letter against Hasidism and various other anti-Hasidic edicts that followed in its wake.[19] Ya'akov Yosef knew he had to quell the emerging antagonism among many of the unlearned Jews against the rabbinic elite by viewing them as providing an essential function in the Jewish community. Given his status as a well-respected rabbinic leader and a member of that elite class (unlike his master the Besht, who was not well regarded in those circles) he was well situated for such a task.[20] One could posit that these two challenges, both of which have been noticed by scholars, serve as the pillars of his theological and sociological project.

Most Hasidic literature is printed as abbreviated or extended homilies on the weekly Torah portion. While this may be partially due to printers' decisions (most Hasidic masters did not publish their own work and much of it was published posthumously and in limited editions), the appearance of Hasidic literature, beginning in 1780 with *Toldot Ya'akov Yosef* on the Pentateuch, gave the educated Jewish public an entire literature devoted to spiritualistic commentaries and meditations on the Bible.[21] Biblical characters were brought to life and constructed as models of piety from this new Hasidic perspective. Rabbinic literature (Talmud and Midrash) was freely deployed alongside kabbalistic ideas to present this new way of Hasidism which, though pietistic in nature, departed significantly from the ascetic pietism of the past and offered its readers a way of serving God joyously. This is not to say that Hasidism invented this genre. Collections of learned homilies and extended commentaries on the Bible surely existed between the end of the classical period of medieval biblical exegesis and the emergence of Hasidism. Hasidism's innovation here is the way it made these homilies on the Bible the very foundation of its intellectual focus and the centerpiece of its spirituality.

This new orientation is carefully constructed, and even spearheaded, by Ya'akov Yosef in his various works, particularly in his *Toldot Ya'akov Yosef*. In fact, as I demonstrate below, Ya'akov Yosef spends much time in this work building his Hasidic perspective by questioning the continued relevance of the Bible and presenting the approach of his master as the solution that will save the Bible from obsolescence, obscurity, and even heresy.

It is unclear how much of this focus on the Bible is driven by the fact that the two dominant sources of Jewish spiritual life—Talmud and Kabbalah— were largely inaccessible to the unlearned masses he wanted to reach. The Bible, on the other hand, was something most moderately educated Jews knew—not deeply and often not very well—but they had enough familiarity with the narrative to be drawn in. And such a book could be studied alongside the weekly Torah portion read in synagogues on Shabbat. Although it is true that one who is not well versed in the entire body of Jewish meta-halakhic literature will often have difficulty deciphering some of Ya'akov

Yosef's terse and referential writing, his work is also interspersed with more palatable and tangible explanations and teachings that he heard directly from his master, the Besht, which often become touchstones for his more learned explanations directed, perhaps, toward his rabbinic audience.[22]

His work thus exhibits the complexity of writing *for* two very disparate communities *about* very disparate communities: the rabbinic elite and the masses. On the one hand, he wanted to introduce the Besht and his way to the rabbinic elite whose exposure to Hasidism was largely through the sometimes bizarre and often uninformed behavior of some young followers in their towns and cities. Yet he also wanted to give the unlearned public a text that would affirm their role and introduce them to the Besht's ideas in a more nuanced way than they may have heard orally in stories or parables.

Biblical Relevance: "What was, was! Why do we need to know this?"

There is an oft-cited passage from the *Zohar* that if the narrative of the Bible is merely a collection of "stories," that is, if the Bible is "merely" literature in the colloquial way in which we understand that term, there are other literatures more compelling and more interesting (*Zohar* 3:152a). In short, the *Zohar* contests what became a more modern description of the Bible as "the greatest story ever told." As a "story," the *Zohar* suggests, it is far from the "greatest story ever told"; moreover, even if it is a great story, it is not told particularly well. The *Zohar* presents this as a justification of its own esoteric project: that each story, each character that the *Zohar* describes, each episode, passage, even each word in Scripture, points to a higher spiritual reality.[23] In short, the Bible is holy to the extent to which it can be unlocked by the esoteric teachings in the *Zohar*. This self-justificatory approach had a deep impact on the history of Kabbalah; it is used in a slightly different way and to different ends by Ya'akov Yosef in his *Toldot Ya'akov Yosef*. As mentioned above, Ya'akov Yosef adopted the late medieval model of scriptural exegesis by beginning his commentary on any weekly portion with a series of questions which then become the template of his homily (*drash*). But the similarity to medieval exegesis ends there.

Unlike most late medieval commentaries, the question that appears most often in the *Toldot* is why, in fact, this particular episode is written in the Torah at all! This takes numerous forms. Sometimes Ya'akov Yosef begins, as in the story about Sarah's postmenopausal pregnancy (Gen. 18:9–15), by saying, "These are just stories [*sipurei devarim be-alma*]; what happened, happened [*mah de-havei havei*]!"[24] On Jacob loving Joseph more than his other sons, he asks, "Why mention these stories in the Torah? What happened, happened."[25] These kinds of statements, and there are many, are almost always followed by, "If the Torah is eternal [*niṣḥi*], how is this relevant for all times [*be-khol 'et uve-khol zeman*]?" This is not only used when discussing biblical stories, but also in reference to the description of commandments (*mitzvot*).[26] For example, regarding the sabbatical year (*shemittah*), he notes,

> There are many problems to address [*veha-sefakot rabo*] [in the Torah's description of the sabbatical year]. Regarding the question, "What is the difference between the sabbatical year [*shemittah*] and Sinai?" (*b. Zevaḥim* 115b) we [already] know Rashi's explanation.[27] Second, since the sabbatical year is one of the 613 *mitzvot*, how is it relevant in our time [which it must be] given that the Torah and its *mitzvot* are eternal?"[28]

This is a particularly interesting case, as it may be an example where Ya'akov Yosef's question of scriptural relevance ("Why is this written? What happened, happened.") may challenge the question asked by the Midrash and cited by Rashi (discussed below). Although it is arguably the case that all classical biblical exegesis tries to make Scripture cohere, I argue that Ya'akov Yosef—illustrated in his uncharacteristic question—is making a stronger claim. His concern is not about scriptural coherence but about its relevance to any reader at any time in history.[29]

The question of textual relevance may be moot for medieval exegetes. Given the assumption of the divine origin of the Torah, relevance is precisely about understanding the text. But although Ya'akov Yosef and much of subsequent Hasidism accepted the divine origin as true, that was a necessary but not sufficient condition for the relevance of the text—to understand the text is to understand divine will. If we accept that piety and devotion stand at the center of Hasidic spirituality, the text must serve those human needs. While contextual interpretation (*peshat*) might provide sense to a particular biblical episode, it does not by definition make the episode relevant to the life of the reader. If relevance, as opposed to sense, cannot be provided, it is not clear to Ya'akov Yosef why it needs to be part of a divine and eternal document. Hence the question, "Why is this written in the Torah?" What seems different here than in classical Midrash or medieval exegesis (*parshanut*) is not the desire for relevance per se; that exists in both Midrash and *parshanut*. Rather, it is the exclusivity of relevance such that if a text cannot be made to speak to the reader it has no purpose whatsoever. Hence, "Why is this written in the Torah?" In the *Toldot*, and I would argue in Hasidism more generally, the interpreter of the biblical text serves as a bridge—not between the text as such and the reader but between the text and the one who reads it in order to know how to serve God. Beyond the first-tier dimension of *knowing* what the text says or knowing *what* to do, Hasidism is focused on a second-tier question: *how* to do what one is commanded to do.

The Midrash on the sabbatical year cited by Rashi asks why the laws of *shemittah* immediately follow a description of the theophany at Sinai. The midrashic answer cited by Rashi is to teach us that just as all the details of the laws of *shemittah* were given at Sinai, so, too, were all the laws of the Torah given at Sinai in all their details, even though the Torah is often circumspect about many of the details of these commandments. This addresses two distinct, and distinctly, rabbinic issues. First, it resolves a seemingly unclear, and jarring, transition in Scripture from the laws of *shemittah* to the mention of Sinai. Second, it bolsters rabbinic legislation (the details of *mitzvot*) by rooting the entire rabbinic project in the theophany at Sinai, something the rabbis obliquely proclaim in the first chapter of *Ethics of the Fathers*. The rabbinic sages use Scripture's ostensible disjuncture between Sinai and *shemittah* as an occasion to champion their own project. Ya'akov Yosef surely agrees with this project, and yet here he appears somewhat dissatisfied with the rabbinic answer and follows his citation of the Midrash by asking about the general relevance of *shemittah*, regardless of where it is situated in the scriptural narrative or what it tells us about rabbinic legislation. In other words, according to Ya'akov Yosef, the rabbinic explanation may be a necessary condition, though an insufficient one, to explain why these two factors (*shemittah* and Sinai) are juxtaposed.

One reason for what I take to be the intentional juxtaposition of these questions—why not ask the more general question first, as is Ya'akov Yosef's custom, and then cite the midrashic question?—would be that Ya'akov Yosef wanted to suggest that Rashi's reading is inadequate here. Although it resolves a textual anomaly and supports the rootedness of rabbinic legislation under the aegis of Scripture, it misses the more fundamental point of why we need to *read* the Torah in the first place; that is, it does not explain what *shemittah* might *mean* to a reader for whom its original or literal meaning is irrelevant. Because *shemittah* is a commandment limited to the territory of the Land of Israel (*Erets Yisrael*), Rashi's approach fails to integrate *shemittah* as a source for Jewish devotion in a nonterritorialized Judaism. Ya'akov Yosef may be suggesting that without an answer to *this* question Scripture cannot serve as a template for devotion and (here I admittedly speculate) cannot, therefore, survive the weight of modern (heretical) critique. He then goes on to ask a series of additional textual questions, but the question of relevance remains at the center. Ya'akov Yosef subsequently brings to bear a series of rabbinic texts to answer this question, suggesting that his question is already implied in classical literature if one reads it with this query in mind. It is this question as an interpretive lens that he claims is the Hasidic innovation. And the application of this innovation inaugurates a fundamentally new reading of Scripture.

Ya'akov Yosef's concern with biblical relevance is not rhetorical; it holds what I take to be his main interpretive and theological concern. In many cases the question of relevance is followed by a variation of the theme "this can be explained in two ways [bi-shnei panim]." Sometimes, albeit not always, this is followed by a citation from Maimonides, juxtaposed with an oral tradition from the Besht (shama'ti mi-mori). This technique suggests that Ya'akov Yosef may be trying to situate the Besht as an alternative to a more conventional approach to Torah (the citations from Maimonides are almost always from his legal code and not his philosophical works). Maimonides is often set up as the standard and then (re)read to conform to the Besht's understanding. Here is one example of his use of a classic Maimonidean principle.

> Now when Pharaoh let the people go (Exod. 13:17). The questions [sefekot] here are self-evident along with the obvious question [safek yadua'] "Why are these stories written and how do they relate to every individual and at all times?" I can explain this in two ways, as Maimonides writes, "The middle path is the straight path. If one leans to one extreme one must go to the other extreme and remain there for some time until he uproots his first (extreme) trait after which he can return to the middle path."[30]

Ya'akov Yosef then goes on to apply this Maimonidean (really, Aristotelian) principle of the "golden mean" to explain why God has to send Israel in a roundabout way in order to get to where it needed to be. But perhaps we can also find a subtler message here about "two ways" to serve God. The conventional model until Hasidism was one of pious asceticism and the division of society between the elites and the masses. (As an Aristotelian, Maimonides supported such a position). Hasidism suggests (at least in the Besht's portrayal imagined by his early disciples) as a non– or even anti-ascetic pietism and supports a more integrative relationship between the elite and the masses.[31] The Toldot Ya'akov Yosef works with this notion of "two ways" in at least two, perhaps three, directions: first, the explicit notion of "two forms of worship"; second, the division of two communities (the elite and the masses); and, perhaps third, the notion of two ways of reading (for textual clarity and for devotional guidance).

The notion of two different forms of worship (although these are never defined as conventional and Hasidic, that seems implied) looms large in the *Toldot Ya'akov Yosef* and is often introduced by asking about the relevance of a biblical episode. Commenting on the verse describing Lot in Sodom, "But they said, 'Come close, and go!' they said, '[he, Lot] came here as an alien'" (Gen. 19:9). Ya'akov Yosef asks, "Why write the story of the Sodomites in the Torah at all and how is this relevant to every person at all times?" He then explains this "in two ways," offering two interpretations of how proximity—to God or to one's neighbor—can be dangerous. In the first way, he cites from what he only calls *ketavim* (writings) about the recitation of the bedtime *Sh'ma*. His second way is based on a Tosafot from the talmudic tractate *Shabbat*.

From his ensuing discussion, the reference to the anonymous *ketavim* is clearly a kabbalistic source, likely from the Lurianic Kabbalah (Lurianic literature has numerous lengthy homilies on the bedtime *Sh'ma*) about two types of fear of God.[32] The point here is that one should be aware that if one comes too close (whether to God or to a friend) that proximity can often result in distance. (He cites the phrase *raṣo va-shov*—"*running toward and retreating*"—from Ezekiel's vision of the angels [Ezek. 1:14].) Hence one needs to be cautious as one approaches spiritual or relational intimacy. In the second way, he uses the Tosafot's suggestion that God had to "hang the mountain over Israel's heads" (at Sinai) because even though they had already said, "We will do and we will understand" (Exod. 24:7), the theophany might be so traumatic that they would recant their initial commitment. He continues:

So it is with the exodus from Egypt that resulted in extreme intimacy [*kiruv gadol*]. Afterward, things returned to their natural course. So, too, with a person's worship of God. First it is "come close" and then "go" from a distance . . . as I once heard a parable of a father and son: When he teaches his son to walk, he first holds his hand and afterward, when he becomes accustomed to walking, the father removes his hand. So, too, the son "comes close" and then "goes."[33]

In this "first way" one has to exhibit caution so as not to undermine one's desire for God by always keeping a safe distance. Intense proximity is discouraged. In the "second way" one throws caution to the wind in order to achieve an experience of extreme intimacy that is then followed by a natural separation and stabilization even as that separation, following the father and son analogy, retains a sense of intimacy, albeit from some distance. His example is Israel's intense (ecstatic?) experience of the exodus and then the retreating process of forty-nine days between that event and the theophany at Sinai, which corresponds to the forty-nine days of the *Omer* as an organic progression from Passover to Pentecost (Shavuot).

Notably, here the way of caution is exhibited through a kabbalistic text, and the way of experimentation and religious enthusiasm is exhibited through the classic talmudic commentary of the French Tosafists. The first may describe the non-Hasidic elite who were critical, or at least wary, of nascent Hasidism's ecstatic expression of spiritual intimacy, while the second "way"—the Beshtean or Hasidic way—is illustrated through a reading of traditional talmudic commentary. It seems that here Ya'akov Yosef, almost always addressing two distinct audiences in his work, curiously justifies the Hasidic way through the texts of the non-Hasidic community and justifies the non-Hasidic way by using a kabbalistic text more commonly deployed for the purposes of conveying the Hasidic message.[34]

If this reading is plausible, it would support my claim that Ya'akov Yosef structured his homilies and took considerable care in choosing which literary genre to use to make his views known. Here we see his two principles at work. First, this is all prefaced by the fundamental question of his exegetical enterprise (two ways of reading Scripture), that is, "why do we need these [biblical] stories anyway." The stories in the Torah are only justified when they can serve as templates to describe some element of human devotion. Second, he describes two modes of devotion, the Hasidic way and the non-Hasidic way. Here, unpredictably, he uses the Tosafists to exemplify the Hasidic form of worship and the Kabbalists to describe the non-Hasidic form of devotion. We do not know whether this is an intentional reversal. If it is (and it surely could be), it may be how he illustrates the third manifestation of "two ways," that is, toward two distinct communities. By exemplifying the Hasidic way of devotion through a comment by the Tosafists, he may be communicating to his non– or anti-Hasidic rabbinic readers that the Besht's approach is rooted in the very rabbinic tradition they hold dear.

One final example explores a well-known disagreement between Hasidic and non-Hasidic Judaism on the relationship between one's thoughts and actions in regard to divine worship. The standard formula has it that the non-Hasidic pietists argue that one should empty one's distracting thoughts (sometimes defined as the "evil inclination" or *yetser hara*) before undertaking the performance of a *mitzvah*. The Besht counters this by arguing that one should engage in acts of divine worship even (or precisely) with these distracting thoughts and that the power of one's worship will elevate these thoughts to their (holy) root above. Commenting on the verse, "So on that day [bayom hahu] Esau started back that day on his way to Seir. But Jacob journeyed on to Succoth and built a house there" (Gen. 33:16, 17), Ya'akov Yosef writes: "One could ask, why does it say 'on that day'; second, what do we learn from this; third, how is this relevant to every individual at all times?"[35] The first question is the classic medieval question about seemingly extraneous words or phrases. The second question is transitional, serving as a bridge to the third question that takes us beyond the medieval exegetical agenda and into the realm of Hasidic reading. The questions are immediately followed with, "I heard from my master [the Besht]" about a passage from the *Zohar* stating that Israel was only being exiled after they disbelieved in God and David.[36] Ya'akov Yosef then continues with a drawn-out kabbalistic interpretation of this passage that is not directly relevant to our limited concerns but returns to his initial question later in the homily. I pick up the text on the following page where he returns to his initial question, why write "on that day," implying, I assume, that Esau and Jacob went their separate ways "on the [very] same day."

I can now explain my question "what was, was." There are two types of divine worship which constitutes a fundamental principle [klal gadol] . . . One is that a person must purify one's thoughts first and then perform the mitzvah, in action or words, in order to be pure without any extraneous distractions. We see this in the verse, "And Isaac went out walking [i.e., to pray] in the field close toward evening [lifnot erev] (Gen. 24:63). When Isaac went out to pray he was careful to remove and to turn away [from all distractions] as it is said, lifnot erev. This [the verb lifnot literally means "to turn"] refers to all his evil and extraneous thoughts in order that his prayer may be pure. . .

The second way, which is deeper [penimiut yoter], is illustrated in the Mishna *Ethics of the Fathers*, "Do not say 'when I have time I will study,' perhaps you won't have time. . ." (m. Avot 2:4). The simple meaning suffices. "When I will push away my extraneous thoughts I will organize my study schedule but now I am busy." Do not say this, perhaps you will never have time and thus never study. The same is true for prayer . . . I heard from my master [the Besht] on the verse, "I have considered my ways and I have turned back to your decrees" (Ps. 119:59). That is, one should commence with Torah and prayer *with* the evil inclination, that is, "not for the sake of heaven," and, in this way, the evil inclination will not protest against you [on high] and you will conclude "for the sake of heaven." This is the meaning of the verse, "I have considered my ways and I have turned back to your decrees . . ." What comes from this [interpretation] is that one must trick [*lignov da'at*] one's evil inclination into joining him at first and then afterward one must be strident and make it all "for the sake of heaven" . . . Even though this is dangerous, as one enters into the exilic state of the evil inclination by joining forces with him . . . Nevertheless be scrupulous so that you can develop [*la'alot*] and pray to God that He should aid you against this evil inclination. In that case, this way is superior to the first way.[37]

This well-known teaching of the Besht has been examined by many. I wish to draw attention to the way it is born from a rereading of the verse in Genesis 33. Going back to the Besht's question on the words in Genesis 13:16 "on that day [*ba-yom ha-hu*]" citing the *Zohar* (3:77b), the Besht (as conveyed by Ya'akov Yosef) suggests that this locution ("on that day") refers to the day of redemption.[38] In other words, at the time of redemption Esau and Jacob will go their separate ways *but not before.* Hence the first way of serving God by waiting to deflect all distractions before enacting a *mitzvah* is futile because it is impossible (and hence inappropriate) in this exilic existence. Trying to separate one's extraneous thoughts before engaging in devotional acts is not a product of appropriate caution but the opposite, an act of hubris.[39] Here he deploys the Mishnah in *Avot* 2:4 about waiting until one has time before undertaking a regime of study. In this homily, he illustrates this point with the reference to the biblical passage of Jacob "journeying on to Succoth to build a house there" to refer to the Temple in Jerusalem or the period of redemption. What may be implied here is that the exile continues precisely when one does *not* engage with the evil inclination in order to uplift it, since nonengagement with one's evil inclination will result in delinquency in one's devotional life.

This may also apply to Jacob's commitment to have a reunion with Esau, which frames the biblical episode in question. One must engage the evil inclination in order to separate from it. This comes across even more strongly in his reading of another Mishnah from *Ethics of the Fathers*, "Who is a wise man? One who learns from everyone" (*m. Avot* 4:1). Ya'akov Yosef writes, "From 'everyone' includes learning from one's evil inclination [*yetser ha-ra*]."[40] To offer a reading that would situate "on this day" solely within the context of the biblical story (this is common in medieval Bible exegesis) is the old paradigm that Ya'akov Yosef is contesting, not because it is false per se but because in his mind it does not, and cannot, bring Scripture (back) to life. This, according to Ya'akov Yosef, is precisely what the Besht, and Hasidim more generally, were coming to remedy.

Hasidism's whole new approach to worship, what Abraham Joshua Heschel referred to more broadly as "a new approach to Torah,"[41] is founded on the seemingly extraneous words "on this day" in what appears to be a story that, in Ya'akov Yosef's rendering, is not on its face necessary to the biblical narrative. I read Heschel's locution "a new approach to Torah" in a hyper-literal rather than colloquial way—a new approach to *reading* Torah, a new approach to the Bible.

The innovative nature of Hasidism (or lack thereof) has been discussed by many scholars. Most of these discussions revolve around concepts such as the role of the tzaddik, the centrality of prayer over study, or the anti-ascetic nature of Hasidic worship. What has not received adequate treatment is the way Hasidism, in developing its approach to worship, is also offering a new way to read Scripture. My suggestion here is not simply to note that Hasidic ideology is born from its reading of Scripture. That is obvious. By prefacing so many of his observations with "Why do we need this at all?" Ya'akov Yosef is *reintroducing* the Bible as the primary template for Jewish spirituality and, in doing so, is reinserting the Bible into a traditional Jewish world that was dominated by the study of Talmud and codes. The *Zohar* turned to the Bible as a way to found its esotericism and cosmology. Ya'akov Yosef does so to teach his readers a new way to serve God, a new way to be human, not simply by using biblical archetypes as exemplars but by suggesting that without the Besht's new way of creating biblical relevance by making the Bible about human devotion ("for all individuals, at all times") the eternal nature of the Bible is threatened—that is, without reading it primarily for its devotional import, the Bible could not withstand its modern critique.

Although biblical criticism had not yet reached maturity in the latter part of the 18th century and the Jewish Enlightenment was still some decades away where Ya'akov Yosef lived, that he stressed the need to confirm the Bible's eternal nature (*niṣḥiyut*) by reading it as pointing outside its own narrative marks an important and underexamined dimension of Hasidism's innovative spirit.[42] Whether this was a direct response to Bible criticism or perhaps a more unconscious move generated by a sense of modernity's looming challenge is not known. But given that the *Toldot Ya'akov Yosef* is a work explicitly written for more than one audience, we should not discount the possibility that its polemical tone extended beyond the topical debate between the rabbinic elite and nascent Hasidism. There may be a veiled triangulation here. Without explicitly acknowledging this, most Hasidic literature subsequent to the *Toldot* adopts this practice, although the foundational question—"Why is this relevant?"—is rarely rehearsed. It is simply taken for granted.

Conclusion

My argument here is that we need to examine Hasidism through a wider lens than just as another manifestation of the Jewish mystical tradition. The hermeneutical contribution of Hasidism, while surely deeply informed by Kabbalah and pietism, largely lies in its focus on the Bible as the template of Hasidic spirituality. This "innovation" is cultivated by Ya'akov Yosef in his *Toldot Ya'akov Yosef*. Ya'akov Yosef does more than simply base his Hasidic ideology on Scripture. He begins his exegetical enterprise by marking a flaw, if you will, in the very nature of how Jews read their Bible. The Bible had become disconnected from the lives of its readers because the exegetical frame that surrounded it did not present the Holy Writ as a template for devotion but rather as a divine text whose internal fissures and ambiguities required clarification and whose narrative (sometimes) needed to be justified. These concerns are shared by classical biblical exegesis (and its subsequent consumers) and modern Bible critics, using different methods and yielding different—often opposite—results. By the late 18th century, traditional readers of the Hebrew Bible were often, consciously or not, responding defensively to the accusation of the Bible critics against the divine origin of the Pentateuch. Early Hasidic masters are not often counted among these defenders. I argue here that Ya'akov Yosef may be doing so not by openly engaging Bible criticism—of which he likely knew almost nothing—but by criticizing the traditional approach of biblical exegesis that he believed undermined the argument of the Bible's eternality.

By consistently asking—and in a loud voice—"Why is this written?" Ya'akov Yosef challenges the traditional trajectory of biblical exegesis by suggesting that the Bible can only be saved if it points to the present, to the devotional needs of each reader in every generation (*bekhol et uve-khol zeman*). Although there were precedents to this reorientation (precedents he often cites), Ya'akov Yosef was doggedly devoted to making this the centerpiece of his approach and, given that the *Toldot* was the first Hasidic book in print, the approach of much of Hasidic literature that followed. We need to read the Bible in this way, he implies, not only to bring the Bible to life but (also) to save us from the misdirected piety that had developed over the long period of exile. For Ya'akov Yosef, the Besht comes to offer us a new lens through which to read the Bible and to worship God, and both are mutually dependent on each other. That Hasidic masters and their publishers seemed to follow this advice, coupled with the ultimate success of the movement against its traditional and progressive detractors, resulted in, among other things, a revivified Bible and a reenergized Judaism.

NOTES

I dedicate this chapter to Rabbi Chaim Brovinder, with unending gratitude.

1. For classic studies in these areas, see Immanuel Etkes, "The Study of Hasidism: Past Trends and New Directions," in *Hasidism Reappraised*, ed. Ada Rapoport-Albert (London: Littman Library of Jewish Civilization, 1997), pp. 447–264; Rachel Elior, *The Mystical Origins of Hasidism* (Portland, OR: Littman Library of Jewish Civilization, 2006), pp. 195–205; and Zeev Gries, "Hasidism: The Present State of Research and Some Desirable Priorities," *Numen* 34, no. 1 (1987): 97–108; 34, no. 2 (1987): 179–213.

2. This is the topic of Moshe Idel's *Hasidism: Between Ecstasy and Magic* (Albany: State University of New York Press, 1995), esp. pp. 31–146. One salient response to Buber's view of Hasidism can be found in Rivka Shatz-Uffenheimer's essay "Man's Relation to God and World in Buber's Rendering of the Hasidic Teaching," in *The Philosophy of Martin Buber*, ed. Paul Arthur Schilpp and Maurice Friedman (La Salle, IL: Open Court, 1967), pp. 403–34. For an examination of this debate, see Jerome Gellman, "Buber's Blunder: Buber Replies to Scholem and Shatz-Uffenheimer, *Modern Judaism* 20 (2000): 20–40. Scholem's essays on Hasidism have recently been collected in one volume and published as *The Latest Phase: Essays on Hasidism by Gershom Scholem* [in Hebrew], ed. David Assaf and Esther Liebes (Jerusalem: Am Oved, Magnes Press, 2008).

3. Elior, *Mystical Origins*, p. 37.

4. See Yohanan Petrovsky-Shtern, "Review Essay: *Hasidei de'ar'a* and *Hasidei dekokhvaya*: Two Trends in Modern Jewish Historiography," *AJS Review* 32 (2008): 141–67.

5. For a useful and general introduction to the critical study of the Hebrew Bible, see Jacob Weingreen, *Introduction to the Critical Study of the Text of the Hebrew Bible* (New York: Clarendon, 1982), esp. pp. 1–10, 25–37.

6. Although the Bible serves as the template for the classical mystical text, the *Zohar*, it does so in a different way than in Hasidism. In brief, the *Zohar* uses the narrative of Scripture to describe its metaphysical system. On medieval Kabbalah more generally, Gershom Scholem writes, "In conclusion it should be said that the conception of the Torah as a fabric woven of names provided no concrete contribution to concrete exegesis. It was, rather, a purely mystical principle and tended to remove Torah from all human insight into its specific meanings, which are, after all, the sole concern of exegesis. But this did not trouble the Kabbalists. To them the fact that God expressed Himself, even if His utterance is far beyond human insight, is far more important than any specific 'meaning' that might be conveyed" (Scholem, "The Meaning of Torah in Jewish Mysticism," in idem, *On the Kabbalah and Its Symbolism* [New York: Schocken Books, 1969], p. 43).

7. An exception to this can be found in many Modern Orthodox and Ba'alei Teshuva yeshivot, where medieval Bible commentaries are studied seriously and systematically. I had the privilege of studying in Yeshivat ha-Mivtar in Jerusalem for more than four years with Rabbi Chaim Brovinder (among others), where scriptural exegesis was taken as a serious course of study.

8. See, for example, Eliezer Schweid, *Filosophia shel ha-TANAKH ki-Yesod Tarbut Yisrael*, published in English as *The Philosophy of the Bible as a Foundation of Jewish Culture*, trans. Leonard Levin (Brighton, MA: Academic Studies Press, 2008).

9. On Hasidism and the influence of modernity through the Jewish Enlightenment, see Raphael Mahler, *Hasidism and the Jewish Enlightenment* (Philadelphia: Jewish Publication Society of America, 1985); and Marcin Wodzinski, *Haskala and Hasidism in the Kingdom of Poland* (Portland, OR: Littman Library of Jewish Civilization, 2005). On a Hasidic polemic that directly addresses Mendelssohn, see the anonymous Bratslav treatise *Kinat ha-Shem Ziva'ot* (Lemberg, ca. 1870–85). For a brief discussion of this text, see Mendel Piekarz, *Studies in Braslav Hasidim* (Jerusalem: Mosad Bialik, 1972), pp. 197–202.

10. For one such tradition, see Abraham Kahana, *Sefer ha-Ḥasidut* (Warsaw: Levin-Epstein, 1922), p. 105; cited in Samuel H. Dresner, *The Zaddik* (New York: Abelard-Schuman, 1960), pp. 38–40. Most of the material on Ya'akov Yosef's relationship to the Besht is taken from *Shivḥei ha-Besht*, ed. Avraham Rubenstein (Jerusalem: Reuven Mass, 1991), pp. 99–110. *Shivḥei ha-Besht* was first published in 1814, and its historicity regarding the biographical figure of the Besht has been the subject of scholarly scrutiny; see, for example, Moshe Rosman, *The Founder of Hasidism: A Quest for the Historical Ba'al Shem Tov* (Berkeley: University of California Press, 1996).

11. The standard edition of the *Toldot Ya'akov Yosef* is printed in two volumes; all references here come from the 1973 Jerusalem edition (ed. Gedalyah Nigal and Mosad Harav Kook). Newer annotated editions have appeared in the past decade. The *Toldot* is divided into three distinct but linked parts. The introduction is more than a short précis of the book; it is, in fact, a small book unto itself. It seems to have been constructed as a prolegomenon to Hasidism more generally, touching on many themes that became popular in Hasidic writing. In this regard, the introduction resembles the introduction to the *Sefer ha-Zohar*, which doesn't introduce a book as much as a spiritual movement. The second part of the book contains homilies according to the weekly Torah portion. The third section is a collection of teachings that Ya'akov Yosef heard from his master, the Besht. His other works include *Ṣofnat Pa'aneaḥ* (1782) and *Ketonet Pasim* (1866). On various significant dimensions of the editorial process of the *Toldot Ya'akov Yosef*, see Zeev Gries, "The Hasidic Managing Editor as an Agent of Culture," in Rapoport-Albert, *Hasidism Reappraised*, pp. 149, 150.

12. See Mendel Pierkarz, *Be-Yemei Ṣemikhat Ha-Ḥasidut* (Jerusalem: Bialik Institute, 1978), pp. 15–16.

13. See Gedalyah Nigal, *Manhig ve-Edah* (Israel: Yehuda, 1962), p. 19. *Toldot Ya'akov Yosef* was printed in two locales, Karetz and Miedzyboz, in the same year (1780); both editions were initially printed without approbations.

14. For some examples of Ya'akov Yosef's citations of Alsheikh, see *Toldot Ya'akov Yosef*, pp. 9b, 55a, 116a, 142a, 234b, 267b, 268b, 307a, 661a. For Lunshitz, see *Toldot Ya'akov Yosef*, pp. 90a, 102b, 443a, 724a. This is not an exhaustive accounting.

15. In general, see Zeev Gries, "Kabbalistic Literature and Its Role in Hasidism," in idem, *The Book in the Jewish World, 1700–1900* (Portland, OR: Littman Library of Jewish Civilization, 2007), pp. 69–90. Moshe Idel similarly suggests that, aside from kabbalistic Hasidic circles such as Zhidatchov-Komarno, early Hasidic masters "understood this classic [the *Zohar*] of Jewish mysticism the same way they approached other books of Judaism, namely as pointing to the values of devotion, ecstasy, and exaltation" ("Abraham Joshua Heschel on Mysticism and Hasidism," *Modern Judaism* 29 [2009]: 92).

16. See Dresner, *The Zaddik*, pp. 113–40.

17. Ibid., pp. 148–72.

18. See, for example, Ya'akov Yosef, *Ben Porat Yosef* (Lemberg, n.d.), p. 106a.

19. For this and many other documents against the Hasidim, see Mordecai Wilensky, *Hasidim u-Mitnagdim* [in Hebrew] (Jerusalem: Bialik Institute, 1970). On Ya'akov Yosef's attack against the "learned community" focused on the method of casuistry (*pilpul*), see, for example, *Toldot Ya'akov Yosef*, pp. 141b, 163b; and *Ben Porat Yosef*, p. 91a.

20. Yet it seems that Ya'akov Yosef's previous reputation did not protect him from vehement attack. Soon after its appearance, *Toldot Ya'akov Yosef* was the victim of sharp criticism by the anti-Hasidic forces, perhaps most forcefully by the anti-Hasidic polemic *Zemir Aritzim*; see Mordecai Wilensky, "Criticism on the Book *Toldot*" [in Hebrew], *The Joshua Starr Memorial Volume* (New York, 1953), pp. 183–89; and Dresner, *The Zaddik*, pp. 66–68. More strongly, scholarship reveals that it was likely burned in Vilna, Krakow, and Brody.

21. On the relationship between Hasidic literature and printing, see Zeev Gries, *The Book in Early Hasidism* [in Hebrew] (Israel: Hakibbutz Hameuchad, 1992), esp. pp. 17–68.

22. He is often quite open about his method; see, for example, *Toldot Ya'akov Yosef*, pp. 86b, 103a, 131b; and Nigal, *Manhig ve-Edah*, pp. 92, 93.

23. This is aptly stated by Abraham bar Hiyya in his *Megillat ha-Megalleh* (Berlin, 1924), p. 75: "Every letter and every word in every section of the Torah have a deep root in wisdom and contain a mystery from among the mysteries of [divine] understanding, the depths of which we cannot penetrate"; cf. Scholem, "The Meaning of Torah in Jewish Mysticism," p. 63.

24. *Toldot Ya'akov Yosef*, p. 59b.

25. Ibid., 102b.

26. See, for example, ibid., pp. 3b, 4a, 70b, 111b. Cf. Nigal, *Manhig ve-Edah*, pp. 19–20. Nigal spends considerable time on the question of relevance regarding the *mitzvot* but almost ignores the fact that these kind of statements in *Toldot Ya'akov Yosef* are made more frequently regarding the narrative of Scripture.

27. Rashi asks, "'What is [the connection] between *shemittah* and Mount Sinai?' Behold, all the *mitzvot* were given at Mount Sinai. Rather, just as with *shemittah* all the details were given at Sinai, so, too, all the details of all the *mitzvot* were given at Sinai." See also the *Sifra* to Lev. 1:1 and Rashi on Lev. 25:1.

28. *Toldot Ya'akov Yosef*, p. 414a.

29. Daniel Boyarin discusses the idea that one of the goals of Midrash is about "filling in the gaps" of the biblical narrative and, in doing so, making the narrative more coherent (*Intertextualty and Midrash* [Bloomington: University of Indiana Press, 1994], pp. 1–20).

30. *Toldot Ya'akov Yosef*, p. 164a.

31. The conventional wisdom about Hasidic populism has been challenged in Ada Rapoport-Alpert, "God and the Tzadik as the Two Focal points of Hasidic Worship," *History of Religions* 18 (1979): 296–324.

32. See, for example, Meir Poppers, *Pri Etz Hayyim* (Jerusalem, 1988), pp. 319–44.

33. *Toldot Ya'akov Yosef*, p. 61a.

34. On the dual nature of Torah, speaking to two distinct audiences, see *Toldot Ya'akov Yosef*, p. 57b.

35. *Toldot Ya'akov Yosef*, p. 97a.

36. *Zohar* 2:175b.

37. *Toldot Ya'akov Yosef*, pp. 98d, 99a.

38. Ibid. 97b.

39. A very different reading, albeit one that makes similar moves can be found in Nathan of Gaza, "*Drush ha-Menorah,*" published in *Be-Ikvot Mashiah*, ed. Gershom Scholem (Jerusalem: Tarshish Books, 1944), pp. 97–99.

40. *Toldot Ya'akov Yosef*, p. 99a.

41. See Abraham Joshua Heschel, "Hasidism as a New Approach to Torah," in *Moral Grandeur and Spiritual Audacity*, ed. Susannah Heschel (New York: Farrar, Straus, Giroux, 1996), pp. 33–39.

42. See Wodzinski, *Haskala and Hasidism*, pp. 9–33.

7

Christian Kabbalah

ALLISON P. COUDERT

Until relatively recently the academic study of the Christian Kabbalah has been pretty much the stepchild, dare I say *mamzer*, of Kabbalah studies. For the "real" Kabbalah was considered to be the Jewish Kabbalah, and whatever Christians made of it was bound to be derivative, even illegitimate. But I am pleased to say that this dismissive evaluation has changed, especially during the last decade, and it can safely be said that the Christian Kabbalah is now a legitimate field in its own right—so legitimate, in fact, that in 1999 Moshe Idel, David Ruderman, and Guy Stroumsa organized a year-long seminar at the Institute for Advanced Judaic Study (University of Pennsylvania) on the interaction of Christians and Jews in Europe, which included a discussion of the Christian Kabbalah. But this is a relatively recent development and one that occurred long after I began graduate studies more years ago than I care to remember (or admit). Back then, even the Jewish Kabbalah did not appear on the radar of scholars interested in European history in general or the history of science in particular, the fields which I chose to study. And here let me warn any potential graduate students who might read this chapter: be careful when you select your thesis adviser, for that person may end up exerting more influence on your life than your parents or future spouses. This certainly was the case for me when I arrived at the Warburg Institute in London to work under the direction of Frances Yates.

Yates is best known for her work on Giordano Bruno and *The Art of Memory*,[1] but she is also remembered, especially by scholars of Judaism, for stressing the importance of the Kabbalah. Moshe Idel, for example, described Yates's willingness to admit the formative role of the Kabbalah in Renaissance and post-Renaissance history as "courageous . . . and quite extraordinary."[2] Yates's interest in the Kabbalah had a profound effect on me, for she introduced me to a course of study that has influenced my entire scholarly life. In fact, writing this chapter brought back both fond and frightening memories. Put yourself in the place of an eager, if ignorant, college graduate, taught to regard Francis Bacon as the father of modern science only to discover upon her arrival

159

Figure 7.1. Aleph. Courtesy of Wellcome
Library, London.

Figure 7.2. Beth. Courtesy of Wellcome
Library, London.

at the Warburg Institute that not only was he a Renaissance Magus—what, I
wondered, was that?—but also a devotee of Hermes Trismegistus, of whom I
had never heard. And what about having your adviser suggest to you that you
write your thesis about one of the leading Christian Kabbalists of the 17th century, a man with the curious name of Francis Mercury van Helmont (1614–
1698), when you had never heard of the Jewish Kabbalah, much less the Christian one. And imagine your reaction when you opened the first book written
by your new object of research only to find a complete set of illustrations of
Hebrew letters such as those shown in Figures 7.1 and 7.2.

What, I wondered, could possibly be going on here? I soon discovered
that van Helmont believed that Hebrew script presented exact representations of the movements made by the tongue as the letters were pronounced.
I remember trying this out in the British Museum reading room—the man
next to me was singing, so my mutterings were hardly audible. I concluded
that the theory worked better with *bet* than with *alef*, but I basically ended

up utterly mystified and decided that I would ignore this aspect of van Helmont's thought and concentrate on something more directly related to the subject I had come to study, namely, early modern scientists, or natural philosophers as they were called at the time, and the scientific revolution. Only after a few months of research did I realize that van Helmont's theory of Hebrew would become a central part of my doctoral thesis and that as I tried to make sense of his so-called natural alphabet of the holy Hebrew language I would find myself deeply involved in the study of the Christian Kabbalah and its relationship to the scientific revolution. Let me add here that I should have realized how important this book was as soon as I discovered that it had been written by van Helmont when he was incarcerated in the dungeons of the Roman Inquisition on the charge of "Judaizing."

Figure 7.3. Frontispiece of Alphabet of Nature. Courtesy of Wellcome Library, London.

As you can see from the frontispiece of *Alphabet of Nature* (Figure 7.3), van Helmont worked on the book while a prisoner. Sitting at a small table in his cell, pen in one hand and calipers in the other, he is portrayed measuring the movements made by his lips, teeth, and tongue as he pronounces different Hebrew letters.[3] I came to learn that investigating the Kabbalah could be extremely dangerous for Christians for the reasons I outline below, namely, because the Kabbalah presented ideas about God, humanity, and the universe that did not fit into the Christian emphasis on the uniqueness of the Christian revelation, original sin, and the need for divine grace to achieve salvation or an eternal Hell.

But even though I followed in the footsteps of Frances Yates, it was a hard sell to convince scholars that esoteric subjects like the Kabbalah had any relevance to science as it developed in the 17th century. For at the time I began my graduate studies, most people (and this included most scholars) believed that modern science emerged only when rationalist Enlightenment philosophers rejected religion and the kind of mystical traditions represented by the Kabbalah. In fact, during my time as a graduate student, scholars of what is now described as "esoteric" thought were routinely relegated to the "lunatic fringe of the British Museum Reading Room," to quote John Saltmarsh, and described as being "tinctured with. . . lunacy," to quote Sir Herbert Butterfield.[4] But these curt dismissals of esoteric currents of thought seriously misrepresent the forces that contributed to the scientific revolution and the transition from the premodern to the modern world. As my dissertation, along with subsequent publications, eventually argued, the Christian Kabbalah deserves to be recognized for the positive contribution it made to promoting key ideas at the core of modernity: first, that we are in charge of our own destiny and that of the world; second, that it is possible to gain knowledge of both the divine and natural world and to use this knowledge to improve the human condition; and, third, that experiment is a legitimate way to read the so-called Book of Nature and glorify God.[5] In fact, as scholars have now shown, esoteric currents of thought were and still are an integral part of the Western intellectual tradition and not simply an unimportant, fringe phenomenon.[6] But to turn to the Christian Kabbalah.

The Christian Kabbalah

As recent scholarship stresses, despite the very real anti-Semitism that existed in early modern Europe, Christians and Jews interacted in ways that were extraordinarily significant in fostering both the idea of progress and the ideal of toleration, twin pillars of our modern, religiously pluralistic, and scientifically oriented society,[7] and the Kabbalah played a significant part in this process. Kabbalistic ideas had been introduced into Christian circles as early as the 12th century in the writings of Raymond Lull (1232–1315), a Majorcan writer, philosopher, and mystic who became a Franciscan friar after having lived a profligate life as a young man.[8] By the 15th century it became possible to speak of a specifically "Christian Kabbalah." This first appeared in the Renaissance court of Cosimo de' Medici[9] (1389–1464), a wealthy businessman and banker who was the first of the Medici dynasty that virtually ruled Florence throughout most of the Renaissance. Noted for his patronage of the arts and culture, Cosimo established and funded a Platonic Academy among the philosopher-scholars. The *wunderkind* of the Academy was the young scholar Giovanni Pico della Mirandola (1463–1494), who began to study kabbalistic texts with the assistance of several Jewish teachers—Samuel ben Nissim Abulfaraj, Yoseph Alemano (1435–1504), and the converted Jew Raymond Moncada, also known as Flavius Mithradites (fl. 1470–1483). In 1486 Pico published his *Nine Hundred Theses*, in which he set forth the maxims for an ecumenical theology that he had culled from Jewish, Christian, Muslim, and pagan sources.[10] In Pico's view, this theology reflected the so-called *prisca theologia*, or first theology, that God had imparted first to Adam in the Garden of Eden and again to Moses on Mt. Sinai. Some one hundred of Pico's theses were derived from Kabbalah. In the preface to his *Theses*, Pico expressed the kabbalistic idea that the world could be perfected through human effort. Nowhere in Pico do we find the Christian emphasis on our irreparably fallen and sinful nature, on our incapacity to help ourselves, and the need for divine grace. A decidedly unorthodox and optimistic view of humankind emerges in Pico's pages—for example, Pico argues that human beings could become anything they choose to be from beasts to angels[11]—and, as a number of scholars have argued, this view contributed to the idea of progress characteristic of the later scientific revolution and Age of Enlightenment.[12] Pico's exhilaration was short-lived; he thought he could convince the Pope to accept his philosophy, but he could not. One has only to remember that a mere thirty years after Pico's optimistic attempt to unite men under the aegis of a single ecumenical philosophy, the Reformation began, which plunged Europe into a bloodbath of religious division and hatred for the next 150 years.

The Kabbalah did not disappear in the hostile atmosphere of the Reformation, however. In fact, the Reformation had the unintended effect of bringing Christians and Jews into closer contact than ever before. Luther's insistence that Scripture alone was the word of God encouraged Protestants to turn to Jewish commentaries when the text proved difficult to understand. The Protestant search for "real" Christianity—meaning, before it had been corrupted by the Catholic Church—also encouraged a closer look at Jewish sources, and this led many Christians to "Judaize" in the manner of van Helmont. The study of the early centuries of Christianity created greater awareness about the way that key Christian concepts, such as Jesus' nature—whether he was divine or human or both—and fundamental doctrines like the Trinity and the atonement had evolved over time. This realization encouraged, at least among some Christians, a skeptical, less dogmatic approach to doctrine.[13]

Christian Kabbalists provide an example of how dangerous the Protestant emphasis on Scripture proved to be for dogmatic assertions of any kind. Gershom Scholem was aware of the way that Christians had used and abused the Kabbalah to undermine the faith of some Jews, but, as far as I know, he never investigated the subversive influence the Kabbalah exerted on Christianity.[14] The Kabbalah's subversive influence was, however, pointed out by Ernst Benz, who emphasizes the religious no-man's land that many Jews and Christians found themselves in as a result of their kabbalistic studies. As Benz says:

> It frequently happened that, starting from Judaism, Jewish Kabbalists took a step towards Christianity; but they never arrived at a complete acceptance of Christian dogma. Inversely, the thinking of Christian Kabbalists, starting from a Christian perspective, often evolved in a manner that led to conflict with the traditional doctrine of their Church and ecclesiastical authorities. In this way, esoteric groups of Jews and Christians found themselves in a frontier region beyond the borders of their respective religions.[15]

That the Kabbalah clearly could undermine key components of Christian belief is demonstrated by the work of such eminent Christian thinkers as Johannes Reuchlin, Giordano Bruno, Cornelius Agrippa, Francesco Giorgi, Paracelsus, and Jakob Boehme, all of whom were influenced by kabbalistic thought in one way or another and all of whose various philosophies were unorthodox in major respects. The example I know best to illustrate the way in which the Kabbalah undermined Christian dogma and contributed to the growth of tolerance and ecumenism involved the publication of the *Kabbala denudata*, or Kabbalah Unveiled, in the late 17th century.

And this is where we get back to the subject of my doctoral thesis, Francis Mercury van Helmont, who was a close friend and collaborator of Christian Knorr von Rosenroth, who edited this two-volume work with van Helmont's assistance. The *Kabbala denudata* offered the European public the largest collection of kabbalistic texts published in Latin before the 19th century.

Figure 7.4. Frontispiece of Kabbala Denudata. Courtesy of Wellcome Library, London.

The *Kabbala denudata* is particularly rich in Lurianic kabbalistic texts, and it was on the basis of these that the editor dedicated the book to the "lover of philosophy, the lover of Hebrew, and the lover of chemistry." This is clearly a strange combination by modern lights—philosophy, Hebrew, and chemistry?—but not for the editor, who saw the Lurianic Kabbalah as a key to unlock the two great books that God had provided, the Book of Scripture and the Book of Nature.[16] This is the basic iconographic message of the frontispiece of the first volume of the *Kabbalah denudata* (Figure 7.4).

In the frontispiece one sees the figure of a beautiful maiden with flowing hair and Grecian robes, gazing skyward as she runs along a narrow ledge of earth separating the sea from a cave toward a doorway marked "Palace of Secrets" (*Palatium Arcanorum*). In her right hand, which is stretched out over the swelling waves, she holds a burning torch, under which is written "the sea of concupiscence" (*mare concupiscientiarum*). In her left, she carries a scroll representing the Scriptures, on which is written "she explains" (*explicat*). A great circle of light breaks through the clouds and darkness, and within this light are three circles, which in turn enclose three smaller circles. These stand for the ten kabbalistic *sefirot*, or the ten faces (*parṣ uphim*) of the hidden deity as He revealed Himself in the act of creation. In this Christian-kabbalistic synthesis, they are arranged in the form of a Trinity. Where the sea meets the sky the words "metaphysics of the gentiles" (*Metaphysica gentiles*) are written, suggesting that gentile wisdom has clear limits—it does not reach to, or come from, heaven as the Kabbalah does. The editor of this text, Knorr von Rosenroth, attributed the divisions among Christians to their misplaced dependence on Greek wisdom, which far from being the source of true philosophy had simply muddied the pure waters of divine Hebrew wisdom.[17] The female figure in this complex landscape is, of course, the Kabbalah, and the keys hanging on a cord from her waist indicate that the Kabbalah alone is able to unlock the secrets of both the Old and New Testaments.

This frontispiece emphasizes the encyclopedic nature of the Kabbalah. Not only does it provide a theology that will unite Christians, Jews, Muslims, and pagans, but it offers a morality that calms the passions besetting the soul (illustrated by the lurching of the ship on the stormy sea and the force of the wind exerted on the bent tree trunk). In addition to doing all this, the Kabbalah provides an entrance to the "Palace of Secrets," or true natural philosophy, represented by alchemy and chemistry. And here one needs to remember that throughout European history Solomon's temple was considered a repository of all the arts and sciences. The reason why Knorr dedicated the *Kabbala denudata* to the lover of chemistry—in addition to the lover of Hebrew and philosophy—should now be clear. The Kabbalah provided the metaphysical key to the physical world of nature. Thus the Kabbalah unlocks the secrets of the two books that reveal God, the Book of Scripture and the Book of Nature, since both books—the first dealing with the upper world and the second with the lower—are intimately linked. This great truth leads to another, namely, that the perceived gap between the material and spiritual realms, or matter and spirit, is nonexistent. Matter and spirit are simply different modes of a single entity. Through the process of *tikkun*, or restoration, matter will eventually be restored to its original spiritual perfection.

The *Kabbala denudata* presents a philosophical and theological framework for understanding how the world came into being and why it had degenerated to its present state. In addition to this, it offers an analysis of what could be done to restore creation to its original perfection and describes the role that we are expected to play in this process. In the Kabbalah we are held responsible for maintaining the connection between God and the world. Moshe Idel comments on the extraordinary scope this gives to human activity. As he says:

> The focus of Kabbalistic theurgy is God, not man; the latter is given unimaginable powers to be used in order to repair the divine glory or the divine image; only his initiative can improve Divinity. . . the Jew is responsible for everything, including God, since his activity is crucial for the welfare of the cosmos.[18]

He labels this kabbalistic view of our function in the universe, "Universe Maintenance Activity!"[19] R. J. Zwi Werblowsky goes even further, suggesting that in the Lurianic Kabbalah the role of humanity and God is inverted as we become God's savior:

> This is spiritual activism at its most extreme, for here God has become a real *salvator salvandus*. But to the Jew, Israel's exile became meaningful because it was seen as a participation in the profounder exile of God, and God Himself required Israel's active participation in the redemption of Himself and His people. It is not surprising that in this kabbalistic system the personality of the messiah played a relatively minor role. He was not so much a redeemer as a sign and symbol that the redemptive process had been achieved. In fact, the messianic doctrine of Lurianic Kabbalah comes close to the structure of an evolutionist scheme.[20]

All these ideas appear in the *Kabbala denudata*, which provided its readers the intellectual rationale for restoring the world to its idyllic state before the Fall. It was not enough, however, simply to contemplate restoring the world to its original perfection; concrete action was required. For all their interest in the abstruse theology of the Kabbalah, von Rosenroth and van Helmont were not thinkers cloistered in ivory towers. Their interest in the Kabbalah was inextricably tied to their active engagement in the world of politics, science, and religion. Von Rosenroth acted as Chancellor for Prince Christian August of Sulzbach during the same period that he was collecting, editing, and publishing kabbalistic texts, practicing alchemy in the laboratory which he and van Helmont set up in Sulzbach, collaborating with Helmont on various books dealing with penal reform and the rediscovery of Hebrew as a natural language, and translating Latin scientific texts into German. Von Rosenroth's work as a translator was deeply rooted in his religious and kabbalistic vision of a world restored to its original pristine condition through the cooperative efforts of human beings. Translating was therefore part of von Rosenroth's larger project of breaking down the barriers between Latin and vernacular culture in the interest of enlisting as many people as possible in the task of *tikkun*. Knowledge had to be communicated and shared. It could no longer remain the exclusive province of a few privileged intellectuals and scholars. Like von Rosenroth, van Helmont was deeply immersed in politics at the same time as he pursued literary and scientific endeavors. He was instrumental in publishing his father's chemical writings, as well as a number of works promoting his brand of ecumenical kabbalistic natural philosophy. Both men were reputed to be skilled chemists, possessing formulas for miraculous medicines, and they were often consulted on medical matters. In their daily lives, theory was not divorced from practice; scholarship was a means to the greater end of the common good.[21]

What I have emphasized in this chapter is how practical and in many ways down to earth—quite literally—an esoteric encyclopedia like the *Kabbala denudata* could be. Von Rosenroth and van Helmont were decidedly not interested in how many angels could dance on the head of a pin, and however abstruse their discussions about the intricate doctrines of kabbalistic thought were, their interest in it was dedicated to improving the human condition as well as the state of the natural world. This was the driving force behind their manifold activities. In the minds of von Rosenroth and van Helmont, as in the minds of many of their contemporaries, there was no separation between their religious beliefs, intellectual pursuits, and active political lives. Ancient kabbalistic texts could and did provide the blueprint for an ideal future, one in which humanity would, for the first and only time since the Fall, experience the harmony, peace, and brotherhood that God had originally envisioned for them. And this would come about through human effort and human ingenuity. This shift from the divine to the human plane fostered a new and more optimistic vision, a view that in many cases led them to reject the concepts of original sin, of an eternal hell, and of an irredeemably corrupted world. It is for these reasons that I believe that the

Kabbalah should be recognized for its contributions to the Enlightenment belief in science as a progressive social force.

Evidence suggests that the *Kabbala denudata* was read by a number of eminent Christian philosophers, theologians, and scientists, who were influenced by its ideas. Gottfried Wilhelm Leibniz, for example, was a close friend of van Helmont and knew von Rosenroth's work well. Some of you may know Leibniz from the scathing, hilarious, but very much mistaken view of his philosophy presented by Voltaire in *Candide*. Here Leibniz is satirized in the character of Dr. Pangloss, the fatuous philosopher, who, no matter what awful thing happens, reiterates his philosophy that this is "the best of all possible worlds." Nothing could convince Dr. Pangloss that his optimism was misplaced, not a shipwreck, a very, very bad case of syphilis, a botched execution by the Inquisition—only botched because an earthquake intervened—or the fact that he regained consciousness just in time to avoid being dissected. But Leibniz was not the fool Voltaire made him out to be. He did not, as Voltaire claimed, believe that this world was the best possible as it presently is, but only because it had the capacity to become increasingly better, largely through humanity's rational and scientific endeavors. If Leibniz really believed that this world was the best possible as it now stands, what would explain his lifelong concern with improving the world, first, by restoring religious unity and, second, by devising innumerable projects for all kinds of socially useful inventions. Leibniz's calculator is perhaps the best known, but he also proposed plans for such things as a high-speed coach, which would run along rutted tracks on something like ball bearings, a scheme for draining water from the Hartz mines, an inland navigation system, the manufacture of porcelain, the exploitation of waste heat in furnaces, tax reform, a public health and fire service, steam-powered fountains, street lighting, a state bank, and isolation wards for plague victims.[22] What cemented the friendship between Leibniz and van Helmont was their mutual concern for making the world a better place. Together, they worked to invent such mundane but important things as a better wheelbarrow, more efficient cooking pots, and, my favorite, shoes with springs for fast getaways. As I have argued in my book *Leibniz and the Kabbalah*, key areas in Leibniz's philosophy, and this includes his profound interest in restoring the world to its original perfection, can be understood in an entirely new light if his knowledge of the Kabbalah is taken into consideration.[23]

Many other examples show that the Kabbalah played a role in shaping European thought. John Locke, for instance, excerpted passages of the *Kabbalah denudata* to keep among his papers, and he discussed kabbalistic ideas at length with van Helmont. Like Leibniz, he, too, collaborated with van Helmont on various scientific inventions. Even Sir Isaac Newton read the *Kabbalah denudata*, although most scholars now think it was his negative reaction to it that influenced his philosophical and theological ideas.[24] German Pietism was an offshoot of Lutheranism initiated by Philipp Jakob Spener (1635–1705) that emphasized Bible study, personal devotion and faith, and pious living. It spread to other Protestant denominations, influencing the Anglican John Wesley to establish Methodism and Alexander Mack to found the Brethren movement. Pietists were also influenced by von Rosenroth's translations, and they, in turn, influenced such German idealists as G. W. F Hegel and F. W. J. Schelling.[25] The last great work of Christian Kabbalah was written by Franz Josef Molitor (1779–1861) and received high praise from Scholem, despite its Christological approach.[26] The influence of the Kabbalah on European Masonry is another area that is beginning to be studied. The reach of the Kabbalah across European history is indeed long. One of the latest figures to be tarred by a kabbalistic brush is Joseph Smith, the founder of the Mormons. Lance Owens, himself a Mormon, and John Brooke have provided new evidence to support Harold Bloom's contention that Mormonism is a revived form of Kabbalah. Owens believes that Smith's extraordinary sermon, known as "The King Follett Discourse," was directly related to Smith's friendship with a converted Jew knowledgeable in the Kabbalah. In this discourse Smith discussed several extraordinary doctrinal innovations, among which were that men can become gods and that many gods exist, ideas Owens believed that Smith derived from the Kabbalah.[27]

Given all these examples, it is high time that the Kabbalah, with its optimistic philosophy of perfectionism and universal salvation, be recognized for the impetus it gave to ideas that have become so fundamental in the modern world, namely, that we are essentially good and can and must use our innate abilities to improve this world. The belief in our human power and perspicacity arose from many different sources, but the Kabbalah surely should be recognized as one of these.

NOTES

1. Frances A. Yates, *Giordano Bruno and the Hermetic Tradition* (London: Routledge and Kegan Paul, 1964); idem, *The Art of Memory* (London: Routledge and Kegan Paul, 1966).

2. Moshe Idel, private communication.

3. Francis Mercury van Helmont, *Alphabeti ver naturalis hebraici brevissima delineatio . . .* (Sulzbach, 1667), ed. and trans. Allison P. Coudert and Taylor Corse (Leiden: Brill, 2007).

4. Herbert Butterfield, *The Origins of Modern Science* (New York: Macmillan, 1952), p. 98.

5. Allison P. Coudert, *The Impact of the Kabbalah in the Seventeenth Century: The Life and Thought of Francis Mercury van Helmont* (Leiden: Brill, 1999).

6. In recent years two societies have been founded devoted to the study of esotericism, the Association for the Study of Esotericism (ASE) and the European Society for the Study of Western Esotericism (ESSWE). There are now two journals devoted to the subject, *Aries* and the online journal *Esoterica*.

7. Allison P. Coudert and Jeffrey S. Shoulson, eds., *Hebraica Veritas? Christian Hebraists, Jews, and the Study of Judaism in Early Modern Europe* (Philadelphia: University of Pennsylvania Press, 2004).

8. Ramon Llull, anglicized to Raymond Lull, is best known for his *Ars magna* (1305), which offered a method for discovering and presenting knowledge in a logical way. The major impetus behind his work was the goal of converting Muslims and Jews to Christianity. Cf. J. N. Hilgarth, *Raymond Lull and Lullism in Fourteenth-Century France* (Oxford: Oxford University Press, 1972); Paolo Rossi, *Logic and the Art of Memory: The Quest for a Universal Language*, translated with an introduction by Stephen Clucas (London: Athlone, 2000).

9. Cosimo de' Medici appointed Marsilius Ficino (1433–1499) to head the Platonic Academy. Ficino made the first complete Latin translation of the works of Plato as well as a translation of the works attributed to Hermes Trismegistus, the legendary Egyptian sage and contemporary of Moses.

10. Stephen A. Farmer, *Syncretism in the West: Pico's 900 Theses (1486): The Evolution of Traditional Religious and Philosophical Systems*, with a revised text, English translation, and commentary (Tempe, AZ: Medieval and Renaissance Texts and Studies, vol. 167, 1998).

11. Pico's Oration can be found at http://www.historyguide.org/intellect/pico.html.

12. See Frank L. Borchardt, "The Magus as Renaissance Man," *Sixteenth Century Journal* (1990): 57–76; Frances A. Yates, "The Hermetic Tradition in Renaissance Science" in *Art, Science, and History in the Renaissance*, ed. Charles S. Singleton (Baltimore: Johns Hopkins University Press, 1968); and M. V. Dougherty, ed., *Pico della Mirandola, New Essays* (Cambridge: Cambridge University Press, 2008). See also the references in footnote 19, below.

13. Jerome Friedman, *The Most Ancient Testimony: Sixteenth-Century Christian-Hebraica in the Age of Renaissance Nostalgia* (Athens: Ohio State University Press, 1983).

14. Gershom Scholem, "Zur Geschichte der Anfänge der christlichen Kabbala," in *Essays Presented to Leo Baeck on the Occasion of His Eightieth Birthday* (London: East and West Library, 1954).

15. Ernst Benz, "La Kabbale chrétienne en Allemagne du xvi au xviii siècle," in *Kabbalistes Chrétiens: Cahiers de l'Hermetisme*, ed. Antoine Faivre and Frederick Tristan (Paris: Éditions Albin Michel, 1979), pp. 111–12 (my translation).

16. From antiquity to the present, theologians, philosophers and scientists have described nature as a book written by God, which, if read correctly, could provide human beings with crucial knowledge about God and the world. Reading the Book of Nature along with Scripture was considered essential for obtaining a deeper understanding of God's power and wisdom. This idea was emphasized by scientists (or "natural philosophers," as they were called before the 18th century) as a way to promote and legitimate a positive attitude toward nature and its study.

17. *Kabbala denudata*, 2 vols. (Sulzbach: 1677, 1684; reprint Hildesheim: Olms, 1974), vol. 1 (2), p. 75.

18. Moshe Idel, *Kabbalah: New Perspectives* (New Haven: Yale University Press, 1988), p. 179.

19. Idel, *Kabbalah*, p. 170. On the importance of human activity in the process of *tikkun*, see Gershom Scholem, *Major Trends in Jewish Mysticism* (New York: Schocken Books, 1954), pp. 244–86; idem, *Sabbatai Zevi: The Mystical Messiah* (Princeton, NJ: Princeton University Press, 1973), chap. 1; R. J. Zwi Werblowsky, *Joseph Karo, Lawyer and Mystic* (Philadelphia: Jewish Publication Society of America, 1977), pp. 97–99; David B. Ruderman, "Hope against Hope: Jewish and Christian Messianic Expectations in the Late Middle Ages," in *Essential Papers on Jewish Culture in Renaissance and Baroque Italy*, ed. David B. Ruderman (New York: New York University Press, 1992), pp. 299–323, esp. pp. 313–15.

20. R. J. Zwi Werblowsky, "Messianism in Jewish History," in *Essential Papers on Messianic Movements and Personalities in Jewish History*, ed. Marc Saperstein (New York: New York University Press, 1992), p. 48.

21. Allison P. Coudert, "Seventeenth Century Natural Philosophy and Esotericism at the Court of Sulzbach," in *Mélanges d'Histoire des Religions réunis en l'honneur de M. Antoine Faivre par ses éleves, collègues et amis*, ed. Joscelyn Godwin and Wouter J. Hanegraaff (Louvain: Peeters, 2001), pp. 27–46.

22. R. W. Meyer emphasizes Leibniz's commitment to practical reforms and improvements in *Leibnitz and the Seventeenth-Century Revolution*, trans. J. P. Stern (Chicago: Henry Regnery, 1952), pp. 118–20.

23. Allison P. Coudert, *Leibniz and the Kabbalah* (Dordrecht: Kluwer, 1995).

24. Matt Goldish, "Newton on Kabbalah," in *The Books of Nature and Scripture*, ed. R. H. Popkin and J. E. Force (Dordrecht: Kluwer, 1994), pp. 89–103.

25. *The Mystical Sources of German Romantic Philosophy*, trans. Blair R. Reynolds and Eunice M. Paul (Allison Park, PA: Pickwick, [1968] 1983); Jürgen Habermas, "Dialektischer Idealismus im Übergang zum Materialismus: Geschichtsphilosophische Folgerungen aus Schellings Idee einer Contyraktion Gottes," in idem, *Theorie und Praxis* (Frankfurt am Main: Suhrkamp, 1971), pp. 172–227; Ernst Benz, "Schellings theologische Geistesahnen," in *Abhandlung der Akademie der Wissenschaft und die Literature* (1955), pp. 231–307; idem, *Schelling. Werden und Wirken seines Denkens* (Zurich: Rhein-Verlag, 1958); Christoph Schulze, "Schelling und die Kabbala," *Judaica* 13 (1957): 65–99; idem, "Zimzum in European Philosophy: A Paradoxical Career," *Jewish Studies in a New Europe: Proceedings of the Fifth Congress of Jewish Studies in Copenhagen 1994 under the Auspices of the European Association for Jewish Studies*, ed. Ulf Haxen, Hanne Traunter-Kromann, and Karen Lisa Goldschmidt Salamon (Copenhagen: C.A. Reitzel A/S International, 1998), pp. 745–56.

26. Katharina Koch, *Franz Joseph Molitor und die jüdische Tradition, Studien zu den kabbalistischen Quellen der "Philosophie der Geschichte,"* with an appendix of unpublished letters by F. von Baader, E. J. Hirschfeld, F. J. Molitor, and F. W. J. Schelling (Berlin: Walter de Gruyter, 2006).

27. Lance S. Owens, "Joseph Smith and Kabbalah: The Occult Connection" (available at http://www.gnosis.org/jskabb1.htm). John L. Brooke, *The Refiner's Fire: The Making of Mormon Cosmology, 1644–1844* (Cambridge: Cambridge University Press, 1994).

III

Contemporary Concerns

Kabbalah at the
Turn of the 21st Century

JODY MYERS

Neither the scholars who penned the first academic studies on Kabbalah nor the next two generations of disciples expected that it would ever be necessary to write a chapter such as this. The standard textbooks treat 19th-century Hasidism as the latest expression of Jewish mysticism.[1] Many could not imagine that in their own time the cryptic medieval Aramaic and Hebrew texts laden with archaic symbolism could be a serious resource for spiritual engagement. Yet, since the last third of the 20th century, kabbalistic concepts and symbols have been found within conventional Jewish congregations and emerging religious movements of all kinds, by individuals from an extraordinarily diverse background, and in spiritual literature and the arts.[2] It is impossible to coin a single label for these new permutations of Kabbalah. The term most commonly used, "popular Kabbalah," is problematic. Kabbalah is not popular in the sense of being widely accepted, for it is not. Generally, at this time people who are engaged with Kabbalah are either those who are uncomfortable with normative religious institutions, practices, and doctrines, or they are Orthodox Jews. All these people are unquestionably unconventional and represent a small minority. Sometimes the term "popular" is used to distinguish current teachings from earlier ones because of the erroneous belief that previous forms of Kabbalah were at all times esoteric, elitist, and unchanging. Contrary to the impression that contemporary Kabbalah enthusiasts have updated premodern concepts, it is the case that some, unhindered by the pressure to conform, have made great efforts to replicate older teachings and express them quite close to what experts regard as "the original."[3] Of course, adaptation cannot be avoided when older teachings are applied in a later time. Often the term "popular Kabbalah" is meant as a pejorative ("pop Kabbalah") or as a means of distinguishing the false from the authentic. Such judgments of authenticity are social constructs and not appropriate for academic writing.

Furthermore, the current involvement with Kabbalah occurs in a variety of social settings. There are only a few congregations in which Kabbalah is the predominant component of the group's doctrines and behaviors. A few such communities exist in Israel, and in the Diaspora there are some real and virtual communities that are parts of the larger, international kabbalistic movements known as Kabbalah Centre (founded in 1969) and Bnei Baruch (founded in 1991). Still unclear, because these are so young, is whether the second generation of followers will be able to produce a third. More commonly Kabbalah appears as one of a number of resources used by individuals or by groups who come together for spiritual purposes on a regular or occasional basis. Not all who study Kabbalah or perform kabbalistic rituals are Jewish or regard their activities as subsumed within Judaism. In some of these cases, people may even follow traditional religious precepts and appear to be Orthodox Jews while they deny any connection to Judaism.

In order to give a sense of Kabbalah at the turn of the 21st century, I will first describe how Kabbalah became attractive and widely available. I will then suggest six reasons for the revival of Kabbalah and illustrate these points with examples from current teachings and practices. The focus of this chapter is on North America.

Pathways to the Revival of Kabbalah

The current renaissance did not occur suddenly, but it did follow decades of general Jewish neglect of Kabbalah as a spiritual resource. First, in reaction to what they regarded as the improper popularization and distortion of Kabbalah, European Kabbalists restricted publication and study of these teachings, and although such strictures had been voiced for centuries, they began to be enforced. Second, Jewish leaders influenced by the Enlightenment and by the possibility of integration into European society regarded Kabbalah as an embarrassment and an obstacle. Consequently, in Ashkenazic society, study of Kabbalah became concentrated in Eastern Europe among Hasidic Jews and among non-Hasidic scholars of the Mitnagdic tradition. Eventually, however, the cultural suppression of Jewish studies in communist regimes and the death tolls of the Holocaust ended Europe's contribution to the production of Kabbalah.

In North Africa and the Middle East, the heartland of Kabbalah study since the 16th century, Jewish communities continued to produce Kabbalah scholars, promote the veneration of Kabbalists, and support the use of kabbalistic symbols and rites in religious life. The extent and intensity of these expressions diminished, however, under the impact of modernization and immigration. A number of Kabbalists (including some from Europe) seeking a more supportive environment relocated to Jerusalem in the first few decades of the 20th century,[4] but this surge of creativity was not long-lasting. The eviscerating effect of secular Zionist culture and the postwar migration of Middle Eastern and North African Jews to Israel severely limited the position of Kabbalah at mid-century. Not until the 1970s did it begin to revive noticeably. In 1977 Israel's socialist Labor Party, which had been dominant since the Mandatory period, lost control of the government to a coalition of secular conservative nationalists, *mizraḥim* (Jews from Muslim lands), and religious Israelis. Since that time, these groups have wielded substantial influence. The augmented government investment in religious institutions and the assertion of a different cultural ethos are evident in the increasing respect for Kabbalah and the institutional structures supporting its proliferation.

The situation in North America has been quite different. Jews who were devoted to Torah scholarship and a rich Jewish religious life did not generally move to the New World prior to World War II. The relatively small percentage of North American Jews who followed *halacha* struggled to perpetuate their loyalties to the next generation and support the study of the Bible, Talmud, and law codes. Kabbalah was outside their capabilities and, except for some immigrants from Eastern Europe, their interests as well. Historians have learned of a few men trained in Kabbalah who arrived on the American continent prior to World War II and sought to propagate their teachings. All had difficulty rearing disciples and finding readers for their writings. Rabbi Levi Krakovsky, one of these Kabbalists, reported in dismay his discovery that American Kabbalah enthusiasts believed that Kabbalah stemmed from non-Jewish origins.[5]

Non-Jews who regarded Kabbalah as a component of a larger spiritual tradition must not be overlooked when accounting for the late-20th-century revival of interest in Kabbalah. Their activities represent a more advanced stage of the innovative approaches to religion and science from Renaissance Italy that blended Christianity with Kabbalah and occult teachings. These ideas took on new life in the late 18th century among Western Europeans who criticized the religious establishment and religious orthodoxies. An important theoretical foundation was laid by the Swedish thinker Emanuel Swedenborg (1688–1772). He taught that one must not read the Bible literally but rather as a code that establishes correspondences between the physical world and the divine realm; the former had been created in the image of the latter, and both received outpourings of divine energy. These points are found in Kabbalah as well.

A number of spiritual philosophies and religious practices grew from these foundations in Europe and North America, where they produced a variety of "metaphysical religions."[6] The most important of these for the dissemination of Kabbalah was the Theosophical Society, founded in 1875 by Helena Petrovna Blavatsky (1831–1891) and Henry Steel Olcott (1832–1907). In Theosophical Society teachings, kabbalistic texts were drawn upon to support the above principles as well as the belief in reincarnation, although reinterpreted elements of Hindu and Buddhist religious traditions played a far larger role. Theosophists rejected the notion that the teachings found in Kabbalah originated in Jewish society and were the "possession" of the Jews; they taught, on the contrary, that Kabbalah was simply one particularized expression of the universal spiritual-scientific wisdom found among many authentic sacred traditions that had been suppressed and pronounced heretical for centuries.[7] The Theosophical Society and its spin-off organizations established learning centers, held public lectures, and published books that included translations and interpretations of Kabbalah for a wide audience.[8] Masonic lodges exposed their members to this literature and to kabbalistic symbols. Prior to the second half of the 20th century, these organizations were more influential than religious Jews in bringing kabbalistic ideas and symbols into American religious life.

The New Age movement that began after World War II in Great Britain is in large part an elaboration and expansion of theosophy and similar metaphysical philosophies. The moniker comes from the commonly held belief that the present civilization is dying and giving way to a new Age of Aquarius, an era of universal brotherhood with the potential for great intellectual and spiritual progress and environmental healing. New Age ideas moved to continental Europe, Israel, and the United States, gaining strength in the 1970s. New Age theorists did not possess much knowledge of Kabbalah, but they would refer to it as being aligned with their views, and they encouraged the production and consumption of books on the subject.[9]

Another path to kabbalistic spirituality, ironically, was academic scholarship. German scholars of the 19th century began to use the academic methodologies of philology, philosophy, and history to research and analyze literature they regarded as evidence of bygone Jewish mysticism. This field of study was aggressively advanced by Gershom Scholem, who moved to Palestine from Germany in 1923 and eventually became a professor of Jewish mysticism at the Hebrew University in Jerusalem. American Jews were introduced to his research in 1938, when the Jewish Institute of Religion brought Scholem to New York to deliver a series of lectures that were later published as *Major Trends in Jewish Mysticism*. This scholarship was not meant to nurture people's religious lives. Nevertheless, academic studies of Kabbalah eventually were, and still are, used as a resource by people exploring ultimate issues or hunting for material to be used for self-expression. One of the earliest examples of this was the utilization of Kabbalah by Jewish "Beat" artists and poets who resided in Los Angeles and the San Francisco Bay region. During the early 1960s they produced art, poetry, and essays incorporating symbols and Hebrew letter combinations that they found in *Major Trends*.[10]

These three sources of Kabbalah—the teachings of Jewish Kabbalists, metaphysical religious literature, and academic scholarship—were drawn upon during the late 1960s during the religious transformation that accompanied the American political turmoil of the time. A sizable number of young people voiced dissatisfaction with their parents' religious lives and with conventional modes of practicing established religions. They accused religious leaders and institutions of being unresponsive to social ills, overly focused on buildings and institutional preservation, and spiritually vacuous. Some looked for new approaches or revived neglected elements from within their inherited religious traditions. Many religious rebels deliberately looked outside their heritage. They experimented with a variety of newly available religious options such as Buddhism, Hinduism, nature-centered and Native American religions, New Age, and all types of meditation and mysticism. College-aged Jews were disproportionately represented among this cohort.

In response, a few rabbis and educators devised strategies for drawing alienated and unlearned Jews back to Judaism. A number of American Orthodox rabbis recognized that Kabbalah contained many of the features that the young found attractive in "foreign" religions. Rabbis Zalman Schachter (later Schachter-Shalomi, b. 1924) and Shlomo Carlebach (1924–1994), Chabad emissaries assigned to American college campuses, were the first of these to include kabbalistic teachings and ecstatic practices in their "outreach" work.[11] In 1969 Rabbi Philip Gruberger (later Philip Berg, b. 1929), a recent student of the late rabbis Levi Krakovsky and Yehuda Brandwein, founded the Research Centre of Kabbalah to publish the kabbalistic writings of others and his own New Age version of their lessons. Rabbi Aryeh Kaplan (1934–1983) began in 1978 to add translations of kabbalistic texts and essays on Kabbalah to his extensive writings directed toward potential or actual "returnees to Judaism" (*ba'alei teshuva*). By this time, courses in Jewish Studies were entering American college curricula, and academic works on Jewish mysticism became more available and increasingly utilized for spiritual, artistic, and literary ends.

The American public's awareness of Kabbalah grew rapidly during the 1990s. Key to this was the organization that grew out of the Research Centre of Kabbalah, known as the Kabbalah Centre. Founded originally as a means of reaching out to Jews in Israel as well as North America, the Kabbalah Centre in the early 1990s revised its lessons and publications to appeal to a North American audience unfamiliar with Jewish concepts and practices. When non-Jews began to frequent Kabbalah Centre classes and ceremonies, the organization's directors expanded their mission to include a universal audience. Celebrity followers—Madonna is the most important—drew extraordinary publicity to the Kabbalah Centre and induced many people to explore its offerings. Prompted by antipathy for what they regarded as the Kabbalah Centre's indiscriminate outreach, aggressive recruitment methods, and exploitative treatment of its devotees, Jewish religious leaders began offering their own "kosher" Kabbalah courses and writings. With the expansion of Internet technology, a tremendous array of kabbalistic writings and images, past and present, have become available and are growing rapidly.

The Allure of Kabbalah

For Jews of the late 20th and early 21st centuries, Kabbalah has cultural value because it is perceived as esoteric, antiestablishment, and spiritual. Further, because it lacked a powerful authoritative defender, it could easily be adopted and adapted. Contemporary audiences have invested it with specific features that make it useful for their religious lives.[12]

1. As a source for constructing an alternate theology and view of the cosmos

Kabbalah presents a view of God that can be interpreted as complex and dynamic. There is the *Ein Sof*, the limitless, infinite, unknowable, indefinable divinity. The *sefirot* are ten stages in which divinity is progressively more manifest in increasing clarity. Some Kabbalists teach that these represent the inner life of God as it is progressively more revealed; other Kabbalists regard these as ten attributes of God, and the human being as comprised of the same ten attributes; still others say that these are the divine emanation within created reality; and others simply call them the instruments of God's creation. These ten *sefirot* may be imagined all together as a tree of life, as forming a divine body, as a group of male *sefirot* and female *sefirot* erotically drawn to or alienated from each other. Divine energy continually flows between them and into our physical world. The sefirotic structure is parallel to our world, and the two worlds are in dynamic relationship to each other, intimately connected. Another image used by Kabbalists for the layers of reality are the Four Worlds of emanation (*atzilut*), formation (*beri'a*), creation (*yetsira*), and action (*asiya*). Hence Kabbalah may be regarded as an alternative to theism and as a spiritual outlook in which divinity and the sacred are not distant and transcendent but immanent and in-dwelling.

The rejection of pure theism is attractive to many seeking alternatives to the prevailing religious outlooks. They find implausible the image of God as a judge or a king who rewards and punishes, rules, commands, and gets angry. They might not find credible *any* image of the sacred personified as a being, male or female. Many accept the Freudian critique of theism as merely human beings' projection of earthly authority onto a supernatural realm. These complaints about theism did not appear for the first time in the 20th century, of course. But with the rebellion against institutionalized Christianity and Judaism and with the mass immigration to the United States during the 1960s of Asian immigrants bearing nontheistic views of the sacred from Buddhism and Hindu teachings, dissatisfied but spiritual-seeking Americans realized that there were alternatives to theism. Kabbalah could be used to provide a Jewish option.

Nontheistic perspectives are also appealing because they are nonauthoritarian. The absence of a ruling deity is important in an era when people see only too well the blunders and immorality of political and religious authorities. The *sefirot* appear as a collective of attributes that operates automatically, according to the distinctive natures of the individual *sefirot*, rather than as an authority figure who commands or rewards and punishes people because they followed this or that ritual or were good or bad. In addition, Kabbalah can easily be understood to present divinity as in-dwelling and immanent rather than separate and transcendent, and this, too, is an outlook much in favor among spiritual seekers. It seems harmonious with feminism and the less rigid gender divisions that have come into favor. People have adapted the feminine images and the erotically charged narratives in kabbalistic texts to express the more nurturing, compassionate, and sensual outlook and practices that they want and need.

There are many examples of this. The current fascination with the *sefirot* is evident in visual art, where one can find many images of the *sefirot* as ten spheres symmetrically arranged in the "tree of life" or overladen upon a human body. These may be used for sheer decoration, as a focal point for meditation, as a reminder for the sacred force embedded in the cosmos, or as a type of amulet.[13] For some, references to *Shekhinah*, the divine feminine presence of God, are an important element in worship, ritual, and study. Since the 1980s people—male as well as female, Jews as well as non-Jews—have called upon the *Shekhinah* in healing prayers or in acknowledging the phases of the moon or the seasons of the year.[14] For many, the concept of the Four Worlds is central. As in premodern Kabbalah, it may describe the structure of reality starting with *Ein Sof*'s emanation of the *sefirot*, the divine chariot-throne and higher angels, the world of angels, and our own material world. Quite common, though, are adaptations of Hasidic teachings that interpreted the Four Worlds to refer to the four inner aspects of the psyche from the most receptive to the spiritual to the least receptive. This language enables the individual to create a more conscious awareness of his or her state of mind and activities as they connect to spiritual reality.[15]

2. As a Source for a Nonliteral Approach to Scripture

To the Kabbalist, the words of the Torah are holy, but they are symbols of a deeper message. They are a coded version of the knowledge of what came before creation, what will come after, the inner life of God (the sefirotic structure and dynamics), and a guidebook to the relationship between the "upper world" and our own. The *Zohar* explains this by comparing God's word to a beautiful maiden's clothed and veiled body. Those who read the stories of the Torah are seeing only the veils. Under the outermost layers are the moral and philosophical teachings. Under those are the body and the heart of the Torah, the Kabbalah, which contains the most precious, essential element. Studying Kabbalah, one learns the code within the Torah's words and sees how it points to hidden wisdom contained within.

Such a nonliteral approach may be quite exciting to many, even those who regard the literal meaning with great reverence. A nonliteral approach, however, is particularly useful to people who believe that the Torah's stories are farfetched, the events ahistorical, the miracles unbelievable, or the ancient outlooks irrelevant. In this sense, Kabbalah functions like Midrash that "rescues" the Torah by identifying it with other, more acceptable meanings. One can regard the Torah as a source of spiritual truth and a guide to living a holy life without subscribing to the principle of biblical inviolability or other conservative orthodoxies. Indeed, Kabbalah study becomes a highly challenging activity requiring great intellectual skills and the ability to gain access to one's intuition and subconscious.

Previously, only those with knowledge of Hebrew or Aramaic and the tutelage of a master could gain insights from kabbalistic literature, but the publication of translations designed for the American spiritual-seeking audience facilitated the development of new approaches to Torah study.[16] Eventually, these found their way into mainstream Jewish institutions. For example, the 1993 ArtScroll edition of the Torah, *The Chumash: The Stone Edition*, which is used widely in American Orthodox synagogues, contains alongside the standard commentaries an additional commentary that includes kabbalistic interpretations among the insights from rabbinic literature.[17] Arthur Green's abridged translation of the 19th-century Torah commentary of the Gerer Hasidic rebbe, *Sefat Emet*, has been used in the curriculum of the Institute for Jewish Spirituality, an organization that arranges study retreats and networks for Jewish clergy and educators (Reform, Reconstructionist, and Conservative) in order to strengthen the "vitally needed stream of contemplative Judaism."[18] The online Chabad website contains many options for learning Chabad's perspectives on Kabbalah and even making it part of one's study of the weekly Torah *parashah* through the "Kabbalah on the Bible" audio classes.[19]

3. As a Source for Alternate Forms of Worship and Understandings of Religious Practice

Prayer is modeled on the human experience: requesting, asking forgiveness, praise, thanking. This makes sense for theism, but prayer has to be reconceptualized in nontheistic contexts. Jewish kabbalists were committed to following the prescribed system of prayer, and they understood the words as tools to activate and balance the *sefirot*, to elevate oneself in order to cleave to God, to weaken the power of evil, and the like. Beyond reciting the liturgy, Kabbalists recommended a variety of practices that could be considered worship, such as contemplation of divine names, voiced chants, and tearful laments. These older rites have been revived and revised. One example is in the Kabbalah Centre, which has produced a liturgy based on the prayer book attributed to the Kabbalist Isaac Luria and the *kavanot* (prayer intentions) of Shalom Shar'abi. In the communal worship services, called Connections, the words of the prayers are regarded not as a means of personally or communally addressing God but as weapons to wage war against the negativity within the soul, human society, and nature; or as vehicles that draw positive divine energy into these realms.[20]

Similarly, contemporary interpreters of Kabbalah draw upon older teachings to describe prayer and *mitzvot* as vehicles for connecting to the upper world, for infusing one's life with the power of the sacred, or for restoring the *sefirot* to a more harmonious balance. For example, in the Jewish Renewal movement, participants use dance, music, and food to evoke the *sefirot* and the Four Worlds, enacting the emanation of the *sefirot* or the dramatic union or separation of *Tiferet* and *Shekhinah*.[21] In the kabbalistic movement called Bnei Baruch, the primary activity is a communal study of texts written by the Kabbalist Yehuda Ashlag. Those in the movement believe that when all participants are motivated by a deep desire to connect to God at the highest spiritual level, their souls are refined toward the ultimate objective of adhering to God.[22]

Because of the immanentist understandings of divinity they associate with Kabbalah, contemporary interpreters may infuse daily life with cosmic significance. Meditations employing kabbalistic concepts have been constructed that turn mundane activities such as exercising and waiting in line into opportunities for contemplation of the sacred.[23] Finally, Kabbalah has proven to be a fertile resource for people who regard spiritual objects and signs in their environment or on their body as a meaningful expression of spirituality. For example, there seems to be a large interest in kabbalistic *shevitis* (pictures composed of Hebrew letters designed to focus one's attention and be a reminder of God's presence), amulets, and items to be worn upon the body.[24]

4. As a Science

Medieval Jews believed that Kabbalah provided an accurate guide to the operations of the universe, and this belief has reappeared in the modern era as the conviction that Kabbalah contains within it the most advanced scientific knowledge and is the authoritative guide to the mysteries of the universe. This is not simple biblical fundamentalism or the explicit rejection of science; on the contrary, it is an expression of the desire to equate one's faith with science. For example, some argue that long before physicists theorized that the universe was created through a "big bang," Kabbalists were teaching the same through the doctrines of *tzimtzum* (contraction) and *shevirat ha-kelim* (the breaking of the vessels).[25] Kabbalah, in short, provides an access to an enlightened understanding of the cosmos that scientists will only painstakingly achieve. Such modern devotees of Kabbalah avidly read about the latest scientific breakthroughs and pride themselves on their grasp of them relative to most people. This position toward science and faith is not unique to Kabbalah; it is a distinctive feature of New Age spirituality and of metaphysical religions in general. Writings and lectures integrating science and Kabbalah can be found in explicitly Jewish sources as well as those broader ones.

GEMINI - May 22/Jun 21
Gemini, you can't help but feel giddy over what is to come. Others will soon be caught up in this infectious feeling. Money matters take priority later in the week.

CANCER - Jun 22/Jul 22
Hold on to your horses, Cancer, because it is going to be a bumpy ride the next few days. When you think everything will smooth over, it starts up all over again.

LEO - Jul 23/Aug 23
Leo, a moment of inspiration comes when you weren't even looking for it. Take the opportunity to do something fun with your ideas rather than focus energy on work.

VIRGO - Aug 24/Sept 22
Virgo, you are back on track and the feeling is exhilarating. Right now you feel like your life has purpose and you're shooting through goals left and right. Tackle romance next.

productivity.

SAGITTARIUS - Nov 23/Dec 21
Sagittarius, you may want to make a resolution to change a few things about yourself that seem irksome to others. The same old strategy isn't working so give a new one a try.

CAPRICORN - Dec 22/Jan 20
Capricorn, a battle of wills leaves you licking your wounds. Now you may need to regroup and find a new way to mend fences. Put finances on the side for a while.

AQUARIUS - Jan 21/Feb 18
Aquarius, you may have been stepping aside and letting others take a leadership role in important decisions. But you have missed out on essential information. Get involved once more.

PISCES - Feb 19/Mar 20
Others may not know just how capable you are at handling things, Pisces. Show them just how effective you can be.

Stop by Betsy Paul Properties (address below) to view this one-of-a-kind painting and purchase raffle tickets for a chance to win.

Myles is an accomplished and intuitive artist. She re-

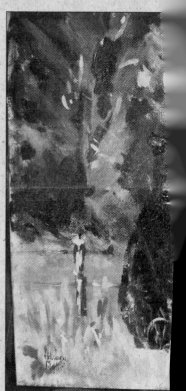

This painting by Adrienn fire raffle prize.

Final movie of season

The final movie of the seaso ring Harrison Ford and Diane Albert Carlton-Cashiers Com day, Oct. 20 at 3 p.m. The f newsroom.

It is rated PG-13 and runs 1 popcorn are free. Donations g brary programs. For further d tion guidelines prohibit publ call the library at 828-743-02

	8			2	7		5	
					6			
		7					2	9
		1				9	8	
	5					3		4
		8						
		9			2			
		2	6	5				1
4					3	2		

Level: Intermediate

Furthermore, the "science of Kabbalah" does not only pertain to the physical sciences but to the operations of the mind, the emotions, and the body. The conviction that Kabbalah is an authoritative source for psychology and physiology is based on the belief that the human being was created in the image of God, and the *sefirot* are a map of the human being as well as the knowable aspects of divinity. From this perspective, there is no real boundary between the mind and the body, and between human beings and divine creative and destructive energy. Consequently, kabbalistic teachings can be used to generate meditations and other spiritual activities that can heal; typically, these are understood as means to activate a person's immune system or other innate healing powers.[26] Outside of healing modalities are those who use kabbalistic teachings about the *sefirot* and Four Worlds as a guide to accessing and empowering the human mind on its cognitive, subconscious, and emotional levels to connect to God. Some draw from kabbalistic teachings universalist conclusions that all human beings, regardless of their religion, are capable of this spiritual height; others build upon older doctrines of differentiated human souls to affirm that Jews and other nations have different spiritual capabilities. Many find in the teachings of Carl Jung, especially his concept of the collective unconscious and its root archetypes, an echo of kabbalistic teachings. For example, Ariel Bar Tzadok, who identifies his work as within the Sefardic tradition, teaches his students that Jung, like other founding figures in the science of psychology, "were adepts in Kabbalah study and adapted many of its teachings into their secular scientific understandings of the workings on the mind."[27]

5. As a Positive, Forward-Looking Outlook

The many different kabbalistic schools of thought differ as to the cause of this world's imperfection and to the extent to which it reflects imbalance within the sefirotic structure or the power of demonic forces. Kabbalists agree, however, that people can bring greater harmony to the *sefirot* and that, ultimately, they can advance the future repair (*tikkun*) of the cosmos and the bridging of the chasm between the physical and spiritual realms. These expectations have at times been expressed as messianic activism; that is, in activities designed to bring the messianic era as it has been envisioned in Jewish tradition—such as returning the dispersed Jews to Zion, erecting a theocratic Jewish kingdom there, and the like. During the last third of the 20th century, messianic enthusiasm in Israel emerged and still remains a factor in political and religious life, and some of this is expressed in kabbalistic terms.[28] In North America, such messianism has appeared noticeably only in Chabad Judaism. The seventh Lubavitcher rebbe, Menahem Mendel Schneersohn (1902–1994), believed that the social acceptance and political achievements of U.S. Jews signaled the imminent redemption. Chabad Hasidic doctrines, which are partly an outgrowth of kabbalistic teachings, provide a rationale, and behavioral prescriptions, for Jews and non-Jews. Under Schneersohn's leadership and after his death, Chabad teachers have committed themselves to the task of strengthening Jewish life and instructing non-Jews in their proper roles, and Kabbalah instruction is an instrument to achieve these ends.[29]

When Kabbalah is utilized to construct an optimistic, forward-looking religious outlook, however, it will generally be expressed among Americans in individual rather than communal or political terms. Kabbalistic narratives and teachings are full of drama, passion, and promise, and they are very inviting to people seeking a vital, meaningful religious life. The element of optimism with regard to this life and the promised future is especially attractive to Americans because of the "can do" attitude that runs so strongly through the national culture. It also has been easily absorbed into the New Age conviction that individual and collective efforts will transform human consciousness. One exemplar of this outlook is the teacher of "mystical Judaism" David Cooper, who believes that this approach "brings a new vitality to each moment and opens up for us an infinity of possibilities . . . to live, to fix ourselves, to change the world for the better."[30] People drawn to this type of religiosity express it in relatively private ways, such as focusing on their individual spiritual journeys, interpreting their dreams, or speculating about their past and future incarnations.

6. As a Source for Specific Answers to the Problem of Evil

Jewish clergy and educators have commonly responded to the existence of evil, disease, and suffering by attributing them to human behavior, and when that answer is inadequate, to God's inscrutable will. Kabbalistic teachings can provide a more specific response, as when the cause of evil is attributed to the divisions and imbalances that occur among the *sefirot*, or to the inauspicious position of the stars and planets. In later Kabbalah, evil is identified as broken shards (*kelippot*), trapped within our world, hindering the free flow of divine effulgence. Belief in reincarnation of souls became in Lurianic Kabbalah a central doctrine that accounted for the good and evil that inexplicably occurred to the undeserving; these were rewards and punishments for the deeds of one's past lives.

These teachings can provide explanations to people and directions for improving their situation.[31] Some people find it comforting to hear that one's suffering is a direct mirror of divine disharmony, for it testifies to one's importance within the cosmos, preserves the belief in an essential justice, and refutes what for some is the nagging worry that life may be merely the result of random events. Present-day followers of Kabbalist Yehuda Ashlag (in the Kabbalah Centre or Bnei Baruch movements) find truth in Ashlag's teaching that the swollen ego is at the root of all negative experiences. Some people regard as empowering the idea that their misbehavior during their current or former lives caused their current distress. Astrology remains credible to many, and it is central to New Age spirituality. Whether one's sorrow is the consequence of the stars, divine forces, or human conduct, kabbalistic teachings can supply some options for improving one's situation. Kabbalistic literature, or teachings reputed to be based on "authentic Kabbalah," can supply recommended behavioral changes, meditations, rituals, clothing, or amulets that ensure a better future.

Kabbalah has been revived and discovered, broadcast and "let out of the bag." It cannot be stuffed back in or denied its place in the resources available to Jews and non-Jews. Although many attribute great allure to Kabbalah because they believe it has been restricted to elites and associated with the esoteric, they still regard it in such exotic terms even though it is currently widely available. More and more knowledge of Kabbalah is being taught to people with less and less grounding in Judaism. New formulations are appearing in response to current events and as a result of the extraordinary cultural sharing of our global era. Just how Kabbalah will mutate and expand because of that exposure is still a mystery.

NOTES

1. Still widely cited is Gershom Scholem, *Major Trends in Jewish Mysticism* (New York: Schocken Books, [1946] 1961), in which the final chapter is titled "Hasidism: The Latest Phase." Also definitive and also concluding the history of Kabbalah at the same point is Moshe Idel, *Kabbalah: New Perspectives* (New Haven: Yale University Press, 1988).

2. That creativity in interpretation of kabbalistic texts and the use of Kabbalah in ritual and behavior during the 20th century was not the focus of academic study is examined in Boaz Huss, "Ask No Questions: Gershom Scholem and Contemporary Jewish Mysticism," *Modern Judaism* 25 (2005): 141–58. The enormous revival of interest in Kabbalah in Israel and North America eventually prompted research. Some of the first studies of this phenomenon are Boaz Huss, "All You Need is LAV: Madonna and Postmodern Kabbalah," *Jewish Quarterly Review* 95 (2005): 611–24; Jonathan Garb, "*The Chosen Will Become Herds*": *Studies in Twentieth Century Kabbalah* [in Hebrew] (Jerusalem: Shalom Hartman

Institute, 2005); and Jody Myers, *Kabbalah and the Spiritual Quest: The Kabbalah Centre in America* (Westport, CT: Praeger, 2007).

3. Indeed, some objections to contemporary kabbalistic expression emerge from discomfort that older, decidedly nonrational beliefs and practices have been revived and that these are not in conformity with presentations of Kabbalah made by modern rabbis who have "cleaned up" older teachings. On this point, see Matt Goldish, "Kabbalah, Academia, and Authenticity," *Tikkun Magazine* 20, no. 5 (September/October 2005): 63–67.

4. Jonatan Meir, "Wrestling with the Esoteric: Hillel Zeitlin, Yehuda Ashlag, and Kabbalah in the Land of Israel" [in Hebrew], in *Yahadut: Sugyot, Keta'im, Panim, Zehuyot: Sefer Rivka*, ed. Efraim Meir and Haviva Pedaya (Beer Sheva: Ben Gurion University Press, 2007), pp. 595–602.

5. Three such Kabbalists have been identified: Levi Isaac Krakovsky (1891–1966; see Jody Myers, *Kabbalah and the Spiritual Quest*); Yehuda Yudel Rosenberg (1859–1935; see Ira Robinson, *Rabbis and Their Community: Studies in the Eastern European Rabbinate in Montreal, 1896–1930* [Calgary: University of Calgary Press, 2007]); and Benjamin Wolf Rosoff (1869–1957; see Stephen R. Simons, *Benjamin Wolf Rosoff: The Messiah of Brownsville*[Ph.D. dissertation, Brandeis University, 2002]). On the paucity of interest in Kabbalah by U.S. Jews through the mid-20th century, see Herbert Weiner, *Nine and a Half Mystics: The Kabbalah Today* (New York: Collier Books, 1969).

6. Catherine L. Albanese, *A Republic of Mind and Spirit: A Cultural History of American Metaphysical Religion* (New Haven: Yale University Press, 2007), p. 7.

7. A succinct statement of this outlook may be found in a Theosophical Society review critical of a Jewish approach to Kabbalah (Levi Krakovsky's 1939 book *The Omnipotent Light Revealed*) as too narrow and parochial; see *The Theosophical Forum* (March 1940): 236–37. I thank Boaz Huss for this reference. On the history and teachings of the Theosophical Society, see Bruce F. Campbell, *Ancient Wisdom Revived: A History of the Theosophical Movement* (Berkeley: University of California Press, 1980).

8. For example, Elias Gewurz, a member of the Krotona Lodge of the Theosophical Society in Hollywood, California, authored *The Hidden Treasures of the Ancient Qabalah*, vol. 1, in 1915, which was published by the Yogi Publication Society and Masonic Temple of Chicago, Illinois, in 1922. For more references to theosophical publications on Kabbalah, see Boaz Huss, "'The Sufi Society from America': Theosophy and Kabbalah in Poona in the Late Nineteenth Century," in *Kabbalah and Modernity: Interpretations, Transformations, Adaptations*, ed. Boaz Huss, Marco Pasi, and Kocku von Stuckrad (Leiden: Brill, 2010), pp. 167–96.

9. Wouter J. Hanegraaff, *New Age Religion and Western Culture: Esotericism in the Mirror of Secular Thought* (Albany: State University of New York Press, 1998), pp. 13, 263, 322–23.

10. Christine A. Meilicke, "The Forgotten History of David Meltzer's Journal *Tree*," *Studies in American Jewish Literature* 22 (2003): 52–71. See also her article "Abulafianism among the Counterculture Kabbalists," *Jewish Studies Quarterly* 9 (2002): 71–101; and Harris Lenowitz, "The Appearance of Hebrew Script in Art: Three from the Golden West," presentation at the Thirteenth Annual World Congress of Jewish Studies, Jerusalem, 2001.

11. Shaul Magid, "Jewish Renewal," in *Encyclopedia of Religion*, 2nd ed. (Detroit: Macmillan Reference, 2005), pp. 4868–74. Schachter-Shalomi and Carlebach had already started their outreach to college-aged Americans in the late 1940s at the request of the sixth Lubavitcher rebbe, Yosef Yitzchok Schneerson.

12. This section of the paper has benefited from suggestions made by my students at California State University, Northridge, in particular Orly Barad, Andrew Belinfante, Anna Bishop, and Shahnee Chen-Zion.

13. Among the first to invoke *Shekhinah* in prayer were Jewish Rosh Hodesh (new moon) groups. The first published edition of sample ceremonies is Penina V. Adelman, *Miriam's Well: Rituals for Jewish Women around the Year* (New York: Biblio, 1986).

14. For a discussion of the place of *Shekhinah* in Jewish Renewal worship, see Chava Weissler, "The Meanings of Shekhinah in the Jewish Renewal Movement," *Nashim: A Journal of Jewish Women's Studies & Gender Issues* (fall 5766/2006): 53–83.

15. For an extensive application of the Four Worlds, see Jay Michaelson, *God in Your Body: Kabbalah, Mindfulness, and Embodied Spiritual Practice* (Woodstock, VT: Jewish Lights, 2007).

16. One of the earliest was Aryeh Kaplan's *The Bahir: An Ancient Kabbalistic Text by Nehunya ben ha-Kaneh* (New York: Weiser, 1979); a number of Kaplan's English translations have been made available in other European languages.

17. Nosson Scherman, *The Chumash: The Torah, Haftaros, and Five Megillos* (Brooklyn: Mesora, 1993).

18. Arthur Green, *Sefat Emet: The Language of Truth* (New York: Jewish Publication Society, 1998); the online site for the Institute for Jewish Spirituality may be found at http://www.ijs-online.org/.

19. Kabbalistic material in Chabad is spread throughout the website http://www.chabad.org; the Torah *parashah* link contains the audio series.

20. Myers, *Kabbalah and the Spiritual Quest*, pp. 115–17.

21. Chava Weissler "Performing Kabbalah in the Jewish Renewal Movement," in *Kabbalah and Spiritual Revival: Historical, Sociological and Cultural Perspectives*, ed. Boaz Huss (Beer Sheba: Ben-Gurion University Press, forthcoming).

22. A description of this activity and its cosmic effect is not immediately apparent in a perusal of the Bnei Baruch website at http://www.kabbalah.info. For more information, see Jody Myers, "Kabbalah for the Gentiles: Diverse Souls and Universalism in Contemporary Kabbalah," in Huss, *Kabbalah and Spiritual Revival*.

23. For example, see Elizabeth Clare Prophet, *Kabbalah: Key to Your Inner Power* (Corwin Springs, MT: Summit University Press, 1997); Tamar Frankiel, *The Gift of Kabbalah: Discovering the Secrets of Heaven, Renewing Your Life on Earth* (Woodstock, VT: Jewish Lights, 2001); idem., with Judy Greenfield, *Minding the Temple of the Soul: Balancing Body, Mind, and Spirit through Traditional Jewish Prayer, Movement, and Meditation* (Woodstock, VT: Jewish Lights, 1997).

24. Critics scorn these items as examples of the commodification of religion and proof of the purely commercial motives of certain contemporary teachers of Kabbalah. Without discounting their judgments, I want to point out that they are overlooking the historic economic functions of religion and dismissing a style of religious expression that is not unique to our era.

25. Among those making this association is Daniel Matt, translator of the Pritzker edition of the *Zohar*, in his *God and the Big Bang: Discovering Harmony between Science and Spirituality* (Woodstock, VT: Jewish Lights, 1996).

26. On Kabbalah Centre strategies for healing bodily ailments, see Myers, *Kabbalah and the Spiritual Quest*, chap. 5. See also Jason Shulman, *Kabbalistic Healing: A Path to*

an Awakened Soul (Rochester, VT.: Inner Traditions, 2004); and Catherine Shainberg, *Kabbalah and the Power of Dreaming: Awakening the Visionary Life* (Rochester, VT: Inner Traditions, 2005).

27. Ariel Bar Tzadok, *Walking in the Fire: Classical Torah/Kabbalistic Meditations, Practices & Prayers* (Tarzana, CA: KosherTorah, 2007), p. 16. Bar Tzadok explains his psychological-kabbalistic approach in "Sefer Devekut: The Book of Attachment to G-d," in idem, *Walking in the Fire*, pp. 29–80; this is also available online at http://www.koshertorah.com/PDF/devekut1.pdf (accessed May 25, 2010).

28. Garb, *The Chosen Have Become Herds*, pp. 37–51.

29. Elliot R. Wolfson, *Open Secret: Postmessianic Messianism and the Mystical Revision of Menahem Mendel Schneerson* (New York: Columbia University Press, 2009). On the outreach to non-Jews, see Myers, "Kabbalah for the Gentiles."

30. David A. Cooper, *God Is a Verb: Kabbalah and the Practice of Mystical Judaism* (New York: Riverhead Books, 1997), p. 249.

31. These conclusions are based largely on the many interviews I conducted for Kabbalah and the Spiritual Quest.

9

Gender in Jewish Mysticism

HAVA TIROSH-SAMUELSON

Kabbalah is a distinctive intellectual strand within Judaism that functioned as a self-conscious program for the interpretation of rabbinic tradition.[1] Rooted in esoteric speculations of the rabbinic period, Kabbalah emerged in the Middle Ages as the theory of Judaism as well as a way of Jewish life that fathomed the depth of divine mysteries, charted the paths for interaction with God, including a mystical union with God, and harnessed divine energy for the redemption of the world. Kabbalah envisioned God as a unity within a plurality of ten dynamic powers—the *sefirot*—arranged in hierarchical order and organized in the shape of the human body. Each of the named *sefirot* reveals a certain dimension of the infinite deity (*Ein Sof*) that remains concealed and inaccessible to human knowledge. A rich symbolism, developed on the basis of Jewish authoritative sources, was employed to express the dynamic interaction between the *sefirot* that manifest the creative power of God.

The doctrine of *sefirot* seems to undermine Jewish monotheism not only because it fathomed God as a plurality of forces but also because the sefirotic system was conceptualized in terms of masculinity and femininity.[2] More specifically, according to Kabbalah God is androgynous: the upper nine *sefirot* represent the masculine principle and the tenth *sefirah*—the *Shekhinah*—is the feminine facet of God.

"Masculinity" and "femininity" can be ascribed to each and every *sefirah*, since these are relational aspects that change their action in response to changing circumstances: "masculine" describes the principle of giving, whereas "feminine" pertains to receiving. Thus Kabbalah expressed the metaphysical principles of Form and Matter in Aristotelian philosophy in the form of a mythic narrative. But Kabbalah goes much further to express the metaphysical story in sexual language, since the relationship between the *sefirot* is understood as the mystery of creation and procreation. For this reason, the relation between the masculine and feminine principles of the Godhead is depicted in familial terms: *Ḥochmah* (Wisdom) functioned as

"Father" to *Binah* (Understanding), the "Mother" and *Tif'eret* (Beauty) is "Son" to *Malkhut/Shekhinah* (Kingship), who is considered as "Daughter." The latter two *sefirot* (i.e., *Tif'eret* and *Malkhut*) also function as "Husband" and "Wife" to each other, and they stand at the center of the kabbalistic familial drama.

Created in the image of God, human beings mirror the structure of the Godhead. Composed of a material body (*guf*) and a nonmaterial soul (*neshamah*), human beings reflect the structure of reality: that which is manifest (*nigleh*) covers that which is concealed (*nistar, sod*), but in the hierarchy of being, knowledge, and religious value, the concealed is always superior. Although all human beings are structurally the same, Jews are unique because their soul is presumed to be of a higher level of existence than the souls of all other humans. Thus, while the deeds of all human beings impact the well-being of the world and ultimately of the deity, only Jews (or, more specifically, only adult Jewish circumcised males) have the ability to unite with the feminine aspect of God—*Shekhinah/Malkhut*—and bring about the unification of the divine female and male that had been separated since the first sin of Adam, perpetuated by ongoing human sinfulness. As recipients of divinely revealed Law, the Torah, the Jews were given the regimen that enables them to live in holiness and to reach a greater level of intimacy with God than all other humans. By performing the commandments with the proper intention (*kavanah*), the Kabbalists not only can attain a mystical union with God, but they can also affect the union between the feminine and masculine aspects of God. Thus the kabbalistic performance of the commandments impacts God: the unification of the divine couple, *Tif'eret* and *Shekhinah*, the divine union (*hieros gamos*), results in the emanation of divine vitality (*shefa*) to the world. This flow of blessed energy redeems all levels of reality—the human, the community of Israel, the cosmos, and the Godhead—reconstituting reality into its primordial perfection. The kabbalistic worship is therefore about empowerment: through their worship, humans empower God, enabling God to redeem and be redeemed.[3]

This brief summary makes clear that the kabbalistic worldview revolves around sex, sexuality, and gender. Indeed, kabbalistic theosophy, anthropology, psychology, ethics, and religious praxis are all expressed through gendered symbolism, pertain to the mysteries of creation and procreation, and are imbued with erotic energy carried out within the institution of marriage.

Needless to say, the academic analysis of Kabbalah could not ignore sex, sexuality, and gender, but the treatment of these topics reflects larger trends both in the study of Kabbalah and in the culture at large. Prior to the rise of feminism in the 1970s, these topics were discussed as part of the objective, historically, and empirically based attempts to provide the relevant data about Kabbalah so as to interpret this intellectual movement scientifically. Gershom Scholem, the leading scholar of Kabbalah during the first two-thirds of the 20th century, rejected psychological and psychoanalytic approaches to kabbalistic speculation and did not reflect on the impact of Kabbalah on the perception of women in Jewish society. Toward the end of Scholem's life and especially after his death in 1982 feminism has transformed Western culture and especially the academy, including Jewish Studies.

The feminist critique of Western culture in general and of patriarchal Judaism in particular compelled scholars of Kabbalah to place sex and gender at the center of their approaches to Kabbalah. The French postmodernist variant has made the most impact on the study of Kabbalah, perhaps because its critique was directed against the psychoanalytic theories of Sigmund Freud and Jacques Lacan and their understanding of the role of sexuality in the individuation and maturation of the Self. Under the sway of French feminists, especially Luce Irigaray, Elliot R. Wolfson has offered a comprehensive, well-documented theory that the God of the Kabbalist was a male deity with feminine characteristics rather than a deity that comprises two separate principles, one male, the other female. According to Wolfson's reading of Kabbalah, the female aspect of the divine, the *Shekhinah*, was but an extension of the male God. Wolfson's powerful interpretation of Kabbalah has not been endorsed by all, and several alternatives were proposed by other scholars of Kabbalah. This chapter surveys the major interpretations of gender in Kabbalah, highlighting the interplay between historicism, feminism, and psychoanalysis.

Historicizing Gender

As we have seen, all discussions of new directions in Kabbalah scholarship must begin with the legacy of Gershom Scholem, since he shaped the modern study of Kabbalah. His essay, "The Feminine Element in Divinity," is still a seminal study of the main literary motifs of *Shekhinah* symbolism.[4] The essay originated in the lecture that Scholem delivered in the Eranos Society in Ancona, Switzerland, in 1952. This lecture and ten others were delivered in German right after World War II, when Europe was barely emerging from the devastation of the war and the destruction of Jewish life in the Holocaust. Jewish Studies did not yet exist in the secular universities of North America, so if Scholem, who had left Europe to settle in Palestine in 1923, was to reach an international audience, this was the best possible audience.[5] The Eranos Society, founded in 1933, included internationally renowned psychoanalysts (e.g., Carl Gustav Jung and his student Erich Neumann) and scholars of the comparative study of religion (e.g., Mircea Eliade). But Scholem deliberately rejected either psychoanalysis or the comparative study of religions and instead remained staunchly committed to the rigorous historical method which he, ironically enough, inherited from the proponents of the academic study of Judaism (known in German as Wissenschaft des Judentums), notwithstanding his scathing critique of this movement.[6] Committed to the history of ideas, the essay traces the evolution of the concept of *Shekhinah* from its inception in rabbinic sources through later Midrashim to its appearance in the *Sefer ha-Bahir* (Book of Brightness), the first medieval text of kabbalistic theosophy, and its elaboration in the *Zohar* and later in Lurianic Kabbalah. The essay identifies the major themes, images, and linguistic resonance of kabbalistic discourse on the *Shekhinah* and explores their change over time.

As a historian of ideas, Scholem was primarily preoccupied by the attempt to explain "the emergence of the female *Shekhina*."[7] Although Scholem structured the essay chronologically and provided the ancient sources of the medieval concept, he insisted that in medieval Kabbalah "a new concept of the Godhead begins to be developed . . . this new concept often takes up old themes of the rabbinic tradition, combining them rather peculiarly into a new understanding, reinterpreting them and placing them in unexpected contexts."[8] The novelty of the kabbalistic concept of the *Shekhinah* was twofold: first, the fact that the *Shekhinah* was not identical with God but was a female entity, and, second, that the *Shekhinah* was identified with the national symbol of the Congregation of Israel (*Knesset Yisrael*). How could this change be accounted for? Because of his commitment to historicism, Scholem resisted the temptation to adopt Erich Neumann's theories of Great Mother symbolism to Kabbalah and instead theorized that the kabbalistic myth of the *Shekhinah* reflects the impact of ancient Gnostic thinking that penetrated Jewish sources. (The precise identity of the ancient Gnostics is still a matter of considerable scholarly debate; but, for Scholem, Gnostic thinking meant sharp dualism of spirit and matter and a negative attitude toward the physical world.) Therefore, Scholem labeled the Kabbalists as "medieval Jewish Gnostics"[9] who reinterpreted the rabbinic tradition along these dualistic principles. *Shekhinah* symbolism, says Scholem, unmistakably reminds one of "the Gnostic hymns about the bride who is 'the daughter of light, upon whom rises the radiance of kings, whose appearance is sublime and filled with charm and grace, and who is adorned with the beauty of purity.'"[10]

The lecture on the *Shekhinah* does not explain how the Gnostic material entered Jewish sources and why it surfaced in the 12th century in early Kabbalah because Scholem had done so in his other works, especially *Origins of the Kabbalah*.[11] Beyond thematic parallels between ancient Gnosticism and medieval Kabbalah, Scholem considered the revival of Gnosticism in the heretical movement of the Cathars as the primary cause for the appearance of Gnostic themes in Jewish kabbalistic sources such as the *Sefer ha-Bahir*, Provencal Kabbalah, and the Kabbalah of Jacob and Isaac ha-Cohen of Castile. Beyond the influence of the Cathar heresy, Scholem entertained the idea that *Shekhinah* symbolism has interesting parallels in the concept of the Church as the body of Christ (*corpus Christi*),[12] but he did not develop this suggestion. Responding to a question from the audience about the parallel between the *Shekhinah* symbolism and the image of Shakti in Indian Tantric religion, Scholem was quick to state: "I believe that we can discern quite clear differences between the two conceptions—differences no less profound than their affinities."[13] His need to accentuate the uniqueness of Kabbalah and his resistance to comparative generalizations were part of a larger claim about the nature of mysticism and the inadequacy of cross-cultural analysis, both of which are related to Scholem's Zionist commitment.[14] In short, for Scholem the *Shekhinah* symbolism was important because it provided the data for his reconstruction of the historical sources of Kabbalah more than for what it meant to kabbalistic practitioners who developed the myth or to Jewish society that lived by it.

Scholem's student Isaiah Tishby further elaborated the literary motifs of the *Shekhinah* symbolism in his *Mishnat Ha-Zohar* (1959), an anthology and Hebrew translation of many zoharic texts arranged thematically with excellent introductions.[15] In the section devoted to the *Shekhinah*, Tishby discusses her status in the sefirotic world, her separation from the *sefirot*, especially her "husband," *Tif'eret*, because of human sins, her relationship to the realm of Evil (*Sitra Aḥra*) ruled by Samael, her dominion of the created world, and her relationship with the People of Israel with whom she shares exile. In greater detail than Scholem's essay, Tishby elaborated the imagery, semantic range, and thematic richness of the kabbalistic discourse but shied away from offering an explanation of the gendered symbolism, since he endorsed the explanation of his revered teacher. In terms of gender categories, Tishby (like Scholem before him) noted the depiction of the *Shekhinah* as a creative as well as destructive force and her ability to act both as a feminine (i.e., receptive and passive) and masculine (i.e., emanative and active) power. But precisely because Tishby regarded Scholem as the authoritative interpreter of

Kabbalah, he did not venture a different explanation of the *Shekhinah* symbolism, nor did he concern himself with the impact of this symbolism on the religious life of practitioners.

What did it mean for Kabbalists to believe that God has a feminine dimension if the Jewish tradition refers to God primarily in male terms? Did Jewish practitioners pray to a masculine or a feminine deity? These questions would come to the fore only in the 1980s, after Scholem's death, when Moshe Idel introduced phenomenology and the comparative study of religion to the study of Kabbalah. I discuss Idel's methodology and his approach to the *Shekhinah* symbolism below; for now let me note that Scholem's interpretation of the *Shekhinah* symbolism remained the foundational study on this topic, even though new theories were proposed to explain the symbolism of the *Shekhinah*, fueled both by the new studies of Gnosticism after the discovery of Coptic texts in Nag Hammadi, Egypt, in 1947, and by the efflorescence of the comparative study of religion.

In 1998 Peter Schäfer, a leading scholar of the mystical literature of the rabbinic period, the Hekhalot and Merkavah literature, published "Daughter, Sister, Bride, and Mother: Images of the Femininity of God in the Early Kabbalah," which was incorporated in his book, *Mirror of His Beauty: Feminine Images of God from the Bible to the Early Kabbalah*.[16] In this study, Schäfer "reexamines Scholem's explanatory model which suggests that the concept originated in the Gnostic systems of the first centuries of the Christian era." Schäfer reaches a paradoxical conclusion concerning Scholem's research: on the one hand, Schäfer holds that even though most of the Gnostic sources were unavailable to Scholem and his understanding of Gnosticism was limited, his intuition about the Gnostic character of the *Shekhinah* symbolism, especially in the *Sefer ha-Bahir*,[17] was correct. On the other hand, Scholem erred, so claims Schäfer, in seeking to explain the feminine element of God by turning to the heresy of the Cathars, especially those centered in the French town of Albi and known as Albigensians. Instead, Scholem should have paid attention to a much more immediate religious phenomenon: the veneration of the Virgin Mary. Looking at the articulation of the Marian doctrine in the writings of 12th-century theologians (e.g., Peter Damian, Herman of Tournay, Bernard of Clairvaux, Godfrey of Admont, Hildegard of Bingen, and Peter of Blois), Schäfer notes "striking parallels with the increased emphasis on the feminine aspects of divinity in the Kabbalah."[18] Like the Virgin Mary, the *Shekhinah* functions as a mediator between God and humanity, an intercessor on behalf of humankind, and a restorer and redeemer of humanity.[19] Rejecting Scholem's "quest for origins" or any simplistic notion of "influ-

ence," Schafer argues for a "dynamic theory of influence," in which both part-
ners, namely, Judaism and Christianity, are engaged in a "continuous *process*
of the digestion, transformation, and recreation of traditions in ever changing historical circumstances."[20]

Schäfer reasons that because Jews in 12th-century Provence lived in close
proximity to Christians, they could not have been oblivious to the "explosion of Marian theology and the veneration of the Virgin, which was taking
place literally before their eyes."[21] On the basis of one comment from Gregory
of Tours, Schäfer even ventures to suggest that Jewish children could have
been schooled together with Christian children. (This conjecture has a very
low degree of probability because Gregory lived in the 6th century and the
relations between Jews and Christians in medieval Europe changed remarkably during the intervening centuries.) But regardless of how Jews came to
know about the veneration of Mary, Schäfer highlights the degree to which
the *Shekhinah* functions like the Virgin Mary, namely, as a salvific figure who
has been deified. Schäfer's analysis of that salvific activity of the *Shekhinah*
invests this symbolism with decidedly Christian overtones. The *Shekhinah* is
indeed the savior of humanity as is the Virgin Mary who by the 12th century
was identified with Christ and even elevated to the Holy Trinity.

How does the femininity of the *Shekhinah* relate to her salvific function?
The ideal state for God and for humans is androgyny, but that state did not
last forever. As much as human beings were split into male and female entities, so did God have to suffer "from the separation of his male and female
components. His feminine part, so essential for the nourishment and vitality of the inner divine life, was split off from its masculine companion. This
split is clearly associated with the creation of the mundane world of human
beings."[22] The christological overtone of Schäfer's readings becomes more
evident when he states that "'gender difference' must be introduced into
the originally androgynous and unified nature of God" in order to facilitate
"God's 'gift' to humanity. If he had not split off from himself what essentially belongs to him, humanity would not be able to get close to him."[23]
Since humans are the cause of the separation of the feminine and masculine
dimensions of God, the mending of the separation is possible only through
humanity. "This is the gist of the many parables of [the *Sefer ha-Bahir*] that
portray the Shekhinah as 'mother' and is expressed most graphically in the
parable in which the king hates his spouse because her children behave badly.
When the people of Israel fulfill the will of their father, not only are they
brought closer to God, but they empower the Shekhinah to return to her
original state. More precisely, when Israel unites God's name (in the *Sh'ma*)

the tenth Sefirah will be reunited with the third Sefirah, the place of her origin. God will be made one again; his original androgyny will be restored . . . the restoration of God's original androgyny means the abolition of creation or, rather, the inclusion of creation in God's eternal unity."[24]

Like Scholem's before him, Schäfer's exposition of the gender symbolism is historical rather than psychoanalytic. Presumably, Jews adopted the logic of the Marian cult because they found the alternative theories of the rationalist philosophers to be profoundly unsatisfactory. These philosophers (Saadia Gaon, Judah Halevi, and Judah al-Barceloni) identified the *Shekhinah* with the Glory of God (*Kavod*) but insisted that it is a created luminous entity that was not identical with God. Even Maimonides, who did allow the term *Kavod* to refer to God Himself, "removed any hint of corporeality from the image of God," and all medieval philosophers "were successful in eliminating any trace of his male and female character left over from the Bible or the subsequent Jewish tradition."[25] For Schäfer, then, the gendered doctrine of *Shekhinah* in Kabbalah corrected a lacuna in Jewish religious philosophy by offering a much deeper reflection about the human condition, especially human sexuality.

Schäfer's book was well received by the academic community in America,[26] but several scholars of Kabbalah, especially in Israel, were most critical of it. In 2004 Moshe Idel, for example, charged that Schäfer "completely ignored all the rich kabbalistic material of the Early Kabbalah from Provence and Catalonia that is relevant, which can be precisely dated and located, but which does not support his parallels from the Christian world."[27] In 2007 Daniel Abrams elaborated this critique, rejecting the notion that the authors of the *Bahir* invented the "feminized" *Shekhinah* under the influence of the cult of Mary."[28] In yet a later study published in 2008, Abrams extended the critique to the worldview of the *Zohar*, demonstrating that it was largely a "clear polemic against the autonomy of the masculine and feminine in Christian traditions, such as the Virgin Mary and Jesus."[29]

Most remarkable about Schäfer's treatment of the subject was that he was silent about two extremely relevant scholarly endeavors. Schäfer utterly ignores the vast scholarship of Elliot Wolfson on gender which contradicts his analysis, although Schäfer does mention Wolfson's essay on the *Bahir*, an essay on Hellenism and Judaism, and a collected volume on myth and hermeneutics.[30] The vast relevant feminist literature (theoretical and historical) that pertains to the medieval veneration of Mary is also glaringly absent from Schäfer's study. Because he is a superb scholar, admired worldwide for his erudition and exacting scholarship, it is hard to believe that his silence is accidental or the result of academic sloppiness; it is more reasonable to view it as a deliberate attempt to discredit views or approaches with which he disagrees. That a book on gender symbolism in Kabbalah could be published in 2002 without any reference to feminism is astonishing, since feminism revolutionized all academic disciplines, including Religious Studies and Jewish Studies.

Feminism and the Symbolism of the Shekhinah

The so-called second wave of feminism emerged in the early 1960s and flourished in the following two decades as both a social movement and an academic endeavor. By the end of the 20th century no dimension of human society (e.g., law, politics, economics, medicine, and even science) remained immune to women's demand for equality and inclusion, and no academic discipline could ignore the simple feminist research question: What about women? Feminism also thoroughly transformed contemporary Judaism when Jewish women became active interpreters of their own tradition as rabbis, teachers, academic scholars, and communal leaders. Within Jewish Studies, which began to flourish in American universities as a direct result of Women's Studies and Black Studies, the study of Bible, rabbinics, history, literature, Jewish sociology, demography, and ethnography were all transformed when scholars began to inquire about women and use gender as a category of analysis. The impact of feminism on the study of religion has been profound since the 1970s; because Judaism was now studied in departments of Religious Studies, it was inevitable that the first feminist critics of Judaism would emerge either from departments of Religious Studies in secular universities or from women trained in divinity schools attached to secular universities.

For Jewish women who studied Judaism, the feminist revolution posed a serious challenge, since one could not ignore the feminist critique of patriarchy illustrated most painfully in the Jewish religion. Three main options were available to Jewish women: first, one could reject Judaism outright because of its oppression of and hostility to women and endorse secular feminism as the only promise for equality and justice for women;[31] second, if one wished to practice Judaism within traditional parameters, one had to work for an internal change of Jewish perceptions of women, rituals, and prayer, thereby reinterpreting and reconstructing Judaism;[32] and, third, Jewish feminists could create their own distinctive egalitarian religion that was rooted not in the command of the oppressive Father God but in the rhythm of nature and its mysteries as practiced by women whom Western culture rejected as "witches."[33] How a given Jewish woman would respond to feminism and how she would position herself vis-à-vis Judaism was an intensely personal decision that reflected her particular background and existential issues. It was the individual woman who would have to define how creative or radical she wants and needs to be and how she prefers to express her Jewishness. Regardless of the personal struggle that gave to Jewish feminism, Jewish women, since the 1970s, have produced a significant body of literature (theological, historical, homiletical, and even philosophical) critiquing the Jewish religion for its marginalization of women but also offering women positive ways of being Jewish that honor and cherish the female voice in Judaism.[34]

The feminist revolution compelled Jewish women to look closely at their relationship to the religion of their fathers and take an existential stand. Those who tried to change Judaism from within found the *Shekhinah* symbolism especially attractive because it provided a ready-made female God-language. In fact, the *Shekhinah* appeared to be the goddess that feminists such as Carol Christ claimed is needed if women are to express themselves religiously as Jews.[35] For example, Rita Gross, a Jewish scholar of comparative religions who specializes in Buddhism and Hinduism, reminded her readers that all God-language is but a linguistic convention that tells us more about the community that generates the language than about God. She strongly advocated the adoption of female God-talk to Judaism, because it will finally end the "oppressing and eclipsing of women."[36] Her essay begins with a reference to *Shekhinah* symbolism. Judith Plaskow, the most influential Jewish feminist theologian, likewise refers to the symbolism of the *Shekhinah* in her attempt to construct an egalitarian Judaism.[37]

Jewish feminists were not alone in appropriating the symbol of the *Shekhinah* to the project of reconstructing Judaism. From the very beginning they were supported by men, especially by Judaic scholars who agreed with the judgment that Judaism has mistreated women, but who also maintained that the tradition contains images and language that can be most useful to the feminist. I have in mind Arthur Green in particular, at the time a professor of religion at the University of Pennsylvania and president of the Reconstructionist Rabbinical College in Philadelphia. In 1979, he delivered a speech to the Women's Rabbinical Alliance titled "Bride, Spouse, Daughter: Images of the Feminine in Classical Jewish Sources." The speech was printed in 1983 in an important anthology of Jewish feminists, *On Being a Jewish Feminist*, edited by Susannah Heschel,[38] who was then a graduate student at the University of Pennsylvania. The short essay made three crucial observations: first, it argued that female God-language is not just the concern of women but also of men, since men need the feminine as much as women need the masculine imagery. Second, Green agreed that the images of the feminine in Judaism were created by men and that, as such, they reflect the sensibilities of men. Third, he proposed that "in the search for the kind of intimacy, tenderness and warmth that people wanted to express in talking about the relationship between God and Israel, they could not remain in the domain of the all-male universe where they lived their public lives."[39] The essay went on to discuss the feminine images in Kabbalah literature, focusing on the image of Torah as feminine and the image of the *Shekhinah*, who is "described as daughter, bride, mother, moon, sea, faith, wisdom, speech, and a myriad of other figures."[40] This elegant speech ended with a call for the creation of "a truly feminine, a truly Jewish, spirituality [as] one of the urgent tasks of our age."[41] The "point of origin" for this reconstruction of Judaism would be kabbalistic sources. Clearly, for Green, feminism would not only transform the role of women in contemporary Jewish society but would also effect a thorough reconstruction of Judaism for women and men alike.

For the following three decades Green continued to make Kabbalah accessible to the general reader, and the feminine motifs continued to be featured highly in his exposition. In 2002, he published a large essay in which he endorsed the approach of Schäfer concerning the impact of the cult of the Virgin Mary on the making of *Shekhinah* symbolism. But if Schäfer focused on the discourse on Wisdom, Green looked at the discourse on the Song of Songs in both traditions.[42] Like Schäfer, Green pays close attention to the historical context of 12th-century Provence where the *Sefer ha-Bahir* emerged, and his conclusion resonates with that of Schäfer: "the female figure of *shekhinah* may be seen as a Jewish response to a great popular revival of Marian piety in the twelfth century Western church."[43] The essay provides detailed support for this claim, but, unlike Schäfer, Green often refers to the work of medievalists whose scholarship on the Marian cult was informed by feminist sensibilities.[44] Also unlike Schäfer, Green does not ignore the extensive scholarship of Wolfson, since he had reviewed it, albeit critically, several years earlier.[45] In his 2002 essay on the *Shekhinah* and the cult of Mary, Green goes out of his way to state in a footnote: "My agreement with some of Wolfson's readings of the sources (as well as my great respect for his scholarship) is greater than is obvious from the polemical expressions of our positions in those statements."[46] Although Green and Schäfer support each other's conclusions about the relevance of Christianity for the interpretation of kabbalistic gender imagery, it is the scholarship of Wolfson that shows what Kabbalah truly means when one applies the critical tools of feminist scholarship.

More than any other scholar, Elliot R. Wolfson, who has been most critical of Schäfer and Green,[47] has introduced the categories of feminist theory and gender studies into the study of Kabbalah. Since the late 1980s, Wolfson focused on the *Shekhinah* symbolism in kabbalistic literature as the cornerstone of his interpretation of Kabbalah.[48] But whereas Green holds that Kabbalah offers the basis for a feminine rereading of Judaism, Wolfson has argued that when kabbalistic texts are read with the critical tools of feminist analysis, it becomes clear that the feminine in Kabbalah is "but an extension of the masculine."[49] According to Wolfson's analysis of numerous texts, kabbalistic symbolism did not posit a deity in which two equal potencies, one masculine and the other masculine, were seeking to reestablish the primordial parity and balance but rather a male androgynous deity whose feminine aspects will be restored to masculinity in the end of days. In the redeemed state the female will be reincluded in, or folded back into, the male; the feminine will be restored to the masculine, and gender differentiation will be overcome. In this drama, the male Kabbalist plays a central role because it is his religious worship, and especially the study of Torah, that facilitates the reinclusion of the female into the male deity, and the locus of the drama takes place in the *Shekhinah*, the gateway to the Godhead. Wolfson's close reading of the *Shekhinah* symbolism revolves around one particular symbol, the *atarah* (diadem), focusing on the fact that this Hebrew word also denotes the corona of the circumcised penis. It is the unpacking of this particular symbol that exposed the profoundly masculine and phallocentric nature of kabbalistic theosophy, making it unusable for a feminist reconstruction of Judaism.

Wolfson has written on gender in Kabbalah for more than twenty years; although his interpretation has become more theoretically sophisticated over time, his basic view has not changed. To understand it, we need to consider three factors. First, Wolfson is committed to a psychoanalytic interpretation of sexuality as articulated by the French disciple and critic of Freud, Jacques Lacan. When Wolfson discusses the phallic nature of kabbalistic theosophy and shows that even the most feminine activities of childbirth and nursing ascribed to the *Shekhinah* as mother are but phallic activities, he has in mind not the male biological sex organ but the psychoanalytic term "phallus" as understood by Lacan. Wolfson explains:

> The word "phallus" refers to an imaginary symbol, the "signifier of desire" rather than the physical organ. This is not to suggest that there is no relationship whatsoever between the symbolic phallus and the biological penis

in the entire Lacanian psychoanalytic theory or kabbalistic theosophy. The point is, rather, that the fascination with and emphasis placed on the *membrum virile* in both systems of thought . . . lies in the fact that this organ serves as the semiotic marker that gives meaning to the other in the construction of the identity of the same.[50]

Both kabbalistic theosophy and its decoding take place not on the earthly level of human embodiment but on the imaginary level of representation. This is why neither Kabbalah nor Wolfson's interpretation thereof can be accused of crude pornography, although I might add that for pornographic literature or visual representation to be effective, the imagination must be involved. The psychological process that explains why pornography works as sexual stimulation may not be irrelevant to kabbalistic literature, but that need not concern us here.

The second point to keep in mind is that Wolfson reads Kabbalah not only with Lacan in mind but through the lens of Lacan's own disciple and critic, the French feminist Luce Irigaray.[51] She subjected all of Western philosophy to a thorough critique, accusing Western philosophers of androcentrism, namely, the tendency to reduce reality to the male perspective of it, positing the male as the standard of humanity. The female is either judged as inferior or lacking in some respect, or is made to be absorbed into the sameness of the male. Androcentrism has made it impossible for Western philosophy and culture to appreciate the female on her own terms and to allow her true independence.

Irigaray highlights the shortcomings of both Freud and Lacan, whose binary understandings of the Self were rooted in the paradigm of male sexuality from which they generalized about all humanity. In contrast, Irigaray offers an interpretation of human sexuality, and of the human Self more generally, whose point of departure is female sexuality that is not binary but pluralistic, all-encompassing, and joyously playful.

Wolfson adopted Irigaray's feminist critique and applied it to his analysis of the *Shekhinah* symbolism, showing it to be decidedly androcentric, namely, a projection of male standards and sensibilities. The way in which Wolfson's analysis of Kabbalah is feminist is explained below.

A third relevant factor is that French feminism is part of a much larger intellectual movement, namely, postmodernism, although their relationship is quite complicated.[52] Philosophically speaking, Wolfson's reading of kabbalistic sources is deeply indebted to Derrida's Deconstruction, which, in turn, is rooted in the philosophy of Martin Heidegger. The basic Heideggerian insight, which is common to the postmodernist outlook, is the claim that reality is ultimately linguistical. Language is not simply the technique we employ to understand reality; it construes reality as much as it veils reality. Now, "if language is the veil through which the veil must be unveiled, the unveiling itself is a form of veiling that will be veiled in the unveiling . . . There is no naked truth to be disrobed, for truth that is truly naked—divested of all appearance—is mere simulation that cannot be seen. Apparent truth, truly apparent, is disclosed through the concealment of its disclosure."[53] Through myriads of texts, Wolfson illustrates this principle, which I may remind us all, was fully understood long ago by none other than Hayyim Nahman Bialik in his famous essay "Gilluy ve-Kissuy ba-Lashon."[54] Wolfson goes beyond this basic Heideggerian point to adopt Derrida's analysis of language in which writing precedes speech; with Derrida he states that in Western culture both writing and speech manifest phallocentrism and logocentrism.[55] Exposing these tendencies is the task of the postmodern reader, as Wolfson surely is, since he is more informed by postmodern writers than any other scholar of Kabbalah.

If we keep these factors in mind, we can understand why Wolfson claims that the *Shekhinah* is included in a male deity and that the union between the *Shekhinah* and *Tif'eret* is but a reconstruction of a male androgynous being. According to Wolfson, this understanding is manifested in the real symbol of the male Jewish body—circumcision—and it is the circumcised Jewish body that reflects the body of the divine male in the sefirotic realm. The *Shekhinah*, the feminine aspect of the supernal *anthropos*, is included in the male entity; ultimately, God is a male androgyne.

Let us reflect now on the extent to which this reading is feminist. Feminist writings always include two moves: first, the critique of the past (canons, practices, rituals, and ideas) in the name of a present, presumably more just position, and the construction of an alternative. Wolfson is indeed a feminist because he is informed by feminist writings and because he applies the feminist critique of androcentrism to Kabbalah. But Wolfson is also an honest historian, and he cannot bring himself to take the next step that feminists expect of him, namely, the constructive step; he cannot in good conscience offer Kabbalah as the foundation for the creation of contemporary egalitarian Judaism, as did Green, because Wolfson maintains that Kabbalah, as it has come down to us, is inadequate to serve in that role. In Wolfson's analysis, theosophic Kabbalah, and rabbinic Judaism in general, was persistently sexist, depicting women "as morally intellectually and physically inferior to men."[56] As a historian, Wolfson reminds us that Kabbalah was developed in male fraternities and that some of these men were "communal leaders and others occupying positions in close proximity to the seats of power and influence."[57] It is therefore historically misleading to position Kabbalah as supportive of the female in Judaism or as envisioning parity between men and women either on earth or in the divine world. Rather, the Jewish intellectuals who created Kabbalah shared the dominant scientific theory of their day, which recognized only one sex rather than two and which viewed the woman as but an extension of the male, thereby erasing the otherness of the woman. As a feminist and a Jew who cares about equality, Wolfson not only refuses to offer Kabbalah as a panacea for the inequality between men and women in Judaism, he also states that "Kabbalah . . . is in need of mending that cannot be attained by way of apologetic thinking or obfuscation shaped by winds of political correctness."[58]

This pessimistic and honest assessment of the situation has not been universally accepted, nor have Wolfson's psychoanalytic, postmodernist, and feminist sensibilities been universally shared. Let us now turn to several alternative theories: the approaches of Yehuda Liebes, Melilah Hellner-Eshed, Moshe Idel, and Charles Mopsik, who either dispute Wolfson's reading directly or reject the application of psychoanalysis and feminism to the interpretation of Kabbalah. By contrast, Daniel Abrams and Devorah Gamlieli are very supportive of Wolfson's approach and apply psychoanalytic and feminist paradigms, although they reach different conclusions than Wolfson's about the feminine in Kabbalah. I will also mention other scholars of Kabbalah who contributed to an understanding of gender, even though they did not articulate a full-fledged theory.

Kabbalah and the Eros of Judaism

The responses to Wolfson's readings of Kabbalah among scholars in the United States and in Israel reflect in part the varying receptions of feminism and feminist theory. In the United States, where feminism has transformed the academy and public ways of being Jewish, Wolfson's work was criticized by such scholars as Arthur Green because it disrupted the contemporary reconstruction of Judaism on the basis of Kabbalah.[59] If Wolfson's reading is correct, *Shekhinah* symbolism could not really be used to create a more egalitarian Judaism. In Israel, feminism impacted the academy only in the 1990s. During the 1970s, feminism entered Israel as a political discourse that gave rise to a political party which failed miserably in the elections of 1977 because of the mistaken perception that Israel does not really have a gender problem. The socialist roots of Israeli society and culture presumably guaranteed equality between men and women in all spheres of social life, and the ethos of the pioneers generated a different kind of woman who has little to do with the female of the bourgeois Jewish family in Europe. In reality, of course, the story is much more complex, as many new studies have made clear,[60] but I maintain that the different reception of feminist theories in Israel accounts for the tendency to emphasize a more balanced relationship between the male and female principles in the world of the *sefirot*.

In "Zohar and Eros" Yehuda Liebes, who is not immersed in feminist theory, suggested a reading of the *Zohar* as an erotic text. In this chapter, the term "eros" is a broad category that encompasses desire, creativity, playfulness, passion, and emotion.[61] In Liebes's reading, the *Zohar* of the *Sefer ha-Zohar* emerges as a creative energy that accounts for the beauty of the world as well as for human creative impulses. Liebes was the first scholar to suggest that the *Zohar* was a product of a kabbalistic fraternity in Castile and that the persona of Shimon bar Yochai is the literary representation of the ideal mystic and leader of the group, who could have been Todros ben Joseph Abulafia, although Moshe de Leon of Guadalajara was the primary author/editor of the main part of the text.[62] If the *Zohar* is a collective product, the psychoanalytic paradigm, especially in the interpretation of Sigmund Freud, is more difficult to apply, although the psychoanalytic theory of Carl Jung and its focus on universal archetypes cannot be ruled out. The main contribution of Liebes's study is to shift the focus away from the symbolism of the *Shekhinah* or the particular symbol of the diadem/corona and to offer an interpretation of the zoharic material in which there is a considerable degree of playfulness and humor. In this reading, the female is still a love object that can generate male creative desire.

The *Zohar* depicts a group of scholars led by Rabbi Shimon bar Yochai who are engaged in the study of Torah while strolling in the imaginary landscape of the Holy Land. Scholars of Kabbalah have largely moved away from talking about the *Zohar* as a single-authored book and accepted Liebes's theory of it as fluid anthology that came into existence over several centuries,[63] even though Moses de Leon was most likely the central figure in writing it.

Melilah Hellner-Eshed, Liebes's student, elaborated his insights about the *Zohar* as a collective product of a kabbalistic fraternity in Castile in her book *A River Issues Forth from Eden: On the Language of Mystical Experience in the Zohar*.[64] Her study is a major contribution to the reconstruction of the life of the zoharic group as "Awakened Ones" (another term for "Enlightened"), who see the Torah as their lover and cause her to arise and give her secrets to her lovers. According to Hellner-Eshed, "this is a mutual erotic arousal of the student and of the Torah. In their arousing activities the members of the group bring about the ultimate awakening of the deity, which is like a cosmic law according to which the supernal world arouses and emanates in response to the arousal of the earthly world, the world of human beings."[65] Eros is the constitutive element of the group and the power that creates the *Zohar*.[66] The mystic is illuminated and awakened by the textual experience of the esoteric interpretation of the biblical text. This act in turn arouses desire above and below in a relationship which reflects the erotic play between the maiden (the Torah) and her lover (i.e., the male mystic) in the famous parable of the "maiden without eyes."[67] In the erotic myth of the *Zohar*, the task of the mystical homilist is to identify with *Malkhut/Shekhinah* and to be filled with divine light which he experiences in the homilies of the Torah.[68] Hellner-Eshed refers to Wolfson's contrary interpretation, but she holds that "the perception of femininity and womanhood in the *Zohar* is more complex and multifaceted."[69] Unlike Wolfson, she hears an "expecting space that wishes to be filled; she does not hear privation, penetration and erasure of existence so as to be integrated in the male."[70] Hellner-Eshed notes that the *Zohar*, although written by men, is surprising "in its ability to capture the erotic posture of females," and the whole erotic play of the *Zohar* is "very subtle, gentle, gradual and joyful."[71] She does not consider zoharic techniques of interpretation to be aggressive (the posture she attributes to Wolfson's interpretation of the *Zohar*) but rather "to be loving since the meaning is enriched through the disclosure of that which was covered."[72] As a woman, albeit not a feminist, Hellner-Eshed is able to identify with the mystical activity of the zoharic group even though she admits that the group understands itself like a knightly order, a monastic order, or a Gnostic cult in activity, namely, a male fraternity that excludes women.[73] The gist of her alternative reading of the *Shekhinah* symbolism is that the erotic play that constitutes the act of Torah study should be viewed as a relationship between two subjects (the Kabbalist and the Torah/*Shekhinah*), thereby disputing Wolfson's reading in which the *Shekhinah* has no identity of her own because She is a mere passive, receptive force. Hellner-Eshed, however, makes no use of psychoanalytic theories (of any kind), and she has no interest at all in feminist readings.

Hellner-Eshed's analysis of gendered language in the *Zohar* is largely supported and complemented by a short study of Ronit Meroz that highlights the "ambivalence that characterizes the self-consciousness of the kabbalists."[74] According to Meroz's analysis of the major imagery in the *Zohar*, the doe,[75] the power of male Kabbalists is characterized by passivity: they can accomplish their spiritual task in the world (i.e., bring harmony to God) only if and when they appropriate feminine characteristics. Salvation (*geulah*) can come about only because of femininity, since it contains sufficient desire and dynamism to change the world, but for the (male) Kabbalists this passivity is found only in men rather than in women.

Hellner-Eshed and Meroz are students of Yehuda Liebes, but the person who has dominated Kabbalah Studies in Israel in the post-Scholem years is Moshe Idel, a close friend and colleague of Liebes. In 2005, the same year that Wolfson published his massive *Language, Eros, and Being*, Idel published *Kabbalah and Eros*, in which he elaborated the meaning of eros in Kabbalah by going well beyond the zoharic material, which was the primary focus of Wolfson, Liebes, Hellner-Eshed and others.[76] Idel is deeply informed of all intellectual trends in Western thought, whether psychoanalysis (Freudian or Jungian), structuralism, poststructuralism, or feminism, but he rejects any attempt to impose these schemas on kabbalistic texts in order to legitimize preconceived ideological commitments. Feminism, in particular, is deemed inappropriate for the interpretation of Kabbalah, either when it reads "feminist triumphalism" into the kabbalistic texts or, conversely, when it highlights Kabbalah's inherent androcentrism which makes it vulnerable to feminist critique. Eschewing any form of ideological dogmatism, Idel jealously guards the autonomy of Kabbalah against potential distortions of its meaning.

Idel is well acquainted with all the existing scholarship about sex and gender in Kabbalah, citing its major contributors by name and referring to their works in the notes and bibliography.[77] Yet he takes issue with several interpreters. For example, he criticizes Gershom Scholem's inability to see that *Knesset Yisrael* functioned as a hypostasis in the rabbinic corpus[78] and also Raphael Patai's treatment of the figure of Lilith in the zoharic corpus.[79] Likewise, he is critical of Arthur Green's and Peter Schäfer's claim that the kabbalistic cult of the *Shekhinah* reflects the impact of the cult of Mary that emerged in 12th-century France.[80] More polemically, he argues with Wolfson's reading of kabbalistic texts, especially the *Zohar*, in light of the feminist reworking of Lacanian psychoanalysis articulated by Luce Irigaray.[81] He also dismisses the views of David Biale and R. J. Z. Werblowsky who regard the kabbalistic discourses on sex and sexuality as expressions of ascetic mentality.[82] In short, the purpose of *Kabbalah and Eros* is, so to speak, to set the record straight about Kabbalah, both because sexuality is so central to the kabbalistic worldview and because of the recent scholarly interest in sexuality in Kabbalah. To replace all these readings, Idel argues that Judaism is, in general, a "culture of eros"[83] and that Kabbalah only manifests and intensifies the erotic impulses of Judaism. Contrary to Wolfson's negative interpretation of the female in Kabbalah, Idel argues that, in Kabbalah, erotic energy is expressed within, and strengthens, the institution of marriage, deepening the halakhic obligation imposed on Jewish husbands to satisfy their wives' sexual needs. The erotic impulse of Kabbalah explains how it empowers its practitioners and why this tradition enhanced Judaism.

Eros is not the exclusive provenance of Kabbalah. But the phrase "culture of eros" is rather vague, because "eros" connotes a range of related concepts: desire, attraction, passion, seduction, lust, love, affection, friendship, pleasure, and enjoyment. The book does not offer a conceptual analysis of the differences between them but rather a taxonomy of "types of eroticism" in kabbalistic texts. Idel documents the emergence of the feminine power in Judaism and argues that the symbolism of the *Shekhinah* in medieval Kabbalah should be understood not as a Jewish response to the 12th-century cult of Mary but as an elaboration of pre-kabbalistic midrashic views about *Knesset Yisrael* as a metaphysical reality. He then analyzes the various expressions of the androgynous myth in Jewish mystical texts, highlighting the similarities and differences between the Platonic version of this idea and the kabbalistic variants. Thereafter, Idel moves on to discuss "the erotic dramas taking place between the human community and the divine sphere"[84] when Israel is both "a corporate personality and a feminine counterpart of God,"[85] that is, when Israel functions as God's concubine. In a separate chapter Idel examines the principle of "metastasis," namely, the transformation of reality on the human and divine spheres, by looking at the history of one tale told by Rabbi Isaac of Acre (14th century), and the following chapter focuses on cosmoeroticism, namely, the notion that "all entities in the world, not only humans, participate in the erotic impulse."[86] In this chapter the interplay between philosophy and Kabbalah is most evident, especially in the prophetic Kabbalah of Abraham Abulafia, a Kabbalist who opposed the doctrine of the *sefirot* and developed his mystical system on the basis of Maimonides' philosophy as the mysticism of German Hasidism. In his concluding remarks, Idel organizes the evidence of the previous five chapters into three "models" in an attempt to generalize about Kabbalah, notwithstanding its resistance to generalizations. The book includes an appendix, in which he examines additional kabbalistic texts that undermine attempts to read Kabbalah through the lens of feminist critique. Although admitting that Kabbalah did not improve the status of women in Jewish society, he adduces evidence for egalitarian intentions in kabbalistic texts, the efficacy of female intention (*kavanah*) in the reproductive process, and even the association of the demonic with the male "while the power that is capable of purifying it is that of the female."[87]

Idel's organization of the material is meant to illustrate the methodology: generalizations about Kabbalah should only be derived inductively on the basis of textual evidence. His taxonomy, however, is by no means neat. In some cases, the object of desire (God, Israel, or Torah) determines the type of eroticism, while in other cases an aspect of the erotic orientation (e.g., androgyneity, or the time and place most propitious for sexual activity) defines the type of eroticism. Furthermore, some types of eroticism are merely mentioned without receiving sufficient exposition. More problematic is the fact that the final chapter organizes the data into three major models: "theosophic-theurgic," "ecstatic," and "talismanic,"[88] even though these models are already presupposed in the analysis of the data in chapters 1 through 5. Since Idel's numerous works have shown that these three models, or "relatively solid structures," cut across the history of Kabbalah, he organizes the final reflection according to the themes of the book: the existence of the feminine aspect of God, the dynamic of androgyneity, Israel as God's concubine, the transformative power of eros, and love as a cosmic principle. Be this as it may, the very identification of models in the final chapter proves that Idel also generalizes about Kabbalah, because generalizations are unavoidable in historical reconstruction.

Out of his close reading of select texts, certain arguments about the place of eros in Kabbalah and in Judaism in general emerge from the analysis. First, Judaism cannot be simplistically understood as a monotheistic religion. Rather, Judaism harbors a ditheistic or binitarian impulse from the earliest rabbinic times. The God of Israel is not the God of the philosophers, a noncorporeal intellect engaged in self-contemplation; instead, He is a passionate God whose tumultuous inner life is dominated by the dynamics of androgyneity as well as by His relationship with Israel, the concubine of God. Second, except for a few notable exceptions (i.e., some Sabbatean sects and Frankism), Kabbalah did not function as a subversive force in Judaism but rather as a force that deepened the commitment of Jews to halakhic norms. In Kabbalah the erotic energy is expressed within and strengthens the institution of marriage, deepening the halakhic obligation imposed on husbands to satisfy their wives' sexual needs. Third, the erotic impulse of Kabbalah, especially in the theosophic-theurgic Kabbalah, explains how Kabbalah empowered its practitioners and why this tradition enhanced Judaism. Since Kabbalists performed all Jewish rituals with specific intentions that linked the prescribed acts to the sefirotic world, they believed that Jews could participate in God's inner life and bring about the redemptive unification of the male and the female aspects of God. Fourth, while Kabbalah absorbed the influences of other religious traditions and schools of thought, Kabbalah is also different from them and should be understood on its own terms. On the whole, although Idel rejects feminist methodology, especially the distinction between sex and gender,[89] the book actually confirms a feminist insight: Idel's analysis of kabbalistic imagination gives us only the male perspective. Even if Kabbalists included female intention in the sexual act as Idel claims, women's desire, intentionality, imagination, and concerns remain inaccessible to us. Kabbalah indeed was produced by men and for men, reflecting the sensibilities of men, but, in direct contrast to Wolfson, Idel holds that Kabbalah insists on equality between men and women. In his analysis of the symbolism of Jerusalem in kabbalistic literature, which is part of a new study of kabbalistic views of femininity, Idel unambiguously refutes Wolfson's theory when he states: "Nowhere in the texts adduced above, or in others I am acquainted with, has the role of the feminine hypostasis designated as Jerusalem been attenuated by absorbing it into the male potency, neither in the present nor in the eschatological future."[90] Clearly the approaches of Idel and Wolfson diverge significantly, but the goal of this essay is not to adjudicate between them.

Idel's attempt to present a balance between the masculine and feminine dimensions in kabbalistic theosophy was supported by another important Kabbalah scholar, Charles Mopsik, who lived and worked in France until his untimely death in 2003. Kabbalah scholarship in France has always displayed a distinctive flavor, and Mopsik's treatment of sex, gender, and sexuality in his *Sex and the Soul: The Vicissitudes of Sexual Difference in Kabbalah*, is no exception.[91] Considering Kabbalah "a medieval form of Jewish mysticism," Mopsik presents Kabbalah as a critique and distancing from Jewish social dictates and hence from their implications for behavior and identification."[92] The kabbalistic discourse on gender was totally unfamiliar to the historians of gender such as Michel Foucault and Thomas Laqueur, and Mopsik thus diminished the validity of their claims. The main goal of his study is to reconsider the issue of passivity and activity which was a major bone of contention among Kabbalah scholars, beginning with Scholem.[93] Mopsik correctly notes that these characteristics are always dependent on function and that a given *sefirah* can be passive in one regard and active in another, that is, it can act as feminine or masculine.[94] The same is true with regard to the human soul. The world of the *sefirot* is indeed androgynous, but to understand it correctly one must inquire how each of the *sefirot* "emanates and receives in a specific way."[95] Mopsik's interpretation of androgyny conflicts with Wolfson's argument, according to which the *sefirot* are a "male androgyne," and he cites especially Rabbi Yosef of Hamadan as an example that refutes Wolfson's reading. The polarity of male and female also resides in the "human individual who does not have a single sexual essence, rather the two poles reside constantly in him or her."[96] According to Mopsik, the Jewish esoteric tradition attempted to take the dynamic relationship between masculinity and femininity in a positive way and "elaborate a complete anthropology that incorporated this duality without retreating into concepts involving the fusion of genders."[97] He adduces examples from the entire Jewish mystical tradition and concludes that,

> Kabbalistic writings of the Middle Ages and in the sixteenth century contain a wealth of interpretation both of biblical text and actual daily existence, which enabled these authors to construct a system of gender difference that was complex to the point of paradox, where the reversals, the combinations and the distortions all found a legitimate and intelligible place. In their eyes, outside appearance is never an accurate reflection of [inner] reality and it is this inner reality which is the key to human relations and identities. On each level there is an interplay of forces moving now closer, now farther away. In this arena of freedom, social and religious norms based on appearance and the needs of inner reality clash and coalesce. The possibility for an interaction and a constructive dialogue between them depends on the survival of a tradition and individuals' ties to timeless collective value.[98]

Mopsik's emphasis on the positive interplay between feminine and masculine is in accord with the approach of Liebes and Idel, but it has not prevailed in the scholarship of Kabbalah. His characterization of Kabbalah as the medieval phase of Jewish mysticism, however, is generally accepted, since all scholars agree that the category "Jewish mysticism" is larger than the medieval chapter and includes other intellectual movements such as Sabbateanism and Hasidism. The practitioners of these movements or of Kabbalah more specifically did not themselves use the phrase "Jewish mysticism" to talk about their own worldview. This category was invented by modern Jewish scholarship of the late 19th century on the basis of Christian usage, and the phrase was taken for granted in 20th-century scholarship, including this volume.[99]

Psychoanalytic Readings of Kabbalah and Sabbateanism

Although Kabbalah Studies in Israel has been dominated by the historicist legacy of Gershom Scholem, psychoanalysis has begun to make its impact in the work of Daniel Abrams, an American student of Elliot Wolfson who settled in Israel, and Devorah Bat David Gamlieli, an Israeli student of Idel. Both of them offered full-fledged theories about female subjectivity in Kabbalah, but their interpretations of Kabbalah refer to different psychoanalytic schools and two different types of feminism. Whereas Abrams, in continuity with Wolfson, reads Kabbalah through the lens of Irigaray's feminist rereading of Lacan's psychoanalysis, Gamlieli reads Kabbalah through a particular school of psychoanalysis, known as object-relations, and the engagement of an early generation of feminists, Carol Gilligan and Nancy Chodorow. The ironic situation is easy to see: Abrams, a man who is at home in postmodernism, including the French feminist version thereof, offers an egalitarian reading that is meant to free not only women but also men from harmful gender and sex stereotypes. By contrast, Gamlieli, who is a traditional woman formally trained in psychology as well as Kabbalah, endorses the pioneers of feminist psychology and moral theory whose views were quite different from Irigaray's postmodern reading. But regardless of their different points of departure, both Abrams and Gamlieli offer positive readings of female power in Kabbalah that stand in conflict with Wolfson's interpretation.

In *The Female Body of God in Kabbalistic Literature: Embodied Forms of Love and Sexuality in the Divine Feminine*,[100] Daniel Abrams engages feminist scholarship on rabbinic Judaism and Kabbalah; his goal is to "find out how much the kabbalistic interpretation of ancient Jewish literature was aware of the problematic nature of gendered symbolism in the rabbinic corpus."[101] Abrams begins with the vast scholarship of his teacher Wolfson, as well as the critique by scholars who rejected either his emphasis on the male character of the sefirotic union (namely, the androcentrism of Kabbalah) or the excessive focus on (male) embodiment, which allegedly turns a "delicate heterosexual eroticism into a reductionist sexual contact between two bodies."[102] Abrams dismisses both criticisms because they do not offer any discussion of gender as a methodological tool and do not appreciate the centrality of the body in kabbalistic symbolism. The purpose of his book is to reexamine the sexual and erotic discourse of Kabbalah with the help of Irigaray's writings in order to identify a line of thought that cherishes the female body as an ideal to the perfection of the human as a *female androgyne*.[103] In other words, although Abrams uses the same approach as Wolfson, he reaches the opposite conclusion. Abrams is not interested in fitting Kabbalah into modern feminism of this kind or another; instead he wants to challenge the assumption of contemporary readers of Kabbalah (including Wolfson) that Kabbalah has no positive statements on the female body because the texts were written by men and for men.[104] Thus Abrams's close reading of texts offering kabbalistic traditions that discuss the feminine body of the deity is intended to correct the feminist critique in Jewish Studies and remove the discussion of the deity from the purview of women only.

Abrams admits that the kabbalistic texts do not present "equality between the sexes"; indeed, the erasure of sex differences is not the goal of Kabbalah. To the contrary, the goal is to "recognize and cherish sexual differences as the basis for the acceptance of the other as Other," both socially and theologically.[105] According to Abrams, the medieval Kabbalists were fully aware of the distance between themselves and the talmudic rabbis; they chose to bridge that distance through the writing of pseudepigraphic, esoteric homilies in which they projected themselves into the literary and ideational world of their ancestors while revolutionizing the rabbinic outlook. The myth of the *Shekhinah* is one example of such a revolution. But how should we understand that myth? Did the Kabbalists recognize God as male *and* female, two principles that complement each other, or is the feminine aspect but a projection of the male imagination? Wolfson, as noted above, argues for the second view: the female exists as a real projection of the male; her destiny and hope in this masculine myth is to be included in the act of restoring the human body in order to build the male androgyne. This approach accounts for the dependence of feminine imagery on the male body and the essential connection in Kabbalah between the doctrine of evil and the existence of the male as an independent entity. This is why it is rare to find positive images of the female body in the world of the *sefirot* as depicted in kabbalistic literature.

Abrams does not consider this the end of the story. While acknowledging that kabbalistic tradition is replete with negative imagery of the female and negative evaluation of the feminine, he also shows that Kabbalah presents positive images of the female body and speaks about the arousal of desire in the *Shekhinah* by using female sexual anatomy: the breast, the vagina, the labia, and the clitoris. In Abrams's detailed reading of kabbalistic sexual imagery, Kabbalah is shown to be an extended fantasy of the body, especially the female body. Kabbalah recognizes not only the essential role of the female in human reproduction but also female subjectivity, initiative, emotion, and pleasure. The novelty of the Kabbalists was the recognition of female arousal as a *condition for* the unification of the deity through the symbolic performance of the commandments. Abrams's interpretation of kabbalistic sexuality is informed by Irigaray's feminist theory, but it also challenges Irigaray's critique that juxtaposes sex against gender because, in so doing, Irigaray perpetuates what is wrong with patriarchy. For Abrams, Kabbalah offers a positive view of the female body that can be celebrated not only by women but also by men because they acknowledge the female other *for its own sake as a full-fledged subjectivity.* These images do not present the female as an aspect of the male body, nor do they look at the female as a separate Other that represents Evil in the sefirotic world. Rather, the female, which is indeed described as the Other Side (*Sitra Aḥra*), is not a negation of the male or a projection of the male but rather is enshrined through images of the distinctive female body; through her unique body parts a distinct selfhood that characterizes her alone is exposed. The female as a woman is depicted to have erotic desire manifested in the sexual arousal of her body through detailed depiction of erotic zones.[106]

Abrams admits that the Kabbalists tended to see God as a male and understood religious dynamics as males, but they were also revolutionary enough to offer female imagery. Indeed, in Abrams's reading, Kabbalah appears as an elaborate fantasy, or meditation, about the female body. He thus responds to Irigaray critically because she posits sex against gender, which he believes perpetuates the distorted patterns of patriarchy. Irigaray maintained that by paying attention to the distortion of patriarchy, Western society will become cognizant of the inequality in the attitude toward the Other and the discourse about the Other in the past and the present. Abrams retorts that recognition of differences between the sexes is not just the business of women but of all human beings. His goal is to show that the Kabbalists cherished these differences and had no desire to erase the female from their gaze as Irigaray (and Wolfson in her footsteps) have suggested. The sources that Abrams amasses highlight the female body, the male body, or the union between man and woman that rely on the complementarity between the male and the female. This shows that Kabbalists believed that their theurgic work can empower not only the masculine *sefirah Yesod* but also the *Shekhinah* directly.[107] In short Kabbalah, according to Abrams, recognizes not only the place of woman in intercourse but also her initiative, her feelings, and her bodily pleasures.[108]

The openness toward psychoanalysis is most evident in the recent study by Devorah Bat David Gamlieli, who studied Kabbalah with Idel and Liebes and psychology with Shmuel Ehrlich at the Hebrew University. But her *Psychoanalysis and Kabbalah: The Masculine and Feminine in Lurianic Kabbalah* does not privilege Irigary's feminist reworking of Lacan's theories, and it is doubtful that she is versed in them.[109] Instead, she offers a thorough application of psychoanalytic principles to Lurianic Kabbalah that draws on theories of the object-relations school of psychoanalysis (e.g., D. W. Winnicott, H. Kohut, W. R. D. Fairbairn, and W. R. Bion). To the extent that Gamlieli is interested in feminist theory, it is Carol Gilligan and Nancy Chodorow that shaped her views rather than French feminism.[110] Showing how kabbalistic gender categories are rooted in the identification of Form with male and Matter with female in Aristotelian philosophy (which was introduced to Judaism by Maimonides), Gamlieli's psychoanalytic rereading of Lurianic Kabbalah shifts the focus of the divine drama (i.e., the events of *tzimtzum*, *shevirah*, and *tikkun*) from the cosmic arena to the psychological arena of human Self. She argues that Luria articulated a deep theory of the Self that requires the proper relationship between the "feminine" and "masculine," that is, between the finite and the infinite, the passive and active, the material and the spiritual. Lurianic Kabbalah was not about the evolution of the cosmos but about the formation of the Self in a way that anticipates the interrelational insights of object-relation psychoanalysis.

Gamlieli uses the paradigm of the object-relations school of psychoanalysis to interpret the Lurianic myth.[111] In essence she claims that the Lurianic myth is not about cosmology but about metaphysics and psychology, which are two sides of the same coin. Luria explains two different modalities in the human psychological makeup: "Being" (*havayah*) and "Doing" (*asiyah*). Being originates in *Ein Sof*, which is thought to be the essence of the Self, relating to continual being, unity, and wholeness. "Doing" has its source in the material dimension and physical laws imprinted in nature at creation. The *Adam Qadmon* (Primordial *Anthropos*) is the archetype or prototype for humanity, and the processes that Luria describes take place in each and every human being. Thus each person spends life alternating between these two experiential states of consciousness—"Being" and "Doing"—in a long process of building the Self. What does that have to do with gender? The answer has to do with Gamlieli's interpretation of the Lurianic concept of *tikkun* as the inclusion of the male and female. In the act of *tikkun*, the female aspect becomes *equivalent* to that of the male. The female aspect is the vessel that contains selfhood, or Being. It requires a vigorous advocate during the lengthy processes of its formation into the vessel that contains the consciousness of unity, for until the culmination of these processes, it acts within a consciousness of separation, finiteness, and negation that result as evil in the world of "Doing." For Gamlieli, Lurianic Kabbalah was a much needed correction of Rabbinic Judaism because Kabbalah provided insights into unseen psychological processes. Since the psychological growth of the Self is possible only through action in the social-moral sphere, the myth of Lurianic Kabbalah is inherently linked to kabbalistic ethics and the actual lived reality of kabbalistic communities.

Gamlieli is not alone in focusing on the positive portrayal of the *Shekhinah* in Lurianic Kabbalah. Her reading receives some support from another student of Idel, Jonathan Garb. Garb offers an interesting fusion of history, phenomenology of religion, and cultural studies in his essay "Gender and Power in Kabbalah: Theoretical Investigation," in which he argues that the status of the female in Kabbalah changed in Lurianic Kabbalah as a result of deeper transformation in European society concerning the status of women.[112] Garb's point of departure is Wolfson's analysis that took the *Shekhinah* to be "entirely passive and receptive vis-à-vis the power of the male *Sefirot*."[113] Instead, Garb offers another model where the *Shekhinah* as a female force is perceived as a source of power for a male mystic. This understanding of the *Shekhinah*, he suggests, may even have some impact on how certain Kabbalists (for example, Joseph Karo) imagined concrete women.[114] Garb claims that the second model (i.e., the *Shekhinah* as a source of power) emerged in the 16th century in the Kabbalah of Isaac Luria in Safed as a result of a historical shift in the Renaissance understanding of women.[115] Although his documentation and analysis of this shift is somewhat weak, the argument is very suggestive. In Safedian Kabbalah the righteous Kabbalist (the earthly *tzaddik*) stands in, as it were, for the supernal *Tzaddik* (*sefirah Yesod*) in intercourse with the *Shekhinah*; he thereby arouses the desire of the *Shekhinah* to dwell in him and to bestow her influx on him. Garb persuasively argues that to understand gender relations one must examine them as power relations, but, notably, "an interaction between male and female powers may commence in an asymmetrical manner yet result in a rather egalitarian exchange."[116] This view, which echoes Foucault, supports the interpretation of Idel and Mopsik who present the relationship between male and female in Kabbalah as egalitarian and fluid. But speaking as a historian of Judaism, Garb speculates that the gendering of the rabbinic myth of the *Shekhinah* was the response of Kabbalah to the Maimonidean philosophy, which in turn reflected the impact of Islam.[117] Ironically Garb, who focused on the immediate historical context as a cause of change in 16th-century Kabbalah, ends his analysis echoing Scholem's "quest for origins."

The gendered symbolism of the *Shekhinah* stood at the center of consciousness, culture, and ritual practices of the Safed community. One Kabbalist who contributed greatly to this was Moses Cordovero, who headed a Portuguese congregation in Safed and led the study of the *Zohar* as a means for salvation. Cordovero and his mystical cohorts believed that they were tested by their ability to correctly decipher the mysteries of the *Zohar* and that they were ready to take upon themselves to worship the *Shekhinah* so as to facilitate her reunion with her husband, *Tif'eret*. In his *Ma'ayan Ya'akov* (The Fountain of Jacob), the fourth section of his *Sefer Elimah*, Cordovero unpacks the mystery of *Malkhut/Shekhinah* through an exposition of the zoharic myth. In 2009 five female scholars of Kabbalah—Bracha Sack, Shifra Asulin, Melilah Hellner-Eshed, Esther Liebes, and Leah Morris—engaged this rich text, exploring the theological significance of its sensual and sexual symbolism.[118] While these studies illustrate how women have successfully entered the field of Kabbalah Studies in Israel, they also make clear that their textual scholarship has little interest in or familiarity with feminist theory or gender studies.[119]

These learned studies contrast not only with the feminist informed reading of the *Zohar* by Ruth Kara-Ivanov Kaniel, already mentioned above, but also with the studies of Joseph H. Chajes who has uncovered the "mystical prowess of a number of sixteenth – and seventeenth-century Jewish women," which he has reconstructed from "tantalizing, if meager, material . . . in an impressive range of biographical, inspirational and encyclopedic works."[120] Focusing on reports about female spirit possession as reported by Hayyim Vital and other male mystics and rabbinic authorities, Chajes, in a good feminist fashion, managed to "reveal glimpses of a mode of religiosity largely, but not entirely, buried under layers of cultural bias and literary artifice."[121] Chajes's pioneering work recovered the activities of several Jewish women who were venerated for their actions as mediums, healers, and diviners.

Undoubtedly, the Safed community manifests some of the profound changes in Jewish culture. But if Garb explains the shift by looking at the status of women in Renaissance Europe, Abraham Elqayam, a scholar of Sabbateanism, locates the major change in the sexual revolution that transformed Jewish society in the 17th century, undermining rabbinic sexual strictures and norms.[122] Elqayam identifies the causes of the profound crisis experienced by European Jewish society in the second half of the 17th century and the first half of the 18th century in several possible developments: the general sociocultural crisis of Europe in the 17th century, the dissemination of kabbalistic ethical literature to the general public as a result of printing, and the conflict that ensued when the kabbalistic ascetic mentality confronted the more lax sexual mores of the general public and former *conversos*. Whatever the reason, the breakdown of sexual norms and mores was reflected in the unique, psychotic behavior of Shabbatai Zevi, the messianic claimant of the mid-17th century and even more so in the sexual theology of his propagandist, Rabbi Abraham Nathan Benjamin Ashkenazi, known as Nathan of Gaza. In a brilliant reading of Nathan's writings, Elqayam offers an intriguing exposition of Nathan's paradoxical and highly sexual messianic discourse that addressed the inner conflict in Nathan's own soul between the ascetic mentality of the prophet (Nathan) and the deviant sexuality of his Messiah. The dialogue between these conflicting sexual postures reaches fruition in the discussion of spiritual sexuality in Nathan's writing. To explain this dialectic, Elqayam, in a departure from Scholem and Idel, employs Jungian psychoanalysis, especially as articulated by Erich Neumann. The myth of the Messiah, as articulated by Nathan, is but a psychological mode present in the soul of Nathan himself. The myth manifests the conflict between the oppressive persona that followed the ascetic mentality of Lurianic Kabbalah and Shabbatai Zevi's promiscuous sexuality, the "shadow" of Nathan's "persona." The conflict is resolved in the eschatological moment when the corporeal "Law of Creation" (*Torah de-Beriah*) will be replaced by the "Law of Emanation" (*Torah de-Atzilut*), replacing bodily sexuality and its sinfulness with spiritual love experienced by the Godhead itself. The higher spiritual love is indeed androgynous as embodied by the spiritual Shabbatai Zevi, namely, the archetype of the Messiah in whom the crisis of sexuality is resolved by a new level of individuation.

What was the impact of Sabbatean antinomianism on the status of women? Ada Rapoport-Albert, in a comprehensive, historical study, addressed this question.[123] The messianic-mystical upheaval surrounding Shabbatai Zevi was unique in terms of women, as they were active participants, carriers of the movement's message, and even its heroines. Hundreds, perhaps even thousands, of women envisioned or prophesied the messiahship of Zevi, although few of these testimonies were recorded in writing. Women had direct, unrestricted access to the various messianic leaders; women interacted with men sexually in order to affect a messianic "repair" (*tikkun*) of various sins; women convinced men of the truth of the Sabbatean message; and women took very active roles in all the public activities of the Sabbatean sects, including formal study. Within Sabbatean sects, women could function independently, and they joined the sect on their own accord. A few women (e.g., Eva, the wife of Jonah Valle in Prague and her two married daughters) were known as writers of their own accord and even defended the Sabbatean sect against their detractors. In Sabbatean communities women studied the *Zohar* in order to hasten redemption, and in the Frankist sect the messianic drama not only revolved around the female figure of the Maiden, but it was also realized in the actual activities of Jacob Frank's daughter, Eva.

If Rapoport-Albert's elaborate study indicates the perpetuation of historicism among scholars of Kabbalah, the studies of Abrams, Gamlieli, and Elqayam clearly indicate that kabbalistic scholars today are much more open to psychoanalytic theories and consider it a valid schema in the interpretation of Kabbalah. The commitment to historicism, which had given rise to the academic discipline of Jewish Studies in the 19th century, remains as strong as ever (especially in Israel), even though historicism is fused with other approaches taken from the phenomenology of religion, cultural studies (primarily its Foucauldian strain), and comparative literature. Scholars of Kabbalah are very aware of feminism, but they vary in their application of feminist approaches. Recent scholarship on Hasidism illustrates this point most clearly. Nehemia Polen, an American scholar of Hasidism who is involved in the Jewish Renewal movement, highlights the degree to which women took an active role in the history of Hasidism and even functioned as recognized spiritual leaders.[124] By contrast, Ada Rapoport-Albert shows that Hasidism exacerbated the marginal status of women in Jewish society and even contributed to the breakdown of the Jewish family.[125] In between these opposing readings of many of the same sources, Naftali Lowenthal, a scholar of Hasidism who is also a member of Chabad, offers a nuanced analysis of the role of women in organizing formal education among women in the 19th and 20th centuries and the spiritual underpinning of these efforts.[126] All three use the exacting tools of historical research, but they reach very different views about the role of women in the Hasidic movement reflecting their own Jewish commitments and place in the spectrum of contemporary Judaism.

Conclusion: The Study of Gender in Kabbalah in Retrospect

What can we conclude about the new studies on gender in Jewish mysticism? To begin, it is evident that current scholarship on Kabbalah has been attuned to feminist theory, even though scholars of Kabbalah who employ feminist theories are not necessarily feminists. The scope of feminist theory employed by kabbalistic scholars, however, is limited to a small number of feminist theorists, leaving this vast theoretical discourse relatively unexplored. Although Irigaray is a central feminist theorist, feminist theory cannot be reduced to her work; in fact, many feminist theories dispute Irigaray and accuse her of positing a female essence. No evidence suggests that Jewish scholars of Kabbalah today are really informed about the nuances and richness of feminist theory.

Precisely because feminist theory is so complex and ridden with internal debates, whether Kabbalah is compatible with contemporary feminist sensibilities depends on how one interprets the kabbalistic material and which feminist theorist one privileges. The mere attention to gender categories in

Kabbalah does not render one a feminist interpreter,[127] but it does suggest that attention to the absent presence of women in kabbalistic texts can enrich our understanding of the tradition. As we have seen, Idel, who offers a most positive reading of the female in Kabbalah, actually rejects the application of feminism to the study of Kabbalah. Conversely, Wolfson who highlights the marginalization, even dehumanization, of the female because of Kabbalah, is most influenced by feminist theory. The use of the label "feminist" is thus rather misleading, because feminism itself is not a simplistic diagnosis about the female condition and the political steps necessary to ameliorate it. Feminism speaks in many voices, and feminists do not agree about either the problem or the solution.

The above statement about feminism also befits psychoanalysis. Since Kabbalah theorizes about the inner life of human beings, it is understandable that psychoanalysis (a major theoretical paradigm in the 20th century) is applied to the analysis of Kabbalah. Yet, how one reads kabbalistic texts psychoanalytically depends on which theory one privileges as the appropriate lens. In the past three decades, psychoanalysis has been under severe criticism not only because of new information about how Freud developed the field but primarily because of the developments in the new brain sciences. The narrative structure of psychoanalysis makes it especially suitable to the interpretation of Kabbalah, another mythical narrative. We should also note that Freud, the founder of psychoanalysis, viewed eros as a cosmic force, following in the footsteps of ancient philosophers such as Plato, as Jonathan Lear brilliantly demonstrated.[128] The interaction between psychoanalysis and kabbalistic scholarship, which was already proposed in 1965 by David Bakan[129] but dismissed by scholars of Kabbalah at the time because of their allegiance to Scholem's historicist method, might offer new directions in the study of gender in Jewish mysticism. Yet we should also remember that as profound as psychoanalysis is, the understanding of human inner life today requires that scholars also be attuned to the cognitive sciences and neuroscience. Sometimes (as V. S. Ramachandran has shown in regard to the Freudian theory of repression),[130] contemporary neuroscience offers support to Freud's theories, but in other cases it is very possible that contemporary neuroscience will also debunk some analytic interpretations about the formation of the Self or the acquisition of language. In short, the conversation between Kabbalah and psychoanalysis can be fruitful if it is supplemented with current scientific studies of the Self outside psychoanalysis. Whether psychoanalysis is, in principle, a viable model for the interpretation of mental life is a highly debated question that scholars of Kabbalah should engage.

Sex, sexuality, and gender are at the core of the kabbalistic worldview, and understanding Kabbalah and its immense cultural appeal cannot ignore the role of the feminine. To interpret the feminine aspects in Kabbalah requires the application of feminist theory, but feminism includes both negative and critical dimensions as well as positive or constructive ones. As much as feminism rejects any discussion of the essence of women, so, too, does Kabbalah resist one exclusive interpretation. Kabbalists generated thousands of texts in which they offer numerous interpretations of their shared symbolism. There is no one way to interpret a given kabbalistic text, and even the attempts of scholars such as Idel to identify kabbalistic structures of thought, or ideational models, can always be negated or undermined by some texts that do not conform to the model. Kabbalah is a linguistic art of the Jews, and like all great art it can sustain conflicting interpretations that cannot be reconciled.

As an intellectual historian, I am interested in the history of interpretation and its change over time as a result of changing modes of thought, intellectual fads, and scholarly conventions. In principle, I do not believe that it is possible to offer one definitive reading of Kabbalah, nor do I believe that the search for such definitive reading is good for kabbalistic scholarship. Can we imagine how horrible it would be for culture if we endorsed the notion that the Bible or the works of Shakespeare and Kafka have but one and only one correct interpretation? By the same token, Kabbalah resists one overarching interpretation no matter how good our scholarship. Rather, it is through the conflicting and incommensurate interpretations of these imaginative fantasies that we may come to understand something about the human, about Judaism, and, through the dark glass of language, something about God. If we keep this in mind, we may be able to remember that every interpretation of Kabbalah is subject for revision, debate, and reinterpretation; it is this task of ongoing interpretation that not only perpetuates our scholarly activities but also enables us to approximate what the Kabbalists themselves were doing. I, for one, believe that what matters for future scholarship of Kabbalah and, indeed, for the future existence of Judaism is the perpetuation of the interpretative impulse, which is predicated not just on the knowledge of text but on the love Jews have (or should have) for their inherited textual tradition of which Kabbalah is but one, albeit the most powerful and imaginative dimension. The commitment to the textual tradition and the process of interpretation equally requires the appreciation of the mystery of language and its dialectic of disclosure and concealment, a mystery most deeply acknowledged by novelists such as Franz Kafka, philosophers such as Franz Rosenzweig, poets such as Hayyim Nahman Bialik, psychoanalysts such as Sigmund Freud, and scholars of Kabbalah such as Elliot Wolfson.

If we allow the mystery of language and the power of the textual tradition to do their enchanting work on us, we may be able to survive the challenges of contemporary science and its complementary technology, in which only one interpretation is feasible and only one reading is true. Against this shallow vision of reality, Kabbalah offers us its multivocal, infinite, never-ending interpretative, imaginative, linguistic richness that makes us humans, created in the image of God.

NOTES

1. The generalizations about Kabbalah in this chapter pertain to the dominant strand, the so-called theosophic kabbalah, of the *Zohar* and Lurianic Kabbalah rather than to the Kabbalah of Abulafia and his followers, which is known as "prophetic Kabbalah" or "ecstatic Kabbalah."

2. This statement identifies "monotheism" with Maimonides' definition. It is true, however, that Judaism encompassed prophetic and rabbinic conceptions of monotheism that were quite different from those of Maimonides.

3. Empowering God is the meaning of "theurgy." For systematic analysis of power and empowerment in Kabbalah, see Jonathan Garb, *Manifestations of Power in Jewish Mysticism: From Rabbinic Literature to Safedian Kabbalah* [in Hebrew] (Jerusalem: Magnes, 2004).

4. The original lecture in German was published in *Eranos Jahrbuch* 21 (1952): 47–107.

5. See Joseph Dan, "Forward," in Gershom Scholem, *The Mystical Shape of the Godhead* (New York: Schocken Books, 1991), pp. 3–14, esp. p. 7.

6. See G. Scholem, "*Mi-Toch Hirhurim al Hokhmat Yisrael,*" in *Explications and Implications: Writings on Jewish Heritage and Renaissance* [in Hebrew], ed. Ahuvia Malkin (Tel Aviv: Am Oved, 1982), pp. 385–403.

7. Scholem, *On the Mystical Shape of the Godhead*, p. 160.

8. Ibid, p. 159.

9. Ibid. p. 160.

10. Ibid., p. 168.

11. *Reshit ha-Kabbalah* was written originally in Hebrew (Jerusalem: Schocken Books, 1948) and then translated into German as *Ursprung und Anfänge der Kabbalah* (Berlin: Walter de Gruyter, 1962) and later into English (Philadelphia: Jewish Publication Society, 1987).

12. Scholem, *On the Mystical Shape of the Godhead*, p. 161.

13. Ibid., p. 194.

14. On the relationship between Scholem's scholarship and his ideological commitments, see Hava Tirosh-Rothschild, "Continuity and Revision in the Study of Kabbalah," *AJS Review* 18 (1991): 161–92; and Boaz Huss, "The Mysticism of the Kabbalah and the Myth of Jewish Mysticism" [in Hebrew], *Pe'amin* 110 (2007): 9–30.

15. Isaiah Tishby and Fischel Lachover, *Mishnat ha-Zohar*, 3rd ed. (Jerusalem: Bialik Institute, 1971); English translation, *Wisdom of the Zohar*, trans. David Goldstein (Oxford: Littman Library of Jewish Civilization, 1989). The section on the *Shekhinah* appears in volume 1 of the Hebrew edition, pp. 219–31, and in volume 1 of the English edition, pp. 371–87.

16. Peter Schäfer, "Tochter, Schwester, Braut und Mutter: Bilder der Weiblichkeit Gottes in der fruehen Kabbalah," in *Saculum: Jahrbuch fuer Universalgeschichte* 49 (1998): 259–79; English version, "Daughter Sister, Bride, and Mother: Images of the Femininity of God in the Early Kabbalah," *Journal of the American Academy of Religion* 68 (2000): 221–42; idem, *Mirror of His Beauty: Feminine Images of God from the Bible to the Early Kabbalah* (Princeton, NJ: Princeton University Press, 2002).

17. The *Sefer ha-Bahir* is an anonymous text attributed to the patriarch Abraham. The text began to circulate in Provence at the end of the 12th century, but scholars still debate the time and place of its composition. Scholem's view that the *Sefer ha-Bahir* was composed in Babylonia between the 8th and 10th centuries is largely accepted by many scholars of Jewish mysticism, although there is no way to prove it. More likely it is a product of the European environment in the 12th century, although where it was finally edited is also in dispute. Most scholars view Provence as the editorial context of the book, but Marc Verman proposed Spain as the editorial setting (*The Book of Contemplation: Medieval Jewish Mystical Sources* [Albany: State University of New York Press, 1992], pp. 166–70).

18. Schäfer, *In the Mirror of His Beauty*, p. 11.

19. Ibid., pp. 11–12.

20. Ibid., p. 13.

21. Ibid., p. 239.

22. Ibid., p. 226.

23. Ibid., p. 228.

24. Ibid., p. 228.

25. Ibid., p. 117.

26. The book was awarded the Association of American Publishers Award for Best Professional/Scholarly Book on Religion in 2002.

27. Moshe Idel, "The Kabbalistic Interpretation of the Secret of 'Arayot in Early Kabbalah" [in Hebrew], *Kabbalah* 12 (2004): 89–199, quote at p. 95 n. 32.

28. Daniel Abrams, "The Condensation of the Symbol "Shekhinah" in the Manuscripts of the Book Bahir," *Kabbalah* 16 (2007): 7–82.

29. Daniel Abrams, "The Virgin Mary as the Moon That Lacks the Sun: A Zoharic Polemic against the Veneration of Mary," *Kabbalah* 17 (2008): 7–56, quote at p. 19.

30. Elliot R. Wolfson, *Along the Path: Studies in Kabbalistic Myth, Symbolism, and Hermeneutics* (Albany: State University of New York Press, 1995); idem., "Hebraic and Hellenic Conceptions of Wisdom in *Sefer ha-Bahir*," *Poetics Today* 19 (1998): 147–76.

31. This secularist option was adopted by many women who defined themselves as Jewish ethnically but not religiously; it was also common among the leaders of American feminism, including Bella Abzug and Betty Friedan.

32. This approach is represented by Orthodox feminists as well as by Jewish feminists in academia; when I speak about "Jewish feminism," I have this second group in mind. The works of Blu Greenberg, Rochelle Millen, Judith Plaskow, Aviva Cantor, Paula Hyman, Ellen Umansky, Rachel Adler, Judith Hauptman, Laura Levitt, and many others belong in this category.

33. The most famous example of this option is Starhawk (aka Miriam Simos), who created a new nature-based religion known as Wicca and who is associated with the political Left and with the ecological movement. Her works include *Dreaming the Dark: Magic, Sex, and Politics* (Boston: Beacon, 1982); and *The Spiral Dance: A Rebirth of the Ancient Religion*

of the Great Goddess (San Francisco: Harper and Row, 1979). For an intelligent analysis of Starhawk's earth-based spirituality and commitment to the Goddess religion, see Rosemary Radford Reuther, *Goddesses and the Divine Feminine: A Western Religious History* (Berkeley: University of California Press, 2005), pp. 277–84.

34. This body of work is too vast to cite here, but a few edited volumes can be cited as examples of this genre: Ellen Umansky and Dianne Ashton, eds., *Four Centuries of Jewish Women's Spirituality: A Sourcebook* (Boston: Beacon, 1992); Judith Baskin, *Jewish Women of the Word: Jewish Women and Jewish Writing* (Detroit: Wayne State University Press, 1994); T. M. Rudavsky, ed., *Gender and Judaism: The Transformation of Tradition* (New York: New York University Press, 1995); Miriam Peskowitz and Laura Levitt, eds., *Judaism since Gender* (New York, Routledge, 1997); Hava Tirosh-Samuelson, ed., *Women and Gender in Jewish Philosophy* (Bloomington: Indiana University Press, 2004).

35. See Carol P. Christ, "Why Women Need the Goddess: Phenomenological, Psychological, and Political Reflections," in *Womanspirit Rising: A Feminist Reader in Religion* (San Francisco: HarperSanFrancisco, 1979), pp. 273–87. The impact of Carol Christ's thealogy on Jewish feminism could not be underestimated, since the leading Jewish feminist theologian, Judith Plaskow, worked closely with Christ and edited several volumes in which the early writings of Jewish feminists were published. As Jewish feminism matured, it became independent of the Christian and post-Christian sisters, in part because Jewish feminists had to come to terns with the latent anti-Semitic tendencies of the feminist critique of patriarchy and in part because they realized that Jewish uniqueness and distinctiveness could not be erased by feminist universal analysis.

36. See Rita Gross, "Female God Language in the Jewish Context," in idem, *Womanspirit Rising*, 167–73.

37. Judith Plaskow, *Standing Again at Sinai: Judaism from a Feminist Perspective* (San Francisco: HarperSanFrancisco, 1991), pp. 138–40, 165–66; idem, "Jewish Feminist Thought," in *History of Jewish Philosophy*, ed. Daniel H. Frank and Oliver Leaman (New York: Routledge, 1997), pp. 885–94, esp. p. 890.

38. Susannah Heschel, *On Being a Jewish Feminist* (New York: Schocken Books, [1983] 1995).

39. Arthur Green, "Bride, Spouse, Daughter: Images of the Feminine in Classical Jewish Sources," in idem, *On Being a Jewish Feminist*, p. 250.

40. Ibid., p. 255.

41. Ibid., p. 259.

42. Arthur Green, "Shekhina, the Virgin Mary, and the Song of Songs: Reflections on a Kabbalistic Symbol in Its Historical Context," *AJS Review* 26, no. 1 (2002): 1–52.

43. Ibid., p. 21.

44. Carolyn Walker Bynum, *Fragmentation and Redemption: Essays on Gender and the Human Body in Medieval Religion* (New York: Zone Books, 1991); idem, *Jesus as Mother: Studies in the Spirituality of the High Middle Ages* (Berkeley: University of California Press, 1982); E. Ann Matter, "The Virgin Mary—A Goddess?" in *The Book of the Goddess, Past and Present: An Introduction to Her Religion*, ed. Carl Olson (New York: Crossroad Books, 1983), pp. 80–96; Penny Schine Gold, *The Lady and the Virgin: Image, Attitude, and Experience in Twelfth-Century France* (Chicago: University of Chicago Press, 1985); Elizabeth A. Johnson, "Marian Devotion in the Western Church," in *Christian Spirituality: High Middle Ages and Reformation*, ed. J. Raitt, B. McGinn, J. Meyendorff (New York: Crossroad Books, 1987).

45. Arthur Green, "Kabbalistic Re-Vision: A Review Article of Elliot Wolfson's *Through a Speculum That Shines*," *History of Religions* 36 (February 1997): 265–74.

46. Arthur Green, "Shekhina, the Virgin Mary, and the Song of Songs," p. 36 n. 142.

47. See Elliot Wolfson, *Language, Eros, Being: Kabbalistic Hermeneutics and Poetic Imagination* (New York: Fordham University Press, 2005), pp. 445–46 n. 24.

48. Among Wolfson's numerous studies on gender are the following: "Beautiful Maiden without Eyes: *Peshat* and *Sod* in Zoharic Hermeneutics," in *The Midrashic Imagination: Jewish Exegesis, Thought, and History*, ed. Michael Fishbane (Albany: State University of New York Press, 1993), pp. 155–203; *Through a Speculum That Shines: Vision and Imagination in Medieval Jewish Mysticism* (Princeton, NJ: Princeton University Press, 1994); "The Feminine as Other in Theosophic Kabbalah: Some Philosophic Observations on the Divine Androgyne," in *The Other in Jewish Thought and History: Construction of Jewish Identity and Culture*, ed. Lawrence Silberstein and Robert Cohn (New York: New York University Press, 1994), pp. 166–204; *Circle in the Square: Studies in the Use of Gender in Kabbalistic Symbolism* (Albany: State University of New York Press, 1995); "On Becoming Female: Crossing the Gender Boundaries in Kabbalistic Ritual and Myth," in *Gender and Judaism*, ed. T. M. Rudavsky (New York: New York University Press, 1995), pp. 209–30; "Coronation of the Sabbath Bride: Kabbalistic Myth and the Ritual of Androgynisation," *Journal of Jewish Thought and Philosophy* 6 (1997): 301–44; "Tiqqun ha-Shekhina and the Overcoming of Gender Dimorphism in the Messianic Kabbalah of Moses Hayyim Luzzatto," *History of Religions* 36 (1997): 289–332; "Constructions of the Shekhinah in the Messianic Theosophy of Abraham Cardoso, with an annotated edition of *Derush ha-Shekhina*," *Kabbalah: Journal for the Study of Jewish Mystical Texts* 3 (1998): 11–143; "Occultation of the Feminine and the Body of Secrecy in Medieval Kabbalah," in *Rending the Veil: Concealment and Revelation of Secrets in the History of Religions*, ed. Elliot R. Wolfson (New York: Seven Bridges, 1999), pp. 113–54; "Judaism and Incarnation: The Imaginal Body of God," in *Christianity in Jewish Terms*, ed. Tikva Frymer-Kensky et al. (Boulder, CO: Westview, 2000), pp. 239–54; "Gender and Heresy in the Study of Kabbalah" [in Hebrew], *Kabbalah: Journal for the Study of Jewish Mystical Texts* 6 (2001): 231–62; *Language, Eros, Being: Kabalistic Hermeneutic and Poetic Imagination* (New York: Fordham University Press, 2005).

49. See Elliot R. Wolfson, "On Becoming Female," in Rudvasky, *Gender and Judaism*, p. 210.

50. Wolfson, *Language, Eros, Being*, p. 128.

51. The most relevant readings of Irigaray that shaped Wolfson's reading are *Speculum of the Other Woman*, trans. Gillian C. Gill (Ithaca, NY: Cornell University Press, 1985); and *This Sex Which Is Not One*, trans. Catherine Porter, with C. Burke (Ithaca, NY: Cornell University Press, 1985). The secondary literature on Irigaray is too extensive to cite here, but most useful is Margaret Whitford, *Luce Irigaray: Philosophy in the Feminine* (London: Routledge, 1991).

52. See Rosemary Putnam Tong, *Feminist Thought: A More Comprehensive Introduction*, 2nd ed. (Boulder, CO: Westview, 1998), pp. 193–211.

53. Wolfson, *Language, Eros, Being*, p. 10.

54. Hayyim Nahman Bialik, *Kitvey H. N. Bialik* (Tel Aviv: Devir, 1935–1938), 2:224–26.

55. The term "logocentrism" was coined by Jacques Derrida in order to speak about the Western confidence in language as a mirror of nature. According to Derrida and his postmodernist followers, "logocentrism" captures the Western tendency to believe that

the meaning of a word has its origin in the structure of reality itself so that the word makes the truth about that structure directly present to the mind. The term "phallocentrism" reflects the impact of Jacques Lacan's analysis of language, in which the phallus is the signifier.

56. Wolfson, *Language, Eros, Being*, p. 78.

57. Ibid., p. 78.

58. Ibid., p. 372.

59. See Arthur Green's review of Wolfson in *History of Religions* 36 (1997): 265–74.

60. For a penetrating analysis of gender in Israeli society and culture, see Rachel Elior "'Present but Absent,' 'Still Life,' and 'A Pretty Maiden Who Has No Eyes': On the Presence and Absence of Women in the Hebrew Language, in Jewish Culture, and in Israeli Life" [in Hebrew], *Alpayyim* 20 (2000): 214–70. For a useful volume on gender in various aspects of Israeli society and culture, see Dafna N. Israeli et al., eds., *Sex, Gender, Politics: Women in Israel* (Tel Aviv: Hakibutz Hame-uchad, 1999); Renée Levine Melammed, ed., *"Lift Up Your Voice": Women's Voice and Feminist Interpretation in Jewish Studies* [in Hebrew] (Tel Aviv: Yediot Aharonot and Sifrei Hemed, 2001); Esther Fuchs, ed., *Israeli Women's Studies: A Reader* (New Brunswick, NJ: Rutgers University Press, 2001).

61. Yehuda Liebes, "Zohar and Eros" [in Hebrew], *Alpayyim* 9 (1994): 67–119.

62. Yehuda Liebes, "How the Zohar Was Written," in idem, *Studies in the Zohar,* trans. Arnold Schwartz, Stephanie Nakache, and Penina Peli (Albany: State University of New York Press, 1993), pp. 85–138.

63. See Boaz Huss, *"Like the Radiance of the Sky": Chapters in the Reception History of the Zohar and the Construction of Its Symbolic Value* (Jerusalem: Ben Zvi Institute and Bialik Institute, 2008), pp. 43–83; idem, "The Emergence of *Sefer Ha-Zohar*" [in Hebrew], *Tarbiz* 7 (2001): 507–42.

64. Melilah Hellner-Eshed, *A River Issues Forth from Eden: On the Language of Mystical Experience in the Zohar* [in Hebrew] (Tel Aviv: Am Oved, 2005). All translations of citations from this book are mine.

65. Ibid, p. 99.

66. Ibid., p. 172.

67. This famous parable received considerable scholarly attention, each highlighting a particular aspect that fits into a larger interpretative theory. Compare Michal Oron, "Put Me as a Seal on Your Heart: Reflections in the Poetics of the Zohar, *Saba de-Mishpatim* Section" [in Hebrew], in *Masu'ot: Studies in Kabbalistic Literature and Jewish Philosophy in Memory of Prof. Efraim Gottlieb,* ed. Michal Oron and Amos Goldreich (Jerusalem: Bialik Institute, 1994), pp. 1–24; Daniel Abrams, "Knowing the Maiden without Eyes: Reading the Sexual Reconstruction of the Jewish Mystic in a Zoharic Parable," *Da'at* (Nahum Arieli Memorial Volume) 50–52 (2003): LVIX–LXXXIII; Pinchas Giller, "*Saba de-Mishpatim*: Love and Reincarnation," in idem, *Reading the Zohar: The Sacred Text of Kabbalah* (Oxford: Oxford University Press, 2001), pp. 35–68.

68. Hellner-Eshed, *A River Issues Forth from Eden,* p. 200.

69. Ibid., p. 202.

70. Ibid.

71. Ibid., p. 203.

72. Ibid., pp. 258–59.

73. Ibid., p. 174.

74. Ronit Meroz, "The Passion of Kabbalah: Desire, Passivity and Activism in Kabbalah" [in Hebrew], in *Teshukah*, ed. Shlomo Biderman and Rina Lazar (Tel Aviv: Hakibbutz Hame-uchad, 2007), pp. 116–40, quote at p. 140.

75. *Zohar*, 3:249a–b. Meroz's analysis of the extended symbol of the doe is informed by gender theory as well as medieval intellectual history, but it is not feminist per se. For a strong, feminist reading of this symbolism, see Ruth Kara-Ivanov Kaniel, "Eve, the Gazelle, and the Serpent: Narratives of Creation and Redemption, Myth and Gender," *Kabbalah* 21 (2010): 255–310. I return to this essay below.

76. The following two paragraphs are based on my review of Idel's book published in *AJS Review* 31 (2007): 187–90.

77. M. Idel, *Kabbalah and Eros* (New Haven: Yale University Press, 2005), p. 12. It is important to note that Idel had published several studies on sex and sexuality in Kabbalah, prior to the publication of *Kabbalah and Eros*. For example, "Sexual Metaphors and Praxis in Kabbalah," in *The Jewish Family: Metaphor and Memory*, ed. David Kraemer (New York: Oxford University Press, 1989), pp. 197–224; reprinted in Mortimer Ostow et al., *Ultimate Intimacy: The Psychodynamics of Jewish Mysticism* (London: Karnac Books, 1995), pp. 217–44; "The Wife and the Concubine: Women in Jewish Mysticism," in *Baruch She'asani Ishah? Ha-Isha Bayahadut—Meha-tanach ve-ad Yameynu*, ed. David Yoel Ariel, Maya Leibovitz, and Yoram Mazor (Tel Aviv: Yediot Aharonot, 1999), pp. 141–57; "The Beauty of a Woman: On the Evolution of Jewish Mysticism" [in Hebrew], in *Within Hasidic Circles: Studies in Hasidism in Memory of Mordecai Wilensky*, ed. Immanuel Etkes, David Assaf, Israel Bartal, and Elchanan Reiner (Jerusalem: Bialik Institute, 1999), pp. 317–34.

78. Idel, *Kabbalah and Eros*, pp. 29–30.

79. Ibid., pp. 135–36.

80. Ibid., pp. 45–49.

81. Ibid., pp. 97–103, 128–34.

82. Ibid., pp. 224–33.

83. Ibid., pp. 5, 69.

84. Ibid., p. 104.

85. Ibid., p. 105.

86. Ibid., chap. 4, p. 179.

87. Ibid., p. 250.

88. These terms are central to Idel's classification of Kabbalah. "Theurgic-theosophic" Kabbalah refers to the doctrine of the *sefirot*, in which knowledge of God (theosophy) is prerequisite to the attempt of the Kabbalist to impact God (theurgy). The *Zohar* is the primary example of this type of Kabbalah. "Ecstatic" Kabbalah refers to the reflections of Abraham Abulafia and his school in which the focus is on the mystical union of the human soul with God. And "talismanic" Kabbalah refers to the practice of "drawing spirituality" from the divine world for the sake of human, earthly needs. This paradigm links Kabbalah to magic, and, according to Idel's analysis, it is most common in Hasidism.

89. Ibid., p. 97.

90. Idel, "On Jerusalem as a Feminine and Sexual Hypostasis," p. 43.

91. Charles Mopsik, *Sex of the Soul: The Vicissitudes of Sexual Difference in Kabbalah*, edited and with a forward by Daniel Abrams (Los Angeles: Cherub, 2005).

92. Ibid., p. 9.

93. Ibid., p. 18.

94. Ibid., p. 21.

95. Ibid., p. 25.

96. Ibid., p. 32.

97. Ibid., p. 33.

98. Ibid., p. 50.

99. On the history of the construct "Jewish mysticism" in modern scholarship, see Boaz Huss, "The Mystification of the Kabbalah and the Myth of Jewish Mysticism" [in Hebrew], *Pe`amim* 110 (2007): 9–30; idem, "The Formation of Jewish Mysticism and Its Impact on the Reception of Rabbi Abraham Abulafia in Contemporary Kabbalah," in *Religion and Its Other*, ed. Heicke Bock, Jorg Feuchter, and Michi Knechts (Frankfurt: Campus, 2008), pp. 142–62, esp. p. 145 n. 9.

100. Daniel Abrams, *The Female Body of God in Kabbalistic Literature: Embodied Forms of Love and Sexuality in the Divine Feminine* [in Hebrew] (Jerusalem: Magnes, 2004).

101. Ibid., p. 2.

102. Ibid., p. 4. The reference is to Liebes's critique of Wolfson in "Zohar and Eros."

103. Ibid., p. 5.

104. Ibid., p. 8.

105. Ibid., p. 5.

106. Ibid., p. 7.

107. Ibid., p. 179.

108. Ibid., p. 180.

109. Devorah Bat David Gamilieli, *Psychoanalysis and Kabbalah: The Masculine and Feminine in Lurianic Kabbalah* (Los Angeles: Cherub, 2006). Gamlieli's psychoanalytical reading of Lurianic Kabbalah goes much further than the initial discussion of the feminine in Lurianic Kabbalah by Yoram Jacobson ("The Aspect of the 'Feminine' in the Lurianic Kabbalah," in Gershom Scholem, *Major Trends in Jewish Mysticism, 50 Years After*, ed. Peter Schäfer and Joseph Dan [Tübingen: J. C. B. Mohr (Paul Siebeck, 1992)], pp. 239–74).

110. I cannot explain why Gamlieli is unfamiliar with French feminism, which is deeply indebted to the theories of Jacques Lacan, or why her knowledge of feminism is limited to Gilligan and Chodorow. I suspect that it merely reflects a limited exposure to feminist theory and her own psychoanalytical commitments.

111. The object-relations school of psychoanalysis emerged in England during the 1950s and offered a relational understanding of the human self. The human self is never a self-enclosed entity but a dynamic relationship that evolves through interaction with significant external objects (such as the mother) and their representations (the mother's breast).

112. Jonathan Garb, "Gender and Power in Kabbalah: A Theoretical Investigation," *Kabbalah: Journal for the Study of Jewish Mystical Texts* 13 (2005): 79–107.

113. Ibid., p. 83.

114. Ibid., p. 84.

115. Garb's emphasis on the European relevance of Lurianic gender symbolism stands in conflict with Shaul Magid's emphasis on the particular Ottoman context for the Lurianic corpus that sheds light on the "curiously non-judgmental appraisal of the act [i.e., *mishkav zachur*] and its implicit acknowledgement of the natural inclination for such sexual practices." See Shaul Magid, "Constructing Women from Men: The Metaphysics of Male Homosexuality among Lurianic Kabbalists in Sixteenth-Century Safed," *Jewish Studies Quarterly* 17 (2010): 4–28, quote at p. 5.

116. Ibid., p. 101.

117. Ibid., p 105.

118. See Bracha Sack, ed., *R. Moshe Cordovero, Maʻyan ʻEin Yaʻakov: The Fourth Foundation of the Book 'Elima* (Beer Sheva: Ben Gurion University of the Negev, 2009). I thank Moshe Idel for bringing this book to my attention.

119. These studies stand in contrast to the analysis of Ruth Kara-Ivanov Kaniel mentioned above, which is properly informed by feminist theory and gender studies.

120. J. H. Chajes, "He Said She Said: Hearing the Voices of Pneumatic Early Modern Jewish Women," *NASHIM: A Journal of Jewish Women's Studies and Gender Issues* 10 (2005): 99–125, quote at p. 102. See also idem, "The Female Jewish Mystics: The Evidence of R. Hayyim Vital's *Sefer Ha-Hezyonot*" [in Hebrew], *Zion* 67 (2002): 139–62; idem, *Between Worlds: Dybbuks, Exorcists and Early Modern Judaism* (Philadelphia: University of Pennsylvania Press, 2003).

121. Chajes, "He Said She Said," p. 118.

122. Abraham Elqayam, "To Know Messiah: The Dialectics of Sexual Discourse in the Messianic Thought of Nathan of Gaza" [in Hebrew], *Tarbiz* 65, no. 4 (1996): 637–70.

123. Ada Rapoport-Albert, "On the Status of Women in Sabbateanism," in *Hakhalom ve-Shivro: Ha-Tenuʻa ha-Shabbtait le-Sheluhoteha,*" ed. Rachel Elior, 2 vols. (= *Jerusalem Studies in Jewish Thought*, vols. 16–17) (Jerusalem, 2001), pp. 143–327.

124. Nehemia Polen, "Miriam's Dance: Radical Egalitarianism in Hasidic Thought," *Modern Judaism* 12 (1992): 1–21.

125. Ada Rapoport-Albert, "On Women in Hasidism: S. A. Horodetzky and the Maid of Ludmir Tradition," in *Jewish History: Essays in Honor of Chimen Abramsky*, ed. A. Rapoport-Albert and Steven Zipperstein (London: Halban, 1988), pp. 496–527.

126. Naftali Loewenthal, "Women and the Dialectic of Spirituality in Hasidism," in *Within Hasidic Circles: Studies in Hasidism in Memory of Mordecai Wilensky* [in Hebrew], ed. Immanuel Etkes, David Assaf, Israel Bartal, and Elchanan Reiner (Jerusalem: Bialik Institute, 1999), pp. 7–65 (English section).

127. An example of a nonfeminist treatment of women in kabbalistic literature is Yael Levin Katz, "Seven Prophetesses and Seven Sefirot: Studies in Kabbalistic Exegesis," *Daʻat* 44 (2000): 123–30.

128. Jonathan Lear, *Love and Its Place in Nature: A Philosophical Interpretation of Freudian Psychoanalysis* (New Haven: Yale University Press, 1990).

129. David Bakan, *Sigmund Freud and the Jewish Mystical Tradition* (Princeton, NJ: Van Nostrand, 1958).

130. See V. S. Ramachandran and Sandra Blakeslee, *Phantoms in the Brain: Probing the Mysteries of the Human Mind* (New York: Quill, 1998), esp. pp. 152–57.

Epilogue

Kabbalah and Contemporary Judaism

———— PINCHAS GILLER ————————————————

The English reader of this volume is likely to view its contents within a historical bubble. It has been estimated that 150 years ago, three-quarters of the Jews in the world lived in Eastern Europe. If this population had ever cared to think about the underlying metaphysical presumptions of their lives and culture, they would have drawn on Kabbalah. That is not to say that they *had* to contemplate those ideas, for Judaism has always maintained a becoming reticence about the larger questions that are mainstays to other religions. If they wondered about what would happen after they died, or about the heavenly pantheons addressed in the liturgy and Midrash, how exactly the world was created and when it would end, then their most accessible body of lore was Kabbalah. The rituals attending the observance of the Sabbath, the preparation of the dead for burial, even the muttered incantation "*kein ayin hara*" and the personal *mezuzot* and amulets sold in synagogue gift shops all derive from the intersection of Kabbalah and folk practice. This is true whether they had chosen to be religious or secular or something in between. Of course, it is a truism that secularists, products of the *Haskalah*, or Jewish Enlightenment, advocated a rationalistic approach, citing the social corruption and superstition that was rife in the worldview influenced by the verities of the Kabbalah. The North American, Western European, and socialist *yishuv* communities of what was then Palestine came to be havens for a rationalistic approach. The teachings of Maimonides and other rationalists were elevated over the Kabbalah. Had emigration and the Shoah not decimated the communities of Eastern Europe, they might have clung to kabbalistic verities just as the metaphysical presumptions of Christianity underlie the role of religion in largely Christian nations.

In the academy, particularly in America, the old supposed enmity between philosophical rationalism and Kabbalah continued to play itself out. Jewish studies were slowly admitted into the academy by way of the venue of philosophy, Maimonides gaining entry through a pioneering generation of scholars who had distinguished themselves initially as authorities on Muslim philosophy. Then, in the postwar period, the academy began its entrancement with the revisions of Gershom Scholem. These were purveyed through the venue of the Jewish seminaries, particularly the Jewish Institute of Religion, which hosted the series of lectures that eventually became the model for Scholem's *Major Trends in Jewish Mysticism*.[1]

This volume comes in the midst of an interesting period of transition in the study of Kabbalah. The field is two generations on from the narrative of its founding personality, Gershom Scholem. New questions are being asked, not just in response to Scholem's portrayal of the history of Kabbalah but independently. Scholem set the basic premises of Kabbalah as an area of study. When he and his older colleague, Martin Buber, began their researches, the academy was largely closed to the study of Jewish religion, if not closed to Jews altogether. Enlightened Jews themselves viewed Kabbalah and Hasidism in the way that North American intellectuals might view Pentecostal snake handlers in the Florida Panhandle or late-night televangelists on obscure public-access channels. There was a social gap between the "enlightened" world and the world of the practitioners. Buber and Scholem "dropped out" of Enlightenment Germany with a socially quixotic interest in recovering and exhuming Hasidism and Kabbalah, respectively, and presenting them to the academy, as well as the Jewish community.

In portraying Kabbalah to the eyes of the world, Scholem adopted various strategies to make the field palatable to the academy, adopting notions such as "Jewish Mysticism" and "Jewish Gnosticism" in order to set himself up in dialogue with the academy on these subjects. For example, the ancient Merkavah tradition was portrayed by Scholem and Saul Lieberman as "Jewish Gnosticism" on the basis of its historical coincidence and shared content with the mystery religions and Gnostic heresies of late antiquity. Later, Moshe Idel would make the point that Gnostic ideas could very well have had their origins in Judaism, and therefore the Gnostic tradition itself might really be "Gnostic Judaism."[2] Similarly, scholars seized on the definition of Kabbalah as "Jewish Mysticism." Once Kabbalah was called "mysticism," it could be placed in the continuum of experience defined by the academy as "mysticism."[3] In general, one could say that Scholem campaigned for Kabbalah's place at the table of the academic study of religion and of mysticism in particular. As "mysticism," Kabbalah was portrayed as sharing common properties with other mystical traditions in the religions of the world.

Scholem composed his sweeping review of Kabbalah in response to, and as a participant in, the central historical events of the 20th century. From within the storm, he wrote his narrative. There were fated to be some gaps in his version of the narrative; he was only one man. The seminal historian of the 19th century, Heinrich Graetz, had portrayed the *Zohar* as nothing but a response to Maimonidean rationalism.[4] Similarly, Scholem portrayed Lurianic Kabbalah as an emotional response to the trauma of the Spanish Expulsion. The popularity of Shabbatai Zevi's heretical messianism was widely perceived as a response to the Chmelnicki massacres of 1648–49. Scholem, in turn, portrayed Hasidism as a response to the collapse of Sabbateanism.

Among other things, Scholem became a serial debunker. He viewed the Sabbatean movement as the beginning of Judaism's gear change into modernity. Scholem went out of his way to impugn the authenticity of Yisrael Sarug, who sailed from the Galilee to Italy and brought Lurianic Kabbalah to the Italian neo-Platonists. Later, Ronit Meroz and Yosef Avivi determined that, in fact, Sarug's Kabbalah was authentically Lurianic with some of the terminology adapted to his new audience.[5] Scholem maintained that Isaac Luria's Kabbalah was a psychological response to the trauma of the Spanish expulsion. Since that time, Moshe Idel, Martin Cohen, and others have questioned the idea of a direct relationship between Luria and the Expulsion.[6] Scholem had portrayed the concept of *tzimtzum*, or "divine withdrawal," as a novelty of Lurianic Kabbalah. Idel and Bracha Sack have demonstrated that the image of *tzimtzum* far predated Luria and was present very early in the development of Jewish mysticisms.[7]

This premise that religious phenomena come about as a response to history is itself a product of modernity and the birth of movements that react to historical circumstances. Reform Judaism in Germany, Zionism, socialism, and the other great propellants of Judaism in modernity restructured the given premises of Jewish life. Hence the analysts of medieval Judaism, Scholem and Buber, but also Graetz and others, maintained that the propelling energy of Judaism is one of response to trauma. In fact, in every case there is reason to doubt that Kabbalah is mediated by the vicissitudes of history or is a "response" to an earlier intellectual stimulus.

Since Gershom Scholem set the parameters of Kabbalah study, his narrative has become so powerful in scholarly and popular discourse that some scholars have concluded that they are in a position to cast judgments on phenomena occurring in the field. Elsewhere, the practitioners of Kabbalah in the traditional context are emerging from their hiding places and engaging the outside world, independently from the academic milieu. As a result of these changes, the time may have come to redefine the way that Kabbalah is addressed by the academy, a definition that would bring a new clarity regarding some elements of Kabbalah study.

The popular understanding of Kabbalah is only marginally inferior to the most simplistic, inherited understandings of Scholem's historiography; both are apt to be different from Scholem's narrative. The hapless Kabbalah scholar is apt to find him– or herself being lectured on the subject by nonliterate laypeople. Each of us is bedeviled by cocktail party conversation. One hears, with equal authority, about some long-in-the-tooth entertainer's latest piece of melodrama, or how the *Zohar* was written by Moshe de Leon, or that the doctrine of *tzimtzum* was a response to the Spanish expulsion. Is the first topic really that much more jejune than the last? Was the Ba'al Shem Tov a wild illiterate, or a Sabbatean? Did Rabbi Shimon Bar Yochai "write" the *Zohar* or did Moshe de Leon? Each question misses the real point of its avowed subject. To take one example, the question of Moshe de Leon "writing" the *Zohar* conjures up the image of a Byronic genius spewing out *Leaves of Grass* or *Finnegan's Wake*, because once one posits a single author to the work, one calls to mind the romantic model of the turbulent creative genius. In fact, if the *Zohar* did emerge from de Leon's study, it was in his role as, at best, an ancillary figure, recording the notes of a circle of Kabbalists that remains shrouded in mystery. The circle may have included Todros Abulafia or his son, Yosef, as well as Yosef of Hamadan, Yosef Gikatilla, Yosef Angelet, and other figures arguably stronger and more influential than de Leon. The *Zohar* is described as a "book" by the author of the last stratum, the compositions *Tiqqunei ha-Zohar* and *Ra'aya Meheimna*, and the circle of the anonymous "elder" described in a recent study by Elliot Wolfson.[8] The *Zohar* "book," however, remained a snowballing collection of random homilies collected by aficionados for the first hundred years or so of its development. The studies of Wolfson, Boaz Huss, Yehuda Liebes, Ronit Meroz, Daniel Abrams, and Avraham Elqayam have all served to blur the identity of the *Zohar* as a single composition by a single author, or even a single book.[9] The single authorship of the *Zohar* was a guiding principle of the academic study of Kabbalah until the aforementioned scholars argued for the possibility of multiple authors and levels of composition.

Hence, in the light of subsequent research, it is possible to seriously question the conclusions of practically every chapter of *Major Trends in Jewish Mysticism* for quite empirical reasons. As mentioned, Moshe de Leon might have had rather little to do with the final versions of the *Zohar*. Isaac Luria might have been more influenced by his familial circumstances in the crafting of his kabbalistic system than by the recent Spanish expulsion. Shabbatai Zevi's movement may be better understood as a 17th-century phenomenon of paradigmatic change, much like the thinking of Spinoza, Luther, and Newton, rather than as the natural outgrowth of Lurianic Kabbalah.[10] The possible contributing factors for the spread of Hasidism go far beyond the romanticized figure of the Ba'al Shem Tov, and may include economic and social factors outside the influence of kabbalistic doctrine.[11] This questioning does not, as some might aver, amount to undue "anxiety of influence" on the part of the questioners! There are real problems, which lead to misconceptions that, in fact, have ramifications in the social realm. Hence the revision and reconception of these areas is timely and called for.

Again, we live in a period of transition, and the arc of Scholem's historiography has not prepared us sufficiently for the developments in the field. For example, my conclusions in a recent study of the school of the 18th-century Kabbalist Shalom Shar'abi[12] dovetailed with some ideas proposed by Boaz Huss. Huss has noted that a tendency to reject the present-day manifestations of Kabbalah has continued into the activities of contemporary scholars. For much of the academy, the forms of Kabbalah taken up by the masses are, with the exception, perhaps, of Chabad Hasidism, regarded as false or at least *declasse*. According to Huss:

> This approach is typical of hegemonic Israeli discourse . . . Early kabbalistic literature and the academic investigators who work with it are regarded as worthwhile, authentic and "professional," but contemporary kabbalistic belief and practices (such as prostration on the graves of the righteous, ritual reading of the Zohar and the exorcism of dybbuks) and the kabbalists who believe in and practice them are considered to be the primitives, charlatans and even a menace to modern Western-Israeli culture.[13]

Two impulses in Scholem's school have emerged as problematic at the present juncture. The first of these was the tendency to isolate "true" Kabbalah in the historical past. The second problematic element was the general tendency to define Kabbalah as mysticism, following the frankly christological definition of what mysticism is. The appropriationist anxieties of Israeli social life have played their part in this as well, particularly the coercive tendencies of the religious establishment and rabbinate. To this day, there is far less attention paid to the history and kabbalistic traditions of the Sephardic, North African, and Middle Eastern Jewish communities. The reasons for this reticence to confront North African and Middle Eastern manifestations of Kabbalah are social and historical, dictated by the mores of the academy, as well as the internal politics of Kabbalah study. Kabbalah scholars have largely represented a certain stratum of Israeli society, often (but not always, as in the enthralling work of Havivah Pedaya and Avraham Elqayam) separated from practitioners by social, ethnic and religious barriers. The alienation of non-Ashkenazic and Ashkenazic studies preceded and mirrors the alienation of contemporary Western culture from Islam.[14] This problem was forecast in Scholem's reference to Beit El as the expression of "the Sephardic and arabized tribes,"[15] evidence of his social distance from the pulsing kabbalistic activity going on less than a kilometer away from any of his Jerusalem homes.

Boaz Huss has argued that "Scholem's meetings with contemporary kabbalists left no impression whatsoever on his vast corpus of scholarly work."[16] He rejected the possibility of studying from contemporary sources, even their textual record. Huss maintains that this rejection was an ideological one, influenced by Scholem's embrace of the Zionist mythos, which required the marginalization of all previous ethnic categories and the cultural identity of Diaspora Judaism. According to the devastating critique offered by the late Arthur Hertzberg, "Scholem was quite clearly re-evoking these fascinating shades but ultimately, to use the language of his charge against the scholars of the Wissenschaft school, in order to bury them with due respect. It was part of the Jewish past, the present was Zionism."[17]

Contemporary Forms of Kabbalah

These anxieties have blinded scholars to certain new developments in the history of Kabbalah that have come about as recently as the late 20th century, and some in the scholarly community have been resistant to the examination of contemporary trends in the development of Kabbalah. Contrary to the apparent belief of many scholars, Kabbalah did not cease to evolve in 1948. Chabad, the Kabbalah Centre, Breslav Hasidism, and the Renewal movement represent late, manifestly inelegant interpretations of aspects of the kabbalistic tradition, shaped by modernity and yet emerging from within the closed walls of each sect. All these circles are arguably "popular," as they have been embraced by broader elements of the modern Jewish community beyond the traditional closed circles of classical Kabbalah. The new incarnation of Breslav, in particular, has made inroads in the Israeli youth culture, particularly as embodied in the phenomenon of the post-army trip to India and the sensibilities brought back to Israel by the returning youth. The evangelical groups, by which I mean Orthodox organizations devoted to outreach in the secular world, as well as neo-Breslav and the Kabbalah Learning Centre, have also served to blur the traditionally rigid lines between the religious and the secular in Israeli society. They operate "off the grid" and pose threats to various elements for which the grid is a comfort and a shield.

It is very easy for contemporary scholars to be complacent and tempting to "play the game." It is socially acceptable, in academia, to employ fashionable philosophical approaches and intellectual methodologies that dilute and make relative the teachings of a given tradition. These approaches might be enticing in the humanities; at the end of the day, how much more is there to say about *Tristram Shandy* or *The Purloined Letter*? But the field of Kabbalah remains in its infancy, and thousands of volumes of theology remain without even a first reading at the hands of the academy. So many areas in the field have been unexplored that it is as if the texts that have been assessed are the exceptions to the rule. Whole schools of thought remain ignored by the academy, and they are the living traditions! So much work remains to be done in reconciling the orthodoxies of the world of kabbalistic practice with the orthodoxies of the academy itself if we are to clarify the living traditions in the eyes of living communities, a task that this volume may help to further.

NOTES

1. Gershom Scholem, *Major Trends in Jewish Mysticism,* 3rd ed. (New York: Schocken Books, 1961).

2. Moshe Idel, *Kabbalah: New Perspectives* (New Haven: Yale University Press, 1988), pp. 30–32.

3. Admittedly, this phenomenon had begun well before Scholem arrived on the scene by such figures as Adolph Jellenik, who termed Kabbalah "Jewish Mysticism" in 1853. Buber echoed this view, in 1906, in his initial studies of R. Nachman of Breslav, which he terms "Die Judische Mystik" (Moshe Idel, "On Aharon Jellenik and Kabbalah, *Peamim* 100 [2004]: 15–22).

4. See Heinrich Graetz, *History of the Jews* (Philadelphia: Jewish Publication Society, 1894), 4:10–22.

5. Ronit Meroz, "Was Israel Sarug a Student of the AR"I?—New Research" [in Hebrew], *Da'at* 28 (1992): 41–56; Yosef Avivi, "Luria's Writings in Italy to 1620" [in Hebrew], *Alei Sefer* 11 (1984): 91–134.

6. Scholem, *Major Trends in Jewish Mysticism*, pp. 245–46, 286.

7. Moshe Idel, "The History of the Concept of *Tzimtzum* in Kabbalah Research," in *The Kabbalah of the AR"I*, ed. Yehuda Liebes and Rachel Elior, Studies in Jewish Thought 10 (Jerusalem: Magnes, 1992), p. 89; Bracha Sack, "R. Moshe Cordovero's Doctrine of *Tzimtzum*" [in Hebrew], *Tarbiz* 58 (1989): 207–37.

8. Elliot Wolfson, "The Anonymous Chapters of the Elderly Master of Secrets: New Evidence for the Early Activity of the Zoharic Circle," *Kabbalah* 19 (2009): 143–278.

9. Boaz Huss, *Like the Radiance of the Sky: Chapters in the Reception History of the Zohar and the Construction of Its Symbolic Value* (Jerusalem: Bialik Institute, 2008); Yehuda Liebes, "How Was the Zohar Written?" *Studies in the Zohar* (Albany: State University of New York Press, 1993); Ronit Meroz, "Zoharic Narratives and Their Adaptations," *Hispania Judaica Bulletin* 3 (5760/2000), pp. 3–63; Daniel Abrams, "Zohar, Book and 'the Book of the Zohar': A History of the Assumptions and Projections of Kabbalists and Scholars," *Kabbalah* 19 (2009) 7–142; idem, "The Invention of the Zohar as a Book: On the Assumptions and Expectations of the Kabbalists and Modern Scholars," *Kabbalah* 12 (2004) 201–32; Avraham Elqayam, "Shabbatai Tzvi's Manuscript Copy of the Zohar," *Kabbalah* 3 (1998) 343–87; Ronit Meroz, "The Middle Eastern Origins of Kabbalah," *Journal for the Study of Sephardi and Mizrahi Jewry* (February 2007): 39–57.

10. This is but one of Matt Goldish's conclusions in *The Sabbatean Prophets* (Cambridge, MA: Harvard University Press, 2004).

11. See, in particular, Glen Dynner, *Men of Silk: The Hasidic Conquest of Polish Jewish Society* (New York: Oxford University Press, 2008); and the various works of David Assaf, including *Caught in the Thicket: Chapters of Crisis and Discontent in the History of Hasidism* [in Hebrew] (Jerusalem: Zalman Shazar, 2006).

12. Pinchas Giller, *Shalom Shar'abi and the Kabbalists of Beit El* (New York: Oxford University Press, 2008).

13. Boaz Huss, "Ask No Questions: Gershom Scholem and the Study of Contemporary Jewish Mysticism," *Modern Judaism* 25 (2005): 149–50.

14. Huss has explored the association of Kabbalah with mysticism in "The Metaphysics of Kabbalah and the Myth of 'Jewish Mysticism'" [in Hebrew], *Peamim* 110 (winter 2007).

15. G. Scholem, *Devarim be-Go* [in Hebrew] (Tel Aviv: Am Oved, 1975), p. 71.

16. Huss, "Ask No Questions," p. 141.

17. Arthur Hertzberg, "Gershom Scholem as Zionist and Believer," *Modern Judaism* 5 (1985): 12.

About the Contributors

ALLISON P. COUDERT holds the Paul and Marie Castelfranco Chair in the Religious Studies Program at the University of California, Davis. Among her publications are *Leibniz and the Kabbalah; The Impact of the Kabbalah in the 17th Century: The Life and Thought of Francis Mercury van Helmont, 1614–1698*; and *Hebraica Veritas: Christian Hebraists, Jews, and the Study of Judaism in Early Modern Europe.*

LAWRENCE FINE is the Irene Kaplan Leiwant Professor of Jewish Studies and Professor of Religion at Mount Holyoke College. He is the author or editor of six books, including *Judaism in Practice: From the Middle Ages through the Early Modern Period* and *Physician of the Soul, Healer of the Cosmos: Isaac Luria and His Kabbalistic Fellowship.*

EITAN P. FISHBANE is Assistant Professor of Jewish Thought at the Jewish Theological Seminary. He is the author of *As Light before Dawn: The Inner World of a Medieval Kabbalist* and recipient of a Charles A. Ryskamp Fellowship from the American Council of Learned Societies.

PINCHAS GILLER is Professor of Jewish Thought at the Ziegler Rabbinical School of the American Jewish University, Los Angeles. He is the author of *The Enlightened Will Shine: Symbolism and Theurgy in the Later Strata of the Zohar; Reading the Zohar, The Sacred Text of Kabbalah;* and *Shalom Shar'abi and the Kabbalists of Beit El.*

MATT GOLDISH is Samuel M. and Esther Melton Professor of Jewish History and Director of the Melton Center for Jewish Studies at The Ohio State University. He is the author of *Judaism in the Theology of Sir Isaac Newton; The Sabbatean Prophets;* and *Jewish Questions: Responsa on Jewish Life in the Early Modern Period.* He is also the editor of several collections.

FREDERICK E. GREENSPAHN is Gimelstob Eminent Scholar in Judaic Studies at Florida Atlantic University. He is the author/editor of numerous other titles including *The Hebrew Bible: New Insights and Scholarship* and *Women and Judaism: New Insights and Scholarship*, both available from NYU Press.

HARTLEY LACHTER is Director of Jewish Studies at Muhlenberg College in Allentown, Pennsylvania. His recent publications include "Kabbalah, Philosophy and the Jewish-Christian Debate: Reconsidering the Early Works of Joseph Gikatilla," and "Spreading Secrets: Kabbalah and Esotericism in Isaac ibn Sahula's *Meshal ha-Kadmoni*."

SHAUL MAGID is the Jay and Jeanie Schottenstein Professor of Jewish Studies and Professor in the Department of Religious Studies at Indiana University in Bloomington. His most recent book, *From Metaphysics to Midrash: Myth, History, and the Interpretation of Scripture in Lurianic Kabbala*, won the American Academy of Religion Award for Best Book in Religion in the textual studies category. He is also the author of *Hasidism on the Margin: Reconciliation, Antinomianism, and Messianism in Izbica/Radzin Hasidism*.

JODY MYERS is Professor of Religious Studies and Coordinator of the Jewish Studies Program at California State University, Northridge. She is the author of *Seeking Zion: Modernity and Messianic Activism in the Writings of Zevi Hirsch Kalischer* and *Kabbalah and the Spiritual Quest: The Kabbalah Centre in America*.

HAVA TIROSH-SAMUELSON is Professor of History, Director of Jewish Studies, and Irving and Miriam Lowe Professor of Modern Judaism at Arizona State University. She is the author of *Between Worlds: The Life and Work of Rabbi David ben Judah Messer Leon* and *Happiness in Premodern Judaism: Virtue, Knowledge, and Well-Being in Premodern Judaism*, and is the editor of several volumes, most recently *The Legacy of Hans Jonas: Judaism and the Phenomenon of Life*.

MICHAEL D. SWARTZ is Professor of Hebrew and Religious Studies at The Ohio State University. He is the author of *Scholastic Magic: Ritual and Revelation in Early Jewish Mysticism* and *Mystical Prayer in Ancient Judaism: An Analysis of Maa'seh Merkavah*, and is coauthor of *Avodah: Ancient Poems for Yom Kippur* and *Hebrew and Aramaic Incantation Texts from the Cairo Genizah: Selected Texts from Taylor-Schechter Box K1*.

ELLIOT R. WOLFSON is the Abraham Lieberman Professor of Hebrew and Judaic Studies at New York University. He is the author of several books, most recently *Through the Speculum That Shines: Vision and Imagination in Medieval Jewish Mysticism; Venturing Beyond: Law and Morality in Kabbalistic Mysticism; Luminal Darkness: Imaginal Gleanings from Zoharic Literature*; and *Open Secret: Postmessianic Messianism and the Mystical Revision of Menahem Mendel Schneerson.*

Index

Abarbanel, Don Isaac, 119, 126, 142
Abraham, 42, 78
Abraham ben David of Posquières
  (Rabad), 5
Abraham ben Eliezer ha-Levi, 119, 120
Abraham ben Isaac of Narbonne, 5
Abraham ibn Ezra, 79
Abraham Nathan Benjamin Ashkenazi. *See*
  Nathan Ashkenazi of Gaza
Abrams, Daniel, 15, 57, 198, 205, 212–13,
  234, 213–14, 215, 219
Abulafaraj, Samuel ben Nissim, 163
Abulafia, Abraham, ix, xi, 7, 68–84, 115–16,
  209, 223n1, 228n88
Abulafia, Todros of Toledo, 6, 8, 57, 206,
  234
Abulafia, Yosef, 234
Abzug, Bella, 224n31
Active Intellect, 79–80, 84
Adam, 54, 76, 78, 83, 192
Adam Qadmon, 216
Adler, Rachel, 224n32
Agrippa, Cornelius, 164
Aḥer, 35–36
Akiba, 35–37, 43
Albigensians, 196
alchemy, 166, 168
Alemano, Yoseph, 163
Alkebetz, Solomon ben Moses, 10, 123
Alsheikh, Moshe, 142–43
Alsheikh, Shealtiel, 99
Altmann, Alexander, 95
amulets, 184, 231
'Anafiel, 38, 39
Anav, Raphael, 108

androcentrism, 203–4, 208, 213
androgyny, x, 50, 197, 204, 209–11, 213–14,
  219
Angelet, Yosef, 234
angels, 34, 182
anthropomorphism, 39
anthropos, 76, 204, 216
anti-Christian, 78
apocalyptic, 35
Aquarius, Age of, 178
Aramaic, 55–56
archetypes, 185
ARI. *See* Luria, Isaac
Aristotelian philosophy, 7, 79, 143, 148, 191,
  216
artists and poets, "Beat," 179
ArtScroll, 183
ascent texts, 43
asceticism, 4, 96, 144
Ashkenazi, Hayyim, 99
Ashlag, Yehuda, 13, 184, 187
astrology, 187
Asulin, Shifra, 218
atarah (diadem), 202
atonement, 164
Averroes, 79
Avicenna, 79
Avivi, Yosef, 233
Avodat ha-Kodesh, 124
ayin hara, 231
Azikri, Eleazar, 95, 98, 101

Ba'al Shem Tov, 12–13, 139, 141–45, 148,
  151–53, 155, 234, 235
Bacon, Francis, 159

dreams, 100
Dubnow, Simon, 140

ecstatic, ix, 74, 69–71, 75, 81, 210, 228n88
egalitarianism, 200, 205, 209, 213, 217
Ehrlich, Shmuel, 215
Eibeschütz family, 133
Ein Sof, 6, 8, 51–53, 180, 182, 191, 216
Elazar, 60, 61, 62–64
Eleazar ben Yehudah of Worms, 4
Eliade, Mircea, 194
Elijah, 99, 108
Elijah de Vidas, 101
Elior, Rachel, 139
Elqayam, Abraham, 218–20, 234, 236
Emanations. See *sefirot*
Enlightenment, 134, 162, 163, 176
Enoch, 2, 35
Ephraim of Lunshitz, 142
Eranos Society, 193–94
Eros, 52, 208–9
"eternal Thou," xi
ethics, 101,103
Eucharist, 73
Eva, 219
Eve, 17n46, 54
exodus, 149–50
Ezekiel, vii, viii, 2, 34, 35

Fairbairn, W. R. D., 215
fellowships, 94–95. See also *ḥavurot*
feminism, 193, 198–99, 204–5, 206, 208, 211,
    213, 216, 218, 220–21
Ferdinand, 92
Flavius Mithradites, 163
Florence, 163
Foucault, Michel, 211, 217, 220
Four Worlds, 181, 182, 184, 185
Francis Mercury van Helmont, 160–61,
    164, 167–70
Frank, Jacob (Frankism), x, 219, 133, 210,
    219
Freud, Sigmund, 181, 193, 202, 203, 206,
    208, 221, 222
Friedan, Betty, 224n31
fundamentalism, 184

Gallipoli, 130
Gamlieli, Devora Bat David, 205, 213, 215,
    216–17, 219, 229nn.109–10
Gans, David, 120
Garb, Jonathan, 217, 218
gematria. See numerology
gender, x, 54, 106–8, 191–223
Gerer rebbe, 183
Gerona, 6, 8, 51, 94
Gevurah, 52–54
Gewurz, Elias, 188n5
Gikatilla, Yosef, 7–8, 57, 234
gilgul. See reincarnation
Gilligan, Carol, 213, 216, 229n110
Giorgi Francesco, 164
gnosis, 75, 81, 83
Gnosticism, 194, 195, 196, 207, 232
Godfrey of Admont, 196
grace, 162–63
Graetz, Heinrich, 14, 15, 22,49, 55, 233
Greece, 54, 166
Green, Arthur, 94, 183, 200, 201, 204, 205, 208
Greenberg, Blu, 224n32
Gregory of Tours, 197
Gries, Zev, 140
Gross, Rita, 200
Gruberger, Philip. *See* Berg, Philip
Gruberger, Shraga Feivel. *See* Berg, Philip

halakha, 19, 177
Halperin, David J., 37, 43
ḥashmal, vii
Ḥasidei Ashkenaz, 4–5, 8, 78–79, 209
Ḥasidei de'ar 'a, 140
Ḥasidei dekokhavaya, 140
Hasidism, ix, 12–13, 105, 115, 134, 139–55,
    175, 176, 182, 212, 220, 220, 228n88, 232,
    233, 235
Haskalah, 134, 231
Hauptman, Judith, 224n32
Ḥaverim Maqshivim, 96
ḥavurot, 94–95. *See also* fellowships
Hayon, Nehemiah Hiyya, 131
Hayyim Vital Calabrese, 124
Hebrew language, 19, 56, 76, 79, 161–62,
    165–66, 168

Hebrew University, 178
Hegel, G. W. F., 170
Heidegger, Martin, 203–4
hekhalot, 2–3, 5, 8, 44, 56, 196
Hekhalot literature, 2, 34, 36–38, 40, 43, 45
Hell, 162
Hellner-Eshed, Melilah, 205, 206–7, 208, 218
Ḥemdat Yamim, 132
Herman of Tournay, 196
Hermes Trismegistus, 160
Hertzberg, Arthur, 236
Heschel, Abraham Joshua, 153
Heschel, Susannah, 200
Ḥesed, 52–54
Hesychasm, 72, 86n18
Hildegard of Bingen, 196
Hillel of Verona, 68
Himmelfarb, Martha, 43
Hinduism, xi, 178–79, 181
historicism, 220
Ḥochmah, 52–53, 191
Hod, 52–53
Holocaust, 176, 193, 231
Huss, Boaz, 234, 235, 236
Hyman, Paula, 224n32

Idel, Moshe, 22, 69, 127–28, 159, 167, 196, 198, 205, 208–13, 215, 217, 219, 221, 228n88, 232–33
Incarnation, 80, 83
India, 236
Ines of Herrera, 119
Inquisition, 122, 169; Roman, 161
Institute for Jewish Spirituality, 183
internet, 180
Irigaray, Luce, 180, 193, 203, 208, 213, 214, 215, 220
Isaac Abu Issa, 116
Isaac ben Jacob ha-Kohen, 6
Isaac ben Samuel of Acre, 9
Isaac ha-Cohen, 195
Isaac ibn Latif, 6
Isaac ibn Sahula, 6, 8
Isaac of Acre, 209
Isaac the Blind, 5–6

Isaiah, viii, 34
Ishmael, Rabbi, 35, 37, 41, 43
Islam, x, xi, 11, 21, 37, 56, 72, 79, 217, 236
Israel, 55, 176–77, 180, 205, 218, 220, 231, 235–36
Israel ben Eliezer. *See* Ba'al Shem Tov

Jacob, 145
Jacob ha-Cohen, 6, 195
Jacob Nazir of Lunel, 5
James, William, viii,xi
Jellinek, Adolph, 49, 69
Jerusalem, 92, 94, 123, 211
Jesus, x, 72, 73, 83, 86n29, 116, 125, 164, 198. *See also* Christ
Jewish Institute of Religion, 178, 232
Jewish Renewal. *See* Renewal
Jewish Studies, viii, xi, 179, 193, 199, 214, 220
Jewish Theological Seminary, vii
jihad, 117
João II, 121
John the Baptist, 116
Josel of Rosheim, 123
Joseph, 59, 61, 73, 145
Joseph della Reina, 119
Joshua ibn Shu'aib, 9
Judah ben Barzillai al-Barceloni, 4, 198
Judah Ha-Levi, 8, 79, 126–27, 198
Judah the Ḥasid of Worms, 4
judaizing, 161, 164
Jung, Carl, 185, 194, 206, 208, 219

Kabbala denudata, 164–66, 167, 168, 169–70
Kabbalah, ix, x, 5, 34, 41, 43, 115, 117–20, 122, 124, 126–27, 129, 130, 132–33, 139, 142, 144–45, 150, 154, 231
Kabbalah Centre, vii, xii, 13, 17, 176, 179–80, 183, 187, 236
Kabbalah for Dummies, vii
Kabbalat Shabbat, x, 105
Kafka, Franz, 222
Kalonymus of Speyer, 4
Kaniel, Ruth Kara-Ivanov, 218
Kaplan, Aryeh, 179
Karo, Joseph, x, 9–10, 98, 101, 123, 217